MW00620888

Singing for Freedom

Singing
for
Freedom

⊷⊶✦⊷⊶

The Hutchinson Family Singers

and the Nineteenth-Century

Culture of Reform

Scott Gac

YALE UNIVERSITY PRESS   NEW HAVEN AND LONDON

Set in Adobe Garamond type by The Composing Room of Michigan, Inc.
Printed in the United States of America by Sheridan Books, Ann Arbor, Michigan.

Library of Congress Cataloging-in-Publication Data
Gac, Scott.
Singing for freedom : the Hutchinson Family Singers and the nineteenth-century
culture of reform / Scott Gac.
p.   cm.
Includes bibliographical references (p.   ) and index.
ISBN 978-0-300-11198-9 (cloth : alk. paper)   1. Hutchinson Family (Singers)
2. Singers—United States—New Hampshire—Biography.   3. Antislavery movements—United States—History—19th century.   I. Title.
ML421.H88G33 2007
782.42092′273—dc22
[B]
2006029555

A catalogue record for this book is available from the British Library.
The paper in this book meets the guidelines for permanence and durability
of the Committee on Production Guidelines for Book Longevity
of the Council on Library Resources.

10 9 8 7 6 5 4 3 2 1

*Write and sing about it—you can sing what would
be death to speak.*

*—African-American composer
Joshua McCarter Simpson, 1874*

Contents

Acknowledgments

The journey from typewritten words to book is long and, too often, lonely; the many people and institutions named herein made my excursion bearable and warm.

Early on, the Graduate Center of the City University of New York's (CUNY) Ph.D. Alumni Dissertation Support Fund allowed me backing for travel and photocopying. A CUNY Writing Fellowship provided two years of incredible support, making it possible for me to complete the first draft of this book. In 2001 a Kate B. and Hall J. Peterson Fellowship from the American Antiquarian Society pushed my research in many wonderful new directions; my thanks to John Hench, Tom Knoles, and Caroline Sloat, as well as to fellow fellows Pat Cohen, Hallie Hobson, Karen O'Brien, Joan Radner, Ben Reiss, Cynthia Van Zandt, and Altina Waller. Later in 2001 I moved from Worcester, Massachusetts, to Philadelphia for an Andrew W. Mellon Foundation Fellowship at the Library Company of Philadelphia. Thanks to Jim Green, Phil Lapansky, and the outstanding staff at the Library Company.

Many years as a doctoral student at the CUNY Graduate Center has left me indebted to a number of excellent teachers and friends; I extend my gratitude to Jack Diggins, Ann Fabian, Josh Freeman (who followed me from Columbia), David Jaffee, John Kearns, Karen Lemmey, Kathleen McCarthy, David Nasaw, Jim Oakes, Bob Raber, and Michael Wreszin. And while I am on the topic of friends and teachers, I simply must thank my superb high school history teachers at Ward Melville and an inspiring experience at Columbia University due to Kathy Eden (the first person ever to say something encouraging about my writing—"There are ideas in here," she said; "you just need to learn how to write about them"), Eric Foner, and Theresa Rogers. To Don Fink, my uber-coach, and the people and staff who make Long Course Triathlon Worlds and Team USA memorable, thank you. Homer Mensch, my teacher at The Juilliard School, taught me a remarkable sense of discipline and professionalism—you are one of the greatest.

Staying with music to acknowledge one more debt, I think special recognition is deserved for Rick Benjamin and the Paragon Ragtime Orchestra. You exposed me to the flippant nature of musicians and taught lessons on how miserable life can be on the road. The Hutchinson Family Singers, at times, would have understood what I am talking about.

In 2003 I embarked on what turned out to be an extended postdoctoral education at Yale University thanks to a Special Collections Humanities Fellowship from the Yale University Library and the Mellon Foundation. Many thanks to Norma Thompson and the fellows at Yale's Whitney Humanities Center for two years of lunch, lively discussions, and a fabulous office space. My time in New Haven shaped *Singing for Freedom* in ways that I can't even begin to explain; instead I will send a heartfelt thanks to Alice Prochaska, Jon Butler, David Blight, Jonathan Holloway, my students in history and in American studies, Lloyd Ackert, Scott Newstok, Ken Crilly, Suzanne Eggleston-Lovejoy, Diane Kaplan, Frank Prochaska, and the many librarians who made certain this book is filled with fascinating details. A special mention is due for Writing History at Yale—Aaron Sachs, Adam Arenson, Barry Muchnick, John Demos, and the many readers and writers who spurred fascinating discussions. This book simply would not be as interesting without all of you.

Both the Lynn Museum and the Wadleigh Memorial Public Library in Milford, New Hampshire, house fantastic collections of the Hutchinson Family Singers. My thanks to Diane Shepard and her colleagues in Lynn and Deb Spratt and the rest of the staff in Milford for all of their assistance. I am grateful to the New Hampshire State Library and the New Hampshire Historical Society, especially David Smolen, for access to their wonderful holdings. Thanks as well to those who helped at the Harvard University Library; the Hutchins Library, Berea College; the Syracuse University Library; the Bancroft Library, University of California, Berkeley; the New-York Historical Society; the New York Public Library; and the Columbia University Library.

John Stauffer deserves his own paragraph—counseling me during the writing of this book, John saved me from many errors of judgment and thought. His close readings of the manuscript proved an invaluable resource.

Now it gets really personal. Over the years, no matter what I seem to do, Carol Berkin has remained supportive and still invites me over for dinner. Why? I don't know. But thanks. To Lou Masur: it is getting to the point where I am running out of ways to express how you've influenced my life and work. I am certain the Press won't allot me the space to try.

Ed, Maria, Elyse, and Lenny. Do I deserve such supportive parents and in-laws? No. Thanks for not giving up on me (yet).

There are things that go bump in the night. During those moments I turn to Renee, in hopes that she is awake enough to get up and throw out the cats. Our family is special even though the better half of it is furry. I love all of you.

Singing for Freedom

Prelude

Band of young apostles,
Teaching love and truth,
Onward go, high-missioned,
In your glorious youth!
Onward go, God's blessing,
On your path alight!
Still lift your kindred voices,
As prophets of the Right!
Onward go, undaunted,
Heralds of that day,
When all mankind are brothers,
And War has ceased to slay!
We have seen and loved you!
We have pressed your hand;
We have blessed you, and we bless
In you your native land!
Farewell! God's angel guide you,
Ye young and noble band!

—Mary Howitt, "To the Hutchinson Family," 1846

PROGRAMME.

PART FIRST.

QUARTETTE.
LAND OF WASHINGTON.

Words by G. P. Morris, Esq.—Arranged as a quartette by Hutchinson.

" We love the patriot sage,
    Who in the days of yore,
    In combat met the foemen
    And drove them from our shore ;
    Who flung our banner's starry field
    In triumph to the breeze,
    And spread broad maps of cities, where
    Once waved the forest trees.

QUARTETTE.

Peaceful slumbering on the ocean,
    Seamen fear no danger nigh ;
    The winds and waves in gentle motion—
    Sooth them with their lullaby.

BALLAD.
" THE IRISH EMIGRANT'S LAMENT."

MUSIC BY W. R. DEMPSTED.

Portraying the feelings of an Irish Peasant previous to his leaving his native land,
calling up the scenes of his childhood, under the painful reflection of having buried his
wife and child.

QUARTETTE.
THE COT WHERE WE WERE BORN.

" We stood upon the mountain height,
    And view'd the valleys o'er !
    The sun's last rays, with mellow light,
    Illumed the distant shore ;
    We gazed with rapture on the scene,
    Where first in youth's bright morn
    We played, where near us stood serene,
    The 'Cot where we were born.' "

PART SECOND.

MY MOTHER'S BIBLE.

WORDS BY G. P. MORRIS, ESQ.

This book is all that's left me now,—
 Tears will unbidden start!
With falt'ring lip and throbbing brow
 I press it to my heart.
For many generations past,
 Here is our family tree ;
My mother's hand this Bible clasped,
 She, dying, gave it me.

My father read this holy book,
 To brothers, sisters dear,
How calm was my poor mother's look,
 Who lov'd God's word to hear.
Her angel-face—I see it yet—
 What vivid memory's come !
Again that little group is met,
 Within the halls of home!

SOLO.

RECOLLECTIONS OF HOME.

Ah ! why from our own native home did we part,
With its Mountains and Valleys so dear to each heart,
Ah ! why did we leave the enjoyments of home,
O'er the wide waste of waters, strangers to roam.

TRIO.
"ROCKAWAY."

Words by Henry John Sharpe.—Melody by Russell.—Arranged by Hutchinson.

" On auld Long Island's sea-girt shore,
 Many an hour I've whiled away
In list'ning to the breakers' roar
 That washed the beach at Rockaway."

EXCELSIOR.

Words by Henry W. Longfellow, Esq.

This poem represents the continued aspirations of Genius. Its motto—"Excelsior,"
(still higher,) is a word in an unknown tongue. Disregarding the every day comforts of
life, the allurements of love, and the warnings of experience, it presses forward on its soli-
tary path. Even in death it holds fast its device, and a voice from the air proclaims the
progress of the soul in a higher sphere.

The shades of night were falling fast,
As through an Alpine village pass'd
A youth, who bore, mid snow and ice,
A banner with this strange device—
 EXCELSIOR !

His brow was sad, his eye beneath
Flash'd like a falchion from its sheath,
And like a silver clarion rung,
The accents of that unknown tongue—
 EXCELSIOR !

" Try not the pass !" the old man said,
Dark lowers the tempest overhead,
The roaring torrent is deep and wide,
And loud that clarion voice replied—
 EXCELSIOR !

" O stay !" the maiden said, "and rest
Thy weary head upon this breast."
A tear stood in his bright blue eye,
But still he answered with a sigh—
 EXCELSIOR !

Opening Theme: The Hutchinson Family Singers as Reformers

The stagecoach nearly flipped, throwing the cello from the rooftop luggage rack. No one inside was hurt. The instrument lay on the ground, cracked. In all their years of concertizing, the Hutchinson Family Singers had luckily avoided the personal injury that often troubled rail, road, and steamship travelers. This particular September accident claimed the group's sacrificial lamb, Asa's bass viol (which they also called a cello). Its wooden body, pockmarked from thousands of miles of musical journeying, again needed patching and gluing. After nearly a decade of performing, a driver's unusually sharp turn reaffirmed the utility of Asa, John, and Judson Hutchinson's carpentering skills.[1]

There was no reason for the brothers to continue their travel following the stage mishap. The Hutchinson Family Singers had accomplished everything that they could have ever dreamed by September 1850. Money and international fame was theirs in the 1840s. Then, quite suddenly in late 1849, their sister Abby—an integral part of the Hutchinson Family Singers—married and left the group. In the fall of 1850, the bass viol was not alone in showing wear. Now seemed like the perfect time for the brothers to quit and act upon their frequent vow to retire from music and return to their agrarian roots. A righteous calling as the musical cornerstone of antebellum reform, though, proved to be irresistible. They forged on in many formations: as a trio, as a new quartet with brother Jesse or Joshua, and as the original quartet whenever they appeared in New York, where Abby now resided. Before the stagecoach just about capsized on September 14, the brothers played at a temperance function and, soon, after a visit to New York, they shared the stage at an antislavery function with Gerrit Smith, the political abolitionist who later helped fund John Brown's 1859 raid on Harper's Ferry.[2]

The Hutchinson Family Singers' story details a vibrant cultural space created by waves of reform pulsating through the United States in the first half of the nineteenth century. Starting in 1841, the Hutchinsons transformed themselves from backwoods, church-trained musicians to the most popular musical family in America. They did this at a time when successful native-born musicians were something of an anomaly; a prejudice for European-trained performers, along with a general questioning of the moral worth of entertainment, greatly diminished opportunity for American musicians. The Hutchinsons' musical metamorphosis relied upon, first, the well-liked melodies of blackface minstrelsy and of church hymns to which the group added its own lyrics, and second, harmonized chorus refrains, the standard in today's popular music but quite new to antebellum America. Expounding reform in song and forging a native American identity through their ostensible association with New Hampshire's natural wonders—one of their popular songs rang out, "We have come from the mountains of the Old Granite State"—the Hutchinson Family Singers created a new kind of "sacred" music. The sound of the Hutchinsons was an antiminstrelsy that hushed critics who feared the immorality of entertainment, challenged the European bias of their listeners, and attracted throngs of fans with uplifting reform messages built around familiar tunes.[3]

Works such as *The Narrative of the Life of Frederick Douglass* (1845) and the Hutchinson Family Singers' "Get Off the Track!" (1844)—the group's campaign song for the Liberty Party, the first antislavery political party—announced the full-fledged commercialization of antislavery. For abolitionists, it was a new kind of reform, one that was less controllable, but also very capable. Antislavery works in the North prepared voters for the collapse of a national political dialogue surrounding slavery's expansion in the 1850s. With the vital center—the compromise deals and popular sovereignty—removed from the debate, the question proceeded along its extremes: the perpetuation of slavery or its prohibition (the Free-Soil position) in new additions to the United States. By the time northern cultural consumers were forced to choose between slavery and Free Soil in the late 1850s, they had already tipped their hand through their buying, reading, and performing of antislavery poetry, literature, music, and more.

Efforts of the Hutchinson Family Singers and many other artistic crusaders of the 1840s prepared their supporters for the application of religion and reform found within the pages of Harriet Beecher Stowe's *Uncle Tom's Cabin* (1852), often picked as the definitive expression of antebellum culture and reform. Those who focus on Stowe's accomplishment, though, often miss the larger cultural issue at hand: "There is an embarrassment of riches in reform," said Walt Whitman. Authors like Whitman, John Greenleaf Whittier, W. H. Smith, and Lydia Maria Child appreciated the enormous influence of reform and continually used reform imagery to create texts representative of their age. In these works, the progressive ethos essential to northern Americans in the 1840s—occasionally lost in modern historical accounts focused on detailing the differences between reform groups—is revealed in temperance, women's rights, antislavery, communitarianism, and prison reform, and their combined goals for political, economic, and corporal freedom.[4]

The reform culture prevalent in the 1840s and 1850s, encompassing everything from dietary change to the nation's economic structure, was a countrywide phenomenon with notable exceptions. Antislavery in particular held little appeal for white southerners. The Hutchinsons, who championed nearly every reform, made their name as abolitionist entertainers. Though their American audience did extend as far south as the capital, only a large number of northern politicos and some misguided understanding of their lyrics provided the singers with a warm Washington reception. In places like Baltimore and even in Philadelphia, the Hutchinsons sometimes canceled shows to avoid assault from antiabolition mobs.

Such was not the case when the New Hampshire musicians traveled to Europe. The full scope of American reform culture translated well to the shores of England, Scotland, and Ireland, where a transatlantic liberal community had developed. Here the Hutchinson Family Singers befriended reformers like Daniel O'Connell, leader of "Catholic emancipation"—the cause of Ireland's release from the Church of England; Father Theobald Mathew, a well-known temperance leader; and Hannah and Richard Davis Webb, abolitionists who described the Hutchinsons as "strong against slavery, no compromise there"; as well as luminaries like Charles Dickens, the actor William Charles Macready, the authors Mary and William Howitt, and the poet and philosopher Harriet Martineau. "It was one of the most successful musical entertainments we have witnessed for some time," said the Manchester *Guardian* of the New Hampshire troupe's performance.[5]

The increasing visibility of individual rights at home and abroad in the nineteenth century owes much to the American Revolution, and, in the United States, was further intensified by years of religious revivalism following the nation's founding. No longer "sinners in the hands of an angry God," Americans in the age of revivals found increasing comfort in a more compassionate Christianity and a benevolent God whose son's suffering drew attention to the horrors of pain inflicted on one by an outside force. Though the influence of revivalism has been located in many places, notably antebellum reform movements and politics, one crucial link has been ignored: religious revivals also cast an uncanny affect on American cultural consumers and popular culture. We must look, then, at the religious spectacles known as revivals to understand why cultural works which spoke of reform and of sacred themes sold so well in the 1840s and 1850s. The marketing of a sacred culture—in collections of church hymns, singing schools, church choirs, sacred tracts, and even in revivals themselves—cultivated audiences for a blend of pious domesticity endorsed by American Christianity.[6]

Scholars of American popular music are especially guilty of downplaying the influence of religion. Due in large part to the obvious (and the not so obvious) racial implications of one style, blackface minstrelsy, the music of the antebellum era is most often associated with white imitation of southern black culture. This can make for a wonderfully linear narrative of white musicians' theft of "everything but the burden" from black artists from the 1830s until today. The Hutchinsons' conversion of minstrel melodies into music for emancipation proves the frailty of such a construction. Indeed, the historical record shows that the popularity of performers like William Dempster and the Hutchinson Family Singers forced minstrel groups in the 1840s to downplay some of the racial mimicry in which their genre originated. Many audiences, especially those of the rural North, found the early minstrel display taboo. The sentimentalism of later minstrelsy, such as the songs of Stephen Foster and the toned-down appearance of minstrel sheet music in the late 1840s (which made it more appealing for parlor display), attest to the shift toward a domesticated, more scrupulous musical form. "The songs of the 'nigger' type," said a British reviewer of Christy's Minstrels, "are now of the past, and those presented would have been thought at no distant time ago little in keeping with blackened faces."[7]

During the 1850 trip that was disrupted by the stagecoach crash, the Hutchinson Family Singers were on their way to New York to see famed Swedish vocalist Jenny Lind. Lind had just arrived in America and had received an earthshaking reception. When the Hutchinson musicians finally made it to the city, the international superstars sat side by side in a lavish hotel suite, trading pleasantries. The Hutchinsons offered Lind a gift, a new song written by their brother, Jesse Jr., who often composed pieces for the group. "Welcome to Jenny Lind" turned into yet another Hutchinson Family Singers hit:

> From the snow-clad hills of Sweden
> Like a bird of love from Eden
> Lo, she comes with songs of freedom
> Jenny comes from o'er the sea!

John Hutchinson thought that Lind "seemed very much pleased with the song" and recorded her response: she "spoke of her home and how she longed to go back to it." Later that evening, the Hutchinsons watched the Swedish Nightingale delight an audience of eight thousand.[8]

The exchange between Lind and the Hutchinson Family Singers was rather quaint, but the New Hampshire troupe did not travel to New York to socialize. They had journeyed to change Lind's mind. Frederick Douglass, the group's longtime friend, astutely observed of the Hutchinson Family Singers that they "dared to sing for a cause first and for cash afterward." "Welcome to Jenny Lind," a song of greeting, was part of an antislavery offensive waged on the Swedish vocalist. Urging, "Jenny sing for liberty," and believing that "she comes with songs of freedom," the Hutchinsons prodded Lind to take a public stance against slavery. Their effort failed.[9]

Lind—known as the "Sister of Charity" and the "Angel of Benevolence" for her frequent donations to reform groups and charities—would not speak of abolitionism until right before she left the United States. Long after she finished touring in the South, as she was set to leave the country, the Swede wrote to Harriet Beecher Stowe that *Uncle Tom's Cabin* advanced "the welfare of our black *brethren*." Those within the American antislavery movement were no doubt relieved by her declaration. After all, for many years before her visit, Lind's likeness, usually in the form of a gutta-percha medallion, had been sold to raise money for antislavery organizations.[10]

The Hutchinson Family Singers' relationship with the American antislavery movement began in the early 1840s, when advocates asked the group to create abolitionist tunes similar to the temperance songs that they were already performing. Soon the musicians, regulars at the annual antislavery meeting held in their hometown, stole the spotlight at an 1843 antislavery meeting with their musical offerings. Once the Hutchinsons discovered the power in linking their art to their personal convictions, they never looked back. The group played to integrated audiences in an era when many abolitionists feared such mixing, and they tirelessly fought for abolitionists' right to speak amid the din of disapproving crowds. Long after the Civil War, when the Hutchinsons' brand of reform and culture had lost its widespread appeal, they maintained their idealism as musicians and as reformers.

It is strange, then, that skeptics, in their time and in ours, often point to the enormous amount of money that the group earned as evidence of deceit. How could anyone believe in a righteous cause and actually profit from it? The *Western Christian Advocate,* reporting that the Hutchinson Family Singers collected $30,000 during their ten-month foreign tour in 1845–1846, asked, "How much of that amount was given by professed christians, merely to hear their irreligious songs, which ought to have been given to the cause of missions, or some other religious object?"[11]

The New Hampshire musicians were a bit secretive about their giving, a choice that fueled critics' speculation. When the Hutchinsons built an antislavery hall in their hometown, donated to reform organizations, or simply helped out a friend in need, they did not leak the news à la Jenny Lind or P. T. Barnum. John, Asa, Judson, and Abby were different. Once, the Massachusetts Anti-Slavery Society, concerned that the Hutchinsons were impoverishing themselves by volunteering for their cause, took up a collection for the singers. Immediately the Hutchinsons turned over the money to black antislavery leaders. "Music has charms," the Hutchinson Family Singers wrote in their common journal, "that ought to be cultivated for good purposes, for reform and to help the weary traveler on the road toward Heaven." For many antebellum Americans, the Hutchinson Family Singers' devotion to social improvement was clear. Responding to the *Western Christian Advocate,* the *Christian Citizen* said, "The 'irreligious songs' of the Hutchinsons are more truly christian in their doctrine than ninety-nine hundredths of the pulpit sermons in the land."[12]

It is unlikely that the Hutchinsons collected $30,000 during their ten months out of the country—Asa privately voiced a desire "to earn enough to pay our passage back and have $1000 each beside"— but this much is clear: in a time when laborers were fortunate to earn $300 per year and middle-class Americans brought in roughly $1,000 a year, the Hutchinson Family Singers secured enormous sums for their performances. In 1844 the Hutchinsons occasionally made more than $1,000 per night for shows in New York City, and they played more than thirty concerts in Brooklyn and in New York. That year Asa recorded walking around Baltimore with enough cash to procure the equivalent of a new 2006 Ford Taurus sedan. Seven years later, after buying vast tracts of land in Lynn, Massachusetts, and renovating his family's farm, and soon to found the town of Hutchinson, Minnesota, John confessed that "the reputation of being rich is most trouble to bear."[13]

The sudden wealth available to musicians in the early nineteenth century ensured that some purists would damn the link between music and money. Even Lowell Mason, the well-respected and best-selling composer of church hymns and other sacred music, stood accused of kowtowing to riches. One Mason censurer asked, "What music ever moistened his eye, or except the clinking of silver and gold, ever touched his heart?" As music and reform came up for sale in America—a development later dubbed commodification—many in America needed time to adapt to the sudden availability of nearly everything via the market. So the Hutchinsons were not alone in being targeted for their financial success. But they are in more rarified company in having their reform credentials questioned constantly simply because they profited from their beliefs. The abolitionist leader William Lloyd Garrison—a man never short on detractors—is often celebrated for crafting a career out of brash reform rhetoric; "He cashed it in," said one Garrison scholar who applauded the reform leader's ability to make a living from radical convictions. Too often a line separates the reform work from the reform profits of "traditional" activists while the reform work of cultural activists is intimately and often disparagingly linked to their gains. Like many liberals of their day, the Hutchinsons favored moral and religious issues over making money, but they declined to embrace monasticism.

And it is because the musicians were just as committed to reform as anybody else that they filled a vital role for the antislavery movement during the 1840s. Bridging the significant gaps between various factions, the Hutchinsons functioned as unifiers of abolitionist reform. Time and again they brought together the immediate moralism behind the American Anti-Slavery Society with the practical politics of the Liberty Party even though the leaders of the two groups hardly ever spoke to each other. Garrison and the Hutchinsons did not always agree on antislavery issues either, but the principal abolitionist understood the singers and their music as a sensational tool for American reform; the successful commercialization of the antislavery message assured the movement's vitality. "Never before has the singing of ballads been made directly and purposely subservient to the freedom, welfare, happiness, and moral elevation of the people," said Garrison of the group. "Let the example—become contagious!"[14]

First Variation: The Hutchinsons' Commercial Success and Legacy

In June 1951 the town of Milford, New Hampshire, tackled a bit of a puzzle. Resident Gennaro Sacco had unearthed a clunky piece of metal marked with type while tending vegetables along the Souhegan River on Maple Street. "The Mystery of the Buried Printing Plate" started—Where was it from? How did it get here? Local Patty McLane Botch would eventually identify it as the stamp for page forty-one of Joshua Hutchinson's *Brief Narrative of the Hutchinson Family*.

Milford was the birthplace of the Hutchinson Family Singers and, along with Hutchinson, Minnesota, and Lynn, Massachusetts, the town has served as a curator of the singers' artifacts and their legacy.

By 1891, when John and Abby were still alive, the old Hutchinson homestead in Milford—designated a Landmark of American Music in 1976—already functioned as a repository for Hutchinson Family Singers memorabilia. Here a reporter found prized letters from William Lloyd Garrison and "clippings concerning receptions, orations and congratulations by the Freedmen and colored people generally, also friendly correspondence from distinguished editors and journalists in England and in America."[15]

What the newspaper reporter Cara Reese did not uncover in the late nineteenth century was any evidence of printing plates. The plate, identified more than fifty years ago, still offers up a question: how did it arrive at that spot along the river? Joshua Hutchinson's book, which presents quaint vignettes of each member of his family, was published in 1874 by the Boston firm of Lee and Shepard. We do not know whether Joshua or one of his relatives ever owned the plate, but the Hutchinsons, who paid homage to the Jeffersonian ideal of the virtuous citizen-farmer, certainly would have been pleased that Sacco had harvested it from a garden.

The group's commercial effort successfully saturated cultural markets in the nineteenth-century North, especially those in New England, and it continues to do so, though in a much milder form, to this day. Paraphernalia from the Hutchinson Family Singers, most often sheet music, is readily available and, judging by eBay auctions, still coveted in the twenty-first century. One fan even maintains an extensive Web site for the troupe. Yet the nineteenth-century marketability of the Hutchinson Family Singers runs counter to current perceptions of the antislavery movement. Because abolitionism was loathed in the South and hotly contested in the North, the thinking goes, singing against slavery should have greatly limited the musicians' popularity. A quick look at contemporary newspaper captions reveals another tale. Northern readers eagerly awaited information about the Hutchinsons, and the media indulged their readership:

> "'What are the Hutchinsons doing?' is a question which has been asked us repeatedly."
>
> Miss Abby Hutchinson "has a well proportioned and fully developed physical organization. . . . Her phrenological developments are most desirable."

"In short, the entire family possess musical genius of the highest order, both phrenologically and practically."

"Married. In Milford, Feb. 21, by Rev. A. E. Warner, Mr John W. Hutchinson (Aeolian Vocalist) to Miss Francis B. Patch."

"The Hutchinsons had upwards of 1200 persons at their concert in Springfield, last week."

"The Hutchinson Family instead of having disbanded, as it has been stated, are giving concerts in Boston."

"THE HUTCHINSONS are abroad."

"The popular singers, known as the Hutchinson Family, having amassed comfortable fortunes, have retired to their native hills and bushes of Milford, N.H., to spend the warm season."

"Madame Rumor says the 'nest of brothers with a sister in it,' the 'Hutchinsons,' is about to lose its bright bud. A son of a New York clergyman is soon to take the hand of 'Abby' in marriage."

"OH, SWEET LITTLE ABBY HUTCHINSON is soon to be married to a rank, crazy abolitionist and thus she will retire to the shades."

"*Abby Hutchinson* is married. 'How many poor hearts she will break!'"

"They have become of some note by thrusting themselves into the society of niggers."

"We regret to learn that the 'illness' of Judson Hutchinson, one of the Hutchinson family, is a mind disease."

"Judson Hutchinson, of the Hutchinson Family, has mostly recovered from his insanity."

"The Hutchinson Family—The New York Express says that Judson Hutchinson has not recovered from his insanity. Jesse now is partaking of the same sad calamity. Asa and John are singing in New England. Abby is at home in that city."[16]

Northerners were, at the very least, curious about the Hutchinsons and, if we judge by their purchases of sheet music and concert tickets, they were not, at first, put off by the group's ardent stance against slavery. The Hutchinsons thrived, and not just among dedicated reformers. The music of the Hutchinson Family Singers reached the mainstream in the North, a starkly divided region. From the group's female supporters in Lowell's factories to their fans holding national political office, the cultural work of the Hutchinsons reverberated at many, and at seemingly contradictory, junctures in American life; the power of their art expressed an ability not only to expand the influence of reform ideas but, often, to break down ideological and cultural barriers.

Walt Whitman believed that the Hutchinsons' stage presence and compositions were infused with an innate Americanness which represented the ordinary people of the democracy. Unlike later cultural critics who equated "popular" with "inferior," a good number in the antebellum era believed that the invention of democracy was one of the most world-shattering events in human history. To them, what was popular was often good. For us, what was popular allows angles of exploration into the past that are often cut off when we scrutinize a topic along strict lines of race, class, and gender.[17]

The legacy of the Hutchinson Family Singers does not rest on their celebrity alone. Many musical acts have achieved a degree of popularity. And the Hutchinsons were hardly the first to mix music and social protest. Songs of social significance appeared as early as 2000 B.C. during the Hsia Dynasty in China. In 1640 New York's Governor Bradford had demanded that ballads criticizing the government be burned, while their anonymous composers sidestepped the controversy. What made the Hutchinson Family Singers unique was their combining of social reform, music, and tremendous popularity. That they accomplished this as sincere reformers—in contrast, say, with the famed British singer of the 1830s and 1840s Henry Russell, who disingenuously played temperance songs—only enhances their distinctiveness.[18]

The Hutchinsons' success created a tradition of music-based social reform that started when the Hutchinson Family Singers were still around and remains central to this day: "It was well known that the world-renowned HUTCHINSONS sang 'The Good Time Coming,'" announced the leader of the Amphian Glee Club, a group of three men and one woman, during an 1853 meeting in New York for women and temperance. "By your permission we will sing you the 'Dawn of the Good Time Coming.'" As early in the Hutchinson Family Singers' career as 1844, the music to "The Old Granite State," their famous encore that borrowed from the religious tune "Old Church Yard," was used as the melody for "We're for Freedom Throughout the Land," written by J. E. Robinson. An 1856 book of antislavery music included selections from the Hutchinsons, along with eight adaptations of Hutchinson Family Singers songs.[19]

For generations, schoolchildren sounded out tunes from the New Hampshire singers. Two hundred fifty students sang the group's songs on the New Haven Green in 1844, while youngsters involved with a New York society for impoverished children of seamen offered their own version of "The Old Granite State" in 1852. Educational conferences also resounded with music from the Hutchinsons, such as when the Blakely Family transformed "The Old Granite State" into "Appeal of the Children" and concluded with "The Good Time Coming." The trend of singing the Hutchinson Family Singers in school continued deep into the nineteenth century and probably lingered into the twentieth, as queries appeared in the *New York Times* for lyrics to Hutchinson songs ("The Old Granite State" and "Uncle Sam's Farm") in 1909 and in 1944.[20]

Music by the Hutchinsons may have slowly receded from the public's awareness, but the group's legend would continually grow. William Lloyd Garrison had a dream in the 1850s in which "a spirit" tore his pantaloon. He reported that the same spirit also "beat a drum in his hearing and sang the 'Old Granite State.'" A few years earlier, Henry Wright noted while writing a letter that at the farm where he was staying in Massachusetts, a pianist was playing the Hutchinson Family Singers' "Get Off the Track!" in the parlor. The New Hampshire singers were the voice of a reform generation, evocative of the 1840s in a way that Bob Dylan, Phil Ochs, and Peter, Paul, and Mary were of the 1960s. President Lincoln's portrait artist Frank Carpenter, who also painted Abby Hutchinson, remembered that "'The Old Granite State' became a household word in every town and hamlet in the country." Carpenter was slightly off; the Hutchinson Family Singers were overwhelmingly a regional attraction, appealing to white and black cultural consumers of the North.[21]

The music of the Hutchinson Family Singers confirms that social movements do not proceed solely along political lines. Akin to the climate in 1960s America, the 1830s and 1840s, a time of great cultural expansion and experimentation, forged the Hutchinson Family Singers. So when mid-twentieth-century music critics, trying to explain the sudden rise in socially progressive musicians in the 1950s and 1960s, named one group as the originator of American protest singing, it is not surprising that they singled out the Hutchinsons. The link between the two generations of reformers separated by more than a century was so strong that it earned the Hutchinson Family Singers (or at least their modern re-creation) several appearances on CBS television in 1965. The Hutchinsons' "contagion" had spread indeed.[22]

And why wouldn't civil rights activists look to the Hutchinsons and their antislavery cultural crusade? Long before Marian Anderson was refused access to Constitution Hall because she was black, managers of Philadelphia's Musical Fund Hall broke their contract with the Hutchinsons because the musicians approved of and attracted desegregated audiences. The Hutchinson Family Singers fought against many of the barriers that later generations of cultural reformers would face. It did not hurt that for a long time the Hutchinsons were also held in high regard in popular consciousness; twenty-four years after John Hutchinson died, his name topped a 1932 *Washington Post* list of six "successful people born on January 4."[23]

The key to the Hutchinson Family Singers' triumph was their moral fortitude combined with an uncanny ability to transform the meaning of their often borrowed melodies with catchy lyrics. The Hutchinsons' antislavery anthem "Get Off The Track!" changed the minstrel tune "Old Dan Tucker" from a dim characterization of black society into an abolitionist vehicle; "King Alcohol" transformed the traditional British melody of "King Andrew" into a comical temperance caution; "The Old Granite State," remade a revival hymn into a sacred song about antislavery, temperance, religion, and family. Add to these selections the Hutchinson Family Singers' many sentimental songs (the musical equivalent of sentimental literature) which borrowed lyrics from famous poets, and the group's catalogue implored listeners to identify with the downtrodden, with the powerless—with children, family, and, ultimately, all humankind.[24]

Before we anoint the famous singers as saints, though, we need to

set them against a more unpleasant context. White antislavery reformers rarely lived up to today's standard of human equality. There were a
few, for certain, who did, but many had notions of black inferiority
and even more took on paternal airs when interacting with those of a
different complexion. "I do not understand that because I do not want
a Negro woman for a slave," said Abraham Lincoln, "I must necessarily want a Negro woman for a wife." Historians have explained the future president's remark as everything from hypocritical to the genius of
a "consummate statesman." Yet Lincoln's expression requires clarifica-
tion only if we compare him to the William Lloyd Garrison who demanded in the American Anti-Slavery Society's constitution that
blacks "share an equality with the whites" or the pre–Civil War Gerrit
Smith who founded and funded a biracial community in northern
New York.[25]

Unfortunately, spokesmen for the full equality of races were rare
and, all too often, fleeting. Garrison in the 1840s took the paternalistic
route, according to Frederick Douglass, while Smith lost nearly all his
faith in human equality after the ravages of the war. Nineteenth-century racial science worked against egalitarian ideals, finding myriad
differences among the races; blacks were often thought to be human
but inferior to those of lighter skin. Few were left untouched by such
essentialist thinking. In his autobiographical *Life and Times,* Frederick
Douglass began speaking of racial distinctions he formerly refuted,
claiming that a black man is "naturally" endowed for warmer climes—
he "walks, labors, and sleeps in the sunlight unharmed." And while the
ascendancy of Darwinian theory did change the way that people
looked at race, frequently it shored up existing prejudice. Whites became representative of the "fittest" species, with blacks occupying a
lower rung on the evolutionary scale.

Members of the Hutchinsons come off rather well against such a
background. Whereas Lincoln's famous pledge—that he would, "to
the very last," defend laws forbidding "the marrying of white people
with Negroes"—was not a problem in the minds of most nineteenth-
century abolitionists, it would not have sat well with the New Hampshire musicians. John, Asa, Judson, and Abby had little personal objection to racial mixing, thus earning the moniker "Nigger Minstrels." A
writer, appalled at the biracial Boston audience seen at one of the

Hutchinsons' shows, once suggested that the group should denounce such "amalgamation," believing the sentiment would please the group's fans. This writer for the *Evening Transcript* obviously cared little about the Hutchinson Family Singers' black listeners and supporters. If members of the singing troupe had a reform failing, though, it was an increasingly patronizing outlook toward minorities that seemed to accompany their wealth and their old age, especially in their dealings with Native Americans.[26]

In this book I tell the interwoven story of music, careerism, reform, the transformation of American culture, and one of the greatest musical acts in American history. Following the Hutchinson Family Singers through the nineteenth century as they explored and shaped new openings in American society unveils the centrality of political allegiance to artistic creation in the antebellum era. (The debate over which is more important in exploring the past, culture or politics, is a futile one—these two arenas thrive off of each other.) As grandchildren of the Revolutionary War generation, the Hutchinson Family Singers were integral players in bringing American reform from the Enlightenment offering of Tom Paine's *Common Sense* to the brand of Romantic activism found in their music and in the writings of such authors as Harriet Beecher Stowe. From New Hampshire to New York, from temperance to antislavery, from revivals to political parades to parlors, and from an aspiring musical trio to a wealthy quartet, the Hutchinson Family Singers shepherded in one of the great nineteenth-century phenomena. Ralph Waldo Emerson looked out at what surrounded him and recorded the revolution: "We are in a world for culture."[27]

Part First

———❦———

Chronology

—9 November 1837. Elijah Lovejoy killed by a proslavery mob.

—1838–1840. John Greenleaf Whittier (1807–1892), editor of the *Pennsylvania Freeman,* writes several antislavery poems, including "Massachusetts to Virginia," "Yankee Girl," and "The Hunters of Men."

—13 November 1839. A faction from the American Anti-Slavery Society convenes in Warsaw, New York, in an attempt to create the first political antislavery party in American history.

—1 April 1840. The Liberty Party is formed, with antislavery advocate James G. Birney as presidential candidate.

—6 November 1840. The Hutchinson family, en masse, give their first public performance in Milford, New Hampshire.

—13 November 1840. Annual antislavery meeting held in Milford, New Hampshire. Several members of the Hutchinson family hear Nathaniel P. Rogers, William Lloyd Garrison, Parker Pillsbury, and Stephen Symmonds Foster lecture on social reform.

—1841. John, Asa, and Judson Hutchinson move to Lynn, Massachusetts, after unsuccessfully touring as a musical trio in New England.

—Fall 1841. Frederick Douglass, fugitive slave, moves to Lynn.

—January 1842. John, Asa, and Judson add sister Abby, forming the Hutchinson Family Singers.

—11 August 1842. Nathaniel Rogers, in the *Herald of Freedom,* writes of the Hutchinson Family Singers' abolitionism and suggests that they compose antislavery songs.

—October 1842. Fugitive slave George Latimer incarcerated in Boston.

—4–5 January 1843. The Hutchinson Family Singers' antislavery musical debut at an antislavery meeting in Milford.

—25 January 1843. The Hutchinson Family Singers make their first antislavery appearance in Boston at the annual meeting of the Massachusetts Anti-Slavery Society.

—9 May 1843. The Hutchinson Family Singers debut in New York at the annual meeting of the American Anti-Slavery Society.

—1844. Liberty Party candidate James Birney receives 2.3 percent of the popular vote in the presidential election. Slightly more than 30 percent of the townsfolk in Milford vote for Birney.

—1851. Samuel Joseph May (1797–1871) takes part in the violent rescue of fugitive slave Jerry McHenry in Syracuse, New York.

—1856. South Carolina Representative Preston Brooks (1819–1857) beats Massachusetts Senator Charles Sumner (1811–1874) with a cane after the latest of Sumner's many antislavery speeches.

—11 January 1859. Judson Hutchinson dies.

—14 January 1862. For their singing of antislavery songs to the troops, John Hutchinson and his family are banned from entertaining the Union Army.

—1 January 1863. President Lincoln issues the Emancipation Proclamation, which frees only those slaves in the Confederate States.

—1870. Abby Hutchinson Patton edits and publishes *Camp Meeting Songs of the Florida Freedmen.*

—1874. Joshua Hutchinson, brother of the famed singers, publishes *A Brief Narrative of the Hutchinson Family.*

—1875. Asa Hutchinson's adaptation of "Reign Oh Reign, Massa Jesus Reign!" goes on sale.

—1877. Federal troops leave South Carolina, ending government-sponsored social reform known as Reconstruction.

—24 May 1879. William Lloyd Garrison dies at the age of seventy-three.

—25 November 1884. Asa Hutchinson dies following a sudden illness.

—10 September 1892. John Hutchinson and Abby Hutchinson Patton sing at the funeral of John Greenleaf Whittier.

—24 November 1892. Sixty-three-year-old Abby Hutchinson Patton dies from a stroke.

—26 April 1893. The Danvers Historical Society hosts an Anti-Slavery Commemorative Meeting.

—20 February 1895. Frederick Douglass, seventy-eight years old, dies.

—1896. The Hutchinson family epic written by John Hutchinson, *Story of the Hutchinson Family,* is finally published.

—28 May 1901. John Hutchinson sings and plays violin as a part of commencement ceremonies for the predominantly African-American student body of Howard University.

Exposition: The Civil War and
the Postbellum Problem of Antislavery

In 1890 only John and Abby remained. The two had survived their siblings and many of their reform-minded friends. At sixty-nine and sixty-one years old, John and Abby continued to sing and otherwise advocate for a variety of reforms, especially civil rights, temperance, and women's rights. As part of the antislavery vanguard, they took part in countless events celebrating the role of abolitionists in ending slavery, occasions which in the closing decade of the nineteenth century lacked conviction. The emancipation of nearly four million slaves finalized by the Thirteenth Amendment in 1865 was a highlight in the lives of reformers, including the Hutchinson Family Singers; it was one of those successes fraught with failure.

The abolition of slavery in the United States relied upon the actions of the slaves, politicians, the military, and antislavery activists. That all of these forces came together for a brief moment ensured emancipation as the most astonishing event in nineteenth-century America. Yet nearly thirty years after President Lincoln had sanctioned the Emancipation Proclamation, reformers were left feeling rather empty. They looked at the nation surrounding them, a nation that they had helped to shape, and wondered how much of it was worth celebrating. More than 600,000 soldiers had died in the Civil War, and for what? Capitalism, in a most greedy and exploitative form, was running rampant. The finishing touches were being added to the genocide of Native Americans. And many of the four million emancipated black Americans now lived under a grisly repression.[1]

In their youth, antislavery advocates like the Hutchinson Family Singers held an unwavering belief that "moral suasion"—an appeal to the incorruptible heart in all people—and the aegis of a redemptive, indwelling God assured the triumph of Good over Evil. At the close of the nineteenth century, the Hutchinsons still foisted upon their listeners this ideology derived from the Second Great Awakening. But moral suasion and the sympathy for others that it required had seemingly lost the ability to breach the barrier of race. Many northern white listeners, the same ones who once had catapulted the Hutchinson Family Singers into the limelight, had stopped worrying over the plight of blacks. Black communities, meanwhile, often remained grateful for the musicians, reserving ceremonial spots for members of the group, as when John sang at the 1901 Howard University commencement. Yet even black Americans began casting a wary eye toward the Hutchinsons. Without great influence among a white coalition, the Hutchinsons' music no longer instantiated a biracial reform community. By 1890 the

Hutchinson Family Singers could offer very little to African Americans who increasingly looked within themselves for political action and for protection from an increasingly violent racism.[2]

The Hutchinson Family Singers, along with many other antislavery supporters, spent their final days reconciling their ultimate achievement with the moral disaster that followed. After the war, John, Asa, and Abby—the three remaining members of the musical troupe—tried to help the newly freed men and women, never ending their efforts to eliminate racial prejudice. A national objective to heal the war-torn nation, though, took precedence over lessening racial divides. The new-found cooperation between northern and southern leaders in the postbellum era neutralized the momentum of pre–Civil War reform. Reformer James Freeman Clarke observed, "The North and South are truly one; the American Union, this single root of bitterness [slavery] having been taken away, is vastly more powerful and more united, than ever." Clarke failed to mention that, within an environment obsessed with healing the wounds of war, the gap between races was growing.[3]

As the success of emancipation came to be questioned from all angles, the Hutchinsons and others scrambled to secure their reform legacy. John Hutchinson feared that his life's work would fall prey to obscurity. On the centenary of his parents' wedding in 1900, he visited a subtreasury building on Wall Street. Here, John bought 1,500 one-cent pieces from the final issue of 1899. "I have lived a dozen lives in my seventy-nine years. The world is getting away from me now," explained John to the clerk. "My one wish now is to feel and know that some hundreds of the millions in this big land have in their keeping a memento of my family." With that, John started walking outside, a tried and true nineteenth-century reformer, handing out the last of the 1899 pennies.[4]

The Hutchinsons' lives were not always so nostalgic. When the singers crafted their own brand of fashionable antislavery music in 1843, there was an air of possibility. Someway, somehow, the Hutchinson Family Singers always believed that they could improve themselves and their music so that the world would be a better place. "O there must be a revelation. I think the time is near when the Slave will be free," said Asa at his family's home in Milford. "Mankind will learn how to live and serve the God above. I rejoice in such reformation as the cause of Antislavery is bringing about. It is a part of the true principles of Christ, in fact the foundation."[5]

Comparing the plights of the Hutchinson Family Singers in the 1890s and in the 1840s provides a fresh look at what happened to one of the most hallowed generations in American history. The rise of the Hutchinson Family Singers in the 1840s reveals a complex interaction of personal ambition, religion, reform, and consumerism alongside an antislavery network buttressed by influential leaders, a vast media, and a growing following. At the close of the century—focusing on the ebb and flow of a postwar antislavery meeting that mimicked the events of years earlier—the Hutchinsons' story yields insight into whether abolitionism was a failure, as some have suggested, or a success, as many believe. A fair evaluation should compare the objectives and accomplishments of reformers, and also situate reform aspirations within a particular moment in time. As John Hutchinson discovered in the 1890s, it is difficult for even the most passionate reformer to make a difference without a broad alliance.[6]

Development, Scene One, 1893: The Legacy of the Hutchinson Family Singers and of Antislavery Reform

Those were inspiring days. I look back lovingly upon them; and I find it very hard to realize that so much of it has passed into oblivion, and that whatever remains is merely the cold record of history.

—Lydia Maria Child, letter to Theodore Dwight Weld, July 1880

Everybody now is anti-slavery. It is honorable now to be a child of the man who "cast the first anti-slavery vote in our town"; or called "our first anti-slavery meeting"; or first entertained Garrison as guest, or Abby Kelley, or Frederick Douglass. . . . Everybody now is an abolitionist, or son, or grandson of an anti-slavery parentage, and so all seem to claim equal honor, so far as honor is due, for ridding the world of the sublimest scourge and curse that ever afflicted the human race.

—Parker Pillsbury, *Acts of the Anti-Slavery Apostles*, 1884

Who can measure the influence of their songs of freedom upon the unformed opinions of the youth of the day?

—Frank Carpenter on the Hutchinson Family Singers
in *Peterson Magazine*, 1896

Danvers, Massachusetts, 1893

The air temperature lingered near forty-four degrees, normal for an April day in the Bay State. Soon after disembarking in Danvers, the many out-of-towners welcomed one another and then rushed to reception lunches. At one o'clock long-lost friends and former rivals exchanged more pleasantries, which filled the warm interior of Town Hall. April 1893. Lincoln's Emancipation Proclamation had aged thirty years, and now more than 150 people gathered in this Massachusetts town to relive the excitement of days since past. The meeting began with the clamor and confusion often associated with remarkable get-togethers. But before celebrating their role in ridding the nation of slavery, the reunion's most prominent were to pose for a picture. The guests' lively conversations distracted them from the task at hand, and only the effort of William T. Clark of the Soule Photograph Company, who politely coerced the chatty visitors to stand still, salvaged the customary photo. With one last rush, all were positioned to be in the print.[7]

A flash arced over the men and women poised before the camera, and the moment was secured for future generations. Clark's final product is masterful, capturing the congratulatory spirit and the chaos of the event—certainly no mean feat considering the circumstances (fig. 2). The image is humorous and earnest. The men and women in the photograph stand in two rows, with the row in back placed on a riser. In front of the first row sits a large arrangement of flowers in the middle of which are two larger-than-life portraits—one of William Lloyd Garrison, the other of the Rev. Samuel Joseph May. Two more sizable portraits loom as bookends for the first row; on the left Charles Sumner, and on the right John Greenleaf Whittier. Behind the attendees a very large American flag (presumably the forty-four-star flag that had become official in 1891) envelopes most of those pictured in its folds. A light drops from the ceiling in front of the flag, with two fixtures forming a cross over the guests, a shape accentuated by the way the flag is tied to three supports. Floating above their heads, the lights' white circular sconces hover as halos. Indeed, this was a saintly bunch, as these men and women were the final vestiges of the antislavery vanguard.[8]

The haste of the endeavor is established by (at least) five blurred

Ceremonial Photo of the Danvers Anti-Slavery Commemorative Meeting, 26 April 1893. From *Old Anti-Slavery Days* (Danvers: Danvers Mirror Print, 1893), xxviii–xxiv.

images in a picture embracing forty-three people. Somehow one woman was never identified, her name lost amid the confusion. All the activity was too much for Alfred F. Masury, the young boy caught in the foreground. Alfred turned back, facing the photographer with a thrill of expectation—watching everyone trying to situate, he didn't know what would come next. Then suddenly the camera clicked. A minute after the picture taking, it is easy to imagine Alfred a bit disappointed in his discovery that the excitement had been just for a photograph. When the guests broke from modeling and began a five-hour discourse on how important their lives had been, his distress probably reached a new high.

The Danvers Historical Society had brought everyone together for an Anti-Slavery Commemorative Meeting. Here, members gathered to recall America's "Second Revolution"—the freeing of the slaves—understood by everyone in attendance as a continuation of the nation's independence from Great Britain. William Lloyd Garrison, Jr., Parker Pillsbury, Lucy Stone, and George Putnam are just a few of the notables captured in the photo. Two heads to the left of center in the first row stands the star of the Danvers gathering, John Wallace Hutchinson, one of the founding members of the Hutchinson Family Singers.[9]

The celebrants at the Anti-Slavery Commemorative Meeting surrounded themselves with suggestive imagery. The four men evoked through portrait represented a character that the conventioneers, reformers famous in their own right, deemed particularly worthy of remembrance. A prophet, a preacher, a politician, and a poet: Garrison, May, Sumner, and Whittier. These four had waged antislavery battles in different arenas and occasionally against one another. In 1893 the Danvers commemorators advanced the idea that each had been vital to the success of the movement.

William Lloyd Garrison glares out from an oval print centered prominently before the first row in the photograph. It was an appropriate position, as few would contest his placement within the pantheon of great American reformers. Garrison's was a legacy secured long before the slaves gained freedom. His public life began with his antislavery conversion in 1828 and continued as he placed his stamp on antebellum society through his newspaper, the *Liberator*, and through his stewardship of important antislavery organizations. The impeccably dressed and well-mannered Bostonian quickly developed into one of the leaders of American reform in 1831, when he shook a nation barely able to envision a gradual emancipation with an impassioned call to immediately stop the practice of slavery.

Antislavery located Garrison in the annals of American history, but he espoused many other progressive causes of his era. Pacifism and women's rights were particularly dear to him, and the editor rarely sacrificed one reform for the sake of another. When issues surrounding women in leadership ranks troubled the international antislavery movement in 1839 and 1840, Garrison stood firm in his belief that women were vital to the cause. This was the positive side of Garrison's idealism. His obstinacy made him equally infamous. Garrison believed that slavery unavoidably corrupted politics, and his refusal to work through the nation's political system was legendary. The Boston editor remained steadfast throughout his career, arguing that moral suasion—appealing directly to people to change the way they feel—offered the best alternative to the ballot box or to violence. Garrison's aversion to political affairs separated him from many friends as the climate shifted during the 1840s and 1850s, when antislavery fervor increasingly mixed with national politics.

Emancipation not only freed the slaves, it justified Garrison's cause and quieted his critics. One writer portrayed him as an antislavery bigot while acknowledging that "the future generation will look upon his severity of character, his bigotry, as we look upon the same faults in the grand men who laid the foundations of this republic—as spots upon the reputation of one the noblest men that ever lived." Following the war Garrison was heralded more often as a hero than as a heretic. His death in 1879 further enhanced a legacy soon recorded in an 1885 biography written by his sons Wendell and Francis. Of all the men whose portraits appear in the Danvers picture, Garrison is the one whose reputation needed the least stoking in 1893. At the convention he was represented by progeny as well as portrait. His commemoration was more a ritual than an announcement.[10]

No one guaranteed reverence for the three remaining figures chosen to share the spotlight in the Danvers photo. The Rev. Samuel Joseph May was a Harvard graduate, connected to Boston's elite circles by kin. He left this comfortable network to join forces with William Lloyd Garrison in the campaign against slavery. Already considered a radical when he formed the Brooklyn Temperance Society in 1828 at his church in Brooklyn, Connecticut, the Unitarian minister completely alienated himself by promoting antislavery in the early 1830s. Eventually, only two churches in the greater Boston area, both headed by antislavery sympathizers, allowed May the pulpit. From one of these platforms the ordinarily genial May thundered out his "Discourse on Slavery in the United States" in 1831, a sermon that catapulted him to abolitionism's front line.

From this vantage point—estranged from family and church, but at home among reformers—May lived the rest of his life. With an undying gleam in his brown eyes, he demonstrated that he cared more for his sense of right than anything else. May once, to the consternation of his white listeners, invited a black family to move to the front pew of his church because their number had outgrown the space reserved for them in back. Another time, at a meeting in Haverhill, rocks flew through the windows, and the locals readied a canon while May calmly led his antislavery followers to safety. He fought valiantly for the abolitionist cause throughout the 1830s and became Garrison's closest friend—performing the editor's marriage in 1834 and, over the years, providing counsel. Lydia Maria Child acknowledged May's rectitude by dedicating *An Appeal in Favor of That Class of Americans Called Africans* to the minister "for his earnest and disinterested efforts in an unpopular but most righteous cause."

After two decades of antislavery crusading, years of unfulfilled activism would boil over when May broke his vow of nonviolence in order to ensure the freedom of a fugitive slave. In 1851 May led the unarmed mob that stormed a Syracuse prison to free Jerry McHenry. This placed him at odds with William Lloyd Garrison, yet unlike many who fell from grace in Garrison's eyes, May salvaged the relationship. The portraits of these two friends stood side by side on the Danvers stage, each with its own light casting a soft shadow on the surrounding reformers.[11]

The charged environment which had tried May's pacifist convictions opened a significant space for antislavery politics on a national level. The divide between adherents of moral suasion and those who sought redress through politics opened in 1839, expanded in the 1850s, and was resolved when the Civil War made clear the federal government's crucial role in emancipation. Of the four abolitionists whose portraits were on display in Danvers, two dedicated themselves to political action.

One of the most significant antislavery political figures is positioned on the left side of the Danvers picture, where sits a youthful likeness of Charles Sumner, with flowing hair parted on his right side. Since Sumner's was the only portrait of the four framed in a light color, one's eye follows a line of white beards until it rests on his angled picture, crowned with a wreath and highlighting the left side of the photograph. Sumner fought on behalf of the slave on a national level starting when Massachusetts sent him to the Senate for the first time in 1851. But as many were quick to point out, he was not "an original abolitionist"; Sumner came to espouse antislavery rather late in life.[12]

After graduating from Harvard in 1830, Charles Sumner spent time becoming a lawyer and trying to establish a career at a time when the legal profession abounded with practitioners. In 1837 he left for a long and storied trip to Europe, where he spoke with the explorer and scientist Alexander von Humboldt, the German historian Leopold von Ranke, and the geographer Carl Ritter. Sumner returned in 1840 infused with ideas about the oneness of the universe—that everyone and everything was somehow related. In that vein, on 4 July 1845, with hostilities growing between the United States and Mexico, he began his public career pleading for universal peace, claiming war an unnecessary evil. At an antislavery meeting that year, the future congressman began to stake out other reform ideas, voting against a proposal of William Lloyd Garrison's while enjoying the impassioned debate. Eventually, he would earn an abolitionist reputation: "He put to the hazard his case, his interests, his friendship, even his daring popularity," said C. A. Bartol, "for the benefit of a race of man he had never seen, and who could not even give him thanks." Hooley's Minstrels, Sumner's detractors in the music world, jeered that the senator had "nigger on the brain."[13]

The historical record remembers Sumner best as the victim of South Carolina Representative Preston Brooks's fierce caning in 1856, a classic instance of the proslavery South versus the antislavery North. This episode introduced into the gentlemanly quarters of Congress the vigilante justice so often associated with slaveholders, making Sumner a martyr in the North and Brooks a celebrity in the South. The Danvers organizers' choice of Garrison, May, and Sumner fits well with modern scholarship on the antislavery movement; the three have often been considered central actors in the history of abolitionism. Over the years, the figure in the remaining portrait and his important cultural work have slipped from antislavery chronicles.[14]

John Greenleaf Whittier, the "poet laureate for the abolitionist cause," never looked like a hardened and an impassioned reformer. His tall, slender frame housed "delicate features, eyes of fiery black, and a quick, nervous manner." While many probably recognized his small portrait placed on the right side of the stage, Whittier's poetry, not his face, had served as his public presence. Often reports found him, if anything, "exceedingly bashful in general society." Hypochondria accentuated the poet's shyness, a trait only worsened by real maladies including near-blindness. His reclusiveness was not a terrible burden for a writer, but it was for an abolitionist-turned-politician. Yet no one at the Danvers convention looked at his picture and saw frailty. Whittier may have been weak in body, but anyone who had ever read his writings quickly forgot his physical shortcomings, discovering instead a daring and an emotional activist.

The Quaker poet allied himself with antislavery in 1833 at the insistence of William Lloyd Garrison. Attending the first meeting of the American Anti-Slavery Society in Philadelphia, Whittier, along with Garrison and May, sat on the subcommittee charged with composing the Declaration of Sentiments. From this moment on, Whittier's writings, a blend of moral sensibility and religious themes, earned him the moniker "preacher-poet." One of his first compositions for the cause, "Our Countrymen in Chains!" quickly developed into the centerpiece for the American Anti-Slavery Society's broadside campaign. It starts:

> OUR FELLOW COUNTRYMEN IN CHAINS!
> Slaves—in a land of light and law!
> Slaves—crouching on the very plains
> Where rolled the storm of Freedom's war!

The lines appealed to the "sons of the Revolution," a generation struggling to live up to the promise and deeds of their fathers and grandfathers, who had fought for America's liberation. Nothing stirred this group more than pointing out decline in a nation "where rolled the storm of Freedom's war." Whittier also chronicled events significant to the antislavery world in his work. These poems, shorter and thus quicker to make their point than newspaper articles, served as abolitionist interpretations of current events. "The Sentence of John L. Brown" (originally titled "Stanzas for the Times—1844") was one such piece. Brown, a white South Carolinian, married a slave and aided in her escape from slavery. For these actions Brown was sentenced to death. An international outrage ensued, and protestors pressured officials into lessening the penalty. The writings of the "newspaper-poet" in such situations tied interpretive sentiment to reportage, turning his poems into a valuable source of history. These narratives, beloved by the antislavery rank and file, endeared Whittier to abolitionist leaders.[15]

The success of the antislavery poet was not universally celebrated, though. Whittier was blacklisted from many national political and literary journals because of his reform associations. His initial audience thus did not extend much beyond a select group of New England readers. National recognition for the poet did not come until the late 1860s, when a northern victory rendered antislavery opinions no longer appallingly radical. Even then it was not Whittier's antislavery poetry which was heralded. When he achieved fame, his nature works were upheld, while his abolitionist ones were muted. In the twentieth century he would be listed with such literary greats as Walt Whitman, Henry Wadsworth Longfellow, Ralph Waldo Emerson, Mark Twain, and Emily Dickinson as one of the worthies in American writing. This was not why those gathered at Danvers in April 1893 chose Whittier's image to grace the stage. To them he fit Frederick Douglass's description in 1855: a "brilliant" American poet who spoke "in burning verse." To them Whittier's was a face that belonged on the stage with Garrison, May, and Sumner.[16]

A tinge of irony is buried in the fact that Whittier's and Garrison's images shared the Danvers platform. While the two had been friends in the early days of antislavery, Whittier parted with the man who had drawn him to reform. Their dispute had several causes, not the least of which was the poet's conviction that moral suasion must connect to political action in order for abolitionists to succeed. In this impulse Whittier was hardly alone. Staying true to this belief, he helped found the Liberty Party, and in 1844 he ran for Congress as one of its candidates. Whittier ultimately found Garrison "dictatorial, censorious, intolerant," and the two reformers spent most of the rest of their lives in similar circles, rarely sharing a word.[17]

In the aftermath of the Civil War, a feeling of triumph began to melt away the factional disputes separating abolitionists. Few were willing to let bygones cloud their new sense of self-worth and celebration. Demographics further fueled reconciliation, as those who had enlisted in the 1830s had served the cause for close to three decades—almost half of the average life expectancy for a New Englander—by the time the slaves were freed. They were men and women at the end of their lives. Outside of festive events such as the one in Danvers, funerals served as their most frequent site of reunion.[18]

William Lloyd Garrison tended to many memorial services in the 1870s as an "unofficial minister" to comrades who had withdrawn from the church long ago. Garrison's 1879 death disheartened many abolitionists; they had lost a counselor and a leader. His passing shocked John Greenleaf Whittier into reacknowledging his former friend's best qualities. The poet penned a few lines of praise that were read at the funeral, an event Whittier proclaimed himself too enfeebled to attend. The two men who had started as companions reunited in the forgiving milieu of postwar America.[19]

Thirteen years later, the 1892 funeral of Whittier produced another significant reunion. The poet's death brought together the remaining members of the Hutchinson Family Singers. Fifty-two years after their first performance at the Baptist Meeting House in Milford, New Hampshire, John Wallace Hutchinson and Abigail Jemima Hutchinson Patton sang to honor the famed writer. The Hutchinsons were, at best, casual friends of the poet. Their bond to him was that forged between people of similar circumstance, artists who promoted social reform—a friendship built upon mutual admiration but little private interaction. Over the years, even their most personal exchanges demonstrated minimal affection. John once used a Whittier poem as lyrics for a song he and his family performed for Union troops during the Civil War. The poet, surprised by John's initiative, wryly stated, "I am glad to know that there is *any sing* in my verses." Later Whittier wrote to John that "as one of the old pioneers of the cause, I am glad to acknowledge your service of song" and wished him good luck in the days to come. In 1889 Abby and her husband Ludlow sent a present—yellow sands that they had taken from the Nile River—for the poet's eighty-second birthday, telling Whittier that the gift is a "token of the golden age you have reached."[20]

The superficial nature of their association did not prevent John and Abby from feeling that Whittier was indeed a brother, and, despite Quakers' general discomfort with music, the Hutchinson siblings received permission to sing at his funeral. Among the works performed was George H. Boker's "Dirge for a Soldier," opening with the line, "Close his eyes, his work is done." John wrote two new verses which replaced the references to a dead soldier in the original version of the song. The siblings sang at the large funeral for the likes of General O. O. Howard—the former head of the Freedmen's Bureau—and the jurist Oliver Wendell Holmes. The Hutchinsons had no idea that Whittier's funeral would be their last performance.[21]

Months after the service, Susan B. Anthony wrote to John: "The Farmer's Cabinet of Dec. 1—brings the word that your precious sister Abby has gone before you to the land beyond—and this leaves 'John'—'brother John'—The last of that marvelous band of sweet singers for freedom & equality of fifty-years ago." John, eight years older than Abby, now lived as the sole surviving member from a family of sixteen brothers and sisters. A year before her passing, Abby worried that her volume of poetry, *A Handful of Pebbles*, "will have to go as my last will and heirloom to my brothers' and sisters' children." She was right. John's work, though, was far from done. Which is why he could be found sitting next to the Danvers Historical Society's president, A. P. Putnam, exactly five months after his sister's death. An elderly John is situated comfortably in the commemorative photograph. And he is easy to spot. In an image where others' features are not very clear, one can distinguish the middle part in John's hair and moustache, and even some individual strands of the lengthy white beard attached to his rather somber face. John Wallace Hutchinson had posed for many pictures. A life in the public eye taught him to mind his appearance and, more important for the technology of the day, he had learned how to stay still. In the midst of all the hubbub in Danvers, John was composed and, perhaps, even at peace. Clearly, his portrait belonged amid the antislavery dignitaries.[22]

During their time as the Hutchinson Family Singers, John and his brothers, Judson and Asa, along with their sister Abby, exhibited traits from each of the memorialized reformers at Danvers. They were leaders of antislavery culture, martyrs for their cause, political activists, and supporters of violent means to end slavery, and—like May, Sumner, Garrison, and Whittier—they fought for an integrated America.

By 1893 John had changed from his days as the Hutchinson Family Singers' unflagging cheerleader. He was now the grayed patriarch of Lynn, Massachusetts, who owned considerable real estate upon High Rock, who filled some of his time finding renters for his tenements, who traversed the country with younger women, and who seized the spotlight at any opportunity. In the 1890s John could be found in Washington, D.C., visiting Frederick Douglass, chatting with the president, strolling the streets with senators, and attending the seventieth birthday of Susan B. Anthony; in Lynn, at his own seventieth birthday bash and financing more cottages for his High Rock premises; in Minneapolis with the New York delegation for the Republican National Convention; and in many spots throughout the nation attending the funerals of friends. He sang at nearly all of these events and continued to vocalize for any cause he deemed worthy. The anticigarette campaign was his last beneficiary—"Sings to Save" announced the headline for John's final tour in 1901. His promoters enjoyed playing up his status as the last of a species, a live antislavery advocate and Hutchinson Family Singer, to publicize his shows (fig. 3). The reverence allotted to him in the 1890s was substantial. But being Lynn's most recognizable celebrity never fulfilled John's needs. In his twilight, the famed singer was lonely.[23]

John, then in his seventies, lived under the watchful eye of his daughter, Viola. He once filled his days after the Civil War planning and throwing celebrations which ensured that he would see his dearest friends and siblings, but they were no longer available—either departed or in such poor health as to prevent travel. His parties were now tinged with sadness—a birthday celebration for his late sister Abby, for example. Viola understood his plight, but only to a point. She feared that her father might squander his fortune on some conniving woman, a fear John fueled. From 1894 through 1905, the elderly singer proposed to several younger women—including an offer of marriage to the Boston reporter sent to cover his scandalous relationships. These romantic interludes created plenty of legal trouble, as John, either on his own whim or at his daughter's insistence, broke off several marital engagements. His scorned lovers quickly filed "breach of promise" lawsuits. John, a lifelong supporter of women's rights and women's suffrage, was condemned as a philanderer. "I especially noticed that you and brother John Hutchinson were flirting together the evening we were all in the

COMING.—READ BOTH SIDES.

The mere mention of Mr. Hutchinson's name will crowd the house. Let the young people of to-day ask their parents about the famous Hutchinson Family of years ago. Now one of the ORIGINALS is coming. He has been personally acquainted with ex-President Lincoln. Henry W. Longfellow, John Brown, General Grant, General Sherman, Garfield, Henry Ward Beecher, Mrs. Stowe, Gladstone, Charles Dickens, and many others.

All the scholars will be invited to take part in the Grand Chorus of several Patriotic Songs. It will be a great treat to thus listen to a thousand voices.

Come rain or shine, let nothing keep you away. This entertainment will be the "talk" in every household. A great SURPRISE in store for those who attend.

BORN IN MILFORD.

EXTRA GREAT FUN AND LAUGHTER FOR YOUNG PEOPLE.

Town Hall, Milford,
Thursday Night, Nov. 2.

Mr. Hutchinson will be assisted by Miss Effie Mae Stevens, the favorite soprano of East Lynn fame. Remember that he was born in New Hampshire. This will be your only chance of a lifetime. He will receive a grand ovation. Many extra seats will be provided.

10, 20 and 30 Cents.

1890s advertisement for John Hutchinson. Courtesy the New Hampshire Historical Society, Concord.

Corcoran Gallery," said a concerned Susan B. Anthony to one of her friends in 1900. "I kept my eye on you although I was obliged to stay in my place in the big chair on that elevated platform."[24]

Viola, taxed by these events, tried unsuccessfully to have her father declared legally incompetent. While there was probably a hint of senility setting in with old age, John, the ultimate performer, could still pull it together when in the limelight, and he did so in a Salem, Massachusetts, courtroom. Proving his sanity did not change the drama which inundated the last two decades of John's life. There were the courting quandaries, the deaths of friends and siblings, the loss of a large portion of his memoir manuscript, and a barn fire which killed the oxen ("John Hutchinson's Oxen Cremated," read the headline). But the most difficult ordeal for the singer was not in plain sight. It can't be found in his speeches or in his memoirs, yet it was hinted at within the newspapers: a vast majority of Americans at the close of the century had never even heard of the Hutchinson Family Singers. "Let the young people of to-day ask their parents about the famous Hutchinson Family of years ago," read one of John's concert advertisements. This explains why John felt at home at the Danvers antislavery reunion. Along with the other dinosaurs of the abolitionist days, he remembered, recollected, and reshaped the past. John remained "Famous in Slavery Days," to borrow from the *Washington Post* piece which covered the Danvers celebration.[25]

The time consumed by the photography session in Danvers had pushed back the start of the meeting, scheduled for 1 p.m., until two. At this time the Rev. William H. Fish offered an opening prayer and, following the "amen," the seventy-two-year-old John Hutchinson was asked to sing. The old bard had adjusted swiftly to his status as the only living member of the Hutchinson Family Singers, and he set out alone on "Few, Faithful, and True," joined in on the chorus by his granddaughter Kate and his daughter. After the applause, John, with voice robust even in old age, addressed the convention:

> Dear Friends: This is an impressive occasion and a momentous review. We bid you all a hearty welcome. To the few veterans whose lives have dwindled to so short a span, let

me say, we congratulate you that one more opportunity is offered that will yield sacred remembrance of joys we have tasted and of true friendships we have experienced. . . . Your joys are full and our hearts made glad this day, even though it should chance to be the last. We meet here upon ground sacred to the memory of our ancestors, who, two hundred and fifty years ago, settled and cultivated this soil, deriving title from the aborigines who had so recently vacated their corn fields and hunting grounds. Here, seven generations, bearing the name of Hutchinson, have followed in due succession. From this place heroes of that and many another family went forth to the defence of liberty and were among the bravest at the battles of Lexington and Bunker Hill and in the struggles of the Revolution. We, who have lived since that day of sharp conflicts with the foes of freedom, have rejoiced to hear again the sound of emancipation. And now, in our old age, we assemble with our countrymen here and commemorate the events that establish the fact that the nation could live with chattel slavery entirely eliminated, and right made triumphant.

To start a lengthy closing, John pronounced:

Familiar as household words shall be the names of Garrison, Rogers, Thompson, Phillips, Douglass, Weld, Quincy, Jackson, Burleigh, Sumner, Chase, Wilson, Birney, Foster, Kelley, May, Pillsbury, Putnam, Mott, Purvis, Chapman, McKim, Whittier, Abraham Lincoln and Lucy Stone, with the Tribe of Jesse [the Hutchinson family], and full many others.

The speech outlined the main purpose of John's later years. Where Abby had left her legacy in a small collection of poems, maxims on how to live a godly and good life, John's final mission was to carve a place for his family and friends in the annals of American history. In the 1840s he had awakened to battle for the approaching millennium, an anticipated future of joy and prosperity to be had through the eradication of slavery and other sins then plaguing the United States. The Hutchinsons' songs and actions in the 1840s and 1850s had secured their reform legacy, but the end of American slavery did not ring in an era of peace and justice. John's Danvers speech reflects a man rationalizing the gap between expectation and reality.[26]

The entertainer covered familiar ground in his oration; he acknowledged a common bond with the audience—their pending mortality—and gave everyone a pat on the back for being reformers. John immortalized himself and others by hanging on the coattails of the American Revolution. For a man of John's age, capturing the spirit of the Revolution was uplifting, noble, and necessary to compare favorably to his grandfather's generation. The hoary singer claimed that the members of the Hutchinson family and others who had fought in the Revolution had passed on to their children and grandchildren a notion of liberty that would guide them in their battle against black enslavement in the years preceding the Civil War.

John's conclusion, though, recognized only part of the Revolution's legacy. Speaking of liberty differs from delivering liberty; no American embodies this seeming contradiction better than Thomas Jefferson, who authored the gallant phrase, "We hold these truths to be self-evident, that all men are created equal," and yet could not envision a racially integrated nation. Ultimately, John's grandfathers' generation created a Constitution sustaining slavery. Ending the slave trade in 1808 was an act of justice, but the same document that banned the importation of slaves provided for the perpetuation of slavery through the compromise that counted each slave as three-fifths of a citizen and through an eager protection of private property. Stories of American freedom and liberty sometimes conceal inglorious ends, and John Hutchinson's talk in Danvers was no exception.[27]

In praising his family and his friends by drawing a line from the colonial pioneers to the Revolution to the antislavery movement, John was inspiring, if not outright majestic. But his gasconade also revealed a frightening indifference toward Native America. The great hand of "liberty" which drove his oration ran right over the Indians of New England. John had always understood the world in terms of slavery: temperance fought the enslavement of mind and body by alcohol; labor reform, the enslavement of workers by capitalists; women's rights, the enslavement of women by men; and antislavery, the enslavement of African Americans by white southerners. Native Americans, John believed, fought to avoid slavery, too—an enslavement by whites. Indian freedom, though, would not be acquired through the civil rights and economic progress that John deemed essential for other disadvantaged groups. Indians had to somehow revert in time to be saved.

Like a species already extinct, Native Americans existed, in the minds of many white Americans, back in some primordial North America where they could remain "noble savages" for eternity. This mythical realm served its adherents with an idealized past that helped them criticize modern civilization. Since the 1840s the Hutchinson Family Singers had sung songs such as "Glide On, My Light Canoe," a mournful tribute to a dying and soon-to-be forgotten indigenous people. John clearly wanted no part of blame for the struggles of American Indians. That his Danvers speech erased several hundred years of struggle when describing his ancestors as having derived "title from the aborigines" who had "recently vacated" is therefore not surprising.[28]

The fifty-year span following the Hutchinson Family Singers' 1843 decision to perform antislavery music unveiled a fast-changing nation whose needs for social reform transformed with matching speed, especially after 1865. The ratification of the Thirteenth Amendment removed a foundational evil from American society without bringing about the apocalyptic change that the Hutchinsons and many of their antislavery friends had once predicted. True, the involvement of African Americans in local and national politics in the South during Reconstruction was revolutionary. By the 1890s John Hutchinson and his Danvers supporters knew that those changes had been proven episodic, that freedom for black Americans did not mean justice. When John and fellow reformers celebrated the end of slavery at events like their 1893 meeting, they celebrated a great event, but not *the* great event. Reluctantly, they downsized their vision of emancipation—it was now part of a national story of progress, but no longer a story of eternal salvation.[29]

Many Americans would have agreed with the reassessment made by reformers, and, as a result, the music, literature, and poetry of antebellum reform (with the notable exception of stagings of *Uncle Tom's Cabin*) lost popularity after the Civil War. Most white Americans believed by the 1890s that slavery—whether actual or metaphorical—no longer plagued the nation. Yet as the twentieth century neared, African Americans would increasingly co-opt the language of slavery, giving rise to the creation of a black identity around a shared memory of the slave experience. This imagery would became increasingly relevant to younger generations who had never lived as slaves.

Reformers like the Hutchinson Family Singers found themselves in an uncomfortable position. The Hutchinson family comprehended their world using the language of freedom and of slavery, and they also wished to unite black and white Americans. Yet the very institution that had once integrated and unified certain Americans to a significant extent, now, in the 1890s, drove them apart; slavery was history for some and all too present for others. The horror of the war, along with the culture of individual rights legitimized by the Thirteenth, Fourteenth, and Fifteenth Amendments, created new objectives for reformers—the socially righteous whom activists once believed must turn inward, to God, for social change now had to look out, to government, for assistance. John Hutchinson, his siblings, and his reform friends did not adapt well to a postwar society marred by slavery, yet free of slaves.[30]

The Danvers meeting would continue, but it is well worth our while to prolong our break from those events to dig a bit deeper into John's dilemma. What was he thinking about in the 1890s? It has already been noted that John spent a lot of time in his final years trying to substantiate the legacy of the Hutchinson Family Singers. And starting as early as 1874, John's friends began to look forward to the publication of his memoirs. Upon hearing about John's undertaking, John G. Whittier had immediately insisted that the book include "scenes and adventures of your remarkable career." "Your forthcoming history of the Hutchinson Family I shall read with great pleasure," wrote Gerrit Smith in July 1874, "for I love all the members of that remarkable family."

But Smith's and Whittier's waits were unrewarded. By the time John's book, *Story of the Hutchinsons (Tribe of Jesse)*, appeared in print in 1896, the two had been dead for a considerable time. In the end, John—who received help compiling and editing from Charles E. Mann, the editor of the *Lynn Daily Press*—penned an enormous two-volume memoir. *Story* would greatly influence writings about the

Hutchinson Family Singers, including the only two books ever written about the group (both of which appeared in the 1940s).

But there is a problem. While John claimed to have used his personal diary as a source for the book—a diary which has since disappeared—it looks as if he depended far more upon his memory. In his effort to firmly establish the Hutchinsons as vital to antislavery reform, John Hutchinson wrote a book that one recent scholar calls "notoriously unreliable in factual matters." (That much of the later work on the Hutchinson Family Singers relies on the *Story of the Hutchinsons* has only made the "factual matters" worse.) To understand John's mindset at the 1893 meeting we need to look at his memoirs. What *Story* reveals is an aging cultural giant desperate to be (and to have been) important.[31]

Lost in his postwar letdown, John crafted an epiphanic move to abolitionism for the Hutchinson Family Singers in his book. Confusing the facts, he claimed that meetings with Frederick Douglass and George Latimer (another escaped slave) had pushed the singers to antislavery in 1842. What he had forgotten (or chose to have forgotten) was that the Hutchinson Family Singers were not new to antislavery in 1842 and that their musical abolitionism did not start until 1843. His memoirs spoke to those expecting to hear of a near religious conversion, when, in fact, the Hutchinsons had moved gradually from a private antislavery to a more public abolitionist stance. He ignored the role of annual antislavery meetings in Milford, his family's Baptist revival upbringing, and the responsibility that the abolitionist media had in developing the Hutchinson Family Singers as public reformers. The abolitionist music of the Hutchinson Family Singers was fresh and exciting when they first performed it in 1843, and it was anything but an inevitable event; however, as we shall learn, by 1842 their antislavery leanings were hardly novel.

So Frederick Douglass's personal introduction to *Story of the Hutchinsons* conveys more about the Hutchinsons' value to reform and to reformers than any of John's own writings. Douglass had already included the Hutchinson family in his autobiography, *The Life and Times of Frederick Douglass*, in a list of his most influential friends who "took me to their hearts and homes, and inspired me." In 1896 John failed to remember that the Hutchinson Family Singers' many years of service had earned them the respect of abolitionist leaders from Garrison and Whittier to Douglass and Latimer. The aging musician thus overlooked the time between 1842, when the Hutchinson Family Singers were a troupe of struggling musicians largely disconnected from reform, and April 1844, after the group had rocketed to the forefront of antislavery and when, not having seen "Fred for nearly a year," the Hutchinsons recorded greeting Douglass by "shaking hands, pulling and hauling, loud talking, laughing, embracing."[32]

As John looked to posterity and set the foundation for the Hutchinsons' legacy, he faced a predicament increasingly common among antislavery activists at the end of the century. During the 1893 meeting in Danvers, the Rev. Aaron Porter described their common plight best: "We are too near in time to the early abolitionists to dispassionately judge them on their methods. We are neither artists designing nor skilled workmen building their monument. We are only the burden-bearers, bringing each one his share of the raw material which he hopes will have its place in the finished structure." John mistook his task and built a shaky memorial to the Hutchinson Family Singers; he had transformed himself into a person whose identity depended upon others believing that his life's work had always been enormously important.[33]

John's opening oration met with approval from everyone at the 1893 Danvers convention, for they shared in his values, especially his opinion that their mission, to "establish the fact that the nation could live with chattel slavery entirely eliminated," was accomplished. "The scenes and occurrences of anti-slavery days shall, in our social gatherings, be ever remembered. I cannot express, as I would, the sentiments I feel at such a gathering as this," John said to finish his speech. Applause soon thundered throughout the hall. Gaining approval for antislavery sentiment was so much easier now that slavery was banned. John's task to praise the "old anti-slavery days" provided him the opportunity to feel as if his reform efforts had entirely paid off. His role was that of the dying crusader, a man worth more to the next generation for his memories and his money. At meetings such as the one in Danvers, he felt important again.[34]

The 1893 Danvers meeting was in full swing after John Hutchinson finished speaking, and there was no denying that he was the most prized personality in attendance. Not only was the old bard repeatedly asked to sing, he was continually lauded from the podium. A few hours into the afternoon, George B. Bartlett stood at the lectern to share a poem he had written while imagining an audience listening to "the glorious voice of the great singer who has pleased us so much this afternoon." He read:

> Relics of the mighty past
> Sound the grand old bugle blast.
> Summon to their haunts again
> All these old historic men
> Who in Freedom's blackest night
> Dared to battle for the right.
> Garrison, that fortress strong,
> Refuge sure from every wrong,
> To the shelter of whose name
> Every hunted creature came.
> Phillips, on whose silver tongue
> Eager crowds enraptured hung.
> Whittier, who with mistic lyre
> Quaker souls could rouse to fire.
> Sumner, whose majestic head
> For the cause of Freedom bled.
> Andrew, who to victory sent
> Many a noble regiment.
> Craft, who stole himself away
> From the men who watch and prey.
> Burns, marched back to Southern hell,
> Past the spot where Attucks fell.
> Spring's best blossoms strew his way
> Whose presence was perpetual May,
> Who with consistent courage trod
> The footsteps of the Son of God.
> Parker, with his grandsire's gun
> From the Green at Lexington
> On that "ever glorious day,"

Eager for another fray.
Old John Brown, uplifted high,
Saw the glory in the sky:
What to him were pain and loss
When the gallows gleamed a cross!
These and twenty thousand more
On the fair and shining shore,
When our St. John strikes the chord,
Chant the glory of the Lord.
Whitest souls, with faces black,
Fling the glorious tidings back
From the resurrected land,
Free from Slavery's Iron hand.

Immediately following the tribute placing St. John amid the noblest ranks of reformers, calls went up for the affable songster. The remodeled Hutchinsons who sang at the opening of the convention swiftly sprang to action with the Family Singers' antislavery anthem "Get Off the Track!" A change was made to thrill the audience. John adjusted a stanza to sound,

See the throngs that run to meet us,
At Danvers Hall the people greet us,
All take seat in exultation,
In the car Emancipation.

Those familiar with the Hutchinson Family Singers still relished their lyrical tweaking, but had long since realized that the musicians were "probably accustomed to adapt the line to each new locality." When the song ended and the applause subsided, a few more words were shared about the power of the Hutchinson Family Singers in the days of yore. The speakers firmly believed that none of that strength had been lost. Then, for a while, the commemoration continued with talk of the Hutchinsons relegated to the background. It would not be long, though, before John was asked to sing again.[35]

Parker Pillsbury was one of the few male reformers at the Anti-Slavery Commemorative Meeting to protest the lack of women's suffrage in the United States. After he finished explaining why he hadn't voted in quite some time—the government taxed his wife, who was not allowed to vote, thus breaking a fundamental principle of the Revolution against taxation without representation—John Hutchinson added another song. This time it was "There's No Such Word as Fail." The reasoning for the selection was rather plain. John staunchly advocated for women's rights and believed the movement to be gaining. The song also represented a collaboration between Asa Hutchinson, who had set the music, and the current president of the Danvers Historical Society, George W. Putnam, who had written the lyrics.

After John finished, George T. Downing took the podium and remembered a New York antislavery meeting. At this event, Downing recalled, John and his siblings quashed a disturbance from a menacing group of New Yorkers led by the infamous Isaiah Rynders. Rynders was a political animal connected to Tammany Hall, notorious for his skillful instigation of rioting. A Rynders-summoned proslavery mob had infiltrated this particular antislavery meeting, creating mayhem. Amid the interruptions, the assembly ground to a halt. Downing stated that then, "without any announcement, the Hutchinsons rose in the audience, or rather in the gallery, and with their sweet voices completely tamed the wild beast."[36]

George Downing was not the only one to point out the remarkable calming effect of the Hutchinson Family Singers' performances. When neither Garrison nor Wendell Phillips could silence a mob, "the voices of this family came down from the gallery of the Old Tabernacle, like a message from the sky," said Frederick Douglass shortly before his death, "and in an instant all was hushed and silent." In an era featuring raucous uprisings at reform gatherings, Elizabeth Cady Stanton thought that "perhaps, after one of their ballads, the mob would listen five minutes." The Hutchinsons had discovered a way to contain distractions. Much more than abolitionism as entertainment, the Hutchinson Family Singers' interludes were magical, able to silence antislavery's most vocal adversaries. During those precious moments of peace, the public voice of antislavery returned as the musicians grabbed authority from their opponents and, for a while, gave it back to reformers.[37]

When Downing finished his remembrance, John stood to elaborate on the Hutchinson Family Singers' activities at antislavery meetings. He said that it "was not always convenient for us to be announced from the stage." As long as the Hutchinson Family Singers were in the audience, he continued, "when the opportunity came to do our duty, we did it." He then fought back tears while reading a letter from Abby's husband, Ludlow Patton. Patton expressed regret that neither he nor his recently deceased wife could attend the Danvers gathering in person, assuring everyone, though, that both were there in spirit. Delivering the letter moved John and, feeling a sense of duty once more, he sang another antislavery staple, "The Slave's Appeal":

> Pity, kind gentlemen, friends of humanity,
> Cold is the world to the cry of God's poor,
> Give us our freedom, ye friends of equality,
> Give us our rights, for we ask nothing more.

John's listeners applauded; they simply adored him.[38]

With the meeting slowly winding down, the honorable George W. Putnam made his way to the front of the room. Putnam probably first heard the Hutchinsons in 1842 after moving to Nashua, N.H., just east of Milford. Throughout his life, Putnam displayed a genuine love of music and taught at singing schools in towns like Lowell and Nashua. Putnam was the president of the institution sponsoring the commemoration in Danvers, and it was only appropriate for the eighty-three-year-old to kick off a round of closing remarks: "Gray haired and bent with age—we, a portion of the veterans of the 'old guard of freedom' who still linger on earth, have come here today by the kind invitation of the Danvers Historical Society, to exchange our last greetings, and, with our fellow citizens to commemorate the most sublime event in human history, the abolition of American slavery and the emancipation of four millions of chattel slaves!"

He then invited his listeners to go back sixty years and recall the hypocrisy of America—slavery in the land of liberty. "These things are hard and unpleasant to think of," Putnam insisted and, after praising his audience a few more times, he inquired, "What was the character of these early abolitionists?" Did they always agree? Absolutely not— "They had their sharp angles of character, and they disputed vehemently over the ways and means of carrying out their warfare with slavery."[39]

One cannot deny that "sharp angles of character" still showed in the 1890s. They were, though, mainly absent from the Danvers celebration. The one issue that should have dominated the meeting's discussion was mentioned only in passing by a former slave, the Rev. Peter Randolph. Race relations, he said, could be solved by turning to the brotherhood and unity revealed in religion. Randolph's comment, one suggestive of the racism now facing those who were formerly enslaved, should have elicited some kind of response. It passed without further remark.[40]

Following George Putnam's address, John and his progeny sang the Hutchinsons' signature closing, "The Old Granite State." The assembly at Danvers was not yet over, however. Only after John led the audience in a stirring rendition of "My Country, 'Tis of Thee" did the Anti-Slavery Commemorative Meeting of the Danvers Historical Society officially end.

Five months later A. P. Putnam wrote that "but for the absence of all signs of angry dissent or violent opposition, one might almost have fancied himself transported back to the abolition meetings of long ago." Of John he said that few have "dissolved more of slavery's chains by human voice, than has he; and it is the consciousness of a life so spent that makes age at once happy and interesting."[41]

Scene Two, the 1840s: Music and Antislavery, the Hutchinson Family Singers as Public Abolitionists
Milford, New Hampshire, 1840

"1 Negro woman and two boys *if* slaves," read the 1791 inventory of Portsmouth Captain William Fernald. The document revealed the confusing status of blacks in New Hampshire after the American Revolution; "*if* slaves" they were, then the three would be counted as property, if not, they were free. New Hampshire residents did not really know whether slavery had been abolished in their territory. As in most of northern New England, slavery had never developed deep roots in the Granite State, which was never really more than a place where there were some slaves. Neighboring Vermont was the first state to ban slavery in 1777, and, while New Hampshire's Constitution acknowledged that "all men are born equally free and independent," there was no phrase explicitly prohibiting slavery. An arcane legal procedure, employed from the 1790s on, all but abolished slavery in the state, but to this day no one is sure exactly how New Hampshire governed slavery prior to an 1857 statute banning the practice and granting blacks rights as citizens. The 1790 census listed 157 slaves under the auspices of 123 slaveholders. By 1800, when the population included 182,898 whites and 856 free blacks, there were eight slaves. The 1840 census counted 284,036 whites, 537 free blacks, and one slave, the last ever recorded in New Hampshire.

In the county housing that final New Hampshire slave, leaders of the antislavery movement had started yearly visits to a small, rural community—the Hutchinsons' hometown—called Milford in 1835. On 13 November 1840, the town once again launched its annual antislavery meeting. The reformers there did not focus on the few slaves still in bondage in the state; those who gathered viewed slavery as a social ill, a flaw in the national character to be righted, and a mainly southern scourge. To them abolition was not about changing the legal foundation of slavery; it was about changing the moral reasoning which supported it. If we can alter the way Americans think and feel about the slave system, they mused, then its political and legal buttresses will quickly crumble. "Let us aim to abolitionize the consciences and hearts of the people," said William Lloyd Garrison, "and we may trust them in the ballot-box, or anywhere else." This position predominated within antislavery throughout the 1830s, but the movement, formerly centered upon immediacy and moral suasion (and, before that, colonization), was fragmenting by 1840, a victim of its own success. Having drawn in many new advocates, antislavery needed a more accommodating ideology or it must face unruly divides.[42]

In 1839 one of the largest fissures developed when a group of reformers attempted to establish the first political antislavery organization in American history. Organizers of the new party took advantage of Garrison's avowed refusal to work within the nation's political system, using their position to challenge the abolitionist leader's philosophical and physical stranglehold on the American Anti-Slavery Society. Those who convened in Warsaw, New York, harbored great expectations, but their initial effort failed. Dissuaded by the relative obscurity of the group, the candidates chosen by the convention re-fused their nominations. A few months later, in April 1840, the winds had changed. The Liberty Party was up and running in national poli-tics, with James G. Birney, an antislavery leader from Kentucky, as its presidential candidate.

The creation of an antislavery party considerably affected local politics in Milford. Prior to 1840 the men of Milford had voted for the Whig Party by a two-to-one margin. With the sudden dawn of a third party, no single faction could garner a majority at the annual town meeting. In national elections, the voters of Milford overwhelmingly chose Liberty Party candidates and, later on, their successors in the Free Soil Party. This was typical of the Granite State electorate. New Hampshirites backed the Liberty Party in 1844 more than voters in any other state, when roughly 8.5 percent of the state's ballots read "Lib-erty." In Milford the Hutchinson family and their neighbors gave James G. Birney 30.5 percent of their vote.[43]

When Garrison and his friends from the American Anti-Slavery Society came to Milford in 1840, they had picked a sympathetic spot to hold their meeting. Support for antislavery reform was strong in the New England countryside, reflecting the demographics of the nation in general, and Garrison rightly worried that the founding of the Lib-erty Party signaled a power shift in the antislavery movement. What Garrison and other reform leaders did not appreciate was that many Americans found little or no contradiction voting for the Liberty Party and also supporting the American Anti-Slavery Society. Caught in their own squabbles, antislavery leaders on all sides imparted much importance to the differences between reform organizations while oc-casionally overlooking the growing antislavery backing within New England.[44]

Increasing approval for antislavery did not create a safe environ-ment for reformers. The long tally of violence against antislavery advo-cates already in existence by 1840 only continued to grow. There were notorious events such as the near-lynching of William Lloyd Garrison by a Boston mob in 1835 and the horrific murder of the abolitionist ed-itor Elijah Lovejoy—shot while seeking refuge from a fire set to his Illi-nois newspaper in 1837—yet hundreds of less notable attacks each year truly tested abolitionists' faith. The routine violence faced by antislav-

ery activists was usually not life threatening, but the likelihood of further escalation loomed over them in their daily lives.[45]

Such was the state of affairs for abolitionists in New Hampshire.
While New Hampshire citizens tended to support antislavery more
than those in many other states, their reform inclination was not
enough to secure the region for activists. In 1835 George Storrs, the sole
agent of the American Anti-Slavery Society then responsible for New
Hampshire, was lifted from his knees and thrown out of a church in
Northfield while leading an antislavery prayer. The townspeople in
Canaan once banned an integrated school and then proceeded to haul
the building away by fastening either horses or oxen to it. A Baptist
deacon pounced on Stephen Symmonds Foster and Lewis Ford as they
rose to speak out against slavery in Nashua, a town only ten miles east
of Milford. Quaker officials, though routinely touted for their support
of antislavery and their openness to speakers of all kinds, at times
quelled abolitionist speech too, on one occasion silencing Foster and
Parker Pillsbury by calling in local law enforcement officials to arrest
them. Reactionary violence became so common that the eccentric Foster measured "the success of anti-slavery meetings by the number of
windows and benches broken by the mob and by the quality of eggs
thrown at the speakers." In this he was not alone. "The cause is pro-
gressing," said John Greenleaf Whittier. "I want no better evidence of
it than the rabid violence of our enemies."[46]

Violent opposition hindered many antislavery meetings in the
Granite State in 1840, a year in which the leading lights of the Garrisonian camp considered the region ripe for an abolitionist invasion.
Yet the November Milford gathering would proceed smoothly. The
same town in which Charles Burns's parents had been thrown out of
church for voicing their antislavery concerns hosted a meeting that
Parker Pillsbury recalled as "the best [in] everyway." Milford would
earn a reputation as an "early anti-slavery town" by extending warm-
hearted welcomes to reformers. In 1840 those in attendance supported
the abolitionists' messages, and the Orthodox Congregational Meeting House where they convened remained intact. Not even one egg
marred the event.[47]

Within this agreeable environ, the notables of New England social activism had delivered their ideas—Pillsbury, Nathaniel P. Rogers,

Stephen S. Foster, and William L. Garrison all journeyed through the chill of the New England fall to be in Milford. At the meeting they discussed slavery as a national crisis, chastised churches refusing to condemn slavery, and restated the purity of the American Anti-Slavery Society's principles. They lashed out against the Liberty Party, warning that this attempt to "*new organize*" antislavery was nothing more than a bastardization "of the cause of the slave." They had come to the Granite Town of the Granite State to convince its citizens that their brand of reform was best. And the people of Milford listened to the dialogues around which the meeting revolved and heard some of the movement's finest speakers.[48]

The assembly proceeded like hundreds, if not thousands, of other antislavery conventions. Its significance rests upon who was in the audience. Thirteen people sharing the last name of Hutchinson sat and listened to the reform lecturers on Friday and signed the attendance sheet on Saturday. At least three Hutchinson families resided in town, but the initials "J. W." and "A. B." belonged to the Hutchinson clan out on River Road, where lived John Wallace Hutchinson and Asa Burnham Hutchinson.[49]

John and Asa were nineteen and twenty-one in 1840. At the time, the brothers believed that they would become farmers like most of their older siblings, but the two had yet to develop the means to own farmland. So they continued working on their family's plot. Antislavery meetings in Milford encouraged the Hutchinson siblings' youthful idealism, an impulse first stirred during Baptist revival meetings in the early 1830s. Back then, they began to fashion utopian ideas of a world free from oppressive human relationships. The Garrisonian antislavery speakers, steeped in the practice of revival preachers and using many devices orators had cultivated during the Second Great Awakening, would expand this vision in the 1840s so that the members of the Hutchinson Family Singers and their many cohorts in the reform movement equated their own spiritual liberation with the physical liberation of American slaves. Speaking of moral perfection, of millennialism, and of salvation, antislavery reformers easily communicated with John and Asa's generation.

In Milford, on a rather auspicious day in 1840, the two young

Hutchinsons shared space with the "antislavery apostles," including the high priest himself, William Lloyd Garrison. A small yet significant detail: though John and Asa had not yet chosen a career in music, a week before the start of the antislavery meeting the two had taken part in a concert given by the entire Hutchinson family (the first time that any of the Hutchinsons had performed outside of a church choir or band). With the seeds of reform now securely planted in the brothers too, John and Asa had started down a path which would eventually fuse music and antislavery.[50]

In 1840 they had a long way to go. No one had mentioned any singing at the Milford meeting; antislavery reform then featured animated orators and tireless scribes. Compared with other movements at the time, such as revivalism or temperance, antislavery advocates rarely used music to broaden or hone their message. A majority of antislavery functions thus resembled a lyceum offering more than a temperance gathering, religious revival, political rally, or even a church service. Spectators' attentiveness would be tested with little to change the ebb and flow at abolitionist assemblies. At small meetings, like the one in Milford, this didn't seem to matter. With everyone in such close proximity to the lecturers and with some of antislavery's most eloquent speakers, all ran smoothly. Keeping the undivided attention of larger audiences would prove a much different task.[51]

Many adventures and more than two years were to pass before the Hutchinson Family Singers—thanks in part to a push from Nathaniel Peabody Rogers—forged a veritable link between music and antislavery in early 1843. Rogers, New Hampshire's William Lloyd Garrison, was the influential editor of the *Herald of Freedom*, an antislavery paper founded in 1835 as the *Abolitionist*. A Dartmouth graduate and New Hampshire native, Rogers left a lengthy and successful law career in 1838 to become the editor of the *Herald*, by then the official organ of the New Hampshire Anti-Slavery Society. Rogers's decision to leave the legal profession had been years in the making. Reading pieces by Garrison in the early 1830s first turned Rogers to antislavery, and eventually he and his friends founded the first immediate emancipation association in New Hampshire, the Portsmouth

Anti-Slavery Society. As an editor, he proved to be as hard-nosed and progressive as his more famous counterpart at the *Liberator.*[52]

Rogers loved music. Later he would press his own children to form a singing group (the Rogers Family, a fairly talented bunch, was modeled on the Hutchinson Family Singers), but in 1842 the editor was enamored of the Hutchinsons. Nathaniel P. Rogers and the Hutchinson Family Singers turned out to be an ideal match. Rogers's editorship meant that he could be more than a musical aficionado; he could act the part of the Family Singers' publicist. As John, Asa, and Judson began to tour in 1842, Rogers undoubtedly recognized them from the annual antislavery meetings in Milford. This connection helped earn them a June review in the *Herald.* Here he dubbed the Hutchinsons, who then performed under the name Aeolian Vocalists, "The New-Hampshire 'Rainers.'" Rogers's great compliment, a reference to the very popular Swiss family of singers called the Rainers who enjoyed success in Europe and the United States in the 1820s, 1830s, and 1840s, helped generate a favorable climate for the Hutchinson Family Singers.[53]

But the editor of the *Herald* had put himself in an awkward position. Antebellum papers seldom printed music reviews. Appearing in a New Hampshire antislavery publication only made the Rogers piece more unusual. The fact that the Hutchinson Family Singers had yet to proclaim antislavery sentiment from the stage in 1842 further complicated the matter. To the public they were no more than a bunch of farm kids trying to make their way as musicians. Rogers, aware of this conflict, justified the *Herald of Freedom*'s focus on the singers by stressing in his article that the musicians came from the "anti-slavery town of Milford."[54]

Rogers heard the Hutchinson Family Singers again in July, and this time the brothers had their sister Abby on stage with them. The performance had a tremendous affect. In the *Herald of Freedom*, Rogers identified their musical talent with that of Paganini—the famed Italian violinist and showman who had died only two years earlier—and of the Greek god Orpheus. Their singing, he said, was "truly eloquent and overpowering." He closed the lengthy article with a bold declaration: "If the Hutchinsons come again to Concord, or any where, where these presents may come, I can warrant all true lovers of music, a regale well worth their pains and the trifling ticket price." In his second review of the group, Rogers would leave his *Herald* readership wondering why an antislavery paper embraced the Hutchinson Family Singers.[55]

All was made clear by his next piece on the ensemble, carried in both the *Herald* and the *Liberator*. Rogers finally explained: "Perhaps I am partial to the Hutchinsons, for they are abolitionists." It was a peculiar coming out for the reform-minded entertainers, and yet Rogers was convinced that "it need not affright them to have it announced." He seemed unconcerned with the very real possibility that the Hutchinsons could suffer from such an admission.

Public reform figures active in producing cultural works like John Greenleaf Whittier and Lydia Maria Child felt that all of their writings were slighted because of their antislavery sympathies. (Child even lost borrowing privileges at the Boston Athenaeum as retribution for publishing abolitionist literature.) At the performance that Rogers raved about, the Hutchinsons had taken in eighteen dollars, about fourteen of which was left after expenditures. This, while a good sum, was not nearly enough to make the singers confident of future success, considering that they had "left the people of C[oncord] in extacies." In 1842 the Hutchinson Family Singers were a band of rural entertainers on the cusp of achievement. Almost famous, they saw their recognition increase while their pockets stayed empty—Judson saying that his eyes "become dull" when thinking of the future and John often recording that the group was "short due expenses to night." Rogers's revealing article could have forever banished the musicians to anonymity.[56]

Yet the Rogers review also provided the group a blueprint. And this they would use to capture great reward. Rogers proposed that they compose a "series of anti-slavery melodies, to sing at their Concerts." Certainly aware that the Hutchinsons were already performing temperance material at their shows, Rogers probably considered adding antislavery to the mix a reasonable request. What the editor asked, though, meant more than writing a few new songs. He was asking the Hutchinson Family Singers to break new ground for abolitionists. The Hutchinsons had indeed performed for the temperance movement, but temperance advocates promoted the best-accepted social reform of their day. Antislavery supporters, searching for such levels of respect, had only begun the cultural work necessary to attract a widespread following.[57]

Temperance reformers also had incorporated music into their social activism at a much earlier date. Close ties between the Christian church and the antialcohol movement extended to the adaptation of religious hymns to sound out against drink. The American Temperance Union published many of these in their 1837 journal, and as 1842 rolled around, temperance leaders could confidently state that "the influence of Temperance Songs is no longer to be questioned, as a pleasing, useful, and powerful means of carrying forward our Cause." Music, antialcohol advocates said, positively affected society by morally entertaining Americans, keeping them away from idleness that was thought to cause drinking.[58]

The intricate links between temperance, the church, and antislavery would not, until the Hutchinsons arrived, include music. For years, swirling ideas over the role of religion in the antislavery movement created enough tension to check abolitionists from fully employing music. Quakers, members of practically the founding faith of antislavery, and other abolitionist members of organized Christianity increasingly found themselves at odds with a growing number of abolitionists who believed in Christianity but thought incorporated religion repressive. It seems that each side in this debate brought with it a different perspective on music and entertainment.

Lucretia Mott, a leading abolitionist and Quaker, was thoroughly repulsed by the proposal for music at antislavery meetings. One month before the Hutchinsons were to make their American Anti-Slavery Society debut in 1843, Mott sent out a letter on behalf of her husband and herself: "We are sorry to hear that the Hutchinson family of singers is expected to be there." The Motts found little reason for the organization to descend "to mere excitement to carry on the work." Satisfied with the "high ground" of "rational appeals" at antislavery conventions, Mott feared that music would alienate the meeting's Quaker element. She suggested that organizers somehow confine musical activities to those who enjoyed them and not press them upon all the attendees. Mott would appear at the meeting only because she feared that her absence would mean victory for those wishing to deny women a public antislavery voice. "So," she said, "we shall go."[59]

Mott was hardly the first to reject innovation within the antislavery movement, though her objection revealed a notable fissure. When, in 1840, James Gibbons opposed the sale of antislavery medallions—pieces which further established the visual representation of the reform—he mocked the ornaments: the young could "cut their gums with an Anti-Slavery Medal," while "older folks may use theirs for their *wisdom* teeth." Both Mott and Gibbons responded to the commercialization of reform which led abolitionists through the 1840s and 1850s. A personal aesthetic colored Gibbons's resistance to the use of new media. Mott based her objection to music in religion.

The long and deep connection between Quakers and antislavery reform unveils one reason the antislavery movement initially slighted music. While many Americans' religious upbringing taught them that music was ungodly, this current was much stronger in the Society of Friends, who found "stage plays, horse races, music, and dancing" to be "vain sports and pastimes" for those whose "delight is in the law of the Lord." Mott once used the word *threadbare* to describe the atmosphere at an annual Quaker meeting in Philadelphia. She wrote another telling statement at the same time: "music, very wicked."[60]

Others in the antislavery movement of the 1830s and 1840s disagreed over music too. Black abolitionists like Frederick Douglass pointed to music as a means of resistance and spiritual renewal for those living under slavery. But for many within the white world of antislavery (which in the early 1840s was easily the most powerful abolitionist faction), a troubled relationship with non-Quaker Christian churches further disoriented ties between music and the reform. Many abolitionists labeled northern churches as enablers of slavery for not breaking with their southern counterparts. The most radical of these reformers, called "come-outers"—their name evocative of the Bible's apocalyptic sections: "Come out of her, my people, that ye not be partakers of her sin" (Rev. 18:4)—not only attacked the complicity of the church with the slave system but removed themselves (came out) from organized religion, realizing personal freedom from what they thought an authoritarian institution. This meant that church music—which represented the strongest musical tradition in the United States and the closest thing Americans had to a shared musical language—would be largely distrusted by abolitionists as well.[61]

So Rogers's proposal for a "series of anti-slavery melodies" was more complicated than one might first think. For the Hutchinsons to create a tune heard as legitimate by diehard abolitionists, they had to be sure that the songs shed any overt connection to the church. At the same time, for a tune to ring familiar and for it to be easily learned, the music of antislavery had to draw upon the sacred music tradition—Christian churches had trained antebellum Americans to read and to sing music. The Hutchinson Family Singers solved this dilemma in several ways. First, they borrowed freely and frequently from the music heard in church. They then combined these sacred melodies with original lyrics. Third, the group changed the music enough—by altering tempo and adding harmonized choruses—that the tunes were slightly different, but stayed familiar. The context in which the Hutchinsons performed abolitionist music—antislavery protests, meetings, and other gatherings—tended to downplay the music's connection to organized religion. Lastly, showcasing their individual commitment to musical excellence and to reform at antislavery conventions, the Hutchinson Family Singers energized presentations by linking more to the dynamism of religious revivalism and its successful marketing of the sacred, providing an air of possibility, than to the conservative religious practices to which many antislavery advocates ultimately objected.

The request for antislavery music dared the Hutchinsons on many levels, personally and socially. When they chose to create and perform as abolitionists, they embraced direct action, sang out their antislavery, and expressed their personal liberation, their moral sincerity. We can point to many reasons for the singers' move to antislavery (schooling, religion, family, reform movement infrastructure), yet we can never deny that their decision ultimately rested on an individual level—the Hutchinson Family Singers' brother Andrew, raised in an environment similar to that of his siblings, supported the expansion of slavery through Cuban annexation in the 1850s, and some of the Hutchinsons' New Hampshire neighbors believed that the "Abolition Old Devil is in a fair way to destroy the whole Union and all the people in it." John, Asa, Abby, and Judson selected a different path: the group, soon to declare themselves come-outers, went to work for a perfect Christian world, one uncorrupted by the competitive spirit found among the organized Christian sects. In the words of abolitionist Adin Ballou: "Let us have the spirit of the millennium, and do the works of the millennium. Then will the millennium have already come."[62]

The Hutchinsons' foray into antislavery music began in their hometown, just after Rogers's third review appeared in the *Liberator.* At the end of 1842 antislavery reformers mobilized when Thomas Parnell Beach, a minister who had left his post believing individuals alone best suited to determine issues of faith, was jailed for speaking against slavery during a Quaker assembly. Disgust stirred the citizens of Milford to announce: "RALLY! RALLY!! RALLY!!! Beach Anti-Slavery Meeting at Milford, New-Hampshire, January 4th, and 5th, 1843 . . . Our liberty—your liberty—EVERY MAN'S LIBERTY IS IN JAIL!" Forty-two names accompanied the ad, and three Hutchinsons, John, Jesse Jr., and their brother Benjamin, had endorsed the notice that ran for several weeks in the *Herald of Freedom.*[63]

"BEACH IS OUT!" cheered the headlines shortly before the start of the Milford convention. Thomas Beach could now participate in the Milford assembly originally called to protest his incarceration. Initially a ground for outrage, the meeting promptly adopted a celebratory tone. The change did not catch antislavery advocates off guard. Neither did the terrible snowstorm, a "mischievous Nor'wester," which pummeled Milford that day. The music of the Hutchinson Family Singers was the only thing to cause a stir.[64]

Thanks to the wintry weather, Beach showed late. His delay fueled the meeting's excitement and enhanced the aura surrounding the Hutchinson Family Singers' music which rang out when he opened the door. After surprising reformers with their first selection—a song prepared expressly for Beach—the Hutchinsons continued. Either from the stairs leading up to the balcony or from the balcony itself, the Family Singers repeatedly "burst down upon" the meeting with songs tailored perfectly to the debate at hand. The group fervently supported Beach, the man who in *A Voice from Jail* had upheld the right of free speech as central to personal and social renewal. In rather spectacular style and for their first time, the Hutchinson Family Singers made antislavery music.[65]

Only four months earlier an enthusiastic Nathaniel P. Rogers had beseeched the group to sing for antislavery. Now, in Milford, Rogers claimed that nothing showed "anti-slavery zeal" better than their "popular and striking music of Advent and Revival," which rang out in Milford's Old Meeting House "like trumpet-bursts of music." At a gathering featuring passionate speeches from Thomas Beach and George Latimer, the Hutchinson Family Singers received distinction as "the charm of the meeting." On Thursday morning, 5 January—the final day of the conference—the following was approved: "Resolved, That whatever else of deficiency may be charged on New-Hampshire abolitionism, the Anti-Slavery Host will always look to her for the *music*, so long as her Mountains can send down into the field 'The New-Hampshire Rainers.'" Nathaniel Rogers even spent the night at the Hutchinson family farm. A more smashing success would have been difficult to imagine.[66]

"While I think of it, I suggest to the Massachusetts Society to invite them to their approaching anniversary," said Rogers, quickly promoting the singers following the Milford meeting. "Boston would stand amazed at their mountain melody." The group's transition from singers and private abolitionists to singing abolitionists cultivated a sudden interest in music within antislavery reform. By February 1843 the *Herald of Freedom* published several "Anti-Slavery Hymns and Songs" set to such tunes as "Auld Lang Syne," "America," and the "Missionary Hymn." In all likelihood, the editor did not have to push very hard for the singing troupe.[67]

When William Lloyd Garrison ran the Rogers article about the recent Beach antislavery convention in a January *Liberator,* an accompanying editorial note said that an invitation would be extended to the Hutchinson Family Singers for the upcoming meetings in Faneuil Hall. The Hutchinsons accepted, making their Boston antislavery debut (the group had first played Boston in September 1842) on Wednesday, 25 January 1843.

On the first day of the Massachusetts Anti-Slavery Society meeting, the group sang twice in the morning and then closed out the afternoon session in the famed Boston landmark lined with portraits of leaders from Revolutionary America. That evening they presented another song and, at 11 P.M., concluded the final session of the day. The antislavery convention flowed around the Hutchinsons' music. Thursday followed a similar course, except that on this day they influenced several debates with their music—"the discussion was enlivened by two appropriate songs by Messrs. Hutchinson"—and, again, the late night discussions ended with "a thrilling song." On the final day of the Eleventh Annual Meeting of the Massachusetts Anti-Slavery Society, the Hutchinson Family Singers infused music into some tense debates and sang two songs during the waning moments prior to the convention's adjournment.[68]

Though it was only the second time that the troupe had graced the platform at an antislavery conference, this format, under which the singers opened and/or closed sessions as well as interjecting during disputes, came to represent a standard practice in the years to come. The Boston papers raved. The Hutchinson Family Singers' approach to antislavery meetings worked wonders. Their "enchanting powers . . . made the thousands at Faneuil Hall spring to their feet simultaneously . . . with a cheering that almost moved the old revolutionists from their stations on the wall." Delighting the crowd during one debate, the Hutchinsons took the argument of Wendell Phillips and carried it "heavenward." When Phillips finally finished, the Hutchinson Family Singers rushed the stage and "poured forth with amazing spirit, in one of the maddening Second Advent tunes." The crowd went wild—"the multitude had caught the spirit of the orator and the minstrel bards, and they exemplified it, in their humanized shoutings. . . . Slavery would have died of that music, and that response of that multitude."

As it resounded with shouts for liberty and justice, Faneuil Hall—a "large, dreary place, with its walls and innumerable dingy windows"—filled with an energy not felt in a long time. The Hutchinsons' presence, Nathaniel Rogers reported, "contributed considerably to keeping up the unparalleled attendance, that thronged the hall."[69]

For the next few years an antislavery singing frenzy fueled the Hutchinsons' meteoric rise to fame. But along with larger venues and greater public exposure came increased scrutiny and jealously. Who was paying the group to perform? Who were these Hutchinsons, and what right did they have to interrupt antislavery meetings? These were just some of the immediate doubts stressed after their 1843 Boston performance. Many expressed concern that the Hutchinson Family Singers faked their reform zeal. N. P. Rogers took it upon himself to counter the skeptics. "They are not wandering, mercenary troubadours, who go about selling their strains for bread or brandy," he said, "they were not hired as performers. . . . They were there as Garrison and Boyle were, as Douglass and Remond and Phillips, and the rest of us." His point was clear: the Hutchinson Family Singers were abolitionists. Initially, this was difficult for some to grasp; surely a group of entertainers blemished antislavery in some way. But Rogers did not equivocate. Certain that the Hutchinsons "were not mere vocalists," he would not let the fact that they were entertainers cloud the group's reform work.[70]

Following their Boston debut, the Hutchinson Family Singers set off on a few of their own performances in that city. The group capitalized on their reform-generated publicity with two concerts, private shows unrelated to an antislavery meeting. Nonetheless, William Lloyd Garrison helped them spread the word. A week before the musicians' 28 February concert, a message in the *Liberator* promoted the Hutchinson Family Singers and remarked that the affectionate words of Nathaniel Rogers "barely do them justice." On the same page, an advertisement from the Hutchinsons broadcast a "Vocal Concert. At the Melodeon." For twenty-five cents apiece, or one dollar for the whole family, Bostonians could experience, in Garrison's words, the "moral worth and modest desert" presented by the New Hampshire entertainers.[71]

Two months later Garrison again singled out the Hutchinson Family Singers in order to encourage attendance at the American Anti-Slavery Society's annual meeting: "It will be the source of immense gratification to our anti-slavery friends to learn that those charming vocalists, the Hutchinsons, contemplate being in New-York during the anniversary week, and lifting up their inspiring voices in the cause of universal emancipation at our meetings. We hope they will attract with more than magnetic power."[72]

Admittedly, the *Liberator* advertisement of April 1843 was guardedly optimistic. The Hutchinson Family Singers, after all, had not yet committed to attending the tenth annual gathering of the organization. While every year reformers had felt that this annual assembly needed to be "the most interesting *Anti Slavery Meetings ever held* in the city of New York," there is something about a special anniversary that warrants extra attention. The American Anti-Slavery Society's decennial celebration was no exception, and its organizers searched for ways to make the occasion distinctive. They needed something new and appealing. Something that could top Frederick Douglass, last year's abolitionist phenomenon. At the center of the 1843 frenzy stood the Hutchinson Family Singers, who antislavery leaders hoped would provide the spark for an extraordinary New York convention.[73]

The Hutchinsons were a perfect fit not only for the New York event but for the American Anti-Slavery Society in general. Members of the organization, who had basically presided over the reform cause during the 1830s, were no longer the only major voice against slavery, and they were unhappy with the shift. The American Anti-Slavery Society was at a disadvantage in the public arena. While rivals in the Liberty Party campaigned for office and received a listing on ballots, the heart of the Society's mission—antislavery publications and lectures—lost vitality in the 1840s. Public meetings, as the spell of antebellum religious revivals proved, could enrapture, but despite the Anti-Slavery Society's use of speakers of all styles, their gatherings were not particularly captivating when compared with political rallies or temperance functions. A highly touted family of singers appeared to be exactly what their May anniversary required.[74]

Attending the antislavery meeting afforded the Hutchinsons their first opportunity to perform in New York, an experience they eagerly anticipated. For more than a year, the Hutchinson Family Singers had promoted concerts featuring a variety of new works "which have received the applause of the most fashionable and popular audience in New York." The wording of the ad employed a trick worthy of P. T. Barnum. Readers could not be certain whether it was the performing group or their songs which had received New Yorkers' applause. Prior to 1843 the Hutchinsons had not set foot in Gotham, and their advertising ploy demonstrates the centrality of a New York concert pedigree to the group and to their listeners. It was no great secret that in the sixty-seven years since the nation's founding, New York had edged out Boston and Philadelphia to become America's musical hub. An 1835 article in the *American Musical Journal* put it bluntly: "All talent must fail in America which is not imported via New-York and make its debut in the city."[75]

Asa simply gushed over his first day in the Empire City:

O! *New York* is all that I have had it represented to be! Boston does *not* compare with it for *life* and *business*. The Splendid Street *"Broad Way"* is the most Splendid Street that I ever saw, and then the Grand Park, and the Splendid *water works* where the water is thrown into the air to the height of 25 or 30 feet and then falls in to the Pool again in the most majestic Style. Then the Splendid "Niblos Garden" is worth a journey of 50 miles to see the fine flowers & plants. O New York is the place for me. I have so far, been perfectly at home here.[76]

After a 5 A.M. arrival via Boston steamship, the Hutchinsons spent part of the day touring the city. And nothing in Lynn or Boston measured up to the newly opened Croton fountain fronting City Hall or the sheer madness of the merchants and the multitudes along Broadway. The siblings were so overcome by the majesty of New York that they seemed to forget the purpose of their visit. As the antislavery convention opened on 9 May 1843, the Hutchinsons, who had arrived that morning, strolled through Niblo's Garden.[77]

Located a little below Canal Street at 405 Broadway, the tenth anniversary meeting of the American Anti-Slavery Society started rather traditionally. Within the confines of Concert Hall, orators began to speak out against slavery. Countless moments such as this one triggered Ralph Waldo Emerson's complaint that "eloquence was dog-cheap" at antislavery functions. Overdrawn speech filled the air in the morning at the convention. The crowd was not particularly moved by James Monroe, the first lecturer. Nor was the gallery packed to hear the pleas of any other speaker. Those in New York knew that the Hutchinsons were supposedly in attendance. When Monroe finished, the crowd could not contain its excitement. Thunderous cries went out for a song. And the convention's leaders, knowing exactly who was being called upon, nervously scanned the audience for any sign of the Granite State's songsters. Normally, by now, the troupe would have sprung into action, but the Hutchinson Family Singers were not there. Spellbound by flora at Niblo's, the Hutchinsons forced New Yorkers to wait a bit longer for their unique reform sound. "Nothing was wanting but the melody of their sweet voices to perfect the tone of the meeting," said Garrison, who noted the Hutchinson Family Singers' absence during the morning session as a "disappointment of us all."[78]

The musicians arrived at the meeting in the afternoon and soon revived the crowd. On a rainy Wednesday the Hutchinsons chose to stay sheltered at the antislavery gathering from start to finish. During its course, they sang several times, usually opening or closing a session, and with ever-increasing frequency they broke out in song to punctuate debates. The Hutchinsons were beginning to perfect the art of lyrical improvisation to highlight something special about the place or the time of their performance. Jesse Hutchinson, Jr., first exhibited this talent, and his brothers soon mastered it as well.[79]

In New York their inventive style and their singing in general guaranteed that the Hutchinson Family Singers were the main attraction. After their initial tardiness, the group took the convention by storm. One of the closing resolutions read: "The thanks of this meeting be, and they are hereby tendered to our esteemed friends, the Hutchinsons, for the interest which they have contributed to this meeting by their presence and soul-stirring music." After the final resolution passed, the tenth annual meeting of the American Anti-Slavery Society concluded with a song from the Hutchinson Family Singers.[80]

Two days after the New York convention, the Hutchinsons, again capitalizing on publicity generated by their appearance at an antislavery gathering, performed in Concert Hall, the same space in which the meeting had been held. On 14 May 1843 Asa reported a "first rate Satisfaction" with the previous evening's show and claimed that it had attracted "about 200" New Yorkers. The Hutchinson Family Singers would go on to perform several more times in Brooklyn and in New York during the month of May. At the conclusion of what can only be described as a fantastic first run in the city, Asa observed: "The people of New York are crazy after 'The Hutchinsons.' We have accomplished our 'aimes' for the people are completely charmed. I suppose we might Stop in New York a month and make a thousand dollars each!"[81]

Asa's comment was part ego and part premonition. The Hutchinson Family Singers harbored grand ambitions for their musical talent and reform ideals. In October 1843 the musicians moved to New York for about two months to play more than twenty concerts. For their last two shows at Niblo's Garden in December, somewhere between twelve hundred (Asa's estimate and the listed capacity of the site) and two thousand people (newspaper estimates) came out each night to hear strains from the New Hampshire musicians. They had succeeded in their quest to bring reform-conscious music to a prominent venue. Their profit at these last two concerts alone easily exceeded six hundred dollars a show.[82]

After their January 1843 appearances in Milford and Boston, and their spring concerts in New York, the singing abolitionists had become some of the most sought-after members of the antislavery community. There were pleas: "The Hutchinsons, are cordially and earnestly invited by the Essex County Abolitionists, to meet them at their Annual Meeting"; "Our friends 'of the tribe of Jesse,' from the Old Granite State, are specially invited to be present on this occasion"; "among whom we hoped to be favored with the musical talent of friend Rogers' 'New-Hampshire Rainers,' the Hutchinsons." There were pronouncements: "C. L. REMOND, GEORGE LATIMER, and the HUTCHINSONS, will be present"; "The Hutchinson Family will be present, in full strength. Enough said!" And there was a steady stream of news reporting: that the Hutchinsons led a singing of the "Our Father" in Andover; that they sang their "Friendly Greeting" for the antislavery gathering in Haverhill; and that they "contributed to bring out the people" for an abolitionist picnic in Lowell.[83]

Coverage of the Hutchinson Family Singers at reform events was so extensive that many did not pick up on the group's own growing concert successes. Some in the antislavery movement even worried over the singers' financial state; playing at reform gatherings was presumably unprofitable. During one 1843 meeting in Massachusetts, a collection was taken up to benefit the Hutchinsons. In a move that spoke to the economic realities of the antislavery movement, the white performers immediately donated the monies to two black antislavery activists, George Latimer and Charles Lenox Remond.

Refusing the public donation set a clear boundary—the Hutchinson Family Singers did not need the benevolence of others to survive. By turning around and giving the windfall to their black associates, the group helped out those in need while highlighting the power gap between black and white reformers. In some sense, the division was inevitable. The structure of antebellum American society all but ensured that a white family would earn more than a black one. Leaders of the American Anti-Slavery Society exacerbated these divisions by often treating black abolitionists with a degree of paternalism. Later in the 1840s Frederick Douglass fought against this tendency, making a clean break with Garrison and his organization. Douglass complained that these reformers made him feel like a "thing," and he was right. The upside of commercializing reform is apparent in the works of the Hutchinsons, but a perilous side lurked as well.[84]

Members of the Hutchinson Family Singers exhibited little of this paternalism toward their African-American cohorts in the 1840s, despite the gross economic disparity. Furthermore, the Hutchinsons did accept more subtle forms of support from antislavery organizations. Somewhat hidden in the expenditures for the Massachusetts Anti-Slavery Society's twelfth annual meeting in January 1844 was the "amount paid per order of the Board, for traveling expenses of the Hutchinsons in attending annual meeting," totaling fifteen dollars. This was a decent sum. After all, the organization paid nearly thirty-four dollars just to rent Faneuil Hall. Field agents of antislavery societies, often professional men who had to travel and thus could widely solicit subscriptions to reform publications, were one such group that received reimbursements. Abolitionist leaders clearly felt the Hutchinsons brought more than "delightful and inspiring" songs to the movement, and that they were agents of antislavery in their own right.[85]

Frederick Douglass once said that the Hutchinson Family Singers' "fine talent for music could have secured for them wealth and fame, but, like Moses, they preferred to suffer affliction in the cause of justice and liberty." A noble statement, but the black abolitionist more accurately wrote to John in 1894 that the Hutchinson Family Singers "have dared to sing for a cause first and for cash afterward." Antislavery was, in part, a business, and the Hutchinson Family Singers embarked on a successful music venture beginning in 1843. Combining the reform cause and entertainment was lucrative. P. T. Barnum once offered former fugitive slave Anthony Burns $100 per week to appear at his New York museum. "Tickets for sale at the Anti-Slavery Office," read ads for the Hutchinson Family Singers in Philadelphia.

Moving from the fringe to the cultural mainstream in the North required an elaborate network of the sort that the antislavery movement, when taken as a whole, had developed by the 1840s. The Hutchinson Family Singers probably would never have been well known without the support of Nathaniel Peabody Rogers, William Lloyd Garrison, numerous antislavery organizations and publications, and the thousands of antislavery supporters who lined up to hear them at reform gatherings throughout 1843.

In years to come, the Hutchinson Family Singers would be noted for their unifying brand of antislavery, their celebrity, and their incredible financial success. But starting in January 1843, when the Hutchinson Family Singers first mesmerized antislavery reformers, they became known for opening the door to an innovative kind of abolitionist reform. Music was a new technology in antebellum America—if one thinks of technology as something that changes the world or how the world is experienced—and the four New Hampshire musicians successfully implemented a technological transformation of antislavery. "The happy influence which these Singers will produce upon an audience must be witnessed," wrote the Massachusetts Anti-Slavery Society Committee of Arrangements (which included William Lloyd Garrison and Wendell Phillips), "it can't be described." In June the *Practical Christian* declared John, Asa, Judson, and Abby the most important antislavery phenomena of the year:

> The music of the Hutchinsons carries all before it. It was a most important charm to collect and attach people to the meetings of the Convention. Speechifying, even of the better sort, did less to interest, purify and subdue minds, than this irresistible anti-slavery music. To this and to the great Latimer excitement of last year, may be mainly attributed the increased interest evinced in the late gathering.[86]

Part Second

—+—◊—+—

Chronology

—3 February 1778. Birth of Jesse Hutchinson, father of the Hutchinson Family Singers.

—25 June 1785. Birth of Mary Leavitt, matriarch of the Hutchinson family.

—4 March 1789. The government of the United States of America begins to function under the recently adopted Constitution.

—1794. The town of Milford, New Hampshire, is incorporated.

—7 August 1800. Marriage of Jesse Hutchinson and Mary Leavitt.

—12 October 1800. Death of the grandfather of the Hutchinson Family Singers, Elisha Hutchinson.

—2 February 1802. Birth of first child, Jesse Hutchinson.

—11 October 1803. David Hutchinson born.

—6 January 1810. Zephaniah K. Hutchinson born.

—25 November 1811. The birth of twins Joshua and Caleb Hutchinson.

—29 September 1813. Birth of Jesse Hutchinson, Jr. His recently deceased brother, as well as his father, is his namesake.

—3 October 1815. Benjamin Pierce Hutchinson born.

—December 1816–January 1817. Creation of the American Colonization Society, an antislavery organization formed to "repatriate" American slaves to Africa.

—14 March 1817. Birth of Adoniram Judson Joseph Hutchinson (later known simply as Judson).

—14 March 1819. Sarah Rhoda Jane Hutchinson born.

—4 January 1821. John Wallace Hutchinson born.

—14 March 1823. Birth of Asa Burnham Hutchinson.

—1824. Hutchinson family purchases and moves to Burnham hotel on River Road.

—1827. Lowell Mason, now recognized as a talented composer of sacred music, moves back to New England to pursue a career in music.

—29 August 1829. Birth of Abigail (Abby) Jemima Hutchinson.

—1829–1831. A series of Baptist revivals held in Milford, attracting various members of the Hutchinson family.

—1833. Founding of the Boston Academy of Music.

—1835. Milford Female Seminary opens.

—1837. A financial panic grips the nation. Lowell Mason introduces music instruction to the public schools of Boston.

First Section: Origins of the Hutchinson Family, 1800–1830

They were genuine children of the rugged New Hampshire soil on which they were born. . . . It is hoped that the story of the travels and experiences of the Hutchinson family may be told some day in a form that shall be permanent. Certainly it might be made a very interesting memorial of some stirring days now long past, while as a contribution to the history of the anti-slavery struggle it could hardly fail to possess great value.

—*Boston Transcript,* 9 May 1885

At the dawn of the nineteenth century, the United States—situated on the eastern edge of North America—bound together an island of sixteen territories surrounded by water, antagonistic natives, and foreign possessions. American foreign policy reflected this volatile mixture and, soon, the country would again battle the British, who, this time, set fire to the White House. The nation's precarious place within the global context paralleled its internal divides. An unwelcome factionalization had already replaced the unity of the Revolution, ensuring that the Constitution would remain "a doubtful experiment" for the near future. Three times in the first two decades of the new century the Federalists seriously considered a New England secession; their power was waning, struck a serious blow when Americans elected Thomas Jefferson, author of the Declaration of Independence and leader of the Democratic-Republican Party, to the presidency.[1]

Perhaps the most significant development of the era was the fervor with which the nation embraced geographic exploration and development. Enlarging the country's boundaries became the solution to sheltering Americans from foreigners, natives, and one another. In 1803 the Louisiana Purchase set the stage for the famous expedition of Meriwether Lewis and William C. Clark and affirmed the nation's course of expansion for the next half-century. Funded secretly by the federal government, the explorers traveled by foot, horse, and boat as they mapped a large swath of territory between present-day Illinois and Oregon. The successful expedition detailed diverse matter from flora and fauna to Indians and terrain; the enlarged nation would be generously endowed with resources.

While pointing Lewis and Clark on a westerly course, the Purchase was also important in securing for Americans free navigation of the Mississippi River. Access to the central river created the possibility for thriving western states which would later serve as valuable markets for eastern businesses. But that was not all. With little regulation of slave transfer within the United States, local and federal laws made it easy for southern planters to bring chattel to frontier lands, which inadvertently turned the Purchase into a landmark in the history of American slavery. In the ensuing years, slave owners acquired new plantations and legally secured slavery in many new territories and states. By 1860 the resulting demographic shift could be marked: a majority of American slaves lived in states established after 1790.[2]

Four years before Lewis and Clark set out in 1804, a young couple embarked on a memorable journey of their own. Uncertain of what fortunes, if any, their future together would bring, a twenty-two-year-old farmer named Jesse Hutchinson and Mary "Polly" Leavitt, the fifteen-year-old daughter of a master carpenter, married. Their August wedding united two branches of America's first freedom fighters, as Polly's father and Jesse's father were Revolutionary War veterans. Despite Jesse Hutchinson's lack of wealth, Polly's family judged him a promising suitor. The young farmer had won them over with a discipline and a religious devotion that left the Leavitts confident that their daughter would live in comfort and security. Unbeknownst to the couple or to their parents, the newlyweds had started on a family voyage that would resonate far beyond the hills of New Hampshire, charting a new course within the contours of American culture.[3]

The Hutchinsons resided in Milford, New Hampshire, and were fortunate to have a house to themselves, a gift bequeathed upon the death of Jesse's father. Milford, a rural and somewhat secluded spot, nurtured the Hutchinson family for most of the nineteenth century. Named for a mill site by a ford across the Souhegan River, Milford lies slightly north of the southern border of the state in Hillsborough County. In 1800 the town was new, having been incorporated in 1794 to supply "the inhabitants thereof with all such privileges and immunities as other towns" in the region. Located roughly fifty miles northwest of Boston and thirty-one miles south of Concord, New Hampshire, Milford was then a burgeoning frontier.[4]

In the late eighteenth century, settlers had trickled into the region, continuing a well-established New England migration away from shortages and inequalities of land that arose in more established towns. Elisha Hutchinson, the grandfather of the Hutchinson Family Singers, moved in 1779 from Middleton, Massachusetts, to the area that later became Milford. At the age of twenty-eight, Elisha was older than most of the rural migrants who followed trade routes up the Merrimac Valley to New Hampshire, yet he still represented a migratory impulse that would penetrate deep into unsettled New England.

Milford was small, housing only 139 taxpayers when founded,

blossoming to 939 in the 1800 census. To call the town isolated is slightly misleading, for, like many places in the early nineteenth century, Milford was tied to a multitude of markets both near and far. Two bustling commercial ports, one in Portsmouth, about sixty miles away, and one in Boston, the nation's third-largest city, brought rural residents throughout New England in touch with people and items from the Caribbean, Europe, and beyond.[5]

As country dwellers, the Hutchinsons lived like most Americans, for only a small minority, 3 percent, resided in cities in 1800. A few months into their marriage, when Elisha Hutchinson died, the couple split the inherited farm property with Jesse's bachelor brother Andrew. The house and accompanying land made living as farmers possible, but it was not easy. Nonetheless, the rewards of working their own land brought a degree of camaraderie and exhilaration to the Hutchinsons. Hard work, perseverance, and a Christian home formed the basis of a life well lived for Jesse and Polly. They would do their best to keep their children in touch with these values. With the birth of their first child, Jesse, in February of 1802, the newlyweds' ideas on child rearing were suddenly tested.[6]

The beginning of her childbearing years quickly dragged Polly into a new stage of life. At fifteen, she had been helping with domestic work around her parents' home; at sixteen, Polly was married with a child of her own. Nineteenth-century women began "to fade in a few years after marriage," wrote the abolitionist Cassius Clay, with motherhood leaving "but a wreck of what was once most lovely." Polly would certainly endure years of wearisome child raising. At the age of forty-four, twenty-nine years after she wed, Polly delivered her sixteenth and final child. Hers was an intrepid pace even for the early 1800s, when the average rural woman gave birth to the first of seven or eight children at the age of twenty-four. By the time Polly Hutchinson turned twenty-four, she was already caring for Jesse, David, Noah, Mary, and Andrew—and Zephaniah was due in seven months.[7]

An undated print of Polly in her later years reveals a gloomy, thick woman who had shouldered multiple illnesses and the heavy load of infant care for the majority of her adult life. Adding to her exhaustion, Polly's responsibilities extended beyond conception, birthing, and babysitting. Cooking, mending, milking, and washing were

just a few of the domestic tasks required of the matron despite her repeated pregnancies. While fortunate to have had the assistance of various female family members and the occasional boarder through the
years, Polly never commanded any servants or hired help. Hers was a
busy life that demanded great emotional and physical strength.[8]

But Polly's fortitude had its limits, and her worries filled the
Hutchinson Family Singers' initial trials in music with fear and guilt.
Her anxieties aside, people remembered her as the musically talented
parent in the Hutchinson clan. A Dartmouth professor pleasantly recalled hearing Polly's singing in church and linked her sister, Sarah, to
the preeminent vocalists of the century—Jenny Lind, Madame Mali-
bran, and Madame Sontag. Even though Polly's vocal proficiency did
not translate into encouragement for the Hutchinson Family Singers—she was convinced that her children's musical endeavors manifested a sinful materialism—the musicians pointed to their mother
and her singing as an inspiration.

Yet music took all of Polly's youngest away from Milford; she
openly despised this result. The ugliest scenes revolved around her
youngest child, Abigail. Abby represented the final link to a way of life,
of birthing and of childrearing, that her mother likely found familiar.
So when John, Asa, and Judson whisked their sister away to tour at the
age of twelve, their mother's reaction of sheer panic should not have
been surprising. Polly undoubtedly feared for the safety of her daughter. Perhaps she also thought of Abby meeting a fate similar to her
own—married at fifteen. Whatever the reason, only constant negotiations, during which Polly's three sons promised to return her darling
daughter quickly and safely, could keep the Hutchinson Family Singers on the road in the early 1840s. The traditional matriarch lived in a
different realm from her famous children, more inclined to sing a
hymn, stay at home, and declare that "sweet cream with maple mo-
lasses on boiled corn is excellent." Apprehensive and homespun compared to her public and worldly offspring, the overprotective mother
often made visits home awkward for the Hutchinson Family Singers.[9]

The gap between mother and sons, so prevalent in the 1840s, had
developed long before the musical brothers "stole" Abby away. The division of labor in farming households all but mandated a separation of
work along gender lines. This usually resulted in a corresponding

"emotional segregation." Preparation for domestic life began early in the Hutchinson family. As soon as a young girl was able to carry the wash, watch over a younger sibling, or help with cooking, she was instantly employed. Hutchinson girls trained in housework, spinning, and butter making. Unlike farming families in nearby towns, it does not appear that Hutchinson women were ever a part of a so-called putting-out industry, in which women and children assembled crude items during slow times on the farm. Working in close proximity strengthened the bonds between Polly and her daughters. As a Hutchinson girl started to learn the ins and outs of domestic work, the roles of mother and daughter effortlessly blended together. With the exception of childbirth and nursing, little would distinguish the work of Polly from that of her female kin.[10]

Hutchinson boys, for the most part, learned a different set of skills than those requisite for domestic responsibilities. They cared for livestock, directed plow teams, and assisted with the many odd jobs required in cultivating and harvesting crops. Much like the world of the home which created a set of ideals and bonds among the Hutchinson women, male work on the farm generated a certain solidarity. One initiation into manhood was the tolerance of bodily harm. Asa and John earned marks of distinction during their childhood labors: Asa lost part of a finger to an axe, and John gained multiple scars from a similar implement. Unless specifically directed otherwise, the boys avoided domestic chores, choosing instead, even when they were too young or too weak to perform a certain task, to watch their father and older brothers, and helping in what little ways they could, such as delivering food.

While male chores on the farm were seasonal, women's work—cleaning, sewing, cooking, and child care—was constant. In other rural families, women often helped the men by harvesting in the field or toiling in the barn, but the Hutchinson family makeup so heavily favored men that Jesse routinely ordered one of his sons to assist with work inside the home. The first brother to suffer this fate was Joshua, who was volunteered in 1823 to help his mother. With lard-covered hands set to grease pans, the twelve-year-old probably could have seen his twin brother working the fields outside of the kitchen. As often as the Hutchinson males helped with domestic duties, they never let go of the notion that what they were doing was women's work—Asa, in 1843, explained that he spent part of a break from singing at the family's farm "assisting the womenfolks in their washing."

The division of labor within the household was necessary, but it was not handled in an egalitarian manner. A legal and conventional power that men exercised over women and children structured daily life. Visitors noted the Hutchinsons' home as a "patriarchal premises." This pattern, which kept women inside, men outside, and children wherever their father stipulated, unavoidably affected life in the Hutchinson family. Eventually each of the Hutchinson boys born after Joshua and Caleb would help the family's overburdened women. Polly's sons proved to be inefficient houseworkers. Out of the watchful eye of their father, the boys tended to dally. In the early 1830s John Hutchinson spent a good deal of time obsessively penciling the name of his adolescent love, Caroline Bartlett, on the walls around the wash-room.[11]

Jesse and Polly felt more blessed than cursed by their many children. Humphrey Moore, a minister in Milford, once touted Jesse as a wise farmer, claiming the patriarch to be "making money in raising a family of boys." Fathers and sons were often the only ones to receive public acknowledgment, but every task on the farm proved critical to the success of the family. Without proper clothing to brave the elements, someone to prepare food, or someone to supply food, the Hutchinson family could not have thrived.

Polly and Jesse, bound to a traditional set of values, saw their large family as a sign of health and continuity. Once the foundation of economic stability, large rural families were gradually to lose their advantage as the nineteenth century progressed. Already by the 1820s and 1830s, children had become less vital to farming families that had shifted production toward cash crops. Moving away from subsistence agriculture to specialize in a few valued products earned farmers cash. Cash enabled them to hire help during busy times in the fields and to buy many household staples formerly crafted or cultivated by family members. With hops as their major crop, most of the Hutchinsons' planting and harvesting occurred during limited intervals, burdening the family laborers. Common practice set pay between nine and ten dollars a month for agricultural work, a sum often disbursed through a combination of clothing and cash; Jesse also compensated workers with generous portions of New England rum.

Successfully growing hops did not help the Hutchinson clan avoid a reality facing many rural families of their time—they could not guarantee a farming life for their children. Land in New England was increasingly expensive, and, with such a large brood, dividing the Hutchinson farm among all the children was not feasible. Boys in the family often moved to cheaper lands in the West or looked for employment outside of farming.[12]

The Milford family was trapped between the tradition in which Jesse and Polly were raised—centered around farming or carpentering, domestic work, passing on property, and caring for dependent relatives—and the family lifestyle that developed in the first half of the nineteenth century—centered around the emotional well-being of children, ensuring that they learn self-discipline and conscientiousness to help them manage in an increasingly interactive and self-interested society. When Polly and Jesse wed, the union had required the blessing of their families because it concerned issues above and beyond the love that they shared. Their nuptials set in motion an exchange of property, albeit a very limited trade. Jesse commanded little of such economic authority over his own family. In its place, he gave them all that he had left: guidance on how to live a respectable and pious life.[13]

He accomplished this, in part, through example. Hutchinson family lore records that as a bachelor Jesse enjoyed playing the violin and singing. With his nuptials, however, came an increased sense of responsibility. Jesse believed that music distracted men from the important things in life, like God, work, and family. A devout Christian, Jesse overcame the slothful influence of entertainment by turning his violin into a cigar box. This story was repeated in the family's history many times not only for amusement but to establish Jesse's exacting values. Throughout his life, he preached religion and farming as the only paths to true contentment. A man of puritan conscience with improvement on his mind, he gave his son John the impression that a man was worthless if not dressed before sunrise and, later, Jesse would constantly question the spiritual health of his children when they paraded across the nation as musicians. There was great irony, then, in the mid-1840s, when the Hutchinson Family Singers' earnings could support their family and Jesse abandoned farming for itinerant preaching.[14]

While his body never bore the ravages of nineteenth-century childbirth, Jesse Hutchinson's routine as a New Hampshire farmer was hardly gentle (fig. 4). Milford's soil within the granite-strewn Souhegan Valley did not yield easily to cultivation, and farming has always been labor intensive. A *New-England's Farmers' Diary and Almanac* from the 1820s listed a host of tasks for the industrious farmer each month; work ranged from assessing the quality of one's seed and cutting and splitting wood to cidering, plowing, and settling debts. Of these tasks, producing enough wood was both important and time consuming. Wood largely fueled the economy of the early nineteenth century. The Hutchinson farm required trees for construction and combustion. If there were no more urgent jobs to be done, ensuring an adequate wood supply was essential. Firewood was split and dried, while wood for construction was hauled down to the mill for conversion into a more workable material. Males in the Hutchinson family worked around timber often, and Jesse and Polly's first family tragedy occurred while their eldest son delivered dinner to his father, who was working at the sawmill. A stack of boards caught wind, toppled, and crushed the boy as he excitedly watched the mill operate. Jesse, the son who was about nine at the time, survived the initial impact, but soon died.[15]

Because he was the family leader, the senior Jesse's rigid beliefs often created emotional detachment within the family. The Hutchinson Family Singers met a frightening paternal silence during a brief homecoming in their first year of touring. Jesse refused to speak to Judson when, homesick, the most thin-skinned of all his children surreptitiously left the group to return to Milford. For all of Jesse's severity, he did share an intimate bond with his sons, while Polly remained far closer to Abigail and Rhoda. The brothers' relationship with their father rested upon a generational and parental respect based largely in fear. In no way did any of the brothers wish to disappoint their father lest they become the next recipient of one of his moral cautions. His "strong physical constitution" and iron will made him a formidable patriarch.

The Hutchinson children shared certain traits with their father

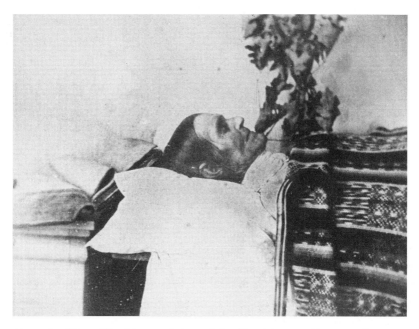

Funeral of Jesse Hutchinson, father of the Hutchinsons. Courtesy the New Hampshire Historical Society, Concord.

which only deepened family conflict; all were set in their ways and did not dither. Their stubbornness, a characteristic seen in the verve with which the Family Singers promoted music and reform, produced disputes but also generated a degree of mutual respect—an acknowledgment of the value of independence—that helped bridge the divide between generations. Ultimately Jesse would be the more supportive parent of the Hutchinson Family Singers. Polly fearfully cried when the children left for life on the road. Jesse sent them off with prayer.[16]

The changes in farming and in family in the early part of the century did not undercut the notion that an agrarian lifestyle was best. While family farming today is frequently viewed as something less than modern—*undeveloped property* is a term used for farmland—a belief that agricultural work constituted civilization (as opposed to the nomadic hunting and gathering of many Indian groups) held fast throughout the nineteenth century. With this stature came impossible notions of self-sufficiency: the independent farmer relied on no one but himself to provide food and clothing for his family. This vision, advocated by presidents and commoners alike, was perhaps the closest early America had to a binding ideology outside of Christianity. Antebellum Americans, though, slowly came to acknowledge the defects within their agrarian ideal at the same time that cash-crop production began to prevail. "An independent farmer," stated the *Farmer's Monthly Visitor* in 1839, was "not altogether independent of the community where he is, or of any business profession. . . . There must be ploughs and axes, and nails, and a hundred other implements which are cash articles, and which are to be bought with the very money received for the produce carried to market."

The flawed agrarian ideal held fast in New Hampshire, where farmers took their work very seriously even though their state's agriculture lagged behind that of the rest of New England. By supporting a variety of organizations, such as the Hillsborough Society for the Promotion of Agriculture and Domestic Manufacture, Granite State farmers ensured a public appreciation of their livelihood. In Milford—which was predominately a farming community before a sudden surge in mining in 1850—the ennoblement of the independent yeoman remained constant. During a dispirited time in his music career, Asa Hutchinson said that, outside of being with family, "My *chief desire* is to be a good Farmer." John Hutchinson, a professional musician who left New Hampshire in the early 1840s for the more industrial Lynn, Massachusetts, found it important to instill in his daughter, born in 1847, the ideal—"We had never lived on a farm," wrote Viola Hutchinson, "but I loved everything pertaining to farm life."[17]

In the first few decades of the nineteenth century, Jesse Hutchinson played the part of the industrious farmer despite relying on outside sources for income and assistance. (And later, family histories and newspaper coverage of the Hutchinson Family Singers would advance the myth that Jesse had been the Hutchinsons' sole economic provider—the quintessential independent farmer—ignoring the valuable contributions of his wife and his children, Jesse's other jobs, and the Hutchinson farm's hired help.) The New England winter, with its crippling cold and harsh winds, left him with plenty of time to pursue additional work. From December until March there was "not much to be

done in the fields" besides ensuring a sufficient wood supply. Jesse's
carpentry, coopering, and shoemaking skills came in handy during
these intervals and were a welcome source of extra money. Bringing
country produce and other wares to Boston was a normal practice for
rural dwellers who relied upon the resources of larger urban markets
for cash. People in Milford frequently saw Jesse atop his "four-ox load"
of barrels on his way to sell whatever he could in Boston.[18]

A host of traders and itinerants, from preachers to singing masters (traveling music teachers), increasingly invaded Milford as the
Hutchinson family grew. And indeed the family appeared to multiply
exponentially. In 1824, with a brood of fourteen, the Hutchinsons
moved three-quarters of a mile to a bigger house along the Souhegan
River, two miles from the center of town and directly across the river
from a road that ran from Boston to Vermont. The new homestead en-
compassed 160 acres, almost the average for a New Hampshire farm,
and the house, originally built as a hotel, was large enough to fit the
growing family. Fruits, hops, cereals, and vegetables were successfully
cultivated on this rather fertile interval adjacent the gneiss-speckled
banks of the river. Eight rooms roughly sixteen by eighteen feet, a full
cellar (with a stairway in back so that the bar boy could fetch refresh-
ments without disturbing the guests), and "convenient" outhouses defined the childhood home of the Hutchinson Family Singers. Wallpa-
per from France decorated the parlor and one bedroom, showing the
impressive reach of foreign goods into rural America. The Hutchinsons' home featured little other ornamentation. Relative to the size of
the house, there was almost no furniture, and the family did not have
the means to buy more items. Doing her best to explain the less-than-
ideal interior decor, Polly offered that her many children were all the
adornment the homestead needed.

Moving significantly affected the family. The Hutchinsons left
behind their oldest sons to tend to their first farm, while the former
owner of the hotel property, a colonel from the Revolutionary War,
continued to live in a small red house upon a hill overlooking their new
fields. Jesse Hutchinson could afford this property only because the
colonel had lost it to debt. Out of consideration for the penniless old
man, Jesse allowed Colonel Joshua Burnham to remain and, for some

nourishment, to pick from the fruit trees during harvest season. Even in his old age John Hutchinson would remember the extraordinary size of Burnham's pockets during apple season.[19]

For all the progress within the Hutchinson family, there had been setbacks as well. To memorialize Jesse, the son who had died at the mill, the Hutchinsons followed common practice and named their next son, born in 1813, Jesse Jr. Of his older brother's unfortunate death John said, it "was the first of many sorrows for his loving parents." Following Jesse, two of Polly's and Jesse's daughters did not survive to adulthood. Mary, their first daughter, died in 1810 at the age of four and, eighteen years later, Elizabeth, the fifteenth Hutchinson child, died at the age of three. Death of a child was a recurring theme in many nineteenth-century households, so in this the Hutchinsons' Milford residence was not unique. The pervasiveness of death, though, did little to lessen relatives' pain. In an age devoid of grief counseling, the Hutchinsons turned to family, friends, and faith to alleviate their suffering.[20]

Polly probably sought the support of her female relatives and close friends. Grieving mothers often received little or no overt support from their husbands during times of crisis. Messages of intimacy and encouragement were employed at key points in women's lives, usually by other women—courtship, marriage, childbirth, child rearing, and death all called the female network into action. After the death of Abby Hopper Gibbons's son, Lydia Maria Child wrote:

> Whatever may be my destiny, you will ever be to me as a dearly cherished sister. Be of good cheer under this temporary affliction; a little more patience will carry you through. I wish I could take part of your suffering for you. God strengthen you, bodily and spiritually, and long preserve you to be a blessing like the sunshine, to all around you.

Focusing on the impermanence of suffering and on fortitude, letters like this were meant to direct a grieving mother to an acceptance of God's will. Religious themes, especially those about a Christian afterlife, constructed the framework within which most advice was offered—"Let us not repine," wrote Fanny Crosby, "but cheerfully sub-

The Hutchinson brothers in 1845. Courtesy The Metropolitan Museum of Art, Gilman Collection, Gift of The Howard Gilman Foundation, 2005 (2005.100.77). Photograph © 1993 The Metropolitan Museum of Art.

mit to the will of Heaven." These notions undoubtedly carried Polly Hutchinson through her darkest moments.[21]

While many men developed close bonds with other men before marriage (fig. 5), after they wed, male relationships tended to take on a more businesslike tone. Throughout bachelorhood men studied and traveled together, forming ties comparable to the relationships shared by women, but male friendships rarely sustained their intimacy. The tone of letters that once revealed the personal angst of courtship and of career development changed over time to distant, polite, and informational correspondence upon marriage. Personal details and requests, if shared, often moved between two men through a female intermediary, such as a sister or a wife. When William Lloyd Garrison's daughter died, he wrote to Wendell Phillips's reclusive spouse, Ann, to request that Wendell speak a few words at the funeral. Married men did not readily share their grief with one another, often preferring to turn inward and to the heavens to lighten their burden. James Gibbons shared his thoughts about his son's death in a journal: "Time only, can enable us to realize the consolations necessary to palliate the force of the blow which paralyzes all power of enjoyment." Garrison wrote that his daughter Lizzie's "emaciated spirit is in that other and better world, which is part of our religious faith to believe a gracious Creator has prepared for his children."

A hardworking, uneducated man from a rural family of moderate means, Jesse Hutchinson largely missed out on the more urbane rituals of close male relationships, and his bachelor days were short. Agricultural life privileged labor over schooling, and school often served as a place to foster cherished friendships. Jesse's marriage thus did not appreciably alter his social network. In difficult times, Jesse could turn to neighbors and fellow farmers, who often helped one another. Their assistance, though, was usually more of a material nature, helping with a fence or in the field. From the scant record found in his son's recollections, it seems that the father of the Hutchinsons turned to his faith for guidance more than to any particular person.[22]

Polly and Jesse never lived completely isolated from each other in times of sorrow, as hope for a future reunion with the dead cut across gender and generations, uniting families through a collective understanding over their loss. John Lewis, a New York school teacher, expressed hope, when his daughter died, that his whole family would "join the dear departed child in realms of endless bliss." The pain affecting grieving relations drove many, in an effort to make sense of their anguish, to weave telling narratives about the deceased. In them, the child was thought innocent and angelic, thus absolved of any fault in his or her demise. Families, like the Gibbonses and the Hutchinsons, believed children to have special powers, not the least of which was prescience. The Gibbonses held that their son had a revelation of his death three weeks prior to the event. Abby Gibbons noted that children are "favored with clearer premonitions of the future than people of advanced years and mature reflection." A similar incident transpired regarding the Hutchinsons' first son. Allegedly, Jesse told his brother on the day of his accident, "David, I don't want to go to the mill today." Jesse's objection probably was a sign only of a child more interested in playing outside than in delivering meals, yet following his death, the Hutchinson family interpreted the remark as a forewarning of their son's awful fate.

Uncovering these omens reassured the pained families. Who else but God could supply a child with such accurate vision? And if God already sided with their child, then there existed a credible chance of reuniting in heaven. The Hutchinsons longed for their "ultimate reunion" with Jesse. Time and a belief in life after death alleviated the family's suffering. "Over the river they beckon to me," said one Asa Hutchinson song, "Loved ones who've crossed to the other side." The sheer number of early deaths in America ensured a spiritual elevation of children that permeated the consciousness of families and provided musicians, writers, and others with significant cultural content.[23]

Second Section: The Hutchinson Children and Some Initial Musical Influences

The Hutchinson family, of course, also focused on their many children blossoming in Milford. David, born in 1803, became the eldest after his brother Jesse's death. David was followed by a third son, Noah, then by Andrew, Zephaniah, Caleb and Joshua, Jesse Jr., Benjamin, Judson, Rhoda, John, Asa, and finally Abigail, born in August 1829. The leader of the youngsters was David, viewed by his younger siblings as the "home dictator." As the oldest son, he was weighed down by many responsibilities, especially when it came to caring for his brothers and sisters. The younger boys came to fear David, trembling "at his exacting words." Complementing David in the early years was Noah, who displayed an uncanny fiscal sense. Noah would help his father manage the family's debt, the majority of which accrued upon the purchase of the Burnham hotel. Andrew and Zephaniah (born in 1808 and 1810) initially showed some vocal talent, but limited family means and a mandate to work quickly undermined any musical aspirations.[24]

Until the twins Caleb and Joshua, nearly all the Hutchinson brothers chose farming—often after earning enough money from jobs in Lynn or in Boston to buy land—as their ultimate pursuit. Some, like David and Zephaniah, moved to the frontier in Iowa and Illinois, while others stayed in Milford or removed to farms relatively close by. Noah, for instance, farmed in Mount Vernon, N.H., where he and his wife raised ten children. Caleb and Joshua largely marked an end to the Hutchinson preference for agriculture. Of the eight Hutchinson siblings born after 1811, only Benjamin spent his life solely as a farmer, living at the family's Milford homestead for his entire life.

Caleb fit comfortably within his family's agrarian tradition. Anyone familiar with Caleb and his even temper could have guessed that he would not challenge the Hutchinson family's way of life. Like his mother and father, Caleb took religion seriously. As a youngster he earned a somewhat dubious reputation for waking napping churchgoers so that they would not miss hearing the word of God. Caleb also sought to downplay dispute, often functioning as the mediator of the Hutchinson clan. Later, with a family of five children, Caleb and his wife, Laura, lived and tilled in Milford.

Joshua took a different route from his twin brother. Not interested in farming, he ambitiously carved out a career developing rural culture. This industry, once the domain of trailblazing itinerants who "enlightened" the countryside selling the products and knowledge of their various skills, increasingly supported the creativity and crafts of locals as the nineteenth century progressed. Joshua's domain was music. After several years singing in the Baptist church choir, an eighteen-year-old Joshua bullied his way to the position of choirmaster in 1829, a position he held until 1843. Joshua was the first Hutchinson son to permanently break from farming, and his success as a music performer, director, and educator proved that cultural interests of a small rural town could support a permanent music presence.

As the nation moved from the margins of the world market on its way to gaining an international commercial standing, many Americans, like the Hutchinsons and their Milford neighbors, turned to family and religion to establish a moral center capable of combating the supposed degenerative forces of business. A separation of home and work, private and public, was part of this safety mechanism. Music, particularly moral music—the sounds of the church that Joshua first taught—worked for and against such separation, mingling public and private, sacred and secular, in performances for worship, for home entertainment, and for public amusement.[25]

Joshua's bold move to a cultural career in rural New England came on the heels of the recent and phenomenal success of the composer and educator Lowell Mason, who had demonstrated that piety, culture, and profits could coexist. Mason, originally from Medfield, Massachusetts, was lured to Boston from Savannah, Georgia, in 1827. Using the unexpected celebrity that accompanied his first publication—*The Boston Handel and Haydn Society Collection of Music* (1824)—which he completed while living in the South, Mason negotiated a handsome salary from three Boston-area churches to serve as their music director.

Mason's route from southern storeowner to nationwide musical preeminence was circuitous. Born in 1792, he exhibited a skill for playing a variety of musical instruments as a youth. But when it came time for him to chose a profession, the young man was at a loss. So when a few of his friends moved south in 1812, Mason left with them, apparently eschewing music to start a business in Georgia.

Much like his father, who operated a store back in Medfield, Lowell Mason worked to promote his own dry goods venture and his public stature in Savannah. At some point between his arrival in Georgia and 1814, Mason experienced a religious conversion, probably at a Baptist revival held in the region. Suddenly Mason, whose early southern letters were informational, began warning his family of irreligion; to his father: "You seem to write like one who had a speculative belief— you believe from education—from custom—but I search in vain for that fervent piety, zeal, & love by which a christian is distinguished"; to his brothers: "Religion is our only rational happiness." Mason's passion led him to found one of the first Sunday schools in Georgia, an interdenominational endeavor which he headed as superintendent from 1815 to 1826.

Alongside his personal business and later, after his store failed around 1819, as a clerk at Planters Bank, Mason started several singing schools linked to his church's educational program. The Massachusetts native was dismayed by what he thought to be a degradation of church music, especially the use of music from lay composers and the use of contrapuntal compositions, which he found too flashy for sacred contexts. In his endeavor to define sacred music, Mason battled both the old and the new. Since the late eighteenth century, musical and religious laymen in New England, particularly New Hampshire Baptists, had filled church services with their own music, often placing sacred lyrics atop popular folk tunes. Meanwhile, in the South, Mason faced musical innovations introduced to the church by African Americans whose practices and souls were welcomed by Methodists and Baptists. Mason's Savannah music school included black children by the 1820s. He did not oppose the new influences out of racial prejudice. For music in general, Mason enjoyed almost anything, but for music in church, he found such devices as polymeter and syncopation, centerpieces of the African musical tradition, distracting from the aim of worship.

Mason's part-time work as a singing-school teacher proved lucrative, and near the end of 1820 the church owed him $650. The pious man worked tirelessly not only to better music in Savannah but to better his own musical ability. During this time, Mason played the organ in church and also started to learn figured bass through a long-distance correspondence with the Boston organist S. P. Taylor. Mason's learning and experiences in this period impressed upon him the need for a tune book better targeted at a new generation of church singers. In the early 1820s Mason capitalized on a connection to Dr. George K. Jackson, organist of the prestigious Handel and Haydn Society in Boston, to publish and market his first book of music.

The success of this publication ensured fiscal stability for that organization and for Mason in the years to come. (By 1839 *The Boston Handel and Haydn Society Collection of Church Music* had earned Mason $12,000—the equivalent of between $200,000 and several million in 2007 dollars.) Even though he lived in Georgia, Mason's tune book vaulted him to prominence within the Handel Society, and after an impressive 1826 lecture on sacred music, three Massachusetts churches jointly offered him a job. Mason's eighteen-month contract to teach and to direct church music was initially worth $2,000 and, shortly after he moved, the Handel and Haydn Society elected him as its president in 1827.

When Mason left the Handel Society five years later, he had demonstrated the centrality of education to the fiscal health of music in Boston. With George Webb and the backing of several prominent Bostonians, Mason created the Boston Academy of Music, which attracted 1,500 students in its first six months. More than 3,000 attended in the next year. Also in 1834 Mason started classes for music teachers in an effort to spread his advances in music pedagogy. The combination of music instruction, music publications, and concerts kept Mason busy and his efforts in the public eye. He had cornered the market on sacred music and on music education in a remarkably short time. "Mr. M. is the master spirit of the age," said one student.

In 1836, with encouragement from Milford's Baptist pastor, Mark Carpenter, Joshua Hutchinson raised forty dollars to pay his trip expenses and fees to attend the annual convention of music educators held by Lowell Mason and George Webb. Mason derived his teachings from William C. Woodbridge (1782–1851), an American disciple of the Swiss educational reformer Johann Heinrich Pestalozzi (1746–1827). Mason, following Pestalozzi, held that music, which provided discipline and orderliness, must be taught to all children. Demonstrating a newfound respect for children, one result of the religious revivals of the early nineteenth century, Mason's pedagogical philosophy showcased four precepts: 1) teach music (a melody or a tune) first and teach musical notation later; 2) cater lessons to a child's mind—teach every aspect of music (melody, rhythm, and expression) as if it were separate; 3) always create a positive environment to encourage mental and spiritual development; and 4) teach children to explore their curiosity and to think for themselves. Mason thought his method "no other than the spirit of the gospel, applied to the work of education."

On top of these lessons on music instruction, Mason also explained how church music should sound. Not surprisingly, he held that sacred works should be very much like the compositions he created—melodies should consist of diatonic tunes (using only the seven tones of a standard scale and few, if any, chromatic alterations) and should demonstrate limited range (preferably no more than an octave); rhythm should be straightforward with little or no syncopation; and harmony should be diatonic and should utilize a major key. Mason composed pieces which heavily favored primary chords and used repetitive texts with symmetrical wording that were syllabically sung within a chordal setting (following the harmonic progression as opposed to a contrapuntal one). Mason's music was popular not only because it was singable but because of the high moral standards which he claimed it upheld. Church music, Mason felt, should never divert listeners' attention away from God.[26]

After attending Mason's class in 1836, Joshua opened his own singing school in Milford. Singing in their brother's choir and growing up within the same household had an immeasurable influence on the members of the Hutchinson Family Singers. Mason's methods and his music spoke to the conditions under which the youngest in the Hutchinson family were raised. While Judson was nineteen years old at the time, John, Asa, and Abby were at the more impressionable ages of fifteen, thirteen, and seven. That the Hutchinson Family Singers played music that was simple, effective, and strove toward a higher purpose is no surprise. Early concert reviews praised the New Hampshirites' clear and precise enunciation, another of Mason's hobbyhorses. Even without the link between Joshua and Lowell Mason, the Boston music mogul loomed large enough in the cultural life of the nation, particularly New England, that he would have undoubtedly affected the New Hampshire musicians. After 1836, though, the Hutchinson Family Singers received a healthy dosage of Mason's musical teachings, with Mason's own success setting the bar for the Hutchinson siblings in their careers as they combined Mason's more learned musical tradition with their earlier backwoods training from New Hampshire's Baptist community.

Joshua's intimate connection to music guided his younger brothers and sister toward stardom while he himself remained obscure. To Joshua's disappointment, he gained a reputation largely through association with his famous siblings. Never satisfied with his limited role in the musical act that he helped train, Joshua tried to seize their spotlight by forming the New Hutchinson Family Singers when his illustrious relations toured Great Britain in 1845–1846. Much like modern-day tribute bands, Joshua's group ultimately failed to capitalize on borrowed fame.[27]

Jesse Jr., born two years after the twins, Joshua and Caleb, gained much more renown for his role in developing the Hutchinson Family Singers. Called the Hutchinson Bard for his lyrical compositions, Jesse occasionally performed with the Family Singers and, over the years, also served as their composer, manager, and publicist. The excitable youngster's uncontrollable energy may have helped earn him the distinction as the second son of the Hutchinson family to reject farming. At some point between 1825 and 1829—when Jesse Jr. was aged twelve to sixteen—Polly and Jesse sent their ninth child away to train at a well-known weekly newspaper, the *Farmers' Cabinet*, published in nearby Amherst, New Hampshire. Jesse spent a few years as an apprentice and then as a journeyman with E. D. Boylston, the paper's owner. As a member of the press, Jesse took part in the growing communication network advancing ties between city and country.

Following his work at the paper, Jesse moved to Lynn, Massachusetts, where he started a stove business and became involved in antislavery reform. Taking a cue from Joshua, Jesse operated a singing school in Lynn while the Hutchinson Family Singers played a series of concerts in town during the 1840s. Jesse was most famous for his lyrical skill. He wrote "Get Off the Track!" the abolitionist anthem of the Hutchinson Family Singers in 1844. Later he composed the words for several songs played at the National Free Soil convention held in Buffalo, New York, in 1848. The Hutchinson Family Singers were fortunate to have had a press-savvy brother who was both connected to reform and capable of writing a hit song.[28]

Of the youngest five children in the family, four were to constitute the Hutchinson Family Singers. The oldest in this group was Judson. On March 14, 1817, the family welcomed a humorous and moody son, Adoniram Judson Joseph Hutchinson. Like many of his siblings, he exhibited a strong determination; as a boy, Judson sold vegetables to raise money to purchase a violin, an instrument he felt he must hide from his father. He was gifted in song and in verse, and his comedic tendencies captured the laughter and hearts of audiences everywhere. An 1851 lithograph on the cover of his composition "The Standing Collar" depicts a half-crazed Judson wryly glaring at the viewer over his violin while wearing a very large (standing) collared shirt (fig. 6).

Judson also harbored a terribly dark side. What demons haunted this talented artist we will never know, but their signs were unmistak-

Judson Hutchinson, "The Standing Collar" (Boston: Geo. P. Reed and Co.).
Courtesy the New Hampshire Historical Society, Concord.

able. In his journal he demarcated depression with an H, followed by brusque slashes. The H stood for the "horrors" that troubled him, a condition that worsened with age. Judson withdrew from the group and from the family in his most dire moments, wallowing in despondency. His suffering was no secret, followed by the public and the press. "He spoke of terrible seasons of depression, which at times came over him," a journalist reported, "and shivered at the thought of some terrible fate which he was sure would some day be his."

Judson's sister Rhoda, born on his second birthday, shared in some of her brother's anguish. She possessed one of the finest voices in the family but was paralyzed by shyness. Joshua thought that excitement simply wore down "the delicate condition of her nervous organism" as each attempt to put Rhoda on stage proved unsuccessful. Her condition, today called stage fright or performance anxiety, cost her the lucrative opportunity to be a part of the Hutchinson Family Singers. Like her mother, Rhoda valued the quietude of home and spent her entire life, which included two marriages, living in her Milford childhood residence.[29]

Two years younger than Rhoda was John, born January 4, 1821 (fig. 7). John was an "intuitively aggressive" child who housed an endless drive. That he developed into the force behind the Hutchinson Family Singers surprised no one. As a child John once decidedly sped up the tempo during a song at singing school, believing that the other children were slowing down. John's teacher kindly reminded him that there could be only one leader. John and Asa, the two dominant personalities of the Hutchinson Family Singers, while similar in appearance (so much so that people often confused the two), were not close. Each was a leader in his own right, and their relationship was tainted by competition. John and Judson, and, later, John and Abby, shared the deepest connections among the four Hutchinson Family Singers.

Polly Hutchinson must have had a special affinity for March 14; in 1823 she delivered her third child in six years on that date. This time it was a boy, whom they named Asa Burnham. He was a child who matured quickly, and the household applauded him for this feat. Asa's early reliability especially appealed to his hardworking father. The other siblings caught on in no time that Asa was their dad's "pet boy." In church the youngster was rumored to have placed his head against

A youthful John Hutchinson. Courtesy The Lynn Museum and Historical Society, Lynn, Massachusetts.

the pews to catch the deep vibrations from the organ—the Hutchinson family explained Asa's tremendously low and accurate bass voice with this tale.

Asa's leadership abilities, moral compass, and vocal range—down to a double B-flat—became the very foundations of the Hutchinson quartet. Asa was "genial, manly, companionable," always looking to help those around him. When the need for a church was felt in his later home of Hutchinson, Minnesota, he went on tour with his family and raised the funds. Upon the death of his first wife in 1875, he created the Elizabeth Chace Hutchinson Memorial Fund of the Minnesota State Temperance Union, to which he assigned his own life insurance policy.[30]

While her brother Asa may have been their father's favorite, Abigail Jemima—Abby—was instantly cherished by the entire family, becoming the "household pet" (fig. 8). Concern over her mother's age, forty-four, combined with the fact that she was "born out of due time," made Abby's 1829 birth a highly anxious event. But all went well and, as the youngest Hutchinson by six years, the newest addition to the family was doted on. Parents and siblings closely watched and protected Abby; after all, the household had already lost two female children. Apparently always a smiling child, Abby encouraged the adoration. The attention prepared her well for the public life that awaited her as a young singer in the 1840s.[31]

First Section (Modified): Milford, the Hutchinson Family, Religion, and Culture

When the members of the Hutchinson Family Singers were growing up—before Joshua led the church choir or Lowell Mason returned to New England—Milford lacked a degree of artistic sophistication, but it was not a cultural wasteland. Rural citizens could and did access instructional works on music and attended classes offered by traveling music tutors. These books, such as Cyrus Phillips's *Musical Self Instructor, Containing Five Hundred Questions and Answers Relative to the Science of Music,* were usually products of itinerant music teachers traveling the backcountry. Replete with musical notation, lyrics, and a set of instructions on how to read and perform, the tune book became a

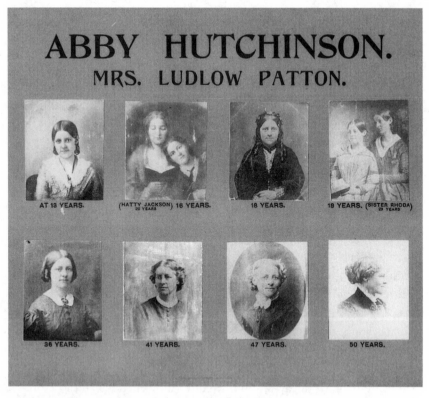

Abby Hutchinson through the years. Courtesy The Lynn Museum and Historical Society, Lynn, Massachusetts.

foundation of musical education and of choral singing in the eighteenth century. Selling music lessons and music books represented the
bulk of income for many American musicians through the first few
decades of the nineteenth century, when they normally had to serve in
many roles in order to get by—indeed, music teachers functioned as
composers, performers, publishers, and distributors. Not until such
acts appeared as the Virginia Minstrels, Louis Moreau Gottschalk, and
the Hutchinson Family Singers did music performance develop as a
specialty and a viable long-term source of income in the United
States.[32]

Singing masters developed tune books for pedagogy and profit;
yet the music instructor would have been hard pressed to market his

wares without strong ties to organized religion. Beginning early in the eighteenth century, churches in America championed music education in response to their congregants' low levels of musical literacy. The emergence of singing masters dates to this period, and they forged a bond with religion that lasted well into the next century. Masters often held class in church buildings, used sacred music as their principal subject, and taught students who went on to perform with or even to lead their church choirs. With the exception of Quakers, all American Christians were singing, making the church the young nation's largest sponsor of music.

Many believe that in the nineteenth century singing masters increasingly separated themselves from the church by introducing secular song to their repertoire. In fact, the music teachers only followed a trend of the time that made secular music—compositions not intended for church service—more and more a part of American life. This trend did not, however, displace sacred music or, more important, sacred themes as a central component of American popular music or of the singing-school experience. The Vermonter Joel Winch recalled attending a singing school in 1802 led by a "Br. Simonds." Winch believed Simonds "had Religion" because he "began his School with Prayer and at the close he called on me to pray." Slightly later in Rhode Island, a young Adin Ballou rejoiced over the opening of a singing school in Cumberland. Ballou's father, though, did not approve, fearing the consequences of irreligious people singing the word of God; his paternal anxiety revealed that singing schools, even in an age when they were supposedly losing their affiliation with the church, taught sacred song nonetheless.[33]

The close knit between culture and religion replicated the bond of church and nation. Churches were, by far, the most active and most stable institutions in rural communities. Whether it was in the church choir, Sunday school, or even common school, children were exposed to a Christian "nationalism as part of the standard curriculum." For country worshipers, the early-nineteenth-century revolutions in the church which culminated in the so-called Second Great Awakening produced a highly emotional religious reaction for which music was well suited. In the New England backcountry, amateur musicians began creating their own brand of sacred music to aid in their expression.

Nowhere was this trend more evident from 1780 through 1830 than in New Hampshire, where members of the dissenting Christian sects, notably Baptists, crafted a new and quite popular style of church music. The Granite State resident Joshua Smith wrote *Divine Hymns, or Spiritual Songs* (1784), a collection of music so admired that it went through at least eleven printings by 1803. Elias Smith, a poor Vermonter who learned basic music skills in eight lessons from his next door neighbor, was another well-liked composer who published numerous hymnbooks between 1804 and 1820. Though working in a tavern and on the farm, Jeremiah Ingalls—a self-taught musician—found time to write *The Christian Harmony* (1805), filled with popular hymns combining well-known tunes and original lyrics. These men and others like them set a do-it-yourself tone for music, especially religious music, in New England. The Hutchinson Family Singers, largely self-instructed as instrumentalists (John and Judson, violin; Asa, bass), were steeped in this rousing environment of music and faith. Eventually the Hutchinsons would reverse the flow from popular folk tunes to sacred music, creating popular music from sacred melodies.[34]

The seemingly spontaneous burst of musical activity sounding out in New Hampshire was only one manifestation of religion that erupted in the region between 1790 and 1830. Active church membership was another, and the Hutchinson family had a lengthy association with organized Christianity. In 1782, prior to the incorporation of Milford, Elisha Hutchinson, the Hutchinson Family Singers' paternal grandfather, was one of the forty-seven members of the South-West Parish of the Congregational Church and part of the group hired to build the Congregational Meeting House three or four years later. By 1788 a church was organized on land that was later incorporated into Milford, and Elisha was chosen as its clerk, a position he held until his death in 1800. Joining a church at the time was more than a simple matter of attendance. Applicants to the Milford Congregational Church had to publicly declare their religious experience either orally or in writing. Elisha's declaration did not have a lasting effect on his family. Elisha's son and daughter-in-law, Andrew and Martha, helped found Milford's Baptist church in 1809. The Hutchinson Family Singers' Uncle Andrew served as a deacon to this Milford institution for years to come. Andrew's brother Jesse, a little more wary of changing his affiliation, waited until 1814 to join the Baptists, a move in which he was joined by his wife.[35]

Baptists, established in regions farther south by the 1760s, gained in New England when migrants moved up the Merrimac and Connecticut river valleys at the end of century. Along with this demographic push came the sudden appearance of self-taught Baptist ministers (along with amateur sacred composers). These untrained religious leaders soon challenged those of more established New England Christian denominations in which social class, education, and wealth remained important markers of spiritual status. Among the largely uneducated population in the frontier regions of New Hampshire, lay ministers plainly communicated divine concerns to their constituents better than their well-trained counterparts who focused on more heady doctrinal issues.

When Polly and Jesse joined the Milford Baptist Church, there was little standardization in the region regarding the faith except for the uniquely Baptist avowal of adult baptism. Reflecting their lay origins, rural New England Baptists differed widely on other issues. Most significant was the question of predestination, which pitted Calvinistic Baptists—those who believed that God foreordained the saved and the damned—against the Freewill Baptists, who held that human free will, the ability to make oneself worthy of being saved, was compatible with the authority of God. (This position is also called Arminianism, after Jacob Arminius, who rejected John Calvin's teachings.) The difference between the two camps was so confused in New England during the early nineteenth century that Edward Lock, minister of the Calvinistic Baptist Church in Gilmanton, New Hampshire, could hold Arminian-based revivals for two years apparently oblivious to the fact that his stance was at odds with his institution. This was not unusual. Benjamin Randall, who founded the Freewill Baptists in New Hampshire, initially thought that universal salvation was the established theology of all Baptists.[36]

In 1780 Randall was wrong. But soon enough most Baptists, and indeed many Christian sects, adopted Arminian worldviews. Baptists, especially early on, governed on a very local level, and so it is difficult to know the precise doctrinal stance of the Milford church without appropriate documentation. In 1817, though, Polly and Jesse named their newborn after the then-famous Baptist missionary Adoniram Judson, known as "Jesus Christ's Man" and, later, "the man who gave the Bible to the Burmese." Judson and his wife set out on a mission to southeast Asia sponsored by Congregationalists in 1812, but once on their way, the two decided that "truth compelled" them to denounce the practice of pedobaptism (the baptizing of children) and become Baptists. Their conversion was a welcome jolt to the growing Baptist community in New England, which suddenly formed organizations to support foreign missions. Judson and his associate Amos Sutton supported the doctrine of free will and general salvation. (After all, without a way for the "heathens" to redeem themselves, a missionary's duty would have been nearly impossible.)[37]

Given the significant Arminianism in New Hampshire, it would hardly be a stretch to imagine the Milford Baptists championing free will. By the 1830s the church definitely espoused the idea, and in the next decade one finds Jesse Hutchinson, patriarch of the family, taking biblical authority into his own hands when he decided to become a revival preacher. The impact of Arminianism and the revivals which often introduced its practice significantly affected New England and the surrounding area, especially upstate New York. In these regions, the kinder and gentler impression of God emergent with freewill belief spurred intense concern for individual souls, promoting a heightened awareness of human suffering. Sin became much more internal, an individual failing that required a change of heart rather than merely a state of divinely sanctioned disgrace. "Adultery" and "fornication" were replaced by "*in*continence," while "acts of drunkenness" became "*in*temperance." Focusing on the personal import of such afflictions, religious beliefs helped many feel a new connectedness to the world around them, which eventually formed the basis for a new legal code protecting the "right of bodily integrity." In the early nineteenth century, the Milford Baptists' newfound compassion manifested in support for foreign and domestic missions to Christianize the unconverted, for temperance societies to stop drunkards from hurting themselves and their families, and even for antislavery to end slaving.[38]

Temperance and missions were central features of the New Hampshire Baptist community—the church formed committees responsible for monitoring antialcohol campaigns, foreign missions, and domestic missions—while antislavery remained more on the fringe. Colonial-era Baptists had dabbled in antislavery, but by the second decade of the nineteenth century there existed a significant number of Baptists against slavery throughout the United States. Prominent Baptist leaders like John Leland openly promoted abolition, while the church's unconventional and exploratory environment also embraced large numbers of blacks. (Methodist congregations, similar in this respect to the Baptists, were 20 percent African American by 1820.) The existence of black Baptists did not signal racial equality in the church. In mixed-race congregations, white men almost inevitably governed. Such policies fed the urge for blacks to establish their own churches— in Boston between 1805 and 1848 blacks founded four religious institutions (two Baptist and two Methodist).

A remote region like southern New Hampshire, though, had virtually no black community and lacked such racial division. The Milford church came out in support of antislavery in 1838 by sending representatives to the first meeting of the New Hampshire Baptist Anti-Slavery Society. The move was liberal but hardly radical for a New England Baptist institution. By 1840 even Milford's First Congregational Church adopted an antislavery resolution, and in 1844 the town's Congregationalists convened an assembly imploring other churches to take action against slavery. As the 1840s progressed, American Christianity as a whole began to divide along moral lines, with the antislavery/slavery debate preeminent, largely removing focus from differences formerly situated in doctrinal disputes.[39]

The Hutchinsons' religious affiliation and its progressive social doctrine did not, in the 1810s, undermine the patriarchal foundation of their family. Colonial Baptists were far more sharing of church governance than their post-Revolution equivalents. As a developing religious community, Baptists had adhered more to the egalitarianism embedded in their congregational practices as women had access to official avenues of power in the church. But as the Baptist Church moved from the margins of American society toward widespread acceptance, women's voices were increasingly silenced. When the founding of the United States categorized women as nonpolitical actors, the

Baptist Church seemingly followed suit. Once the terms *the church* or *the members* described who made important decisions in Baptist congregations; after the Revolution, *men* or *brethren* came into usage.[40]

Jesse and Polly thus joined a religious kinship celebrating spiritual equality that was administered through patriarchy. Women and men, blacks and whites, all were seen as religious equals. When it came to time to make a decision, though, white men ruled. One of Polly's and Jesse's first charges as members of the Baptist Church was to ensure "family religion at home"; Jesse, in 1814, would be the main arbiter of his family's religious decrees. The Hutchinson Family Singers later paid homage to the structure of family and religion in their song "The Old Granite State" when informing listeners that they had obtained their parents' blessing to be musicians and that the singers "bless them in return."

At birth, the Hutchinson children were not automatically made members of the Baptist Church. A parent's affiliation did not dictate her offspring's spiritual inclination, especially for Baptists who believed children devoid of genuine religious experience. So the fact that many of the Hutchinson siblings had no declared affiliation until 1830 was not peculiar. But the children's years of exposure to religious ideas at home, in music, and in school prepared them for their religious conversion. By staying active in the Milford community—particularly in the part of town where the Hutchinsons lived—the Baptist Church exhibited a great influence upon the eventual decision of the children to join their church instead of Milford's Congregationalists or even a church in another locale.

Sunday school was one obvious influence. Through the memorization of moral lessons, hymns, and Bible passages, the children were inundated with religious ideas. This influence seeped into common schools as well, especially in Milford, where the North District school hired Samuel Everett, minister of Milford's Baptist Church from 1824 until 1832, as a teacher. Everett's hiring only furthered the long-standing relationship between the Hutchinsons' school system and local Baptists. In 1806, before the construction of a Baptist church in Milford, the schoolhouse in district two was built as a joint project between Baptists and the community. For the next ten years the building was used as a school during the week and as a Baptist meetinghouse on weekends.[41]

The prevalence of Christian ideas in the lives of young New Englanders cannot be overemphasized. Even in classes not taught by the preacher and teacher Everett, John Hutchinson recalled that the instructors "read the Bible and prayed." The missions of Sunday schools and common schools often overlapped in this way. The Hutchinson children, all of whom except Abby attended the school on North River Road, were thus nurtured in an environment that made little distinction between religion and general education. Moral teachings situated in Christian ideology represented the very foundation of the pedagogical endeavor (Lowell Mason's system of music education exhibited this as well); learning piety was an important part of patriotism. Although John Hutchinson felt that the talk of religion in school did little to foster his "spiritual growth," the religious doctrine he received from his teachers, from the Baptist choir (the group led by his older brother, which he joined three years before declaring his own Baptist faith), and from his parents certainly did not inhibit his enthusiasm during Milford's Baptist revivals from 1829 to 1831.[42]

Intermission (Bridge to Part Third)

—◄◊►—

The year 1835 marked an historical dividing line. The world we now live in came into existence then, and humanly speaking, it is in almost every essential respect a different world from that lived in by the preceding six generations.

—Charles Francis Adams (1807–1886)

Changes in a Northern Land: Religion, Politics, and Culture, 1820–1840

If you had attended the annual convention of New Hampshire Baptists in 1829, you would have heard the bad news. "So far as we can learn the tone of religious feeling in our churches," announced the committee charged with gauging religiosity, "it is generally low. No extensive revivals have been experienced during the past year." Separating church from state during the nation's establishment had slowly unraveled the tax-based support of New England religious institutions and replaced it with congregation-driven financial backing; in the first decades of the nineteenth century, revivals—with the new adherents they attracted—would become the lifeblood of many churches. Smaller Christian sects, marginalized by earlier funding practices, could now compete with the deep-rooted Congregationalists and Presbyterians. Such was the case in Milford, New Hampshire, where the Baptist church vied with a Congregationalist one. Sitting at the statewide Baptist meeting in 1829, listeners understood the import of the committee's testimony: a lack of successful revivals shrank church membership—a potentially crippling fiscal crisis was on the way.

Certain signs that appeared seemingly validated the committee's concern over religious sentiment (and its financial implications). In 1833 Baptist numbers in Milford plummeted from 167 to 124, and then, after being "favored with revivals," surged to 195 two years later. To help buffer these maddening oscillations, Milford's Baptists organized with sixteen other New Hampshire Baptist churches in Nashua, Goffstown, New Ipswich, Dunbarton, and several other nearby places —a decrease in one region hopefully to be countered by an increase in another. By 1835 the so-called Milford Association claimed the second largest membership of all Baptist organizations in the state, its 1,451 adherents representing roughly 19 percent of the church's Granite State constituency. That year a revival hit the town of Nashua so hard that local leaders had to build another church, while at the same time, five other towns in the association continued to be "destitute of pastors" and heard preaching only on rare occasions.[1]

The gross disjunctions in Baptist religious life undoubtedly explains the alarmist nature of those staffing the 1829 Committee on the State of Religion. Their findings, though, had missed a greater trend in New Hampshire. An 1836 report confirmed a decade of growth: "During the ten years, increase of churches, 22; increase of ministers, 29; number erased, 178; restored, 44; baptized, 3552; added by letter, 835; dismissed, 1199; excluded, 264; died, 453. Net Increase, 3373; Total,

8010." Yet expansion did not eliminate the instability. A palpable precariousness continued to plague not only church membership but also church management. Over the ten-year span starting in 1825, each of the state's thirty-six Baptist preachers changed locality. "Truly," concluded church leaders, "we have no continuing city."

The turbulent nature of antebellum religion combined with annual church expenses to undermine any hope of constancy—one pastor cost nearly $500 a year in 1835. (Dartmouth professors who commanded annual salaries of about $700 secured "many comforts with that sum.") Add to these costs the maintenance of church buildings and schools, as well as obligations to other Baptist endeavors, and losing just a small percentage of membership could put a church in severe debt. Baptists depended upon voluntary contributions, and only success in the interdenominational competition for resources translated, as it did in the Hutchinsons' hometown, into something resembling long-term stability.[2]

From 1829 through 1832 Milford's Baptists grew by nearly 25 percent to total 167 members, and almost 20 percent of this growth came from new declarations in the Hutchinson family. Church leaders were quick to explain the increase: "Most of the churches in this Association have experienced some refreshings from the presence of the Lord." The Reverend Samuel Everett's 1831 newspaper ad confirms that these "refreshings" were no accident:

> The Baptist Church in *Milford, N.H.* hoping that by the grace of God it may be the means of promoting a revival of pure religion among them, have appointed a FOUR DAYS MEETING the third week in June next, to commence on Tuesday, the 14th day, at 2 o'clock, P.M. We therefore earnestly invite the ministers of the Milford Association, and other Associations around us, to come and help us. Dear brethren, we trust you will come, and we pray that you may come in the fullness of the blessing of the Gospel of Christ.

Everett's revival succeeded. In 1831 John, Benjamin, and Zephaniah, among others from the Hutchinson clan, officially became Baptists.

The twins, Joshua and Caleb, had joined during another series of Baptist meetings two years earlier. No wonder Samuel Osgood, visitor to southern New Hampshire at the time, reported that the people he met followed "all the formalities of religion . . . to an extravagant extent." He added, "The assiduity with which sacred music is cultivated here is remarkable."[3]

That the Hutchinson children were young adults when they joined the church was normal. In the 1820s and 1830s religious rifts within families were common, and the Hutchinsons'—first, a Congregational/Baptist divide between Jesse and his brother Andrew and, second, after Polly and Jesse became Baptists, one between parents and children—were relatively mild. Polly and Jesse were Baptists for fifteen years before their offspring formally entered the church, but their children did join them in the Baptist faith. The Winch family wasn't as lucky. When Joel Winch was born and as his family moved from Massachusetts to New Hampshire and, finally, to Vermont, his parents did not belong to any formalized faith. By the time Joel was ten, his family had joined the Congregationalists. Joel, though, started working for Samuel Aboat when he turned thirteen, and Mrs. Aboat was Baptist. Joel Winch did not know what to do. He agonized over his spiritual choices—Baptist or Congregationalist—and eventually sought some fatherly advice. Mr. Winch was certain that if his son joined the Baptists, Joel remembered, "the Devil would carry me off Bodily." Joel converted anyway, managed to thwart the Evil One, and later opted to be the Rev. Joel Winch, a Baptist minister.

At the close of the 1830s Harrison Gray Otis noted that "all Christendom has been decomposed, broken into pieces and resolved into new combinations and affinities." The Winch family knew exactly what he meant. Yet there is evidence that Joel's father needed not to have worried so much. Interfaith hostilities may have been a sign of sameness rather than difference. Many found the Christian sects interchangeable—Polly Hutchinson once told her children "that she was an Orthodox, Presbyterian, Congregationalist, Methodist, Universalist, Quaker, Baptist." Familial unity sometimes suffered from the rampant denominational switching of the antebellum era, yet the Winches and the Hutchinsons took part in a system where similarity, hyped as difference in the course of revival excitement, encouraged religious exchanges more than anything else. A loyalty to Christian ideals prevailed alongside unstable attachments to sect.[4]

"What must I do to be saved?" asked Americans at revival meetings. Ministers replied: sinners are obliged to select and to seek salvation. Arminianism and a dramatic emotionalism distinguished early-nineteenth-century revivals at which, day after day, listeners sorted through streams of tales of those who had been lost and then saved. "Tell stories," said revival phenom Charles Grandison Finney; "it is the only way to preach." Those who heard the religious dramas were then in position to undergo their own conversion experience—they were the next story in the making. These "reiterated admonitions and illustrative anecdotes," noted a visitor to a Baptist revival in the 1830s, were the foundation of a meeting's success.[5]

Revivals attracted hundreds, even thousands, of people, figures which make them one of the first mass entertainments produced in the United States. Such popularity challenged revival planners to thwart mob behavior, a prevailing tendency in antebellum society, and to maintain a sacrosanct environment. Revival leaders controlled audiences through a constant variety of activities, from theatrical speeches to picnics and singing. But it was not left at that. Organizers made certain that revival grounds, especially the tenting area housing visitors, minimized licentious contact and fostered a morally respectable environment. If these efforts failed, there were always rules governing proper behavior, prohibiting late-night gatherings, boisterous activities, and every kind of unapproved socializing (all of which transpired on occasion anyway). A refusal to abide by these codes could be met with an expulsion from the meeting area, an edict enforced by arrangements with the local police.[6]

Strictures aside, an event more entertaining than a revival was hard to find in the early 1820s and 1830s, especially in rural America. The art of revivalism is found in oratory (sermons, prayers, and testimonies), song (hymns and other sacred melodies), movement (such as rushing the preacher on stage or even dancing), and, also, perseverance. The most talented preachers read and quickly reacted to the emotions of the crowd. While ministers' performances appeared improvised—revivals looked impulsive and unstructured—it was a "practiced spontaneity" offering leaders several paths through which to move a meeting, each one treading on familiar ground. And if the revival didn't work, a ministerial doggedness kicked in to salvage whatever religious feeling had been stirred. After a meeting had secured forty-seven new followers, Peter Cartwright reported going "from cabin to cabin, taking the names of those that returned to the solid foundation of truth." Cartwright increased his number to eighty-seven.[7]

The link between revival ministers and actors was clear to Americans at the time. One preacher critiqued a camp meeting as "a theater in the open air, on the green sward, beneath the starry blue, incomparably more picturesque than any stage scenery." Innovations like the Anxious Bench—which placed those on the brink of conversion in plain view of the congregation to create a pressurized setting akin to current television talk shows—produced a melodrama within a decidedly sacred setting. Not everyone enjoyed this. Some complained that "the pulpit is transformed more or less into a stage"—which, of course, was the intention. In choosing emotion over intellect and then staging the result, revival leaders crafted a sacred culture capable of competing for attention among those who could select from among a growing number of activities to fill their leisure. The evangelical development of entertainment opened the door for widespread acceptance of cultural productions and, not coincidentally, spoke to the increasingly Romantic notions of American audiences in their quest for affecting endeavors.

The magnetism of revivals especially charmed a younger generation whose early years were infused with moral messages taught at school and at home. John Colby, a Baptist minister, remembered a fifteen-year-old Quaker girl who traveled about fifteen miles to seek conversion. Sensational religious experience proved no match, though, for the girl's mother, who put a quick end to her daughter's jaunt. With Polly and Jesse as avowed Baptists, the Hutchinson children were much easier prey for a Baptist religious awakening, especially with revivals going on only a few steps down the road fronting their home.[8]

Christianity appealed to the Hutchinson family and many of their New England counterparts not simply because it was nearby. The overthrow of British sovereignty in the 1770s left citizens of the new nation wary of those who expected deference. Ministers, in an effort to speak to the post-Revolutionary generation, slowly changed from acting like "fathers" to being "friends." By placing individuals at the center of the religious endeavor, antebellum revivals healed the fracture between the American Revolution—during which persons claiming responsibility for their own fate wound up defeating the world's greatest empire—and Calvinist thought, which upheld the omnipotence of God over humankind. Eventually, revival preachers and other religious leaders nearly overturned traditional church structure by freeing Americans to find religious meaning wherever they saw fit.[9]

The effects of this transformation played out in the Hutchinson family during the 1831 Baptist meetings in Milford. Andrew Hutchinson had remained in Boston to work at his grocery store while religious feelings swept his family. Wanting to be a part of the experience, Andrew, in due course, traveled home, where he and his father went to Milford's "Jordan," the Souhegan River. Here Jesse Hutchinson, who had never held any church position, dunked his twenty-three-year-old son, proclaiming a baptism in the crisp New Hampshire water. The event disturbed Milford Baptists; the rite was performed without witness, and the act of baptism as the full immersion of voluntary, conscious believers was what they thought distinguished themselves from other Christians. Yet they decided to let Jesse's action stand. Andrew was a Baptist.[10]

The so-called democratization of American Christianity went beyond the issues of control which Jesse flouted. After leaving the entertaining environs of a revival, worshipers looked to fill their lives with pious messages beyond those heard in church. Earlier means of marking the faithful were outdated, and new indicators of piety were needed. Eventually, the most pervasive religious source in America developed outside of the revival tent: "The gospel of Christ came filtered down to nineteenth-century Americans through stage plays and through the despised novel and Christmas story, rather than from the drowsy pulpit," said Mark Twain. Songs, books, newspapers, speeches, plays, and pamphlets printed and performed by both sacred and secular establishments spread the word of God throughout antebellum society.

Revivalgoers also reshaped American sacred life by turning their faith on their communities through social reform. By 1850, when this impulse combined with the commercialization of pious material, reform-based cultural productions in theater, music, and literature generated some of the era's best-sellers. No wonder the Washingtonian temperance movement—perhaps the most widely supported antebellum reform organization—skillfully combined "religion, drama, and box-office."

Americans may not have had an official state church, but by mid-century, if not sooner, Christianity became a widespread ritual, a fundamental source of cultural significance. The foundation for the commercial, Christian nation of the late nineteenth century was set. One English visitor reported that in America, "Christianity is in fact understood to be, though not the legally established religion, yet the national religion."[11]

Revolution-era politicians—nervous of replicating things British like a state church—had tried to avoid this situation, refusing to designate a countrywide creed and severing church and state in the Bill of Rights. Religious freedom, it seemed, had prevailed over other faith-based concerns. When some Connecticut Baptists asked Thomas Jefferson for a national day of fasting (to help the nation recoup from a bitter presidential campaign), he famously refused, answering in 1802 that the First Amendment had built "a wall of separation between Church and State." But as the nineteenth century progressed, it became clear that while many believed politics did not belong in religion, they also believed that religion did not necessarily need to be kept from politics. By 1840 the plan for a God-free government outlined by the Constitution had largely failed.

While some church leaders and reformers hesitated to involve themselves in politics—William Lloyd Garrison's absolutist stance against antislavery participation in local or in national politics is one prominent example—others were not troubled by the give and take which makes the art of democratic government. A split in the Covenanter faith in 1833 highlights the divide. Some chose to stay the 1806 Covenanter course, which declared the Constitution an immoral document for denying the word of God as the "Supreme Law of Nations and civil government." Others moved to make politicians liable to Christian belief. "The elective franchise is a great moral lever," said Jane Swisshelm, a Covenanter who became deeply involved with political antislavery; it makes voters, she said, "accountable to God."[12]

Deep ties existed between religion, politics, and social reform. Antebellum reform backed by Christianity required volunteering one's time for temperance or antislavery, a sacrifice of time and money for the greater public good—a forfeiture Americans also asked of their politicians. A nation still steeped in republican political principles openly received the idea of social reform, if not the reform movements themselves. The connection between religion and politics went far beyond the theoretical, and the two largely shared a language and a method. Andrew Jackson's 1829 inaugural speech spoke bluntly about the perfection of man—the president said "that man can become more and more endowed with divinity; and as he does he becomes more God-like in his character and capable of governing himself." The leader credited with stimulating early-nineteenth-century religious revivalism, Charles Finney, was equally blunt: "What do politicians do? They get up meetings, circulate handbills and pamphlets, blaze away in the newspapers, send coaches all over town with handbills . . . all to gain attention to their cause and elect their candidates." Finney went on, "The object of the ministry is to get all the people to feel that the devil has no right to rule this world but that they ought all to give themselves to God and vote in the Lord Jesus Christ as the governor of the Universe." If revival meetings constituted one of the first sources of mass entertainment, political rallies were not far behind. Leaders in both camps worked in public relations, an ongoing experiment in "mass persuasion" within the bounds of a democracy. Twenty years before the Civil War, it was difficult to distinguish between the two.[13]

The Hutchinsons and many representatives of antebellum reform culture, from John Greenleaf Whittier to Harriet Beecher Stowe, easily moved between religion and politics. Evocations of piety in popular music and literature brought sacred shoppers into the ever-widening consumer world. Artists like the Hutchinson Family Singers then directed their listeners to very political causes—in the Hutchinsons' case, each major antislavery party through the election of Abraham Lincoln. In revivalism, popular culture, and politics, the increasing public presence of American Christianity masked antebellum life with a sacred hue.

John Hutchinson crossed music and politics as an older teenager caught up in what would become one of the most memorable federal elections of the century. The voting in 1840 pitted a descendant of the Virginia aristocracy, William Henry Harrison, against the New York political animal and vice president Martin Van Buren. Harrison's Whig Party, for years depicted by Van Buren's Democrats as aloof and representative of upper-income Americans, would make a decided effort to combat this somewhat dubious portrayal. (The Whig Party stood for a larger, more active federal government which the generally proslavery Democratic Party loathed; if the national government could build roads and canals and regulate the mail, it could also police and, perhaps, end slavery.) The ensuing election has since been recognized as a political revival of sorts, its electioneering playing upon the same kind of emotional energy that marked the most successful religious spectacles. And just like the detractors of religious revivalism who decried its theatrics, critics in 1840 likened the political campaign to a magnificent show. One frustrated Democrat wondered whether from then on political parties would be "like a circus company with bands of music and dazzling ponies, clowns with pink noses to make folks laugh & banjo singers, a little lofty tumbling to secure votes." Public extravaganzas proved just as popular in gaining the attention of taxpayers as they had proved in awakening souls.[14]

Both parties in 1840 used elaborate means to get out their message. Several months before the election the Whigs formed local Tippecanoe clubs—named for the 1811 Battle of Tippecanoe in which Harrison waged a successful attack against Native Americans—to cinch support. These clubs published grossly partisan papers and sponsored a variety of community-wide events. The *Harrison Eagle* was one such product of the Nashua, New Hampshire, Tippecanoe Club beginning in June 1840. Both parties created political clubs in an effort to garner local appeal for national politics by linking white men directly to a political institution. For the most part, the Democrats and Whigs offered a similar array of political campaign goods. The Whig Party, though, edged its rivals when using music.[15]

George Julian, the 1872 vice presidential candidate for the Liberal Republican Party, remembered the sounds of 1840 better than anything else from the campaign: "The most distinguishing feature of the campaign was its music," he said. "The spirit of song was everywhere, and made the whole land vocal." Julian continued, "The campaign was set to music, and the song seriously threatened to drown the stump speech. Whiggery was translated into a tune, and poured itself forth in doggerel rhymes which seemed to be born of the hour, and exactly suited to the crisis."[16]

Lynn resident David N. Johnson agreed: "The rallying cry from one end of the country to the other was 'Tippecanoe and Tyler too'":

> What has caused the great commotion, motion, motion,
> Our country through?
> It is a ball a-rolling on, on
> For Tippecanoe and Tyler too—Tippecanoe and Tyler too;
> And with them we'll beat little Van, Van, Van;
> Van is a used up man;
> And with them we'll beat little Van.

So opened William Henry Harrison's and John Tyler's 1840 campaign theme, sung at many an affair and easily found in *The Harrison and Log Cabin Song Book*. The Whig Party left little to chance, so the rolling ball evoked in song actually existed—built by some Pennsylvanians, it stood roughly twelve feet in diameter, painted blue on the ends with stars to symbolize states, and sporting red and white stripes with numerous sayings inscribed in between the lines. By linking lyrics to real objects—in this case, one that smacked of the American flag—the party asked followers to visualize the Whig song as well as to sing it. The national flaglike ball provided a linkage to America's hallowed past and pointed to the Whigs' soon-to-roll-along success.[17]

In the history of the 1840 campaign, the involvement of a twelve-piece band from Milford, New Hampshire, has never figured very prominently. Yet the existence of this band and many others like it throughout the nation connected people to politics through music. The success of these Milford musicians in political settings was manifest. John Hutchinson, who played in the group, remembered it vividly: "How everybody sprang to the doors and windows! the small boys rushing into the streets, following the trail." The band moved energetically down main street showering the town with the election's music. A new world opened to the community, and, for several mem-

bers of the Hutchinson family, the Milford band was their first extended experience performing music outside of a church setting.

The campaign gave those in Milford a new kind of entertainment and lasting memories. John recalled the Whig processions as
"great affairs." Rolling through Milford came "log-cabins on wheels"
(Harrison promoted himself as having overcome humble origins) and
"barrels of hard cider for free distribution to all who came" (despite reports in the *Harrison Eagle* that the candidate had sold his distillery because he thought alcohol was injurious—an acknowledgment of the
political weight of temperance). Putting the final touches on an already
elaborate occasion were the veterans of the Revolutionary War who
drove teams of horses for the Whig festivities. When the wagons and
the music stopped, eloquent orators took over—"How the speakers
worked!" said John.

Yet the old singer, even when writing of the event in the 1890s
with a heightened nostalgia, was not blinded by the liveliness of the
election. When John looked beneath the pomp, he feared that the political message was not what really mattered. "There seemed a good
deal of unnecessary fuss in all this speaking and parade," he said. Eighteen forty was John's first encounter and the first encounter for many
Americans with the new style of political campaigning. The festivities
were less about the partisan message than about securing votes. When
the Milford band played at a political rally in Wilton, New Hampshire, one of the politicians was charged with the task of introducing a
Revolutionary War veteran. The speaker waxed eloquent over the generation of 1776, but, when it came time to present the war hero, turned
in embarrassment to the elderly gentleman to ask his name. The people laughed, for they had been entertained, but John, sitting at a short
distance in the band, was already sensitive to the darker side of political fanfare.[18]

Laughter was probably the most sincere response in Wilton that
day. To be fair, national candidates shouldered a heavy burden. The
parties tried hard to cozy up to voters to bridge the gap between what
was then a distant federal government and its electorate. With no income tax or large infrastructure projects, the post office represented
the most common place for Americans to interact with their nation's
government. Giving away public lands, selecting and removing public

officials, providing exemptions and immunities, and dealing with tariffs made up the business of the national government in the first half of the nineteenth century. The suggestion, then, that many Americans attended the political spectacles as eager audience members—thrill seekers—and not as potential voters is not terribly discouraging. At the very least, elaborate campaign rituals brought people into a public setting where various issues could be debated. At best, the festivities channeled entertainment into political concern and action.

For musicians like John Hutchinson and his brothers, 1840 deepened the possibilities to employ music for public action. Performing on the campaign trail differed from the Hutchinsons' most common concert setting, singing in a meetinghouse. Largely removed from church influence—but not from religious authority—John and other musicians witnessed firsthand the value of American entertainment in public life and played a part in opening a new social space for their craft.[19]

Manufactured Nature

New England changed quickly during the 1830s, and the transformation touched on more than religion, reform, and politics. Milford, a tiny farming community when Polly and Jesse Hutchinson first arrived, was now one of many burgeoning manufacturing towns in the northern countryside. Mechanized labor increasingly took over such tasks as weaving starting in the late 1820s. Women who once partook in outwork weaving ably turned to other handmade products to earn extra cash after the development of the power loom. Manufacturing, though, would greatly alter the lives of the daughters of these women. The opening of large manufacturing towns, like Lowell, drew migrants from the countryside who were no longer tied to family land. Geographic mobility and jobs away from home provided a degree of economic and social independence previously unknown to young men and, especially, to young women. Jesse Jr., Zephaniah, and David were the first of the Hutchinson family to venture toward growing industrial centers in Massachusetts—Lynn and Boston—taking part in a process in which the youth of rural New England moved to areas of economic development.[20]

So much attention is paid to urbanization in nineteenth-century America that cities like New York, Boston, Chicago, and San Francisco often monopolize our attention. Yet in 1860 a good 64 percent of New Englanders still lived in rural settings. Not only was the economic expansion of the countryside vital to the growth of urban areas, providing needed materials and food, it also helped to stem the outflow of manpower and womanpower. A young Harvard graduate, Francis Silsbee, noted when traveling through Nashua (and nearby Milford) in the summer of 1831 that "within a few years" the site had "changed from a small unpopulous village to a brisk manufacturing town. There are several neat houses in Nashua & the Factories add to its appearance." Waterpower provided towns like Milford and Nashua an advantage over other locations, allowing them to extend commercial interests. The development in rural settings of sawmills, then cotton and woolen mills, helped catapult the northern economy into the industrial age. (In the state of New Hampshire, the Amoskeag Manufacturing Company, located in Manchester and founded in 1832, developed into one of the largest and most famous manufacturing sites in the history of early America.)[21]

With factories came disputes over the use of local resources. Many New England towns were soon embroiled in debates over taxes, dams, and roads. New players in the towns' economies, mill owners navigated and negotiated their relationship with the community. Figuring out how to build and bankroll thoroughfares adequate to satisfy the increased demands of mill traffic was central. Noted musician Henry Russell remembered his treks in the 1830s and lamented the "'corduroy roads' of early America"; he faulted their design and construction, believing that "they were formed in a curiously primitive fashion." But by 1850 a greatly improved and expanded transportation network linked New England. As the region was enmeshed with roads, both traditional and railroad, the flow of goods, services, and cultures between city and countryside amplified. "There is scarcely a poor owner of a miserable log hut," said one excursionist, who does not have "a newspaper left at his door."[22]

Tourists took to the muddy New England roads as well, and, starting in the 1820s, many wound their way into the largely unsettled parts of the region. Trips into the wild were much different from the sojourns of earlier American vacationers. Following the lead of the European Grand Tour, well-to-do Americans and foreigners had once spent their time exploring urban areas while quickly traversing rural regions. The retired British manufacturer Henry Wansey's 1794 trip to the United States featured only five days of travel through the countryside as compared to the seven weeks he spent in Philadelphia, New York, and Boston. These early trips revolved around access to various social networks, relying upon letters of introduction for entrée into noteworthy institutions and events. But in the 1820s a different kind of tourism developed, one more reliant on money than upon social connections. Following the canals and roads that supported expanding industries up the Hudson River, continuing along the Erie Canal to Niagara Falls, sightseeing would develop hand-in-hand with industrialization. The focus was no longer upon cities and their many institutions (though West Point happened to be an attraction on the route) but rather upon the experience of traveling the Hudson and the scenery on view during the passage. Nature tourism fast became the antebellum vacation of choice. Landscape was so popular that by the time of the 1829 election, visitors to Washington, D.C., would even flock to the "Transparent Panoramic View of West Point and the adjacent scenery" housed at Pennsylvania Avenue and Thirteenth Street.[23]

The scenic tourism industry boomed in New England before the Civil War as nature and industrialization forged a symbiotic relationship—the industrial infrastructure allowed Americans to fully explore their growing interest in romanticism and the sublime landscape. Locales like Nashua and Milford benefited from growing economies; their factories and mills, along with improved transportation, tied the region to Boston's markets even more securely. Enterprising New Englanders started hotels and inns to accommodate the influx of business travelers to their region, and by the late 1830s, as a factory seemingly sprang up next to each waterfall, so too did a hotel with a set of stairs leading out to a scenic vista—the Romantic visions of nature offsetting the rough advance of industry.[24]

As New Hampshire natives, the Hutchinson Family Singers were well positioned to take advantage of the burgeoning arena that combined nature and culture. Perhaps no single formation dominated nineteenth-century nature tourism more than the Granite State's White

Mountains. By most accounts, the Crawford family set the foundation of White Mountain travel early in the 1800s when they built several crude inns in what later would be dubbed Crawford's Notch. While cut off from most of civilization, their enterprise was tactically sound. The Notch sat at the crux of the most direct trading route between Portland, Maine, and the regions of northern New Hampshire and Vermont. Unfortunately for the Crawfords, commercial traffic could traverse the path only in winter, when a swath of packed snow accommodated large wagon trains. Of course, winters stay long in the mountains, so wagon drivers and lumberjacks were the most frequent guests at the Crawford establishments in the early years.

By the 1820s, though, a different clientele slowly found its way to this remote part of New Hampshire. At the time, Mount Washington was reputed to be the tallest peak in North America. This first lured thrill seekers, but soon the more genteel tourist, nature travelers who thought there was more to the White Mountains than just adventure, followed. The Crawfords quickly adapted to the fast-growing nature industry of the 1830s. Summoning visions of Swiss alpine guides whose cannon-induced avalanches entertained visitors, Ethan Allen Crawford began to greet guests approaching his inn with a blast from his shotgun or a loud burst from a tin horn, regale guests with stories of the mountains, and take them on guided tours of the region's most impressive sights.[25]

Francis Silsbee took a trip to New Hampshire in 1831 following his Harvard graduation, just before commencing a law apprenticeship. Along with a few friends and young ladies (chaperoned, of course), the group took two weeks to explore Maine, the White Mountains, and certain parts of the Connecticut River Valley. On their journey they were treated to bread and cheese carried by their guides in leather wallets. Even when there were eateries, the vacationers preferred to rush their stop in order to continue their travel—scenic tourism was about seeing as much as possible.

By the 1840s, while otherwise offering crude accommodations, the Crawfords eventually changed their food service to placate more demanding travelers; the British author and critic Harriet Martineau reported a veritable feast at Crawford's Notch, consisting of "mutton, eggs, and whortleberries with milk" accompanied by tea and bread.

The Crawfords and their visitors stood at the forefront of changing perceptions of nature and natural scenery which would make the White Mountains a premier vacation spot.[26]

Aside from touring the natural wonders of the region, ranging from the Old Man of the Mountain and Mount Khatadin to Crawford's Notch, White Mountain sightseers enjoyed writing and talking about the things that they had seen. Francis Silsbee told the world in his journal, "I should advise every one who wishes to see the sublime & beautiful to come to the White Mountains." A sixteen-year-old Mary Hale, visitor to New Hampshire in 1840, self-deprecatingly wrote of Crawford's Notch, "It is impossible for a person who has such a weak mind as mine to describe the view that we there had of the beauties of nature." (After seeing the White Mountains in 1844, Asa Hutchinson wrote similarly, "O, we had a good time, too good to try and describe anything I saw on our visit. I haven't the power thus to do.")[27]

The appeal of the wild did not develop by chance—the ideal had been years in the making. Despite Mary Hale's insecurity, she and other nature tourists were well versed in a language to depict what they saw. The mystical attraction of scenic tourism was first spurred by European Romantic writers who ably transformed alpine landscapes from frightening visions into the picturesque or sublime. American readers, familiar with the works of Wordsworth on England and of Byron and Shelley on Switzerland, longed for the creation of a comparable "cult of romantic scenery" in the United States. When the marketing of nature through literature and art developed in America, it focused upon such places as New York's Hudson River Valley and New Hampshire's White Mountains. From 1827 to 1839, the Crawfords' guest books list some of antebellum America's most notable artists and writers, including Thomas Cole, Washington Irving, Ralph Waldo Emerson, Nathaniel Hawthorne, James Russell Lowell, and Henry David Thoreau. Visits by these men earned New Hampshire billing as the "Switzerland of America," luring other famous Americans, such as the politicos Daniel Webster and Charles Sumner, to vacation at the Crawfords' as well.[28]

The results of artist inspiration in New Hampshire are well known. Cole's *Notch of the White Mountains* (1839) and Hawthorne's "The Ambitious Guest" (1835)—which touched on the nationally renowned tragedy of the Crawfords' neighbors who perished in an 1826 mudslide—along with more generally focused works like Emerson's "Nature" (published in 1836, four years after his sojourn in the White Mountains) and works of many lesser-known painters and writers fashioned a nationwide market for scenery, and especially for pieces on New Hampshire. By the late 1840s scenic tourism in the White Mountains was a big business, a phenomenon that pushed frontier families like the Crawfords from their livelihood—the family inn was exchanged for larger, more genteel hotels. Meanwhile, the slow and steady production of landscape paintings and nature writings was replaced by mass-produced scenic prints and guidebooks.

New hotels and well-groomed roads certainly changed the way the White Mountains looked, but the traffic required to fill the accommodations and the railroads that brought visitors to the region made the most dramatic difference. For Henry David Thoreau, the new brand of nature tourism, often featuring areas overrun with tourists, packaged New Hampshire's wonders along with gimmicks: "a ten-pin alley, or a circular railway, or an ocean of mint julep." Connecting the remote state to the nation's railroads also reshaped the way in which vacationing Americans navigated through space and time. Older modes of transportation generally followed the contour of the land, the direction of the wind, or the push of currents. Railroads altered this relationship, plowing through the New England scenery in a straight line. In addition to offering greater speeds and a fairly accurate time schedule (relative to erratic faircoach service), traveling the rails transformed the environment and the perception of the environment in which people lived. Antebellum Americans moved faster and more directly toward their final destinations.[29]

The railroads—or the "roads," as the Hutchinson and others liked to call them—dramatically changed life in Milford. The first quarry opened in the southwest part of town in 1812, yet it was not until the latter half of the nineteenth century that the Hutchinsons' hometown earned a reputation as the Granite Town of the Granite State. Opening the Milford railroad station in 1850 removed the final barrier to the town's full entry into the quarry business. John, Abby, Judson, and Asa did not grow up in a Milford celebrated for its geologic riches, but early stages of the economic shift were present in the

1830s. Residents of the small town suddenly faced an array of choices concerning jobs and public activities. Their economy diversified beyond agriculture, and they began enjoying facets of urban living within a predominately pastoral region. In the years before the Civil War, many out-of-the-way places just like Milford became outposts of "urban civilization" in rural New England.[30]

The new Milford of the late 1830s created a divide among the Hutchinson children. Polly and Jesse treated John, Asa, Abby, and Judson differently from many of their older siblings. The Hutchinson parents had thought of their older children largely as a valuable resource for domestic and farm labor. But changing opportunities for employment during the 1830s forced Polly and Jesse to rethink their obligations to the younger Hutchinsons—to compete in the new environment, John, Asa, Judson, and Abby required a greater educational and economic investment than had their older brothers and sister.

Around 1835 the Milford Female Seminary first opened its doors, and seven-year-old Abby Hutchinson enrolled in the fall of 1836. Expectations for Abby diverged greatly from those of her mother's generation. Polly Hutchinson was to take care of responsibilities around the home and, ultimately, to defer to her husband on issues of child care and religion. Abby, thanks to the availability of many household items that were once made in the home, joined a generation of women who, in theory, had more time to spend mothering. To be successful, Abby needed a better and broader education than her mother had received. Still expected to do household chores, Abby would also be versed in a wide variety of subjects, speak knowledgeably about them, and provide a stimulating environment for her husband and children, who, once at home, were under her care.

The seminary was just the place for Abby and other young women to develop these traits. Here Abby learned that a moral foundation was "the most essential part of education," as the teachers trained their pupils in the proper "social and moral feelings." The Milford Female Seminary exposed the future Hutchinson Family Singer to geology, physiology, European history, and arithmetic. But the subjects that received the most attention were "Vocal Music, and Calisthenics; Reading, Spelling and Composition." More important than any topic was the instruction "given upon female manners and deportment" and the "supervision exercised over the conduct and habits of the young ladies, when not under the *immediate* care of the teachers."

The focus on female education, more liberating than Polly Hutchinson's lack of schooling, did not signal a giant step toward sexual equality. "It is education alone, which shall place woman in her proper sphere," said the clergyman Charles Burroughs in a New Hampshire speech, "bestow upon all her powers a sublime energy and hallowed direction." Samuel Cornish was more succinct: "We expect our females to be educated and refined; to posses all attributes which constitute the lady." Abby's education would prove well suited to a future spent traveling, writing letters, writing in a diary, performing, and being married.

After the close of the Milford Seminary, Abby attended a school for women in Hancock, New Hampshire, and the Edes Female Seminary in Plymouth, Massachusetts, where she continued her education in the spring and the summer months. As the youngest in the family, Abby benefited the most from Milford's increased growth and gentrification. But her older brothers who formed the Hutchinson Family Singers did not miss out. Judson and Asa attended the Literary and Scientific Institution in 1837, also in Hancock, where they trained for work beyond the farm. Though it was not far away, going to school in another place expanded the world of the Hutchinson siblings, perhaps giving them ideas that far exceeded their parents' hopes.[31]

By the start of the 1840s the Hutchinson family's hop cultivation, along with successful business ventures of some of the older brothers in Lynn and in Boston, provided Jesse and Polly with financial stability despite the 1837 depression. Jesse soon surprised his three sons, John, Asa, and Judson, by telling them that they were no longer welcome to live off the family's resources. The three young men, in turn, startled their parents with their career choice. Very few Americans made a living from music performance in antebellum America, and no one from Milford had ever made it to a big city stage.

Part Third

Chronology

—6 November 1840. The Hutchinson family's first ever concert.

—Early 1841. John, Asa, and Judson move to Lynn, Massachusetts.

—13 February 1841. John, Asa, Judson, and Jesse Jr. give a Lynn concert.

—October–November 1841. John, Asa, and Judson undertake a concert tour of New Hampshire.

—December 1841. Back in Lynn, the Hutchinson brothers probably see the world-famous Rainer Family perform.

—29 January 1842. Abby joins John, Asa, and Judson on stage in Lynn.

—4 July 1842. Hutchinson Family Singers play at a temperance gathering in Milford, New Hampshire.

—29 August 1842. Hutchinson Family Singers delight four hundred to five hundred listeners packed into Albany's Female Seminary.

—1 September 1842. The Hutchinsons meet the celebrity black musician Frank Johnson.

—13 September 1842. The Hutchinsons' inaugural Boston concert, at which they meet the music publisher Oliver Ditson.

—2 November 1842. Hutchinson Family Singers' fund-raiser for their grandfather, Andrew Leavitt.

—30 December 1842. William Lloyd Garrison reprints in the *Liberator* N. P. Rogers's article imploring the Hutchinsons to write abolitionist music.

—1843. The Hutchinson Family Singers publish some of their most famous songs, including "Cape Ann," "Excelsior," "King Alcohol," and "The Old Granite State."

—3 January 1843. Beach antislavery meeting in Milford, where the Hutchinsons make their musical antislavery debut.

—11 January 1843. Death of Francis Scott Key.

—5 May 1843. Temperance meeting at the Old Deacon Gilles distillery with the Hutchinsons as the featured act.

—22 May 1843. The Hutchinson Family Singers meet the popular singer Henry Russell.

—June 1843. The Rainer Family leaves the United States.

—18 December 1843. The Hutchinsons' sheet music "Cape Ann" submitted to the clerk of the Southern District of New York.

—19 May 1844. Asa stumbles on a religious meeting led by his father where the ceremony closes with a singing of "My Mother's Bible."

First Section: Music (the Hutchinsons' First Concert)

Mountain minstrels, sweetest singers
Softly float your warbled strains;—
Still the sound about me lingers,
Still the melody remains . . .

—Miss L. A. Fiske,
"To the Hutchinsons," 1845

This chapter is about music—a fall concert; the first steps toward a career in entertainment; the search for an identity—and also about reform, burgeoning fame, and, again, some music: sheet music and some of the group's most popular songs of 1843.

To start, the fall concert: 6 November 1840, a Friday event, the start of what is later claimed to be more than twelve thousand shows given by the Hutchinsons. The Milford citizen and lawyer Solomon K. Livermore spoke on the merits of music to begin the evening. Jesse Hutchinson—"the father," according to the reviewer for the *Farmer's Cabinet,* "not yet crowned with hoary hairs, and whose appearance would place him in active manhood"—then led the large ensemble through a variety of songs.

Though the performance—an offering of the entire Hutchinson clan, Jesse, Polly, and all of the children—seemingly lacked the import of singing during a church service or playing in the Milford band, the group's size, their rendering of sacred song (part of a mixture of secular and sacred selections), and the concert's setting (Milford's Baptist meetinghouse) combined to produce a hallowed atmosphere. If one had unexpectedly walked in on the performance, one might very well have thought the singers part of a religious service. They were not. The Hutchinson family offered music as entertainment, principled entertainment. Enjoying the distraction from their usual evening's activities, the Milford audience thanked the group with a warm reception.[1]

The success of the Friday night concert, still snug in memory, undoubtedly influenced three of the Hutchinson brothers later that year when their father sent them out on their own. Judson, John, and Asa (ages twenty-three, nineteen, and seventeen) opted for a career in music. While older brother Joshua had led the singing school and the church choir for years, his younger siblings harbored a grander musical ambition—winning over audiences as professional performers. Raised in an environment which had popularized composers of sacred music as diverse as the self-taught Joshua Smith and the distinguished Lowell Mason, the Hutchinsons sought to add a significant twist to a New England music tradition with their concert-based dreams.

Music was often thought of as a science in the first half of the nineteenth century, an attitude which had helped make respectable the composing of music and, to a lesser extent, the teaching of music. Musicians themselves did not benefit from this thinking and were often denigrated as lovers of money in a shameful trade. "I declare that I would rather be reckoned the best barber than the best fiddler in England," Lord Chesterfield once warned his son; a like-minded sentiment endured in antebellum America. A prejudice for European-born or European-trained musicians—revered for having special playing prowess, the result of having developed in a more mature cultural setting—added to the woes of American musicians.

When the American-born and -trained performer did triumph in the early nineteenth century (a rare occurrence), it was almost always in a large city. With greater populations and superior concert infrastructure, urban areas served as focal points for the arts. Not surprisingly, blackface minstrels of the late 1820s and 1830s created and acted out their gross caricatures of African-American life within a northern urban society. City patrons made minstrels one of the few successful native acts. Indeed, cultural goods and trends had largely flowed from city to country. In the 1840s the New Hampshire Hutchinson brothers, looking to capitalize on their rustic roots, went from country to city in their quest to garner the worth attributed to composers and teachers of church music, the respect given to European performers, and the popular success of blackface minstrels.[2]

Second Section: A Music Career and the Hunt for an Identity, 1841

The initial step in their musical journey took John, Judson, and Asa in 1841 to Lynn, Massachusetts, where they would soon try their luck on stage. But first, being nearly penniless, and uncertain how they should proceed, the three started working in their brothers' hardware and grocery stores.

Older brothers Jesse Jr. and Zephaniah Hutchinson had removed to Lynn much earlier. Jesse's tenure in the shoe manufacturing town began as early as 1835, when he was twenty-one years old. By 1840 he was at number eight Exchange Street at his stove shop, while his older brother Zephaniah operated W. I. Goods and Groceries next door at number nine. Jesse remained linked to his printing beginnings, as the book publisher Perley and Stoneham occupied the space above his store; the printer's advertisements told customers to come to the "Hutchinson Building," proving that, at the very least, Lynn residents knew of Jesse and Zephaniah. Perhaps the Hutchinsons even owned the building in which the three aspiring musicians toiled upon their arrival.[3]

Working in their brothers' stores was one of the few options open to John, Asa, and Judson. The performance climate dictated that the Hutchinsons, despite their deepest desires, could not simply turn up at the nearest hall and draw in eager listeners. With no celebrity, no European pedigree, and little money to spend on advertising, the Hutchinson brothers were an unlikely sell in concert. The trio realized this, yet hoped that the favorable response of their Milford neighbors signaled promise for them in Lynn anyway. An announcement for a show on 13 February 1841 broadcast their "Family Concert" of "Vocal and Instrumental Music, (Sacred and Secular)."[4]

John, Asa, Judson, and Jesse Jr. performed that Saturday evening, and according to John, "the concert was a great success" in front of a "respectable audience." The Lynn reception, though, did not excite the group. Insecure of their small-town origins, the Hutchinsons desired experience and connections in an established urban center. Nearby Boston, the so-called Athens of America, beckoned.

Despite its high-minded designation, by 1840 Boston, still the nation's center of literature and publishing, had all but lost out to the more cosmopolitan New York as a cultural hub for popular music. Nevertheless, it remained an important site for performers, and a Boston success for the Hutchinsons would mean far more than any applause in Milford or Lynn. Soon the brothers moved to the nation's fifth-largest city, where they sought out Joshua's tutor, Lowell Mason. The eminent Bostonian, whose *Carmina Sacra* had hit music stores in 1841 (on its way to selling more than 500,000 copies by 1853), was well placed, capable of providing the New Hampshire musicians with professional contacts and musical advice. As John remembered their meeting, Mason gave the boys a copy of his most recent publication and immediately went back to work.[5]

Mason did, though, steer the Hutchinson brothers to Boston's Handel and Haydn Society—a choral organization specializing in European art music which he had formerly headed. After one rehearsal with the group, the brothers turned down an offer to join. John later claimed that he and his brothers feared losing their individuality among such robust vocal company. In truth, singing with the Handel Society was not the kind of performance that the Hutchinsons had in mind. The vocal group could connect them to Boston's churches and burgeoning European high art institutions, neither of which the brothers envisioned playing a major part in their future.

With their music career stalling, the Hutchinsons focused on their worsening financial situation. Jesse Jr., still running his stove shop in Lynn, accepted a job as a compositor at the *Advertiser* on Boston's Court Street. Tending bar and other tasks were required of John, who worked with a grocer, while Judson led the local Universalist Society's choir. Through it all, the brothers kept a regular rehearsal schedule, practicing above the store of their brother Andrew, in Boston since the early 1830s.[6]

The big-city adventure was short-lived, and the brothers before long ended their foray. Returning to Lynn, Jesse immediately looked to his store while his siblings immersed themselves in music.

John, Judson, and Asa left Lynn in the fall of 1841 for their first musical tour, a two-month circuit of New Hampshire. Using the family farm in Milford as a base, the Aeolian Vocalists—as the trio initially called themselves—performed in the nearby towns of East Wilton, West Wilton, Wilton Centre, New Ipswich, Hancock, Peterborough, and Nashua in October and November.

Few records remain from this expedition, but the Aeolian label provides a valuable clue to what the Hutchinsons were trying. No instrument represented the Romantic linkage between nature and music better than an Aeolian harp. Remembering his days at Harvard College, Ralph Waldo Emerson said: "The thought, the meaning, was insignificant; the whole joy was in the melody. . . . What joy I found, and still can find, in the Aeolian harp!" The harp, a rectangular box, often three feet in length and a few inches wide and deep, uses the power of the wind to drive strings numbering between three and twelve, tuned in harmony, stretched over two bridges on its body. Sound holes beneath the strings capture vibrations, producing eerie music whose origin is difficult to situate. Americans placed the harps on window sills and outside where changes in the wind sounded different notes, often harmonics, and as the wind intensified dissonances occurred until the strings let out with a ghastly shrill. "I defy you," said the French composer Hector Berlioz on hearing an Aeolian harp, "not to experience a deep feeling of sadness, of surrender, a vague and boundless yearning for another existence."

In 1841 audiences found the Hutchinsons' Aeolian associations weak—their performance was hardly effortless or instinctive, natural, or wondrous; their singing failed to inspire a search for the supernatural within the natural world. And what was most distressing was that their listeners did not believe that an American wind drove the Aeolian Vocalists, despite the group's proclamations to the contrary. One of their earliest handbills read: "When foreigners approach your shores, You welcome them with open doors, Now we have come to seek our lot, Shall native talent be forgot?" Natural and national. So linked were these ideals in the minds of many Americans that the group could not represent the latter without exemplifying the former. Almost two years were to pass before the Hutchinsons figured out how to unleash this powerful combination.

The backcountry tour presented the brothers a bleak but accurate introduction to the lifestyle of traveling musicians. Playing a wide array of secular and sacred songs, the Hutchinsons generated little interest. Barely fifty people showed at one of their Wilton performances—not bad for a country town, but not enough to generate a profit from twelve-and-a-half-cent tickets. Only the trio's use of family and church connections to secure concert spaces for reduced fees mitigated their financial woes. Asa summed up their experience: "Praise was sweet, but pence are sweeter."[7]

A sketch of the troupe performing in East Wilton is most telling (fig. 9). In a crude concert hall—one secured through Deacon Bales, a family friend, who fashioned the "stage" out of a small room—the brothers played and sang on the same level as their rural listeners. Immediately in front of the group sits a crude table, a rough pine board set atop three barrels. Five candles illuminate the sheet music as Asa plays the bass fiddle, John, to Asa's right, sings (sheet music in hand, violin on the table), and Judson plays the violin. The audience members appear attentive despite their unavoidable discomfort from sitting on

The East Wilton concert, 1841. From John Wallace Hutchinson, *Story of the Hutchinsons (Tribe of Jesse),* ed. Charles E. Mann (Boston: Lee and Shepard, 1896), vol. 1, between pages 44 and 45.

wood boards laid over chairs (an apparent design to increase seating). Empty space and coats surround most of the listeners. The East Wilton show did not sell out.

What we see is a rather unimpressive troupe. Perhaps they sang well, but the brothers were not well versed enough to perform from memory. Later, the Hutchinsons' signature, especially at antislavery meetings, was improvisation. John, Judson, and Asa appear young and nervous in front of their listeners, not yet up to the creative task at hand. They probably worried about the small audience which brought a small profit, a dime which was already spoken for, as the trio had yet to pay back their brother Ben a twenty-cent-per-week charge for borrowing his sleigh. With empty pockets, the musicians returned to Lynn.[8]

One of the southernmost cities in Essex County, located eleven miles northeast of Boston, Lynn was the thirty-ninth-most-populated city in 1840, with 9,367 citizens. Lynn's location within an emerging urban area supported by the commercial and financial services of

Boston and the ports of Boston and Salem ensured success for the town's major industry, shoes. The Quaker town was also a hotbed of reforms ranging from temperance to antislavery, which attracted many young social activists like Frederick Douglass, Henry Wright, and Abby Kelley. These movements filled the town with a youthful daring that would welcome the Hutchinsons' eventual move to socially conscious song. Lynn residents also had a proven passion for music. By the mid-1830s the town featured a regular stream of concerts from "Ancient Music" to offerings from their Mozart Society. Citizens of Lynn actively consumed culture and could discourse on the greatest entertainments of their day, from P. T. Barnum's promotion of George Washington's supposed nurse—"We know of no humbug and gross deception that have of late years been so successfully and so long practised as was that of Joice Heth"—to the latest speaker on the antislavery circuit. Among the city's attractions was Henry Prentiss's music shop, opened in 1837, filled with a variety of instruments and sheet music.[9]

Living in Lynn once again, the Hutchinson brothers resumed their nonmusical employ. Asa worked alongside Jesse Jr. at the stove business, now relocated about a half-mile from the center of town to 32 Union Street. Judson and John opened a small grocery next door. (The two bought supplies from Andrew Hutchinson's wholesale business, and the horse and wagon needed to shuttle the goods from Boston cost them fourteen dollars.) In this setting, the siblings uncovered a means for economic survival; their newly acquired stability allowed them their musical dreams. At a rehearsal space on the corner of Union and Silsbee Streets, a quarter-mile west of their storefronts, the Hutchinsons practiced for their future.

Holding down day jobs to fund their music required sacrifice. John, Judson, and Asa apparently cooked their own food and, according to their records, did not socialize much. They added to their rehearsals by singing at the First Universalist Church, where Jesse Jr. worked as chorister. As the focus was on the collective and not on the individual, church performances provided the brothers a more relaxed, public setting in which to hone their instrumental technique and to stretch their voices. Jesse Jr. furthered his own efforts to profit from music by forming a singing school that met twice a week in a chapel.

The cost for twenty-four lessons (twelve weeks) was two dollars for men, one dollar for women.[10]

The Hutchinsons had settled into a routine in Lynn by December 1841, when the world-famous Rainer Family arrived. Then the benchmark for singing families in the United States and in Europe, the Swiss musicians indelibly influenced listeners wherever they performed. The Rainers' rise to stardom began in 1824 near the border of Switzerland and Austria, where a family of singers (three brothers and one sister—later the group consisted of a variety of supposed brother and sister mixes) first played a unique blend of Tyrolean folk and German partsongs. In years following, their performances evoked visions of romantic Swiss vistas and alpine life. A visit to Great Britain brought them much attention in 1827. Here, with the aid of Ignatz Moscheles, one of the best-connected European musicians, they performed for British royals, impressing King George IV and capturing the fancy of the duchess of Kent. The resulting explosion in the number of singing families in England led one critic to complain: "There is no end to our unnatural adoptions—Italians, French, and Germans—the Swiss Family This, and the Dutch Family That, and the Russian Family T'other—Chanteurs Montagnards, Siffluers, and Chinchoppers—Alpine Minstrels, and Bohemian Minstrels, and minstrels from heaven knows where."

An endless stream of emulators was the price of success for the Swiss troupe. Moscheles adapted Tyrolese tunes performed by the Rainers and played them in concert alongside works by his friend Ludwig van Beethoven. Others were more blatantly imitative. Calling themselves the Tyrolese Vocalists, one group of pretenders toured the United States in 1834, the beginning of a family singer craze in America. In 1839 the real Rainers made their way to the States, where they hoped for success among audiences accustomed to lavishing attention upon foreign-born entertainers. Lowell Mason gave them an endorsement: "The excellence of their performance, the peculiarity of their national music, and their own personal excellence and amiability, seem alike to entitle them to the confidence and patronage of the public."

The Rainers were in luck. American music teachers like Mason had used texts highlighting their songs long before the troupe ever set foot in North America. And if Americans knew anything of Switzer-

The Rainer Family, "Tyrolese Melodies" (Boston: Geo. P. Reed, 1841). From the Vocal Sheet Music Collection in the Irving S. Gilmore Music Library of Yale University.

land at the time, it was through images of nature provided by Romantic writers. To their fans' delight, the Rainers' songs worked mainly upon a fascination and wonder with alpine life, and in concert the Swiss vocalists sang about mountain living, yodeled after some stanzas, and always donned their "national costume" (fig. 10).[11]

The alpine act of the Rainers inexorably tied them to the land, and the land, in their case, was Switzerland. Nineteenth-century cultural nationalism thrived on the inseparability of artist and place. Beethoven's music was thought the pinnacle of Germanic thought and progress. Blackface minstrelsy, an imitation of black life in the South, was seen by some as the very essence of America. The presumed value of experience to artistic creativity fueled the commingling. Solon Robinson said in 1845 that the famed Norwegian violinist Ole Bull, then touring the United States and playing many "American" tunes, could have learned much if he had experienced a recent snowstorm that Robinson himself had recently braved. Bull, who performed music associated with "the solitude of the prairie," "would have been able to play the tune in much greater perfection," Robinson thought, had he actually subjected himself to the stormy plains. The violinist, though, no matter how many melodies he played from the United States, would always be seen, at his core, as Norwegian. Later, during Jenny Lind's visit to the country, she would sing many traditional American songs, yet no one mistook the Swede as a representative of America. Her efforts delighted crowds who believed Lind to be reaching out to them, proclaiming American culture and society worthy of her attention.

There was more to cultural nationalism than music written in a particular place or written by a particular national. Obvious connections to American nature included by the composer Anthony Heinrich in his large orchestral work titled *The War of the Elements and the Thundering of Niagara* (c. 1841–1843) went largely ignored. Part of this had to do with innovation; Heinrich's was a difficult piece, not intended to be readily accessible to its listeners. *War of the Elements* also challenged people to hear an American art-music composer—a Bohemian emigrant, no less—as on par with European composers of the same tradition. The prejudice against American artists whose work was understood to be inferior to that of Europeans was only magnified for those who composed within what was believed to be a distinctly European genre.

Musical acts and music deemed representative of the United States often shared one trait—a close association with the land. Heinrich had sought after this connection from the start. His first work, *The Dawning of Music in Kentucky; or, The Pleasure of Harmony in the Solitudes of Nature* (1820), set him on the path. But popular song, not symphonies (or, like *Dawning of Music,* large collections of art-music songs and pieces for violin and piano), ruled the mid-nineteenth century.

There were many ways to draw the correlation between place and nation. One was to herald workers of the land or their music. Occasionally, someone like the Boston Transcendentalist Margaret Fuller would declare the music of slaves and Indians to be the country's first national art, but the social realities of racism, enslavement, and genocide more often prevented these cultural offerings from standing as symbols for white antebellum Americans. Farmers, representatives of the most glorified profession of their time, presented a much different case. Agricultural work summoned curative and restorative images of America in the minds of many citizens. Farming was the closest the nation had to a "common" experience; it was thought the backbone of the nation in a way that mid-twentieth-century Americans envisioned working at General Motors or Ford. In the Rainers, the musical agriculturists from the Alps, many white Americans believed that they saw something they admired in their own nation.

The Rainers understood the power and value to their music of nationalism and posed as organic entertainers whose music and talents sprang forth from their native land. American newspapers continually reported the natural bond between the singers and their country: a Baltimore writer thought that they displayed all the "sweetness and mildness peculiar to German music," characteristics only accentuated by "the grace of their national costume, the simplicity of manner, and the total absence of effort in their style of singing." Not only did the Rainers make performing look easy, they made it look Swiss (or German, or Tyrolean, depending upon the inclination of the reviewer). As the Rainers showcased their identity in the United States, Americans awaited the time when a national culture would arise from their land:

"There is great pleasure in any entertainment that is truly national," said Fuller, and, borrowing from the speeches of the Scotsman Alexander Kinmont, she supposed that a nation's ills could be cured by "good music, good songs, and good paintings, which were all new, and truly native."[12]

Some of the Hutchinsons attended a Rainer Family performance, most likely the Lynn show in December 1841. The Rainers, at the peak of their popularity earlier in the year, had just suffered a difficult blow: Ellena Rainer had married and left the troupe. Her departure forced the musicians to hire a boy, Jon Hagter, to substitute. No longer able to promote their "family" singing, the group went by the new name Lewis Rainer and Company, though most in the media continued to recognize them as the Rainer Family. Ellena's move may have lessened the mania which surrounded the group, but when the Swiss entertainers left America in June 1843, they had become as renowned in the New World as they were in the Old.[13]

The Hutchinsons, awakened to the family singing model after seeing the Rainers, tried their luck twice on the Lynn stage in January 1842. The *Lynn Freeman and Essex County Whig* carried ads for both Hutchinson concerts, along with the schedule for Jesse's singing school. John, Judson, and Asa probably performed the first show, with Jesse acting as their manager. Much like their other recent musical endeavors, this Lynn concert was largely unremarkable.[14]

On 29 January the Hutchinson trio performed again, but this time their eleven-year-old sister appeared with them. Outfitted in "a Swiss bodice or a Tyrolean costume," Abby joined John, Judson, and Asa in a concert featuring a technique John later boasted of having taught his siblings: a "Tyrolean style of singing"—a close harmony seamlessly blending all the voices and a well-rehearsed stage choreography. (From concert reports it appears that John chose not to employ improvised "Jodeln," yodeling.) The Hutchinsons had suddenly morphed into one of the many musical acts derived from the Rainers' approach. By the end of February the New Hampshire musicians, highlighting the bonds of the four singers, promoted a series of "Family" concerts "by the AEOLIAN VOCALISTLS!" in Lynn and also in towns in Maine and New Hampshire.[15]

The Aeolian Vocalists appreciated a sudden increase in adulation.

When summer arrived, they planned a tour of New England and New York. But the starting costs alone almost precluded the endeavor. After securing another horse and harness for roughly $70 (to complement the ones John already owned), a carryall (a four-wheeled coach able to hold four passengers) for $75, and a hired hand named Joseph Tarbell for $45, the Hutchinsons felt ready to set out on tour once again.

Totaling $190, their expenses did not stop—horses need food and shelter (about 28 cents a day for oats, $7 for a week for a stable in Albany); carryalls require greasing and occasionally break down (as much as $1.50 per instance); and traveling, even in the 1840s, meant paying tolls (usually between 12.5 cents and 36 cents). When they weren't on the move, the group paid anywhere from $3 a night to $14 a week for a hotel. Of course, their instruments needed replacement strings (Judson and John bought 25 cents' worth in July) and proper stage presentation required fresh outfits (Abby's new dresses cost between $1.33 and $6, while her brothers occasionally purchased themselves $3 worth of hats or pantaloons at $6 a pair).[16]

Outside of borrowing—which they did often from various family members—the only way that the touring siblings offset their debts was through performance. Yet putting on a show triggered more spending. A crier strolling through town to announce the Hutchinsons' arrival charged somewhere around 50 cents, while bills to be posted cost about 75 cents per hundred, a man to hang them, 40 cents. Nearly every stage (whether a church or some kind of hall) required a person to take care of lighting, candles, for which the group was commonly charged $1. The fee for the hall itself varied greatly. For the Hutchinson Family Singers in 1842, expenditures on performance space normally fell in the $1.25 to $7 range. Occasionally, the Hutchinsons lessened their risk by trading a percentage of their take at the door for lodging. Handing over as much as two-thirds of their revenue might sound extravagant, but when exchanged for housing and horse keeping, it was not extreme. Some nights the siblings actually came out ahead when their concerts attracted small audiences. On more fortunate occasions, the Hutchinsons relied upon the generosity of ministers who donated their churches for the group's use. Even the goodwill of Universalists, Presbyterians, and Baptists, though, did not bring the summer tour into the black.[17]

If one thing did go well for the Hutchinson foursome, it was the discovery of their vocal power. On their way from Concord toward Franklin, New Hampshire, the quartet stopped at a tavern to have the wheels of the carryall greased. Normally a fee of six cents applied, but the singers belted out three songs and received a complimentary lube instead. The authority of their singing, only in its infancy in 1842, would soon prove capable of silencing proslavery mobs.

Singing while traveling provided the Hutchinsons invaluable practice time, and their musical caravan made for quite a sight. Passing through Boscawen, New Hampshire, in July, Judson reported, "We sung all the way through which made the natives stare." The natives were not alone in noticing the musicians.[18]

Nathaniel Rogers began his close look at the Hutchinsons in the summer of 1842, reporting in the *Herald of Freedom* that Abby's "powers and skill" clearly marked her as "a legitimate member of this extraordinary and gifted family." Asa agreed with two of the Hutchinson Family Singers' fans, Dartmouth students, who had seen the group both before and after Abby had joined and noted her addition as an improvement. Abby was a hit, no doubt the reason for the Hutchinson Family Singers' growing acclaim. "The young lady *was* good we *know,* for she looked good, and sung good, and the audience felt good," said the *Nashua Gazette.* "We can say of the concert as boys sometimes say when they begin to study grammar, 'good, gooder, *goodest.*'"

The Hutchinsons were still far from their best. Abby's feminine presence certainly helped the musicians form a more complete *family* presentation on stage, and a wholesome life was an issue dear to many in the revival-strewn regions they visited in 1842. But one New Hampshire admirer wrote that "our little White Mountains has got music among its hills, and Swiss singers among its people, as well as Alps among its *uplands.*" As the tour progressed, it was clear that the Hutchinsons had found a niche, but their success was less as the Hutchinson Family than as Rainer poseurs.[19]

At the same time the Hutchinsons embraced the Swiss singers' style, they slowly molded it to reflect more local concerns. "Mr. Masa H. Morey keeps the Temperance Hotel," said Asa at the start of the 1842 tour. "If ever we patronised a temperance house that was *worthy* of

patronage it was this excelent Hotel kept on strict temperance principles." At some point between 1840 and their summer tour of 1842, the
Hutchinsons took up an antialcohol lifestyle with fervor. Abstaining
from alcohol—except for occasional medicinal use—and advocating
against alcohol consumption were to remain central to the musicians
for the rest of their lives. The body-based reform resonated with the
New Hampshire group, who in upcoming years sought to perfect not
only the nation in which they lived but their own corporeal and spiritual health too.

The legendary speaker John Hawkins, according to John Hutchinson, changed the way the New Hampshire entertainers thought
about temperance by introducing them to the Washington Temperance Society. For years the Hutchinsons had listened to antialcohol
messages as part of a Milford Baptist community that declared alcohol
an "unholy leaven" which "should be purged from the Christian
church." Many found the religious temperance movement attractive as
it channeled spiritual belief into community action. But church-cen-
tered temperance was a reform of the reformed. No drunkards were allowed, as religious temperance leaders often welcomed only the sober.
The American Temperance Union, a Boston organization founded by
evangelicals in 1826, not only excluded drinkers from its ranks but did
so in expectation that the current generation of drunkards would die
out and not be replaced. Church temperance leaders feared the result
of putting sinners and saints together and looked less to change the
habits of drunkards than to retain the purity of their current flock. As
successful as the American Temperance Union was—in 1835 the ATU
boasted a membership that included somewhere between 12 and 20
percent of the free population in the United States—its achievement
seemingly focused on the wrong individuals. The Washingtonians
changed this.

In an age that increasingly moved toward a compassionate understanding of others, providing the impetus to extend individual
rights to the abused or to the suffering (the most prominent examples
being revivalism and sinners and, later, antislavery and slaves), it appears inevitable in hindsight that drunkards would receive attention.
The Washington Temperance Society, like religious revivals, placed the
burden of reform on the individual. By creating a movement for

drinkers and nondrinkers alike, the Washingtonians further enhanced the popularity of antialcohol reform. Founded in 1840 in Baltimore by a group of recovering alcoholics, the society removed temperance from its more staid church setting with sinful admonitions and changed it into to an animated, dramatized reform featuring mass gatherings, picnics, parades, and conversions (from drunkenness to sobriety). More so than their church counterparts, the Washingtonians cut across the growing antebellum class divisions.

Years of church-instilled temperance had not led the young Hutchinsons to identify with the cause, but when faced with the grand revival-like exhibition of the Washingtonians, the siblings uncovered a space to meld their religious perfectionism and their musical aspirations. In June 1841 a Cold Water Army of around twelve hundred rolled through Lynn—quite possibly the very event which John would fondly recall years later. Within the First Methodist Church where most of the day's festivities were held, the temperance participants rang out with "a couple of appropriate songs." On 4 July 1842 in New Hampshire, music by the Milford choir—still under the direction of Joshua Hutchinson—and the Hutchinson Family Singers "enlivened the occasion," a Sabbath school and temperance celebration. By the end of that year, the Hutchinsons were showcased at antialcohol meetings. Temperance leaders, when planning a gathering, implored in advertisements: "The Hutchinson Family, they too must be there; for how can a convention dispense with their sweet, and enlivening music?" Soon the Hutchinsons' own ads excitedly proclaimed shows that would "conclude with a Washingtonian Song in full chorus."[20]

Never heavy drinkers themselves, the Hutchinson Family Singers sought a temperance conversion to combine the passion and perfectionism of their 1830s religious revival with their community concerns, but their move also marked the beginnings of a powerful identity for the musical group as political activists. Through such tunes as "All Hail! Washingtonians" and "King Alcohol," the group advanced temperance messages while bringing their personal views to light. An antebellum consumer culture revved by faster and more intricate communication and travel networks worked to the advantage of the singers. The Hutchinsons led the way in the marketing of musical reform messages, part of a broader culture-situated reform then beginning to take shape.

On stage the Hutchinson's temperance did not mix well with the group's Rainer-inspired presentation. Some antialcohol advocates criticized the group: "We think them unwise in attempting to sing Tyrolese music," said a letter to the *Essex County Washingtonian*. In 1842 the Hutchinsons lived between two worlds, exposing both the international and domestic settings of antebellum romanticism; the group's earliest advertisement revealed a desire to be recognized as "American" performers—and their singing of temperance spoke directly to a national concern—yet the Hutchinsons walked on stage in Swiss alpine gear.[21]

Identity was crucial to the Hutchinson Family Singers' concert experience in the summer of 1842. They faced stiff competition not only from the likes of European performers such as the Rainers but from other American outfits, too. In Saratoga Springs, then the vacation spot for the more refined American, the New Hampshire entertainers faced off in early August against Frank Johnson. The black musician was one of the most talented and popular in antebellum America, one of the first American musicians to successfully tour Europe: his 1837–1838 trip to London earned him a silver bugle from the queen. Born in Philadelphia, Johnson led a collection of African-American players from the 1810s until his death in 1844. Johnson and his band would all but doom the New Hampshire singers' shows at the upstate New York retreat.[22]

By mid-August, the Hutchinsons played in Albany, where the Rainers had just visited. The Albany *Evening Journal* reported that "it was a severe trial to these young musicians to be brought so closely in contact with the great talents and established reputation of the Rainer family." The Hutchinsons lost out in this battle as well. A dismayed columnist wrote:

> [Their] tickets were put at 25 cents—half the price of the Rainers; and although their music, vocal and instrumental, was as good and as well performed as the Rainers, and drew from those present the most enthusiastic applause, the audiences were quite slim. Why was this? Simply because they were *American citizens*. . . . Their slim luck, the last time they were here, was occasioned by the title of the family—

The "*American* Aeolian Vocalists." We hope those who object to it, will read it hereafter—The "English Aeolian Vocalists," and patronize them.[23]

Initial failings aside, most observers consider the 1842 Albany visit the defining moment of the Hutchinson Family Singers' early career. In Albany the entertainers first demonstrated the ability to tie together their religious upbringing, their reform zeal, and their family singing style as part of an impressive publicity blitz. John, Judson, Asa, and Abby had come to understand that advertising meant more than posting a few bills and paying someone to ring a bell and shout out concert details. Nathaniel Leavitt, the siblings' maternal uncle, a barber by trade, was hired to help manage marketing and such matters as renting concert spaces and collecting tickets. The musicians then used their newfound free time to socialize with influential community members. One year later, by the time of their May 1843 debut in New York, the Hutchinson Family Singers had almost perfected this promotional machine.

The group chose Leavitt based on kinship, but he was also a well-connected Albany citizen. He had lived, worked, and worshiped in the capital city of New York for some time, and the barber was quite a talker—an important asset for a manager. Asa felt secure under his uncle's aegis: "He is the man." Leavitt was also "the bank"—the group immediately borrowed twelve dollars from their relative and new employee, whose family also provided them a place to stay.

Leavitt was tough, something that the musicians were not. In late August 1842 Nathaniel Leavitt led the Aeolian Vocalists through Troy, Schenectady, Ballston, and other towns near Albany. Sent ahead via "the Carrs," Leavitt not only drummed up business for his nephews and niece, he negotiated with innkeepers and other service providers, helping to keep the Hutchinsons' expenses low. "Col. Leavitt Gave the Tavernkeeper a blowing up," John recorded. "Told him he was an old dutch hog &c &c." Asa observed, "N. K. Leavitt stood at the Door and then I felt as though the people would not go in unless they paid their fee." No hustling, no freeloading. The Hutchinsons' hiring of Leavitt was a timely blessing.[24]

Following several largely unsuccessful August performances in

Albany—including the one that "was as good and as well performed as the Rainers"—the Hutchinsons came away with their largest payday to date. The success story begins at their August 22 "concert of Sacred Music" to a crowd Asa estimated at 350. "After the Concert we by Special invite by 3 Gentlemen of Albany gave a Serenade to the principle Editors in the City. They made us a present of 6.00."

Six dollars was not a tremendous sum, but considering the Hutchinsons' ups and downs during 1842, it was a welcome amount nonetheless. The exclusive session with Albany's elite was well worth the missed sleep, one result of returning to the Leavitts' at 2 A.M. Later in the day, Luke Newland, music store owner, asked the Hutchinsons to remain in town for another week, assuring the singers that he and friends would promote a well-attended concert. The Hutchinsons, ready to leave Albany and close out the summer tour, stayed.

> A strong feeling has been excited in behalf of these youthful vocalists, and we feel as if we could not consent to part with them till we have repaid, in some degree, the neglect with which talents so rare and deportment so becoming have hitherto been treated. . . . On these grounds, we have requested them to give us one more opportunity of expressing our sense of their high deservings. They have therefore consented to remain till Monday the 29th inst. We have procured from the Trustees of the Female Academy the use of the Chapel for that evening, and we sincerely hope that on that occasion our fellow citizens will show abundant proofs of their taste, and also of their liberality.
> Elihu Russell,
> E. Warner,
> Geo. Warren,
> M. M. Van Alstyne,
> Luke F. Newland.

On the same day this plea appeared in the *Evening Journal,* the singers "Serenaded Mr. Thurlow Weed, Editor of the Albany Evening Journal," and also sang for "the Editor of the Albany Atlas." During the week, the Hutchinsons played at a temperance meeting, did some shopping (vests, a fur hat, and a new dress for Abby—a thirteenth-birthday gift), and attended church. Mr. Newland and Mr. Walker battled over where the Hutchinsons would worship (and sing) on Saturday, 27 August. Newland had promised the Presbyterian Church that the family would appear, but the Hutchinsons had already assured Walker that they would attend a different church with him. The two men exchanged "many hard words," and the Hutchinsons left with Newland. Walker returned later to inform the musicians that he had arranged for them to sing at the Reverend Stillman's church that night—an appearance which, Asa noted, had already been agreed to several days before.[25]

One day later, Sunday, 28 August, the New Hampshire singers found themselves in Stillman's church, Trinity Methodist, once again. Here they sang in the gallery with the choir and then, at the pastor's request, blessed the churchgoers with a solo selection. Stillman then notified his congregation that the Hutchinsons were to perform the next evening, and, the singers recorded, he said "that his acquaintance with us was such as to speak very highly of us, and that we did not come from a theatre or any low place but came from respectable situation and had instilled in to us the Essence of religion."

The turnout for the Monday evening concert did not disappoint; both Newland and Stillman attended, with their respective entourages, and between four hundred and five hundred people packed themselves into the Female Academy. "It was Literaly *Crambed*," said the musicians. Singing a variety of tunes from the romantic drama of "The Snow Storm" (a Seba Smith poem about a real tragedy—Mrs. Harrison Gray Blake's sacrifice of her life to save that of her child during an 1821 blizzard in Vermont's Green Mountains) to Judson's lively "Trip to Cape Ann," the Hutchinsons captivated the Albany audience and bragged that "never was an audience better satisfied—No? Never!"[26]

The Hutchinson Family Singers left the venue with more than $110. This was good news since they had borrowed $100 from Leavitt a day earlier. Using their best connections in church, media, and music, the Hutchinsons won out over two other notable acts then in town. The Steyrmark Family offered their own Rainer-influenced show, appearing on stage in native costume from upper Austria near the Steyr River, and Frank Johnson was in town, too. Asa, speaking with Johnson at the Pittsfield railroad station on 1 September, learned that "Sadly he did not do so well in Albany as he Expected." With the Hutchinsons nearly monopolizing the city's elite, Johnson had little hope. But Johnson's troupe, it appears, struck back at the farmers-turned-performers. The Albany happenings had inflated the Hutchinsons' egos—"Good Many people Envy us—yes," they wrote. Johnson's more seasoned musicians undoubtedly found this amusing and chided the arrivistes—"They are a *Rough* sett of Negroes," Asa noted.[27]

One night in the New York capital was no guarantee of long-term prosperity. Nor did the Hutchinsons' one sudden success alleviate their troubles. Only two weeks before the concert at the Female Academy, a resigned Judson spoke: "We have now come to this. We have been singing five weeks and our money is reduced to nothing. We have not enough to pay our bills. Judge how I feel yee who read this. 200 miles from home. No money but .42 cts. Expenses 5 dollars a day." Even the more enduring John worried, mocking Tom Paine's famous quip when writing, "O! Dear what will become of us. These are times that try our soles."[28]

Eighteen forty-two ended on a mixed note for the Hutchinsons. After their Albany high, the siblings conspired to ride their achievement to cities and towns farther south. No doubt New York City had entered their plans. But first they returned to Lynn—Abby and Asa by train, John, Judson, and Uncle Leavitt by carriage. During the opening weeks of September, the siblings celebrated by eating much "roasted beef," buying clothes, and giving their introductory concerts in Boston. The Boston papers generally liked the Hutchinson Family Singers, who, as time progressed, used their family name more often than the rubric Aeolian Vocalists. But there were still cautions: the *American* said that they "err in imitating the Rainers in their positions—hands upon the hips are an uneasy, ungraceful position."

In Boston, the Hutchinsons met "Oliver Ditson the Music Seller." Ditson had just taken over as the exclusive owner of his music shop, and his appearance in the Hutchinson Family Singers' lives was a sign that they had indeed made a name for themselves. Ditson, a music publisher, gave the Hutchinsons "quite a number of good pieces of music." The gesture, though, was not the product of pure benevolence.

Ditson probably hoped that this up-and-coming musical act would promote his wares by singing the songs in concert.

Leaving Boston and continuing around the area, the troupe played at Newburyport, Portsmouth (a profit of $100), Kennebunk, Saco, and Portland, where the *Advertiser* reported: "These singers know evidently what they are about and never forget the first principles of their art. They know that melody should be imbued with feeling (*passion* is the word) and that harmony should be smooth, proportioned and blended."

Eventually, the Hutchinsons returned to Milford and gave "a Concert of VOCAL MUSIC, for the Benefit of the venerable Andrew Leavitt, (*their grandfather,*) a Soldier of the Revolution." The show raised twenty dollars for their mother's father. The group then set out to play in Lowell and in Boston when, without warning, Judson disappeared. Canceling concerts amid the confusion, the three remaining siblings spilt up and searched in two different locations, Milford and Lynn. John, Asa, and Abby feared suicide. After all, throughout their common journal of 1842, Judson had clearly expressed gloom—"Oh I have got the blues by gracious. . . . We are 150 miles from home, amongst strangers. No wonder I have got the ///////."

Overcome by homesickness, especially the long months away from his sweetheart, Judson had absconded to New Hampshire. Unable to withstand a confrontation with his brothers, Judson preferred to slip away in silence. Reunited, the group made it to Lowell for a Thanksgiving concert in the First Freewill Baptist Church on 25 November, taking in about $75. "The Expectation that we the Aeolians had was to go South this *winter,*" wrote Asa back in Milford on the day after the Lowell performance, but the siblings' parents had decided otherwise. Vexed by the separation from her thirteen-year-old daughter, Polly, with her husband's support, strongly protested any long-distance travel. The brothers, keenly aware that the troupe's recent accomplishment relied on Abby, "concluded to Spend the Winter at *Homestead Home.*"

For the time being, the group attempted to play near New Hampshire, an effort stymied by the cold, snowy weather which not only kept listeners inside but hampered the Hutchinsons' mobility. On

3 December 1842 the Hutchinson Family Singers effectively shut down for the rest of the year.[29]

William Lloyd Garrison reprinted an article, "The Hutchinson Singers," from an August *Herald of Freedom* in the 30 December issue of the *Liberator*. This piece by Nathaniel Peabody Rogers notably announced, "Perhaps I am partial to the Hutchinsons, for they are abolitionists," and urged the group to compose antislavery music. "What an agitation might the fourteen Hutchinsons sing up in the land." Rogers asked, "Would the South send on to our General Court to have them beheaded?" The group was determined to find out. The people of Milford scheduled an antislavery meeting at the start of 1843 in honor of the New Hampshirite Thomas Parnell Beach, imprisoned in early fall for his antislavery speech in Newburyport, Massachusetts.

An earlier Beach convention in Danvers had closed with a song based on the popular tune "The Old Church Yard" from the Millerites—a trendy Protestant sect. The Hutchinson Family Singers were playing in Manchester, New Hampshire, at that time, but the use of the Millerite melody for antislavery purposes was soon to be the basis for the Hutchinsons' most popular song. Perhaps Jesse Hutchinson, Jr., composer of that famous tune, attended the Danvers Beach meeting. No matter who initiated the use of "The Old Church Yard," 1842 would close as the year in which antislavery leaders tried to make their movement sing. John A. Collins, prominent in the Massachusetts Anti-Slavery Society, put together *The Anti-Slavery Picknick: A Collection of Speeches, Poems, Dialogues, and Songs,* while another reform songbook, *Hymns and Songs for the Friends of Freedom,* also appeared; they were the first significant musical abolitionist publications since Maria Weston Chapman had compiled *Songs of the Free, and Hymns of Christian Freedom* in 1836.

Nathaniel Rogers exhorted, "Give me some ballad-making, for a revolution, said some of the sages, and you may have all the law making." At the Thomas Beach antislavery meeting in Milford on 3 January 1843, the Hutchinson Family Singers' abolitionist insurgency would begin.[30]

Coda to First Section: Music (Music Publishing and the Hutchinsons' 1843 Hits)

Let us not forget about the music. New York, May 1843. The Hutchinsons, recently catapulted into the spotlight through antislavery performances in Milford, Boston, and New York, had turned into one of the most fashionable musical acts of the year. Yet even the New Hampshire entertainers, self-important from the success, were excited to meet English vocalist Henry Russell. The biggest name in popular music, Russell had just returned from a break in England to resume touring in the United States, where he had been playing since the early 1830s. Luke Newland, the Hutchinsons' Albany acquaintance who later published a notice of this historic meeting, was responsible for introducing the Family Singers to Russell. The Hutchinsons sang for the esteemed Brit and his friend, the poet and lyricist George Pope Morris. Russell offered the group singing advice, complimented Abby's voice, and praised Asa's—"the Bass"—"as excelent." After giving Russell five tickets to their Brooklyn show of the next evening, the Hutchinsons departed.

It worked. The free tickets lured the British musician, and the concert was a good one. Earning the singers $110, their performance, Asa said, roused applause from the many "Clergymen, Doctors, Lawyers, Merchants" in attendance, and also from Henry Russell and "Genrl. G. P. Morriss!!" Asa went on: "Russell reported at Brooklyn that we were the best Singers in *America!!!* (Bragging here.)"

Morris offered the Hutchinsons his famed lyrical prowess and the songs resulting from their union were soon selling. Eighteen forty-three marked the Hutchinson Family Singers' entry not only into antislavery but also into music publishing. The instant that the Hutchinsons became trendy, publishers scooped up rights to their music. At least fifteen Hutchinson Family Singers selections became available during the year: "Axes to Grind," "Cape Ann," "The Cot Where We Were Born," "Excelsior," "Go Call the Doctor and Be Quick," "The Grave of Bonaparte," "King Alcohol," "My Mother's Bible," "The Old Granite State," "Our Father's Hearth," "The Snow Storm," "Vesper Song at Sea," "The Vulture of the Alps," "We Are Happy and Free," and "We're All Cutting." Some, like "My Mother's Bible"—Henry

Russell's 1841 musical setting of a Morris poem—simply rehashed hits of previous years under the Hutchinsons' auspices. But others were compositions in which a member of the Hutchinson family provided either the music or the lyrics or both. Four of these—"Cape Ann," "Go Call," "Excelsior," and "The Old Granite State"—counted among the most popular tunes of the year. Alongside these hits the Hutchinsons added one other top-selling song in 1843. Written by Henry Washburne and Lyman Heath, "The Grave of Bonaparte" fascinated its listeners by telling of the faded glory of the French leader who had died in 1821.[31]

Meeting the music publisher Oliver Ditson in the fall of 1842 had started what would be a lengthy relationship based on music, reform, and marketability. Ditson began business in 1835, and by 1877 he had bought out three of his major competitors, William Hall and Son, J. L. Peters, and Firth, Son and Co. When Charles Healy Ditson—the son who eventually took over—died in 1929, the publishing empire had amassed a fortune of nearly $7 million—an amazing figure calculated in 1931, two years after the great stock market crash, with the bulk of the estate tied to securities. The Ditson success had fueled generosity. Both Oliver and Charles Healy were philanthropists held in high esteem by their employees and welfare organizations. Reform singers and a benevolent publisher made for an excellent match.

Publishing houses like Ditson were quick to learn their customers' latest fancy by following concert trends in New York, Boston, and Philadelphia. Long before one could track sales of recordings or promote songs over the radio, music was sold on the basis of live performance. Between singing at antislavery and temperance meetings and their high-profile city concerts, the Hutchinsons created an incredible buzz. Ditson, Firth and Hall, Henry Prentiss, G. P. Reed, Steven W. Marsh, A. P. Ordway, C. Holt, Jr., Jacques and Brother, and Wm. H. Oakes were some of the publishers that worked with the New Hampshire singers in the 1840s. Suddenly the group's performance of a song prompted the addition of "AS SUNG IN THE CONCERTS OF THE HUTCHINSON FAMILY" on the sheet music cover to boost sales.[32]

Little is known of the group's contracts with publishers, and unlike their concert receipts, which are sometimes detailed in their journals, income from sheet music sales remains elusive. Ditson outlined

an 1864 arrangement in a letter to Asa Hutchinson for the publication
of the war ballad "Tenting on the Old Camp Ground"—"We will allow you 2½ cents per copy on all copies sold + supply you with copies
you want to sell at your concerts for 8 cents per copy." With no way of
calculating the number of pieces sold, gauging earnings for either Asa
or Ditson is highly speculative. (John wrote years later that composer
and publisher had each made one thousand dollars on "Tenting" in the
first two years. This would put the number of copies sold near 20,000,
but John's number is uncorroborated.) Ditson did, however, urge Asa
to "send on the 'Stripes + Stars' + the other songs you refer to as fresh
+ new . . . will publish + allow you the same copyright as on 'Tenting
on Camp.'" The Hutchinson Family Singers' contracts in the 1840s
probably shared much with the later arrangement.

Fans of the Family Singers could purchase Oliver Ditson's copy
of "The Old Granite State" in 1843 for fifty cents or settle for a plainer
cover from Jacques and Brother for the same price. Either way the Hutchinsons' listeners could take the group's music home to duplicate the efforts of their much-loved entertainers. A blueprint of the Hutchinson
Family Singers' sound, sheet music also provided admirers a decorative
piece to adorn their home. In many instances, the sheet music covers
illustrated the entertainers themselves—a feature making them quite
coveted by fans. *Godey's Lady's Book* in 1847 announced "new music"
called "The Spider and the Fly, with a portrait of Abby Hutchinson"
from publisher Charles Holt, Jr. (fig. 11). Antebellum sheet music
functioned much as modern-day posters and recordings by generating
a visual and aural identification with the artist; the proliferation of
sheet music guaranteed that the musical culture of antebellum America was visible and readily heard.[33]

Here are some examples of what reached the Hutchinson Family
Singers' listeners in 1843:

So we hunted and balloed,
And the next thing we did find,
Was the moon in the element,
And that we left behind,
Look ye there!

Jesse Hutchinson, Jr., and S. O. Dyer, "The Spider and the Fly" (New York: Ch. Holt, Jr., 1847). Courtesy the New Hampshire Historical Society, Concord.

> One said it was the moon,
> But the other said nay,
> He said it was a Yankee cheese,
> With one half cut away!
> Look ye there!

Exaggerating sightings of a real object—"a Meeting House with the steeple blown away" for a barn, cheese for the moon, a featherless canary for a frog, a "sugar loaf with the paper blown away" for a lighthouse, and finally the "Evil One" for an owl (after which the singers all run away)—"Cape Ann," also called "Trip to Cape Ann," relies on the natural and the religious for its humor. The song linked the Hutchinsons to the New England landscape, specifically the cape about seven miles northeast of Lynn, Massachusetts, the group's second home. Written by Judson Hutchinson and performed as early as February 1842, "Cape Ann" is perhaps the first composition from the Hutchinson Family Singers.

Calling it an original would be a bit misleading. The jailer's daughter in Fletcher and Shakespeare's *Two Noble Kinsmen* (1613) sings:

> There were three fooles, fell out about an howlet
> The one sed it was an owle
> The other he said nay,
> The third he sed it was a hawke, and her bels were cut away.

An adaptation of the song appeared in Sir William Davenant's version of *The Two Noble Kinsmen* called *The Rivals* (1688). Later records reveal an eighteenth-century American version which also preceded the Hutchinson Family Singers' "Cape Ann."

In August 1842 the New Hampshire group performed the song while capturing their most important audience to date within the halls of Albany's Female Seminary. The sheet music version of Judson's song published by Firth and Hall and "arranged for piano" was dropped off at the "Clerk's Office of the Southern District of New York December 18, 1843."[34]

King Alcohol is very sly
A liar from the first
He'll make you drink until you're dry
Then drink, because you thirst.

For there's rum, and gin, and beer, and wine
And brandy of logwood hue
And hock, and port, and flip combine
To make a man look blue.

He says be merry, for here's good sherry
And Tom and Jerry, Champagne and Perry,
And spirits of every hue,
O are not these a fiendish crew
As ever a mortal knew
O are these not a fiendish crew as ever a mortal knew.

Two thousand would anxiously gather at the Old Deacon Gilles
Distillery for the "Tea Party"—a temperance meeting—scheduled for
5 May 1843, featuring the Hutchinson Family Singers. After spending
the day in Lynn, the Hutchinsons traveled to Salem, where they visited
Charles Lenox Remond, the eloquent antislavery leader, and relaxed
for the special evening ahead. At the antialcohol gathering, following
speeches and songs from others, the Hutchinsons sang "8 or 10 times
with great Applause." Among their offerings was a new song, "King Alcohol," which transformed the traditional British melody of "King
Andrew" into a comic temperance glee using lyrics by Jesse Hutchinson, Jr.

The reformer James Buffum owned the Gilles distillery (converted to a wood-planing mill long before 1843) and lent it out on occasion for celebrations of the temperate revolution. The crowds drank
water and tea while listening to the Hutchinsons. Asa said, "Every face
of the immense crowd indicated happiness, and inexpressible joy at the
down fall of slavery as one thrown upon the people, in the form of
Rum—made at this '*Old Distillery!*'"

"'King *Alcohol*' went finely," the group reported. The borrowed
tune evoked not only memories of the American overthrow of the

British but the strong dislike that New England reformers harbored for America's recent "monarch," King Andrew, President Andrew Jackson, with whom they sparred over states' rights, Indian removal, and a host of other issues. A week later, just after their New York debut at the American Anti-Slavery Society meeting, the Hutchinsons played "King Alcohol" to "tremendous applause" at a New York temperance meeting on 11 May. Sharing the stage with the teetotal luminaries Lyman Beecher, the head of the Lane Seminary, and John Hawkins, the Washingtonian leader, the Hutchinson Family Singers established themselves as notable reformers.[35]

⊷ ⊰⊹⊱ ⊷

> And when I must resign my breath,
> Pray let me die a natural death.
> And bid the world a long farewell,
> Without one dose of Calomel.

Asa sat reading Wooster Beach's *Family Physician; or, The Reformed System of Medicine* in Milford on 6 June 1843. The group had just finished its historic tour through New York, and the bass singer relaxed by reading. Beach had given his enormous—nearly eight-hundred-page book—to the singers when their paths had recently crossed. Originally published in 1842, the book would arrive in a fourth edition in 1844; "I love it," Asa remarked.

Calomel was a mercury compound often used for medicinal purposes in nineteenth-century America, and many, like the Hutchinsons and Beach, believed it to be an unnatural, deathly way to treat the body. The brothers avoided the nostrum and, when seriously ill, sought help at one of the many "water-cure" establishments which had sprung up throughout the nation. Rarely, in less severe cases, the Hutchinsons broke their temperate stance and drank small amounts of alcohol for its believed curative qualities.

Beach's book, Asa thought, was "practicable and that is just what we want. Truth will Stand." Asa linked the doctor's prescriptions for bodily care to part of a larger cleansing effort: "The Abolition of Slavery!—And Moral Reform—Is a part of Christianity. I Glory in the Great reforms of the day—I look forward to the abolition of Slavery in all forms as the hapiest day of my life." Purifying one's body through temperance and the avoidance of such substances as calomel delivered a clean spirit. Enslavement by calomel, rum, southerners, and every other abusive element demanded an immediate purge. To honor the popular man of medicine, the Hutchinsons dedicated "Go Call the Doctor and Be Quick" (also called "Calomel" or "Anti-Calomel") to Wooster Beach.

"Calomel was enthusiastically received," wrote listener Lucy Chase upon hearing the song at one of the Hutchinson Family Singers' concerts. "Go Call the Doctor"—with its melody seemingly borrowed from the "Old Hundred" hymn—was a hit; even a U.S. senator from New Hampshire, Levi Woodbury, took note of it when the Hutchinsons played in Washington, D.C. *Water-Cure Journal* applauded the group's effort. Curiously, when the Hutchinsons toured Great Britain, the Scottish abolitionist Robert Ross Rowan Moore warned them not to play the song "to a London audience."[36]

⊷ ⊶ ≅✦≅ ⊷ ⊶

> I've been among the mighty Alps,
> And wander'd thro' their vales;
> And heard the honest mountaineers
> Relate their thrilling tales.
>
> 'Twas there I from a Shepard heard
> A narrative of fear,
> A tale, to rend a parent's heart,
> Which Mothers might not hear!

The Hutchinsons' debt to the Rainers is clear in "The Vulture of the Alps," music by Judson Hutchinson and lyrics probably by A. S. Washburn. Transforming a scene of mountain sublimity into horror, the song relates the sudden swoop of a vulture capturing a child from his alpine family on a peaceful "sabbath morn." Dramatically written and composed, the work is filled with tremulous musical passages and sudden changes in dynamics, and is perhaps the most complex work ever written by a Hutchinson. "Vulture" is more an operatic piece than a simple part-song for four voices. Judson's work reveals the Hutchinson Family Singers as capable of writing and performing challenging music. Clearly, the musicians borrowed from popular melodies for many of their songs out of choice, not necessity; a recognizable tune enhanced a song's repeatability, making it more accessible, easier to play, to sing, and to remember.

When Asa heard his brothers Jesse and Judson singing the piece on 14 May 1843—two days after Judson had finished it—he called it "a most thrilling composition. I think it is as interesting as anything like music that I have ever heard." Yet hearing the piece was not the same as watching it. "Vulture" is in the vein of other theatrical songs that the Hutchinsons performed, such as "The Snow Storm" and Henry Russell's "The Maniac," reliant on melodrama as much as on music. "'The Maniac' was also sung with more effect than we ever heard from Russell," said the New York *Tribune* in 1843. "Mr. Hutchinson not only sung but acted it . . . with clear adherence to truth and great effect."[37]

⊶ ⋯ ⊱

> The shades of night were falling fast,
> As through an Alpine village passed,
> A youth, who bore, 'mid snow and ice,
> A banner with the strange device,
> Excelsior!

Poets were the early nineteenth century's equivalent of rock and roll stars. Composers in America sought partnership with noted wordsmiths from the beginnings of the new nation. Benjamin Carr's song cycle *Lady of the Lake* (1810) features poetry from Sir Walter Scott; Shakespeare was another Carr favorite. By the 1830s the reputation of American poets had reached a respectable rank. Henry Wadsworth Longfellow was one such author whose work captured the spirituality of the natural world, a "fusion of the real and the unreal," vital to American romanticism. In 1843 the famed poet, born in 1807, taught modern languages at Harvard. The Hutchinsons chose "Excelsior," one of Longfellow's most acclaimed short poems, as the basis for a song. Their "Excelsior" blended the well-respected tradition of poetry with the advancing genre of popular song.

On the Hutchinsons' sheet music, a note from Longfellow explains that "Excelsior" reveals "aspirations of genius. Its motto—'Excelsior,' (Still Higher!)" and that, after the repetition of the word *excelsior,* "a voice from the air proclaims the progress of the soul in a higher sphere." The lyrics tell of a young traveler who ignores the pleas of those around him as he forges on in the night, where he will die, half-buried in snow, ultimately united with the mystical (and, one imagines, moral) power he seeks.

Notions of divinely inspired artists creating brilliance of nothingness dominated the nineteenth century. (Famously, Harriet Beecher Stowe proclaimed that God wrote *Uncle Tom's Cabin.*) The Romantics conceived of art as an essentially solipsistic practice, creativity an involuntary response to inspiration. Isolated genius fashioned innovative work uninfluenced by the world at large. This ideal conceived of a creation shielded from market forces, shrouding composers, poets, and other cultural workers in mystery—a selling point in and of itself.

Longfellow and the Hutchinson Family Singers, of course, were surrounded by an elaborate network of promoters, critics, fans, and other artists who helped shape their work. New creations unavoidably responded to artistic, political, religious, and other conversations of the day. (Beethoven had sought to praise Napoleon Bonaparte in his 1804 Symphony no. 3, a piece that revolutionized symphonic form, but in a rage over Napoleon's becoming emperor—"Now he too," said the composer, "will trample on the rights of man"—Beethoven dedicated the work to a patron instead.) Judson Hutchinson heightened the oblation of "Excelsior" by drawing on his religious upbringing. One newspaper said of the song that it summons "ideas of those ancient and sublime choral Church performances" and that it is "equally calculated, according to the nature of the strain, to subdue or exalt the feelings."

"Excelsior" received widespread acclaim from audiences, especially when the group traveled abroad. Many believed that the song, "breathing the soul of poetry and feeling," was the Hutchinsons' finest, "one of the most beautiful." This was important. Beauty became so central to nineteenth-century cultural consumers that by the twentieth century, composers were forced either to embrace it or to candidly renounce it (à la Arnold Schoenberg and others).

Charles Sumner wrote to tell his "dearly beloved Henry" in 1846 that a mutual friend just heard the Hutchinsons "*six* times" in England, where "their Antislavery songs commended them; but yr Excelsior was more popular than all else. . . . It was always sung with triumph." Others agreed: "We felt, on hearing this, as if, after the departure of the young Americans, it never could be *sung* again," said the London *Guardian,* "that any attempt to sing it must be a failure, so perfect was their performance."[38]

◦—◦ ≣✦≣ ◦—◦

> This book is all that's left me now;
> Tears will unbidden start,
> With faltering lips and throbbing brow,
> I press it to my heart.
>
> For many generations past,
> Here is our Family Tree;
> My Mother's hands this Bible clasp'd,
> She dying gave it to me.

Sunday, 19 May 1844, Milford, New Hampshire. In the morning, Asa went to church to hear the Rev. John Richardson preach. He played his cello to tonally ground the singers during the service. Afterward, he attended a talk on music—"'twas excellent," he reported. On his way back home, Asa stepped inside the "old school house" once used as the primary place of worship for Milford's Baptists. Here he found "a peculiar meeting" at which the leader, his father, "was exhorting the audience to be Christians." A come-outer assembly, no doubt, called to celebrate human spontaneity and the governance of God, which they believed to be blocked by institutions of organized Christianity. This church ceremony closed with a singing of "My Mother's Bible." Asa then walked home.

The Hutchinsons had taken over one of Henry Russell's great hits of 1841 and reworked the chart in 1843 to add their own embellishments to the lyrics of George Pope Morris. Interweaving faith and family, "My Mother's Bible" spoke to a generation of Americans raised in the midst of religious revivals who turned to pious domesticity as a bulwark against the burgeoning public world of commerce. Purchasing a copy of the Hutchinson Family Singers' "My Mother's Bible" from Firth and Hall brought the Hutchinsons' work into the home, muddying clear divisions of public and private, of work and leisure, in antebellum America.

Above all, though, the song, with its sappiness and simple maxims, preached the organization of life around religion. Those at the Milford meetinghouse were just some of many antebellum Americans who redefined the meaning of sacred living and of sacred song. "My Mother's Bible" finishes: "In teaching me the way to live, It taught me how to die."[39]

We have come from the mountains,
We have come from the mountains,
We have come from the mountains of the Old Granite State . . .

David, Noah, Andrew, Zephy
Caleb, Joshua, Jessy, Benny,
Judson, Rhoda, John, and Asa,
And Abby are our names:
We're the sons of Mary,
Of the tribe of Jesse,
And we now address ye,
With our native mountain song.

People often rushed the stage when the Hutchinson Family Singers finished their signature piece, "The Old Granite State." Once, after the group closed a May 1843 concert in New York with the song, fans mobbed the musicians for an hour and a half—"such a rush to Speak to us I never have often witnessed," said Asa. "The Old Granite State" is special in both message and melody. The song condenses the religious identification and family bonds ("We bless our aged parents and they bless us in return") explored in "My Mother's Bible" and "Excelsior," the wondrous association with nature found in "Vulture" and "Cape Ann," the reform messages of "Go Call the Doctor" and "King

Alcohol," in one work, while including the Hutchinsons' first published music-based declaration against slavery.

"The Old Granite State" effectively closed the gap between the Hutchinsons' identification with the Rainers' mountain style and their effort to promote themselves as native American talent. Celebrating their alpine origins in the mountains of New Hampshire and speaking of reform matters directly relevant to 1840s Americans, the Hutchinsons branded themselves as American Romantics. Ludwig van Beethoven's genius sprang from his Germanic origins, the Rainers' from their Swiss upbringing, and the Hutchinson Family Singers' from their wild and free mountain lifestyle in the nature of the Granite State— "We listened to them with much gratification," said the editor of *Godey's Magazine,* "and felt proud of the genius which the green hills of New Hampshire had nurtured and inspired." Indeed, in 1843 the Hutchinsons used nature—quite literally—as the foursome, unlike the many tourists who then flocked to the region, had yet to vacation in the White Mountains; the highest point in Milford, New Hampshire, stands 271 feet above sea level.

Further connecting family, nature, and reform to religion is the song's melody, which Jesse Hutchinson, the lyricist of "The Old Granite State," borrowed from the musically active Christian faction the Millerites. The Rev. William Miller had predicted that 20 March 1843 marked the beginning of the second millennium, the second coming of Christ. Many believed him. And when the day came and went, Miller discovered an error in his calculations, declaring 23 October 1844 as the proper date. In February 1844 John and Asa attended a "Miller Meeting at the Chinese Museum" in Philadelphia, along with four hundred others. Miller and his cohorts apparently "proved quite plainly," John later recalled, "that the end of the world was near at hand."

How affected the Hutchinson family was by Miller's ideas is difficult to gauge. In the 1840s the Hutchinson Family Singers certainly believed the millennium imminent, though perhaps not as imminent as Miller reckoned. By continually doing good works and encouraging others to do good works, the musicians seemed to be preparing for the day when God would directly govern over man.

In music, the Millerites and the Hutchinsons found themselves more closely aligned. Jesse Hutchinson's transparent use of the Millerite tune from the "Old Church Yard" worked magic. Jesse was, perhaps, also inspired by another second advent melody, "The Christian Band," when crafting the lyrics for the Hutchinson Family Singers' most famous song. Intoning, "We have come from the mountains" instead of "You will see your Lord a coming" ("Old Church Yard") or "Here is a band of brethren" ("Christian Band"), the singers created a fanaticism of a different sort from that of the followers of William Miller. Miller's prediction served to heighten the millennialist fervor then sweeping the nation. The Hutchinson Family Singers' borrowings from the Millerites utilized the familiarity of the buoyant tunes to promote their own social reform–minded vision of the millennium, one attached less to a specific date than to the specific deeds found within religion, family, antislavery, and temperance. The Hutchinsons' use of "metrical psalms," wrote an approving British critic, provided them "an antique, primitive, solemn effect"—*solemn* in the sense of deeply earnest or sincere, not gloomy or somber.

Like the Millerite songs, "The Old Granite State" relies on musical and lyrical repetition, especially on references to family and the Hutchinson Family Singers' inspirational upbringing within the backwoods of New Hampshire, to get across its message of family, faith, nature, and reform. In this, the song was very different from Judson's more complex "Vulture of the Alps," but the differences help to explain the song's allure. A catchy tune, one maddeningly repetitive, is easier to replicate and, in an age where the parlor piano functioned as the family radio, ease of performance was a marketing plus.

On the sheet music cover of "The Old Granite State," the group further linked itself to the natural world. Posing with hands on hips (which was how they often performed a cappella works), the four singers stand amid the rolling hills of, one presumes, New Hampshire (fig. 12). Opening the music to the last page, one finds the various verses of the song and discovers that these alpine musicians are "the friends of emancipation," that "liberty is" their "motto," and that they "despise oppression and cannot be enslaved." The Hutchinson Family Singers' vision of the nation—seen through their use of New En-

The Hutchinson Family, "The Old Granite State" (New York: Firth and Hall, 1843). From the Vocal Sheet Music Collection in the Irving S. Gilmore Music Library of Yale University.

gland's nature, piety, and reform in "The Old Granite State"—rang out in a potent fashion.[40]

A closing note: When Francis Scott Key died on January 11, 1843, the Hutchinson Family Singers were in between performances at anti-slavery meetings in Milford and Boston. Scott's poem "Defence of Fort McHenry," sung to the melody of "Anacreon in Heaven," was to become "The Star-Spangled Banner." Written in 1814, the song did not become the American national anthem until a 1931 act of Congress. During that more than one-hundred-year interval, "The Old Granite State" was one of several proposed for the national song. Many in the North, and even some in England, heard the expressions of family, temperance, antislavery, and religion in the piece and thought that it represented the very best that the United States had to offer. But it was hardly evocative of the nation. More so than most things deemed national (which almost inevitably characterize only a part of a country), the Hutchinsons' nationalism was quite regional. The group spoke for a significant number of Americans, but these listeners lived in the North—particularly in New England, but also in New York and in Philadelphia, where the New Hampshire singers enjoyed the support of free black communities. As the 1850s progressed, such regional differences gained in importance as the federal system for political compromise collapsed, leading North and South to an epic cultural clash.[41]

Part Fourth

—·—⊠◇⊠—·—

Chronology

—1821. Mexico gains independence from Spain.

—1829. Slavery abolished in Mexico.

—2 March 1836. The Republic of Texas is established.

—4 April 1841. John Tyler becomes president following the death of William Henry Harrison.

—1843. Jarius Lincoln publishes *Anti-Slavery Melodies.*

—1844. The Hutchinson family's communitarian experiment.

—9 January 1844. The Hutchinson Family Singers perform with the Philharmonic Society in Philadelphia.

—31 January 1844. The Hutchinson Family Singers perform for President Tyler and his visitors in Washington, D.C.

—12 February 1844. The Hutchinson Family Singers visit Baltimore slave trafficker Hope H. Slater.

—18 March 1844. John Pitkin Norton buys a copy of "The Old Granite State" for the Olcotts.

—Spring 1844. "Get Off the Track!" the Hutchinsons' Liberty Party campaign song, is published.

—August 1844. The Hutchinson Family Singers take their first vacation in the White Mountains.

—24 October 1846. Anna Quincy Thaxter experiences her first Hutchinson Family Singers concert.

—27 October 1848. Frederick Douglass defends the Hutchinson Family Singers from a Buffalo music critic in the *North Star.*

I *do* hope that I may spend this year (1844) with (if kind Providence allows me to live) more general benefit to myself and my fellows. I wish that I might forsake all that is evil. I trust I shall refrain from Profanity and every immoral thought or act. I entertain a desire to treat my Brothers and Sisters better and to respect the "Good old Parents," Jesse & Mary, and heed their advise and not be instrumental in bringing them down to the tomb with sorrow.

—Asa Hutchinson, 1 January 1844

Theme: Leisure and Politics in 1844

Though the Hutchinson Family Singers feared a small turnout on 3 January 1844, they knew before showtime that their "antislavery friend" James Miller McKim—a Garrisonian abolitionist—had sold nearly enough tickets to cover their expenses. To the Hutchinsons' surprise, the two or three hundred Philadelphians who showed at the group's performance proved an excitable bunch; Asa called them "one of the most enthusiastic audience ever I saw." About 150 swarmed the singers after the show, and the next day the *Public Ledger* reported that "their performances are something in the style of the Rainers; but the Hutchinsons have greater versatility of talent."

The musical New Hampshirites dared bring their entertainment south from New York in 1844 and, in this vein, they opened the year in the City of Brotherly Love. On 5 January the *Christian Observer*—a Philadelphia paper run by a New Hampshire native, the Reverend Amasa Converse, with whom the Hutchinsons had tea the day before—said that concerts of the Hutchinson Family Singers were "a place where a Christian may be, and not feel that he is doing wrong; for while all their songs are chaste, some are entirely addressed to the pious feelings of the heart." The city's elite Philharmonic Society apparently agreed, asking the group to perform along with them on 9 January and offering the Hutchinsons free and exclusive use of Musical Fund Hall on the 11th.

On the 9th, the Hutchinson Family Singers arrived at 7 o'clock for the concert with the Philharmonic Society. They then waited for about forty-five minutes as the orchestra tuned their instruments and warmed up ("which, by the way," Asa remembered, "was very annoying"). The evening began as the orchestra lit into a "grand overture" while the Hutchinsons sat out of sight from the audience. Then, with the listeners "waiting in breathless silence to see and hear those characters of whom they had heard so much," came what Asa called the "Tug of War." Presumably this was some kind of back and forth between the Hutchinsons and the instrumentalists, a call and response pattern, perhaps, during which the two ensembles interacted. The New Hampshire musicians soon took over the show with some of their solo selections. "Such applause," said the Hutchinsons, "Oh! 'twas deafening."

A trumpeter from the Philharmonic played after the Family Singers, and Mrs. Edward E. Loder—wife of the noted English opera composer—followed him with several songs. (Asa thought Loder displayed "good tones" but "no soul.")

Back on stage again, the Hutchinsons offered several more selections and topped off their night with "The Old Granite State." The *Saturday Courier* declared "the *Hutchinson family*" winners of the Tuesday night happening and added: "Their performances being both vocal and instrumental, are entirely novel, and so popular and effective, that the audience seemed loth to part with them even after the *third encore!*" The event, a surprising presage of twentieth-century collaborations between popular musicians and orchestras, attests to the Hutchinson Family Singers' resourcefulness and their multifaceted talent as instrumentalists and vocalists.

A few days after the concert, members of the Philharmonic Society tried to book the Hutchinsons for another joint project. "But it's no go!" said Asa. By 1844 the Hutchinsons had tired of friends and strangers who invited them to events where, without any advance arrangement, they would be asked to sing. Playing at these gatherings was not remunerated, and sometimes the extra singing led to vocal distress for one or more members of the quartet. The Hutchinsons' "well-known liberality"—a term the poet Nathaniel P. Willis used when asking the group to donate its act for a concert in New York—almost always extended to reform associations, friends, and family. But the Philharmonic Society was none of these. The Hutchinsons made no record of payment for their first shared concert with the orchestra, and, being in such high demand, they said, "We must draw a line somewhere."[1]

A constant negotiation of personal and work boundaries was one of the costs of fame. Asa lamented that "wealth maketh many friends." Their vigilance in this matter, though, had its limits. Like many gifted entertainers, the Hutchinson Family Singers shared a heartfelt connection with their fans. One of their concerts inspired a supporter to dash off a poem to the *Sun:*

> They hail from the lofty granite hills,
> From a free and northern home:
> 'Tis a band of our own loved land,
> Of "the land of Washington."

Such mutual closeness made letdowns inevitable. Before leaving Philadelphia in 1844, the musicians were deeply distressed by news that a young man who had killed himself had attended one of their recent concerts.[2]

"The Land of Washington," mentioned in the homage to the group was the exact piece the Hutchinson Family Singers chose to sing during some free time in Baltimore at the end of January 1844. Shaking "the whole atmosphere with a terrible force" and creating a disturbing echo that Asa found "most deafening," the tune resounded along a narrow staircase in Baltimore's Washington monument:

> I glory in the spirit
> Which goaded them to rise
> And found a mighty nation
> Beneath the western skies.
> No clime so bright and beautiful

> As that where sets the sun;
> No land so fertile, fair, and free,
> As that of Washington.

A relatively new George P. Morris poem formed the song's lyrics, and the visitors who paid the 12½ cent admission to climb the memorial on Monday, 22 January 1844, were undoubtedly startled to hear it. When the Hutchinson Family Singers passed a New York merchant in the stairway, his agreeable demeanor welcomed the troubadour tourists. So the group continued marching up, offering another selection which, given their 228-step ascent, proved an impressive feat of musicianship and fitness.

With the weather "being somewhat pleasant" and with no concert scheduled in the evening, John, Abby, Asa, and Judson had decided on sightseeing in Baltimore, then known as the Monumental City. Climbing the 180-foot statue dedicated by the citizens of Maryland to George Washington was one kind of activity that occupied the singers' leisure. Though construction on the Washington Monument had begun in 1815, it was not completed until 1841. At the time of the Hutchinsons' visit, the site designed by Robert Mills (who later created the Washington Monument in Washington, D.C.) was a new attraction, *the* place to visit in Baltimore. To honor its hallowed ground, the singers judiciously started their hike with verses from Francis Brown's new song based on Morris's words.[3]

The testament to General Washington greatly impressed the musicians, who called it the "Grandest of all monuments." Asa studiously recorded every figure about the site: it was 280 feet above sea level; the diameter was 20 feet at the bottom, 14 at the top; the crowning statue stood 16 feet tall and weighed sixteen tons; and the total cost of the building was $200,000. The bass singer's obsession with numbers was hardly unusual. Antebellum citizens displayed a numeracy far superior to that of any preceding group of Americans. An obsession with facts and figures flooded journals and diaries covering everything from monuments to reform—the increase in almanacs claiming to predict everything from weather to antislavery points to the trend. (Lydia Maria Child's *American Anti-Slavery Almanac, for 1843* is one example.)

Mathematics gave Americans a new way to rationalize the world, and they incorporated it, as Asa did, into their leisure activities as well as their work.[4]

The Hutchinson Family Singers, who in three years had gone from family agricultural laborers to grocery clerks to select members of American entertainment, struggled with their changed lifestyle. But theirs was just a more dramatic shift than that experienced by most Americans. There existed a great difference in the amount of free time a factory worker had when compared to a factory owner, but both faced new options when planning their free time in the antebellum era.

Trips like the one to the Washington Monument were not a part of the Hutchinsons' agrarian childhood. Asa, in particular, held some of the siblings' 1844 activities as damning evidence of moral decline. "If we had good hard farm work to do," he said, "we should not be so earnest to be playing and making nonsensical remarks."

Like many antebellum Americans, particularly those with money, the Hutchinsons now indulged during their time away from work in a wide variety of pastimes. They played card games and ballgames—apparently John could juggle three balls thirty-eight times before dropping them. They attended to music-related and other business—while performing in Hanover, New Hampshire, the Hutchinsons visited a Shaker village, met with friends Cyrus L. Blanchard and Mark True, had Asa's bass bow fixed, and attended a rehearsal of some Dartmouth musicians ("The Voices were very good but rather harsh"). They read books and newspapers—everything from James M. Phillippo's *Jamaica: Its Past and Present* and Lydia Maria Child's *Letters from New-York* to the *Liberator* and the Bible. They wrote letters and recorded thoughts and events in their journals. They went to plays—but only virtuous ones such as *The Drunkard,* a popular temperance offering which they saw twice in 1844. They lent personal support to antislavery and temperance reform. They fraternized with local elites, friends, and fellow musicians—during one trip to New York they met with new antislavery friends, Roswell Goss, James Buffum, Henry Wright, and Mary Gove, as well as visiting with old pals like Luke Newland. And of course they attended church. In the end, Asa retreated from his earlier misgivings over the singer's activities, deciding, "Mankind are capricious and change their thoughts from things of a solemn cast to those of folley!"[5]

The Hutchinsons did their best to infuse their activities with their idealism. In the summer of 1844, more than a year after they first started singing that they had "come from the mountains of the Old Granite State," the sibling quartet followed the trend of the times and actually visited New Hampshire's White Mountains. The Hutchinson Family Singers made the journey together with brothers Zephaniah and Benjamin, John Robert French (then printer of the *Herald of Freedom,* later a congressman and sergeant at arms of the Senate), Caroline and Ellen Rogers, the Boston abolitionist Francis Jackson, the abolitionist and temperance advocate Mary Hersey Lincoln, and others.[6]

Nathaniel P. Rogers's house in New Hampshire served as the gathering point for the travelers. Unable to separate work and vacation, the Hutchinsons gave a concert upon their arrival in Concord. That night they slept in tents on buffalo hides—"in Indian fashion"—on the Rogers property, where Mary Lincoln noted Rogers's deep attachment to the Hutchinson Family Singers "both on account of their reform spirit and their rare musical talents."

The vacationing group, which included John and his wife, Frances (Fanny), and Judson and his wife, Jerusha, as well as Abby, Asa, and Zephaniah with his wife and daughter, left the Rogers family at eight o'clock on Thursday morning, 8 August. Caravan travel, especially with horse-drawn coaches weighed down by excessive luggage, is slow. Taking advantage of the pace, the Hutchinsons sang for many surprised listeners while passing through small New Hampshire towns. And when they reached a female academy in New Hampton, "the girls swarmed out on the balconies and waved their hands and handkerchiefs" as the Hutchinson Family Singers serenaded from the street. "Our time passed most delightfully," recalled Mary Lincoln. "Now we sang, now we chatted, now we walked, now we were silent."

One night the travelers, tired, hungry, and six miles from the next nearest accommodation, stood in front of a "brown and dirty" place, "a rum tavern." The Hutchinsons, still reeling from Nathaniel Rogers's 1843 public exposure in the *Herald of Freedom* of the "pyramids of hop poles" he had found at their family's Milford farm, made certain that their temperance credentials would not be called into question again. Back then they had had to convince their father and brothers to stop growing the most profitable crop on the farm. Now, faced with the prospect of patronizing a rum seller while traveling with Rogers's progeny, Asa proposed a musical intervention: "They might be made to see the wickedness of rum-selling perhaps by some of our temperance songs."

The bass vocalist continued to plead with the group to make some kind of reform effort, but, Lincoln said, "the instincts of us women were against those who wished to stop." So the group did without Asa's confrontational design. As a collective, the travelers would have ample chance to prove their activist mettle. A few days later, all attended an antislavery meeting in Littleton, New Hampshire, where the reformers Abby Kelley and Stephen S. Foster, as well as the Hutchinsons, mesmerized those in attendance.

By 13 August the group had reached Ethan Allen Crawford's inn near the foot of Mount Washington, where they took turns blowing the horn which echoed from "summit to summit." The vacationers quickly figured out that Crawford "tells awfully large stories," but they were so excited over the scenery that they hardly noticed. "Oh! how great and glorious are those heights!" said Mary Lincoln. "The ocean and the mountains! *they* impress me. . . . They are *both* infinite in their sublimity!"

Starting at eight in the morning on 14 August, the Hutchinsons and friends began their ascent of Mount Washington, which they believed to be 6,775 feet above sea level (current measurement puts it at 6,288 feet). Ten southerners, some of whom held slaves, were part of the large hiking company. The Hutchinsons and their friends made sure that these unwelcome tourists knew "that they had got into warm company."

At the top, the Hutchinsons and Mary Lincoln observed with dismay that the "'chivalric' section" of their party imbibed in order to stay warm. "*Brandy* must be there, even on top of these everlasting monuments of God's power!" To counter, the Hutchinsons sang "Temperance Ball," which some found in "glorious harmony with the place."[7]

We don't know how the hikers reacted to the Hutchinsons.

Whether they laughed at the singers or took them to heart, the southerners certainly understood the extent to which the Hutchinson Family Singers would go, even in a nonconcert setting, to try and sing up to their ideals. Today the musicians appear noble for their antislavery, a bit prissy for their temperance. Yet the two reforms inseparably organized the group's public and private lives. "Let us, the Hutchinson family, tune our voices for the cause of freedom, for the overthrow of slavery, for the promotion of Teetotalism and every moral and Christian act," said Asa.[8]

In 1844 the Hutchinson Family Singers came into their own as musical activists. Yet the daring Hutchinsons revealed in their journal writings, and seen at antislavery meetings and in the White Mountains, sometimes came up short. Playing a series of concerts in Washington, D.C., helped the musicians understand why.

John Tyler, who with presidential candidate William Henry Harrison had been a subject of the famous political song with the refrain "Tippecanoe and Tyler, Too," ascended to office as the tenth president of the United States following Harrison's untimely death in 1841. The president was an improbable fan of the Hutchinson Family Singers. As a Virginian, the slaveholding Tyler had helped to balance the 1840 Whig Party ticket, comforting southerners who feared that many antislavery supporters saw an ally in Harrison.

As president, Tyler quickly snubbed the political machine responsible for his position. After he vetoed economic legislation that underpinned his party's ideals, some Whig organizations formally disavowed Tyler. "His Accidency," as critics dubbed him for his means of ascension, was soon a president without serious party obligations. Freed from the compromises required of a national party leader by 1844, Tyler set in motion a plan largely avoided by previous administrations: the annexation of Texas.

Back in 1821, after gaining independence from Spain, the Mexican government had welcomed American settlers. At the same time, Mexico refused to sell the territory of what would later become the state of Texas to the United States. Trouble arose in 1829 when Mexico emancipated all slaves. American émigrés in Mexico, who had predominantly come from the South, refused to free their bondsmen. The Mexican government responded by disallowing any additional American settlers access to their territory. In 1836 Americans living in Mexico declared independence, captured the Mexican leader Antonio López de Santa Anna, and forced him to acknowledge Texan sovereignty.

Texas then turned to the United States for admission. Andrew Jackson, aware of likely northern objections to the annexation due to a growing antislavery sentiment and the fact that Texas would add to the South's political clout, waited until his last day in office to formally recognize the newly formed Republic of Texas. Jackson's successor, Martin Van Buren, wary of the explosive issue, chose not to recommend for Texas statehood.

President Tyler thought differently. Mindful of the fact that Texan leaders had contacted Great Britain for possible assistance and that British help would probably come with some stipulation for abolishing slavery (British emancipation had taken effect in 1834), Tyler's administration proposed not only the annexation of Texas but its annexation as a slave state.

Since 1820 slavery's expansion in the United States had been decided by an imaginary line drawn across the continent at 36 degrees, 30 minutes north latitude (the northern border of Missouri); slavery would be forbidden in states created to the north of this mark and allowed in those to the south. But by the 1840s, as the regional balance in national politics became increasingly enmeshed in the demographics of proslavery versus antislavery, the utility of the so-called Missouri Compromise unwound. The question of slavery and its growth was thus in the air when the Hutchinson Family Singers came to Washington. Months after they left, the issue became the key in the 1844 national election.[9]

But at the start of the year, Washington hosted an odd pairing, antislavery singers and a proslavery, slaveholding president (a man for whom John Hutchinson, a Harrison supporter, had once begrudgingly campaigned). On 31 January 1844—the day after the Hutchinsons were introduced to President Tyler at the White House by Senator Levi Woodbury—the troupe played for Tyler and guests at the president's request.

The Hutchinsons performed six songs that night: "The Land of Washington," "Happy and Free," "Little Farm," "The Origin of Yankee Doodle," "My Mother's Bible," and "The Old Granite State." Obviously in the company of slave owners, the Hutchinson Family Singers also saw alcohol pass freely among the politicians ("sin in high places," they complained). Asa felt assured after their parlor show that listeners understood the Hutchinsons' call for "'Liberty' and 'Washingtonianism'"—antislavery and temperance.

John Tyler's children, whose mother had died in 1842, cried when the group finished "My Mother's Bible," but the singers seemingly struck no chord with their antislavery verses. After "The Old Granite State," Henry Alexander Wise, a staunch proslavery congressman from Virginia who would later sign John Brown's death warrant, enthusiastically shook the performers' hands. The group stood dumbfounded. Just two days earlier in Baltimore their singing of the final verse of the same song "caused some hard feelings and expressions" as they exited the stage. Proslavery listeners then had clearly objected to the abolitionist sentiment expressed in the song. In the president's parlor, reactions were milder. Asa wondered why. What did Wise hear in the line "We despise oppression and cannot be enslaved?"

Misinterpretation of intention plagues all forms of communication, particularly the more artistic kinds. Many listeners have favorite songs without really knowing the lyrics. Others, so enamored with the tune or the chorus, rework the meanings of songs to fit their program. (Bruce Springsteen's "Born in the U.S.A." is often used by American athletic organizations when introducing or celebrating the nation's athletes in international competition, yet the song delivers a stinging portrait of working-class life during and after the Vietnam era.) The fact that Wise and also Tyler—whom the group said "appreciated" all their songs—enjoyed the Hutchinsons does not necessarily slight the singers' reform spirit or make the politicians Hutchinson Family Singers fans.

Perhaps Congressman Wise heard their antislavery verse as a reference to the liberty and spirit of the American Revolution, an idea he certainly would have endorsed. Anyone who followed the Hutchinson Family Singers, though, knew that antislavery newspapers adored them, and a look at one of their songsters quickly would have revealed their abolitionist slant. Concertgoers in 1844 even gifted the group recent copies of the *Herald of Freedom,* the New Hampshire antislavery publication, after some shows.

The Hutchinsons' performance thus exhibited more than just two groups speaking past one another; it displayed the power of a musical form—popular song featuring a harmonized chorus. The sheer emotionalism evoked by the group's unfailing harmony cut through some very real ideological differences as form triumphed over content. Clearly Wise and Tyler had become so wrapped up in the melody and the performance that they found it difficult to raise an objection to the words. Beautiful mountain harmony—enhanced by interjecting responses of "The Old Granite State" chorus propelling the piece ever onward—provided listeners with a diversion from the lyrics. "Seldom has one such an opportunity for realizing what the human voice is capable of, or what these natures of ours are capable of feeling under the spell of simple vocal music," one columnist would note of the Hutchinson Family Singers years later.

Confusion over what had happened in the president's parlor did not dissuade the Hutchinsons, who would "sing 'Emancipation'" at their next concert. One Washington newspaper also reported on "an attempt to hiss their reference to anti-slavery" that "was promptly put down by the good sense of the audience" during another show. "I do rejoice that we are having a moral influence in this city," entrusted Asa to his journal. "The curse of slavery in this land yet rests but soon we may look on this our country and see it is free."

Washington, D.C., was as far south as the singers believed prudent in 1844 for their brand of entertainment. Passing through Baltimore again on their way north, the singers played for former President John Quincy Adams, then active in keeping a discussion of slavery alive in national politics, and also visited the slave pen of a trafficker named Hope H. Slater—a "disgrace to the country," said Asa. John later observed of the captives, "Some were so bleached that you could scarcely trace the Africa blood." As much as they despised slavery, the Hutchinsons did not see the world without difference between races. Some abolitionists paraded former slaves who exhibited a light complexion around the North in an attempt to shock their viewers: "If a nearly white person can be enslaved, then so can you" was the message implicit in the act. But it was more than a scare tactic. That John found it important to note the whiteness of the slaves shows his inclination for those with white skins. Still, after speaking with an elderly black servant who tended the singers' fire at a hotel—a free man whose wife and two children remained in bonds—Asa cried, "O, O, the horrors of slaves and blacks. . . . I must speak out against this damning evil. . . . We will tune our voices for freedom."[10]

The Hutchinson Family Singers returned from their sojourn south dissatisfied with the political climate in the nation's capital. They struck back with their first campaign song, a work nearly impossible to interpret as anything other than an antislavery diatribe; if listeners were going to realize some sort of escape under the spell of this song, it would be an escapism allowing them to envision (and to sing out) their most radical antislavery beliefs. The composition debuted in a concert by a few members of the Hutchinson family (not the Hutchinson Family Singers) sometime in February. Jesse Hutchinson, Jr., then ironed out some details, and "Get Off the Track!" received its public release in late spring. The song fast became the Hutchinson Family Singers' antislavery anthem and was soon available at music stores all over the North.

A pronouncement on the front of the sheet music reads: "A song for emancipation, sung by THE HUTCHINSONS." Jesse Jr. wrote the lyrics and placed them atop the tremendously popular melody of "Old Dan Tucker." Relying on the imagery of a railroad driving across the nation, the song links the story of liberty first revealed in the American Revolution to the "car Emancipation" (fig. 13). The train of freedom analogy is central, as railroads were a relatively new symbol of progress. In a time when science was often viewed as a means to elevate the human condition, the railroad represented the most advanced technology of the day. People stood in fear and in awe at the sound and might of the roads. Powered by steam engines, trains used iron and coal to create a seemingly limitless source of energy and possibility. The promise opened by such technology appeared divine to New Englanders steeped in the millennialism and human perfectionism of the recent religious revivals.

"Get Off the Track!" plays on the triumph of morality over bigotry as the song turns one of the most familiar early minstrel tunes into a medium for emancipation. The Hutchinsons and many of their abolitionist friends despised early minstrelsy for its exaggerations of black character. Yet minstrel melodies were some of the most popular of the

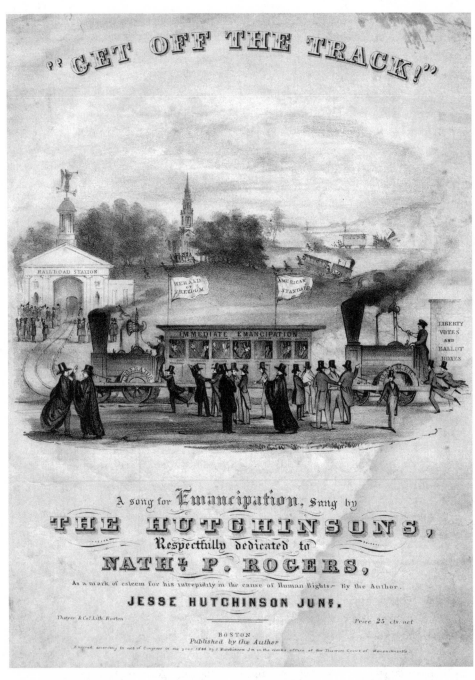

Jesse Hutchinson, Jr., "Get Off the Track!" (New York: Jesse Hutchinson, Jr., 1844). Call #M1622a, Digital ID Number 73866d, Collection of The New-York Historical Society.

day. In "Get Off the Track!" the Hutchinsons enhanced the melody's marketability by making it palatable to those suspicious of immoral entertainment. The *Herald of Freedom* reported of the song that "the people find there is a meaning in the warning."

With its references to the *Liberator*, "Get Off the Track!" steadfastly declares William Lloyd Garrison's brand of antislavery as the train's leading car:

> First of all the train and greater,
> Speeds the dauntless LIBERATOR,
> Onward cheered amid hosannas,
> And the waving of free banners.

The Hutchinsons then name certain Americans—"Merchants, editors, physicians, / Lawyers, priests, and politicians"—who must either jump aboard "the Car of Freedom," "Clear the track!" or else "fall under" the abolitionist convoy. In northern urban centers where the Hutchinsons' success was growing, antislavery sentiment was often the domain of such professions whose members had enough free time and enough money to support reform organizations (in contrast with the abolitionist farmers populating the countryside). "Get Off the Track!" dictates precisely what every reform adherent should do.

For all of its many facets, "Get Off the Track!" is, at heart, a campaign piece. The Hutchinson Family Singers left behind the warm memories of 1840 and the Whig Party, turning to the Liberty Party, the only alternative to the two-party system. But their Liberty backing was not what one would expect from a Garrisonian antislavery promotion. In 1844 Garrison and his cohorts denied politics as a legitimate means for slavery's abolition. With their music, the Hutchinsons looked to do something different—to unify the antislavery factions by linking the two largest divisions through song. In Washington, the Hutchinsons saw ample reason to rally northerners under a broadly defined antislavery and to vote antislavery representatives into office. Abolitionist doctrinal disputes, the Hutchinson Family Singers probably presumed, were the last thing that the movement needed and certainly were not something to parade. Slavery, slavery's expansion, and what to do with the slaves once freed—these were three issues on which many white northerners had opinions. By using broad strokes to simultaneously promote Garrison's American Anti-Slavery Society alongside its arch-rival, the Liberty Party, the Hutchinsons spoke across the boundaries of the reform, trying to consolidate abolitionist sentiment while converting any uninitiates.

The sheet music version irked both the proslavery public and Whig supporters with its cover lithograph depicting a series of railroad cars named "Liberator" and "Immediate Emancipation" pulling "Liberty Votes and Ballot Boxes," while a train in the background identified as "Clay" falls into a ravine. Clearly illustrating their support for both the American Anti-Slavery Society and the Liberty Party, the Hutchinsons also picked a specific target, the beloved Whig politician and presidential candidate Henry Clay, nicknamed Old Kentucky. Jesse's work parodied Clay's campaign song of 1844 of similar title ("Get Out of the Way!") and identical tune, which urged Americans, "Get out of the way, you're all unlucky; / Clear the track for Old Kentucky!" Minstrelsy was not the only resonance embedded in the tune of "Old Dan Tucker."

Many abolitionists despised Clay for two important reasons. The Whig leader, though he believed that slavery injured both bondsmen and masters, had maintained and, in fact, increased his own stake in slavery during the 1820s. (He was to free most of his slaves before his death in 1852.) And in 1839, as the speaker for a national party with his eye on a presidential nomination, Clay had publicly denounced Garrison and his brand of emancipation. "I prefer . . . the liberty of my own race to that of any other race," said Clay, who found "the liberty of the descendants of Africa in the United States" incompatible with that of whites. He said this in part to ensure the support of southern Whigs who feared his gradualist antislavery ideas. But it was what Garrison and immediate abolition meant to politics that truly frightened Clay. A world-class compromiser, Clay worried that the nation was doomed if left to extremists on both sides of the slavery debate. Garrison and fanatical proslavery backers, Clay believed, could ruin the nation.

The Hutchinson Family Singers expected some backlash for releasing the song, since publishers apparently had refused to take it on, forcing Jesse to publish it himself. This is something of note, for music of the Hutchinsons was a hot item in 1844; the blacklisting of "Get Off the Track!" demonstrates the depth of concern over the song's content. Jesse's antislavery ditty quickly became one of the group's most talked-about pieces. At an antislavery convention in Salem, the Hutchinson Family Singers offered "Get Off the Track!" to close on both April 11 and 12. The musicians felt that the tune "went like wild fire," and the *Liberator* reported that they sang their new work "with thrilling effect."

Other responses quickly poured in: "The Hutchinsons Doomed" ran the April 20 headline in Boston's *Morning Chronicle*. Following the Boston *Atlas*'s declaration that the Hutchinson Family Singers' "denunciation of domestic slavery was hardly a sufficient justification to 'get out of the way' so much as to denounce Henry Clay," the *Chronicle* wondered, "How could you, Jesse, 'denounce Henry Clay, the prominent candidate' ever since 1824, 'for the presidency?'" The *Atlas* rationalized the publication of "Get Off the Track!" suggesting that the group must have "fallen into the hands of bad advisers" and warned the public "to regard the aforesaid tribe as from henceforth utterly extinct." Months later, the paper continued its critique, publishing and then blasting the lyrics to the song and, prior to a Hutchinson Family Singers concert in October, wondering "whether they will sing such offensive trash." The *Express* in New York was no kinder: "We had always supposed they had shrewdness enough not to embody so gross an expression of their sentiments in music, intended to be sung in public."

Antislavery bothered those in charge of northern newspapers less than denouncing Henry Clay did. The Hutchinsons shook moderate antislavery Whigs by intoning, "Railroads to Emancipation / Cannot rest on Clay foundation" and putting their support behind the Liberty Party.[11]

To those who agreed with the Family Singers' Clay reproof, the song was a hit. Old friend Nathaniel P. Rogers (to whom the group had dedicated "Get Off the Track!") wrote in June that the piece was one of the greatest ever composed:

> It represented the moral rail road in characters of living light and song, with all its terrible enginery and speed and danger. And when they came to the chorus-cry, that gives name to the song, when they cried to the heedless pro-slavery multitude that were stupidly lingering on the track, and

> the engine "Liberator" coming hard upon them, under full
> steam and all speed, the Liberty Bell loud ringing, and they
> stand like deaf men right in its whirlwind path, the way
> they cried "Get off the track," in defiance of all time and
> rule, was magnificent and sublime ... I should say only
> that is was indescribable. . . . The multitude who heard
> them will bear me witness, that they transcended the very
> province of mere music. . . . God be thanked the Hutchin-
> sons are in the movement.

The Hutchinsons' fate, though, was decided by neither the Boston papers nor the antislavery press. Listeners ultimately sanctioned
the group's music with their continued attendance at concerts and
their ovations for "Get Off the Track!" Reports from New York
recorded "unbounded applause" and "great satisfaction" after the song.
The Hutchinsons' call for the Liberty Party was heard (but only occasionally heeded—the party won 65,608 votes in the 1844 election, a little more than 2 percent, though more than three of every ten voters in
Milford cast their ballots for the antislavery delegation).

In 1843 Jarius Lincoln, an agent of the Massachusetts Anti-Slavery Society, had put together a collection entitled *Anti-Slavery Melodies*. Lincoln felt—and many reformers agreed—that "the Anti-Slavery community needed something of the kind." He may have been
right, but sales of *Anti-Slavery Melodies* faltered. After its publication,
when only $40 worth had sold, not enough to cover his $200 expendi-
ture, Lincoln pleaded with William Lloyd Garrison in the *Liberator* to
help boost the book's sales. But in 1844 the Hutchinsons' success wiped
out any fears that reformers could not hold a public voice in the growing cultural market.[12]

First Variation: Money for Nothing? The Hutchinson Family Singers as Communitarians

Being well off changed the way that the Hutchinsons lived. A windfall
of concert profits, especially from shows in New York City, made it
possible to tour new sites, spend time with friends, and sing songs
which sided with ostensibly risky political ideals. Where once Asa had

joked after tallying the group's money that he was "afraid the *Milford* people will envy us if they hear that we have 34.00 dollars on hand," in 1844, the day after the group visited the Washington monument, he recorded a sum of $894 in his pocket (equal to somewhere between nineteen thousand and several hundred thousand dollars in 2006). The Hutchinson Family Singers had reached a point where they could (and occasionally did) earn more than $1,000 a night. The enormity of this figure is clear—many working families, even those employed in skilled positions, found it difficult to net the annual $500 necessary to keep up with their cost of living.

After three years into a career that had started in 1841, making money was not a problem for the Hutchinson Family Singers. But the group found little comfort in wealth and tried to come to terms with their financial excess. One rumor claims that Judson, apparently on more than one occasion, tossed all his coins and the group's concert proceeds into the audience. During their more rational moments, the musicians promised to "ever conduct ourselves as to meet the countenance of the moral and religious portions of Society"—but they would still feel lacking. Wealth and fame had catapulted the entertainers into a different social sphere. "Oh, well, that may be," admitted the troupe, "but the truth is the Hutchinsons cannot talk as well as they sing and all our friends know it." Money was only one social marker, and it didn't smooth over some of the Hutchinsons' rougher edges, remnants of their rural upbringing.

The question of what to do with their capital lingered for some time. Resonating in the musicians' minds was the 1841 failure of the United States Bank of Philadelphia. They knew that Henry Russell had reportedly lost $30,000 during that debacle. So, back in Milford, in a shot-bag placed inside of an earthen jar and hidden at their parents' farm, one could find the Hutchinson Family Singers' loot in the early 1840s.

If burying the money in New Hampshire did nothing to solve their wealth-based guilt, investing it in their family, community, and future did. Over time, the Hutchinson Family Singers spent $2,000 renovating their family's farm and more than $5,000 purchasing an entire block in Milford. On this strip, the Hutchinsons built rental apartments and also a meeting and performance venue called Freedom Hall

(or Temperance Hall). In the center of town, Joshua Hutchinson operated the family's new store. The ventures of 1844 were the first of many
that the entertainers embarked on during the next few years in Massachusetts, Minnesota, and Colorado.[13]

Hardly alone in worrying about the effects of money and leisure,
the Hutchinsons lived in a time of economic uncertainty. The burgeoning industrial economy wildly swung up and down, while the gap
between the haves and the have-nots grew. This is not simply a phenomenon observed in retrospect by historians. Those who lived in the
1840s were quick to note it; Asa worried in 1844, "We had better not
have our concert admission fees too high for by thus doing we keep
away all the poor and laboring classes who have souls pure as the
Monied Class and who would . . . be profited by its good influence."
The Hutchinsons' tickets—which looked similar to money, as if to say
that the purchaser had merely exchanged one currency for another—
stayed at or near the same price throughout the 1840s. Asa resolved that
the group was stuck in a "deplorable condition": If the entertainers
lowered their prices, they could put their livelihood at risk. But, at the
same time, he realized, "If we sing expressly for the money we cannot
advance one step towards reform as our Aristocratic audiences lead."
Moral conscience and market forces often worked in tension. To make
the two compatible was one goal of the singers—"We cannot be so free
to sing high and lofty sentiments to an audience when we feel bound to
sing to their Pockets instead of their hearts."

Adjusting ticket prices, the Hutchinson Family Singers determined, was not the way to alleviate their moneymaking concerns. Instead, they looked to handle their wealth equitably. One solution surfaced after an 1843 experience with community-centered life at Brook
Farm in West Roxbury, Massachusetts. Formed in 1841, Brook Farm
was intended by its founders to "insure a more natural union between
intellectual and manual labor." Two important ways of realizing utopia, they held, were equal access to education and a more progressive
role for women. Brook Farm believers sought a "true equality without
its vulgarity" where washerwomen, mechanics, and farmers could live
with Harvard graduates, and nobody would be distinguished in one
way or another.

After their visit to Brook Farm, the Hutchinson Family Singers adapted an arcadian model for their own immediate family. Community-centered life offered a chance for the ultimate in social improvement: the creation of a morally enriching environment independent of the individualism and jealousies many believed rampant at the time. With their family experiment, the Hutchinsons were hardly alone. The same economic, religious, and political changes that opened the way for New England's cultural enlightenment gave rise to the "communitarian moment"; the period from 1840 to 1849 boasted the establishment of at least 59 new communities charged with creating socially progressive alternatives to industrial life. This was far more than in any other decade before the Civil War, during which 119 were formed. For economic survival, most of the community experiments derived goods and cash from in-house farming and industry, while sympathetic artists like the Hutchinsons provided uplifting entertainment. Most of the experimental societies proved rich in ideals but poor in cash. Though created to be self-sufficient, communitarian organizations in the 1840s typically survived no longer than two years.[14]

The Hutchinson Family Singers' communitarian arrangement extended no further than their parents and their brothers and sisters (and all their respective families), but the pooling of resources provided the Hutchinsons a clear way to share their financial boon. The group also hoped, no doubt, to use the opportunity to rein in some of what they believed were wayward tendencies among their relatives. Brother Andrew, in particular, dealt in "that miserablest of all traffics, selling rum."

The Hutchinson commune was also a path to a righteous retirement for the now-famed musicians. As part of the plan, the Hutchinson Family Singers would withdraw from the stage to live as farmers. This was not a long-term strategy. The four musicians envisioned switching careers starting immediately in 1844. But like those of a majority of community experiments, the scheme quickly changed.

Jesse Hutchinson, the family patriarch, decided that the luster of farming had worn for him, especially when compared with the life of an itinerant preacher. He excluded himself from the Hutchinson cooperative and signed over his property to his children with the promise that they take care of Polly. The singers soon came to their senses, realizing that the artistic and financial rewards, along with the social influence of their musicianship, surpassed those of any farmer. Straying a bit from the original conception, the Hutchinson Family Singers chose to continue the communal idea but to contribute concert revenue to the family treasury instead of farming.

In April 1844 the Hutchinson Family Singers performed at an antislavery meeting at the Northampton Association, a communitarian society in western Massachusetts. Here they found everything in "a plain, simple, rough, pleasant condition"; the same could not be said of their own community. The split between the entertainment branch and the farming branch of the Hutchinsons sparked great disputes. Why should some in the family journey around the country, especially the nation's great urban centers, while others endlessly toiled in Milford? The obvious answer to the question—that the Hutchinson Family Singers earned a lot of money—was of little solace to the brothers who worked the fields. So while Jesse Jr. participated in debates in Lynn and in Worcester concerning "*the rights of property, and the best means of reorganizing society,*" some of his older siblings, those who had been first in line to formally inherit property, "began to hint that it was not quite fair to deprive them of their interest in the farm."

By May 1844 the Hutchinson family began seriously quarreling over their communal association. The musicians' older brother Benjamin, who lived his entire life on the Milford farm, came out against the experiment, as did John's wife of three years, Fanny Burnham Patch, who, along with Asa, completed the opposition. Judson and Abby agreed with the communal farm's most fervent supporter, John, to continue the venture. Despite intense bickering, the family maintained the arrangement until the end of December. Then typhus struck down Ben and his sister Rhoda's husband. Their deaths, along with increasing protest from the wives of both John and Judson (who had wed Jerusha Peabody Hutchinson, a distant cousin, in July 1844) brought the matter to a head. The Hutchinson family soon abandoned their cooperative and divvied up the property. John found this a messy affair even though the deed transferring the farm to the children had not yet been legalized. During the short-lived trial, the family had accumulated a large number of possessions. Public auction turned out to be the only way to divide the community's legacy (except for the farmland) to everyone's satisfaction.[15]

Communitarian failure did not sour the Hutchinsons on reform. They continued to support small and large antislavery and temperance organizations with their voices and their money. The group gave $100, for example, to the Salem Anti-Slavery Society just before they performed at one of the association's meetings. In 1844 and 1845 the Hutchinson Family Singers appeared in at least nineteen different reform functions, such as antislavery meetings or temperance celebrations. The group often played more than once at larger events, so they totaled roughly 33 reform shows during a span of about 230 concerts. Nearly 14 percent of their entertainments took place at explicitly reform-sponsored galas. Add to this figure the Hutchinsons' countless copies of sheet music and songsters (slim books containing only lyrics), along with their singing of antislavery and temperance tunes at their own concerts, and one realizes the extent to which social reform suffused their career.

Of all the reform efforts the Hutchinsons undertook and supported, perhaps the most telling was the building of the Milford hall, founded on the principles of temperance, antislavery, and come-outerism. The group's creation of Freedom Hall placed a temple of culture in Milford, where the Hutchinson Family Singers' moral authority would be heard. As the 1840s progressed, the group and the culture industry they represented increasingly secured an influential public space.[16]

Second Variation: Hutchinson Family Singers Fans and the Weight of Sympathy

What did it mean to be a Hutchinson Family Singers fan? The group's listeners tended to be from the same age bracket as the performers, and with good reason. The 1840s gave rise to a consumer generation then unparalleled in the nation's history. With production and work increasingly moving out of the home, shopping for goods and services shifted to a more central position in one's daily life. John, Asa, Abby, Judson, and other Americans born between 1815 and 1835 became young adults at a time when consumer activity developed into an awkward hybrid of need, desire, and social distinctiveness.

The Hutchinson Family Singers' own uncertainty of their worth in this changing world marked them: later generations felt more at home in the commercialized nation, and earlier ones bemoaned the tremendous pace of the revolution. Antebellum commerce differed from that of the colonial era as a greater diversity of wares—made possible by more efficient (and often more exploitative) labor practices and technologies—now fueled the economy. Cultural products— from the material, like books, banjos, and pianos, to the more ethereal, like concerts—represented just one facet of this new commercial America.

"Music, like everything else, is now passing from the few to the many," said Lydia Maria Child in 1842, as an ever-increasing number of Americans tested boundaries and affirmed identities through song and other musical efforts. In the North, thanks to Lowell Mason's pioneering effort to teach music in public schools, as well as to the endless work of church choirmasters and other Christian musical leaders, a basic music literacy had become a fundamental part of early education.[17]

The changes from the early nineteenth century through the years before the Civil War were easy to detect. In 1817 a fourteen-year-old Adin Ballou attended a singing school opened by an itinerant instructor named Samuel Frost. Ballou thought that music education was "a desirable privilege" even if he was being trained only to sing in church. To the young teen's religious father and many other parents of his generation, it was a "public mockery." The pomp of revivals, political campaigns, and reform movements, though, pushed Americans toward new understandings of music and of entertainment. Twenty-seven years after Frost taught Ballou the fundamentals of singing, the *New Hampshire Magazine*, "devoted" to "moral and religious reading," ran a piece on "The Claims of Vocal Music." In it the author asserts that musical faculties can be developed in all children, not just in those with special talents, and insists that music education is desirable for everyone. "In the social circle, around the family fire side, and in the hour of solitude" music is a uniquely valuable skill; "it opens to the singer a source of enjoyment to which others are strangers." Since the Boston public schools already offered systemwide musical instruction, the article simply repeated what many had come to accept: that music was a "most important branch of culture in our age."[18]

In a time before recorded sound, music became central because it was easily transferable (you could take your knowledge of singing with you anywhere and apply it to any kind of music you saw fit), entertaining, social, and also a rather common skill. One source for the explosion in musical interest of the 1830s and 1840s was a significant reduction in the cultural divide between the countryside and the city.

Music was one of the activities of urban refinement most quickly adopted by country dwellers. Elizabeth Phelps Huntington once entertained two guests who were "both very fond of musik" in her Litchfield, Connecticut, home by playing guitar while all three sang together. Years earlier, before her marriage, Elizabeth Phelps had shied away from other forms of urban socializing: in Newburyport, Massachusetts, she avoided conversation during an elaborate dinner party. When the aspiring farmer John Pitkin Norton went to a get-together in Albany, New York, he sang with gusto, but he refused to partake in the dancing—"of course, I took no part in that portion of the performance."

Margaret Fuller attributed rural Americans' passion for music to a desire to imitate their urban idols, but she also acknowledged that "singing in parts is the most delightful family amusement." William Ellery Channing predicted that music would provide "every family" with "a new resource" and that "home [would] have a new attraction" when all children learned to sing. He was right. The social aspect of music, which for some was intimately connected to the politics behind certain lyrics, often proved irresistible. "I love music better than ever," wrote New Hampshire resident Adaline Rice Parker in 1841. "We have a number of very good vocalists in Lee and Nottingham, and have had several *social sings*. I enjoyed them exceedingly." More personal than the milieu at large parties, the intimacy of musical offerings in the home blended well with the ideal of a close-knit community, a notion cherished in many rural areas.[19]

The Hutchinson Family Singers, country dwellers singing of family ties along with their religious and reform ideals, played to rural listeners who would adore the group even more after the musicians earned the recognition of urban fans like those in Boston, New York, and especially London. While the Hutchinsons bridged country and city, the New Hampshire quartet and many of their musical compatriots also attracted an economically diverse lot. Edward Jenner Carpenter, a twenty-year-old cabinetmaker's apprentice living in western Massachusetts, filled his free time in 1844 and 1845 with a host of musical activities. Carpenter at first glance could ill afford to spend twenty-five cents on concert outings in the town of Greenfield, yet he still heard performances of sacred music, caught a few black fiddle players, danced, and attended several functions featuring bands or glee club singers. Carpenter's pursuits suggest two observations: first, that musical performances were not the sole domain of the well-to-do, and second, that a remote town like Greenfield hosted such varied musical events. At the same time in eastern Massachusetts, the infatuation of Lowell factory women with the Hutchinson Family Singers began. The Hutchinsons "discoursed sweet music, *so sweetly*," said one in 1844. "They have become great favorites with the public."[20]

Other fans of the Hutchinson Family Singers left more detailed records of the musical revolution. In 1846 the Boston suburb of Dorchester housed about 6,500 people, including one named Anna Quincy Thaxter. Twenty-one-year-old Anna had suffered through the deaths of her mother in 1837 and her father in 1841. As the eldest, Anna ultimately took charge of her brother and sister, and the trio wound up in Dorchester after having lived in Hingham and in Cambridge.

Anna loved to visit friends, take part in card games, read, sing, play piano, and attend concerts and lyceum lectures. Many of these activities, used to fill free time and to break the monotony of daily tasks, were also sponsored in some way by the local Unitarian church. Anna's church's sewing meetings, during which the women crafted items for the poor, linked her and friends to each other and to the Dorchester community.

The women enjoyed these activities and replicated communal reading and sewing in their own homes. To have a man or woman recite Shakespeare or Dickens aloud in the parlor while women were sewing was hardly unusual. One Saturday morning Anna Thaxter visited her friend Lucy, who ironed while Anna read aloud from Gibbon's *Decline and Fall of the Roman Empire.* (Five months later, when she finished it, Anna had little to report outside of the joy of having read a really long book.)

For Anna, though, there were few pleasures as great as listening to or performing music. The Unitarian church sported a choir, offered singing lessons, and provided her weekly opportunities to perform.

Music, especially singing, was particularly well adapted for use in domestic settings. "This evening we sang to Mr. Dafe, sewed & c.," Thaxter recorded. Music seemed the very lifeblood of Anna's existence. It is little wonder, then, that she and future husband Benjamin Cushing shared a passion for music.

For several years, both Anna and her friend Charlotte took piano lessons, and in 1846 they had "a beautiful new piano" at their disposal. The young women's interest in music, cultivated and encouraged by their Unitarian affiliation, was also fed by the latest developments in popular music. To Anna and her associates, myriad musical events were available, yet, unlike Edward Carpenter, the Thaxter group shunned such sordid musical offerings as those presented by Greenfield's barbershop fiddlers. Anna Thaxter took pleasure only in reputable entertainments and remained highly conscious of possible conflicts with her religious beliefs. When neighbors went to a production of the British actors Mr. and Mrs. Charles Kean, Anna recoiled from their invitation: "I did not know how I should feel about it, as I am still somewhat undecided about the theatre." The thought of seeing the famous thespians who often produced works of Shakespeare unnerved the young woman. Luckily, one of Anna's companions offered a comforting solution—"Mrs. Peters invited me to go and hear the Hutchinsons the next time they sang."[21]

Anna Thaxter tracked the many musical performances of Dorchester in 1846. In January she heard William Dempster, the Scottish corollary to the Englishman Henry Russell, perform "Scottish songs, very beautifully," and "enjoyed it, very much." Throughout the year she attended oratorios, parties featuring music, the opera, and the local philharmonic society. She also enjoyed the singing in church and listened to a variety of instrumentalists, from children's groups to solo violinists. Anna once visited a military group camped in a nearby field. She went not to see their arms but, she said, "rather to hear the music. . . . We were so much fascinated by the music."

None of these events, though, could rival the excitement of one fall concert. In early October, Charlotte read aloud an account written by Harriet Martineau of the Hutchinson Family Singers' recent trip to England. On 24 October 1846, five of Thaxter's acquaintances, including Charlotte, went to see the Hutchinsons perform. Anna for some reason did not attend. Greatly influenced by the press writings about the troupe and, no doubt, by her own antislavery beliefs, the twenty-one-year-old was decidedly anxious over the New Hampshire singers—"They have been treated with a great deal of attention in England, and I really want to hear them." A few weeks later Anna got her chance. After having tea at Charlotte's, Anna Thaxter accompanied a group into town. "It was a beautiful, warm, moonlight evening, and the music was delightful," scribbled a tired Anna. "Abby Hutchinson is as simple and natural as possible."[22]

The concert had a lasting effect on the Thaxter group. One month later Anna and friends "practised 'Excelsior'" in the forenoon. The Longfellow-based song was one of many Hutchinson Family Singers' selections available from the publishing firm of Firth and Hall. Thaxter's reaction to the Dorchester show exhibits how newspaper and journal coverage worked hand-in-hand with the Hutchinsons' presentations. The end result was a thirty-eight-cent sheet music purchase (fig. 14). Live performances helped advertise sheet music; sales of music personalized the cultural experience, allowing people to bring home a piece of the Hutchinson Family Singers.[23]

Anna was not the only one caught by the Hutchinsons' potent mix of religion, reform, and consumerism. In 1844 a twenty-two-year-old John Pitkin Norton combined his interest in music and reform with another pursuit, courting. Young Norton, son of a successful farmer, wanted to be just like his dad. So every winter—when the family farm could spare his labor—Norton left to study with leading agricultural minds in New York, Albany, New Haven, and Boston. Everywhere he went Norton linked himself to local music and reform groups. Sometimes the two were one and the same, such as the monthly "Anti Slavery" concerts he attended with a Miss Sarah Porter in 1843.

In 1844, though, before heading off to Edinburgh and Utrecht on a whirlwind farming-education tour, Norton was in Albany attending reform meetings and music rehearsals. On 23 February, Norton's choir decided to sing "'the Old Granite State' of the Hutchinsons to temperance words." Three days later, when he showed up to practice with the Musical Club, Norton learned that most of his cohorts had gone to a College Temperance Meeting instead. His friend Ed later relayed the

HUTCHINSON FAMILY.

		ct.			ct.
1. Cot where we were born.		38 nett.	2. Go call the Doctor, or Anti-Calomel.		25 nett.
3. Excelsior.		38 "	4. Cape Ann		25 "
5. Mother's Bible.		38 "	6. Soldier's Funeral.		50 "
7. Vesper Song at Sea.		25 "	8. Vulture of the Alps.		38 "
9. Axes to grind.		25 "	10. Were a cutting.		25 "
11. We are happy and free.		25 "	12. Our Father's Hearth.		38 "

NEW YORK

PUBLISHED BY **FIRTH & HALL** No. 1, FRANKLIN SQ.
& **FIRTH, HALL & POND** 239 BROADWAY.

Price list on the cover of Hutchinson Family and Henry Wadsworth Longfellow, "Excelsior" (New York: Firth and Hall, 1843). From the Vocal Sheet Music Collection in the Irving S. Gilmore Music Library of Yale University.

news that they sang their adaptation of the "old Granite State" at the temperance gathering and that it was "very fine." Ed also, said Norton, had "the pleasure of escorting Miss Belcher & Miss Bull."

A month later, Norton enjoyed a Saturday evening with the Olcott family. The group urged John Norton to sing, but not wanting to go at it alone, he insisted on singing with Mary Olcott. Never having rehearsed together, he and Mary "made rather poor work" of some songs. Then several others in the room took a stab at singing the "'Old Granite State' from their recollection of the Hutchinsons." Theirs was such a horrific rendition that, first thing next morning, John went to a music store and bought a copy of the sheet music for the Olcotts.

Norton immediately set out rehearsing the Hutchinson Family Singers' work with Mary Olcott. "Her voice is very good," he assessed. "It is a pity that she has not some good teacher in vocal music." Soon John Norton journeyed into dangerous territory. He brought a former love interest, Mary Delovan, in to "practise the 'Old Granite State' again with Mary Olcott." Intending to have Olcott take the lead, Delovan to sing the second part, and to sing tenor himself, John soon realized his folly. Mary Delovan, he said, acted out "one of her old fashioned tantrums." She started teasing the other two, making "the most embarrassing speeches she could think of," and, after storming off, returned and declared her determination to "plague" Norton and Olcott.

Later that day, John Norton and Mary Olcott attended a party together, where they happily sang the "Old Granite State." By April 1844, though, John was set to leave for Europe: "Before I come back however she will be married or engaged in all probability so that there is little hope for me," said the sullen bachelor. "I don't know what has gotten into me to put all this in writing but it is done + I will let it go." During May in Dunham, John tried singing with a young Irish woman. It did not go well, so he left with her a few pieces of music that he had brought from the United States. Their host, Mr. Johnston, "rejoiced in getting hold of the Hutchinson poetry."[24]

It is easy to understand the appeal of the Hutchinson Family Singers for Anna Thaxter, John Norton, and the many other northerners steeped in pious traditions and reform, notably antislavery. But what of the rest? The magnitude of the Hutchinson Family Singers' success during the 1840s suggests three generalizations: 1) that antislavery, though always a highly contentious issue, was nonetheless growing more popular in the North; 2) that the Hutchinsons' medium, the parlor song, and the aesthetic of their music broke through ideological and political barriers; but at the same time, 3) that their performance (and its reception) revealed the limits of reform in song.

In New Haven, Connecticut, the debate over ending slavery would rack one clergy family. "I have no interest in the hot disputes of the day with regard to slavery," said Aaron Rice Dutton, "so at one time I go the 'in time sincere' for abolition, and at anothers I'm a colonizationist and at anothers am a sort-of a halfway between man, neither approving of the measures of the Colonizationists nor of the antislavery society." Aaron's sister Mary was for colonization and criticized the antislavery movement: "They don't want slaves among them any more than we do & would be glad to be free from them." Dorcas Dutton, the family matriarch, harbored fewer doubts: "Many of the most devoted and intelligent Christians in the North" are a part of the Anti-Slavery Society, she said. "Their cause is a righteous one, one approved by God."[25]

No matter how one looks at the views expressed by the Dutton family, all were informed by a stance against enslavement. The problem for the Duttons was the question of how to emancipate and what should be done after emancipation. At Brook Farm, a community littered with reformers, one writer could not recall meeting any proslavery advocates yet thought that no one saw any "real significance and importance" in antislavery organizations. Along these lines, when the Boston *Evening Transcript* covered an 1843 concert of the Hutchinsons, it thought it no great mystery that a group promoting "temperance, emancipation, equal rights, & c." could find "enough maintaining these various opinions to support them and fill a house." But after noting "a goodly number of our colored population" in the audience, the newspaper reprimanded the Hutchinsons and suggested that they sing these changed lyrics: "We support Emancipation, / But like not *Amalgamation.*"[26]

As the antebellum period progressed, more and more northerners came to see the institution of slavery as an evil. In politics the growing dissatisfaction in the North with the expansion of slavery led to serious jockeying for voters between the Liberty Party (and its later manifestations), the Whig Party, and the so-called Independent Democrats (those willing to break with the southern branch of the party). By the late 1850s the newly emergent Republican Party plainly announced its northern bias with the slogan, "Free soil, free labor, free speech, free men."

Of course, institutions are created and sustained by individuals. And while many northerners were quite certain that white slaveholders were wrongdoers and that bondsmen must be freed, ideas about what to do with liberated black men and women ran the gamut from granting legal equality to shipping them to another continent. The Hutchinson Family Singers, whether through small actions like Judson sharing a room with Frederick Douglass during a stay at the Northampton Association or through their compositions and performances, tried their best to get their fans to understand that, as John Hutchinson signed his letters in the 1860s, "We must have a common Brotherhood."[27]

Yet the Hutchinson Family Singers' presentations so fruitfully tied together other prominent themes important in their day that some fans undoubtedly enjoyed the group for what the musicians, in essence, were not. For starters, audiences found the Hutchinsons to be authentic. This meant a lot to antebellum consumers. In the 1860s the English philosopher and critic George Henry Lewes, in his *Principles of Success in Literature,* summarized the importance of authenticity when warning, "No style can be good that is not sincere." Many valued an ideal that the individuals on stage were acting no differently than if they were sitting around at home. Shunning the dramatic posturing of many European performers whose grimacing faces and trilling vocals attracted criticism, the Hutchinson Family Singers looked sincere, believable to their admirers. One reviewer thought Judson "a live Yankee" (which he was) but also found Judson's singing of the "The Bachelor's Lament" so convincing that he observed of the then wedded musician, "He is unmarried." This was a norm for the Hutchinson Family Singers, a group which promoted their farming origins but showed up on stage and on sheet music covers in "superfine black cloth coats and pantaloons," white vests, silk neckerchiefs, collars turned down à la the Romantic poet Lord Byron, and tailored dresses. Dirt, sweat, and manure, the Hutchinsons must have presumed, would not authenticate their performance.[28]

Abby Hutchinson's appearance always seemed more important than that of any other member of the New Hampshire troupe. "A pretty brunette of thirteen" when she started singing with her brothers, "very picturesque in her bodice of scarlet velvet," Abby served as a role model of womanly piety for her female listeners like Anna Thaxter and the Lowell factory girls. She also stood as an icon of womanly piety for male fans who hoped that Abby's goodness might cleanse them of their sins; at the same time, many men lusted after the young singer.

"We measure a nation's social life by its home life," said the minister at the 1875 funeral of Asa's wife, "and we estimate home life by the elevation, or degradation, of women." In an age in which women were idealized as the redeemers of nations and of men, Abby's hallowed position in the performance troupe appeared natural. "Every one who came into her sphere of influence was elevated and refined," said one critic. Following a Thanksgiving concert by the Hutchinsons at a New York prison, an inmate declared, "If we had been devils, and Abby had come along with us, she would have made us wish to become angels."

All of Abby's actions, from her singing and her walk across the stage to her style of dress, were understood to be devoid of the disingenuousness of which European-trained musicians were accused. "She was simplicity itself and totally unspoiled by admiration and applause which her touching singing brought forth," said a biographer. Abby awed fans with the impression that she had nothing to hide. The popular female vocalist was, according to an 1844 description, just like every other free woman in America: "She employs her time in reading, studying, sewing, or housework, as inclination or convenience may dictate; and she is as much at home in either of these, as in charming an audience of thirty-five hundred people." What *Arthur's Lady's Magazine* neglected to mention was that only a select few lived lives comparable to Abby's. She traveled for all but two months of the year and, for a woman, acted as a very public, political figure. Abby was also, at the time of the article, only fifteen.[29]

The young singer personified the "sentimental style" to audiences steeped in ideas valuing simplicity for its supposed link to what is natural or genuine. (After all, as Aristotle once said, "Naturalness is persuasive, artificiality is the contrary.") On covers of the Hutchinson Family Singers' music, Abby is portrayed in a self-effacing garb that was most popular in the 1840s. Her dresses are drawn out, slender at the waist, and ballooning with fabric over her hips, creating the illusion that her upper body sits atop a separate, cushiony platform (fig. 15). With one look, Hutchinson Family Singers fans saw all they needed to know. Abby's clothes alone told audiences that her singing was candid. Contemplating the sum of the female vocalist's stage performance, the Philadelphia *Citizen* could not reckon what to admire most, "the richness and sweetness of her voice," "her perfectly easy, simple unaffected manner," or "her modest and tasteful costume." Ultimately fans marveled over everything. "Even the would-be-fashionables, who think they must applaud the protracted trills of an Italian screamer, have some chords of humanity left, that will vibrate strains responsible to the melting plea of Abby as she so sweetly and feelingly sings."[30]

Cassius Clay, the Kentucky antislavery advocate, once told Abby her voice was "more eloquent than speech in freedom's cause." He was one of many men who admired the songstress for her talent and beauty. Perhaps no one embodied the male fixation with Abby better

THE SHEPHERD'S COTTAGE.

Pastoral Ballad,

SUNG BY

MISS ABBY J. HUTCHINSON.

THE WORDS BY

G. P. MORRIS, ESQ.

THE MUSIC BY

CHARLES E. HORN.

NEW-YORK:
PUBLISHED BY C. HOLT, Jr. MUSIC PUBLISHING WAREHOUSE 156. FULTON ST.

Abby Hutchinson on the cover of "Shepherd's Cottage." Courtesy The New Hampshire Historical Society, Concord.

than Ludlow Patton. Patton was the son of eminent minister William Patton, a founder of New York's Union Theological Seminary. He had trained for the gospel ministry too, but instead embarked on a successful business career that culminated with a seat on the New York Stock exchange and his own firm, Ludlow Patton and Company.

An eighteen-year-old Patton first heard the Hutchinson Family Singers in May 1843, when Abby was a few months away from her fourteenth birthday. Ludlow recalled: "I was thrilled throughout that afternoon by their singing and always, thereafter, embraced every opportunity to hear them sing." He meant that literally. His infatuation with the group, and with Abby in particular, bordered on mania. Starting in the early 1840s and continuing for more than fifty years, Patton clipped every newspaper article on the group that he could find, a collection still extant at Milford's public library. The persistent young admirer, no doubt spared the status of a crazed groupie by virtue of his wealth, eventually married Abby Hutchinson.[31]

Despite Abby's heralded status among the four siblings, the Hutchinson Family Singers were noted for a sensation of harmony in concert that enhanced their being a *family* of singers. "The Hutchinson Family's sense of the vocal blend was not completely new," writes Dale Cockrell. "Its incorporation into an enormously popular commercial music idiom was something novel though." Early in their career, one display of the Hutchinsons' combined vocal prowess convinced an all-male audience in Hanover, New Hampshire, that Hutchinson Family Singers performances were decent enough for women to attend. Listeners saw a "perfect sense of propriety which they exhibit in all their demeanor," and they also heard it: a quick note in *Godey's Lady's Book* read, "They excel in the singing of simple ballads, which they sing in such perfect harmony . . . that there seems among them but one voice, one heart, one soul." "Their chords sometimes grow on the ear like the swelling sounds of the organ," said the London *John Bull,* "and sometimes fade away like the faintest breathing of the Aeolian harp." The Hutchinsons' uncannily collective production was often attributed to their "pure moral and religious" upbringing which rightly steered the group and their "dangerous gift of great musical talent." Others more sensibly thought their excellent harmony "the result of constant practice."[32]

The moral fortitude that the Hutchinsons brought to popular music delivered a noticeable impact. Much as Catherine Ward Beecher's *Treatise on Domestic Economy* and Andrew Jackson Downing's *Cottage Residences* reorganized antebellum domestic space to fit with new visions of home life and leisure, the Hutchinson Family Singers and others reformulated popular song. At the heart of this endeavor stood what later generations have dubbed the "sentimental." Hutchinson Family Singers songs from "The Bereaved Slave Mother" to "My Mother's Bible" depended on an ability to evoke sympathetic responses from the listener (fig. 16). Whether depicting a slave mother watching her child being sold by auction or a youngster realizing the power of a Bible which her now-dead mother had given her, many Hutchinson Family Singers songs found ways for their fans to actualize the emotionalism—the pain and love—of a particular situation. Upon hearing Abby sing the line "Or had she a brother?" from the group's "Bridge of Sighs," Thomas Wentworth Higginson (the white colonel in command of the first black regiment of the Civil War) assumed that the song "not only told its own story, but called up forcibly the infinite wrongs of the slave girls who had no such protectors, and who perhaps stood at that very moment, exposed and shrinking, on the auction-block."[33]

Sympathy was one of the most powerful weapons reformers wielded in the 1840s. White families broken by drunkenness or black families broken by slavery, these texts, images, and songs flooded stores, stages, and exhibitions. That the Hutchinsons excelled at the practice is no surprise. Through their poignant use of sympathy, the Hutchinsons challenged their audiences to think of music as more than an enjoyable, social entertainment. Music, for them, was a civic act intimately guided by a humanistic Christianity.

The success of the Hutchinson Family Singers and similar musical acts pushed popular song toward new territory in the 1840s. At the start of the decade, it looked as if the blatant racial characterizations of early blackface minstrels would dominate the scene. And by the mid-1850s the widespread fame attained by Stephen Collins Foster's songs certainly attests to the sustained accomplishment of minstrel tunes. But the work of Stephen C. Foster differs from T. D. Rice's "Jump Jim Crow" of the 1830s and even Dan Emmett's "Old Dan Tucker" of the early 1840s.

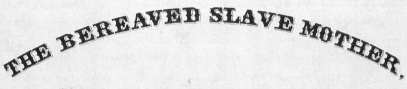

The Hutchinsons, "The Bereaved Slave Mother" (Boston: Henry Prentiss, 1844). Courtesy The New Hampshire Historical Society, Concord.

Blackface minstrelsy was, in essence, a product of northern cities where working-class whites and blacks often occupied similar spaces. As much as audiences in the northern countryside adored urban entertainments, it was not until blackface minstrels toned down the rougher edges of their performances—or, as one scholar has put it, until they domesticated their acts—that minstrelsy moved from its underground origins to truly captivate northern cultural consumers.

To accomplish this, minstrels followed the lead of the Hutchinson Family Singers and other artists whose entertainments enthralled the many "pious consumers" of the North. The Hutchinson Family Singers were never fond of blackface minstrels. One evening, when Asa suggested that the group attend a minstrel concert, John reportedly persuaded everyone to stay at home and hold a "family meeting," at which they sang the church tune "The Old Hundred" and "talked about heaven." Yet even though the New Hampshirites did not interact with minstrel performers, the Hutchinsons' success affected the minstrel genre. In 1844 advertisements for Buckley's Minstrels (who, not surprisingly, also promoted themselves as the Buckley Family) announced, "Their songs are sung in Harmony in the style of the Hutchinsons." But it did not stop there. Over the next few years, images on minstrel sheet music looked more and more like the four well-dressed Hutchinsons, presenting a hint of propriety, while the songs inside continued the racial characterizations of the "rollicking minstrel show." A quick look at the sheet music covers to "Jim Along Josey" (1840) and Stephen C. Foster's "Old Black Joe" (1860) begins to tell this tale (figs. 17 and 18).[34]

Frederick Douglass lived through the evolution of blackface minstrelsy. At first, the former slave and antislavery leader hated the musical form. When defending the "great good" of the Hutchinson Family Singers, he called minstrels "the filthy scum of white society, who have stolen from us a complexion denied to them by nature." Antislavery was hardly the only product made musical in the antebellum era, and Douglass found African-American impersonations done by blackfaced white performers unacceptable. Blackness, he said, was not for sale.

Things quickly changed with the success of the Virginia Minstrels and, later, Stephen C. Foster. Already by the 1850s some would

"Jim Along Josey," as sung by John N. Smith, arranged for the piano forte by "an Eminent Professor" (New York: Firth & Hall, 1840). From the Vocal Sheet Music Collection in the Irving S. Gilmore Music Library of Yale University.

Stephen C. Foster, "Old Black Joe" (New York: Wm. A. Pond, 1860). From the Vocal Sheet Music Collection in the Irving S. Gilmore Music Library of Yale University.

bemoan the loss of the comical racial manner of early minstrelsy—the *Spirit of the Times* thought that blackface performers should set out to accomplish only "what is the legitimate object of their costume and colored faces, namely the personification of the witty Negro." Others, like Frederick Douglass, saw the entertainment in a new light and claimed the songs of Foster responsible: "It would seem almost absurd to say it, considering the use that has been made of them, that we have allies in the Ethiopian songs," said the black lecturer in 1855. "They are heart songs, and the finest feeling of human nature are expressed in them. 'Lucy Neal,' 'Old Kentucky Home,' and 'Uncle Ned,' can make the heart sad as well as merry, and can call forth a tear as well as a smile. They awaken the sympathies for the slave, in which anti-slavery principles take root, grow and flourish."

Alexander Wheelock Thayer agreed: "There is real feeling in some of these songs." Foster—whose opening notes in "Oh! Susanna" are strikingly similar to Lowell Mason's "Missionary Hymn" and who by 1863 could be found writing a collection of hymns and Sunday school pieces—crafted a very different kind of minstrel tune, songs heavily reliant on nostalgia and sympathy:

> The head must bow and the back will have to bend,
> Wherever the darkey may go;
> A few more days, and the trouble all will end,
> In the field where the sugar canes grow;
> A few more days for to tote the weary load,
> No matter, 'twill never be light;
> A few more days till we totter on the road,
> Then my old Kentucky Home, good-night![35]

Finale

Chronology

—15 August 1845. Hutchinson Family Singers embark for England aboard the *Cambria*.

—27 August 1845. Frederick Douglass attempts antislavery lecture on the *Cambria*.

—28 August 1845. *Cambria* arrives in Liverpool.

—10 September 1845 to 3 July 1846. Hutchinson Family Singers perform in England and Ireland.

—29 December 1845. Texas admitted as the twenty-eighth state; slavery is legal there.

—17 July 1846. Hutchinson Family Singers return to the United States.

—8 August 1846. The Wilmot Proviso calls for abolition of slavery in territories obtained from Mexico.

—Fall 1846. John Parker Hale is elected as U.S. senator from New Hampshire (begins his term on 4 March 1847).

—23 February 1847. Battle of Buena Vista elevates victorious General Zachary Taylor to prominence.

—April 1847. Hutchinsons are barred from performing before racially integrated audiences in Philadelphia.

—3 December 1847. Debut of Frederick Douglass's *North Star.*

—1848. Jesse Jr. and Judson Hutchinson, "Eight Dollars a Day." James Russell Lowell, *The Biglow Papers.*

—March 1848. Hutchinson Family Singers' perform at tribute to Henry Clay in New York and are banned from the American Anti-Slavery Society.

—17 May 1848. Hutchinson Family Singers are readmitted to the American Anti-Slavery Society.

—August 1848. Free Soil Party convention.

—7 November 1848. Zachary Taylor, Whig, is elected president over Lewis Cass, Democrat, and Martin Van Buren, Free Soil.

—28 February 1849. Abby Hutchinson marries Ludlow Patton.

—Spring 1849. Publication of Henry David Thoreau's "Resistance to Civil Government" (later known as "Civil Disobedience") in Elizabeth Peabody's *Aesthetic Papers.*

—16 February 1851. Death of Jesse Hutchinson, father of the Hutchinson clan.

—5 June 1851. Harriet Beecher Stowe's first *National Era* installment of the series that, in 1852, becomes the novel *Uncle Tom's Cabin.*

—17 April 1853. Zephaniah Hutchinson dies in Illinois.

—15 May 1853. Jesse Hutchinson, Jr., dies in Ohio.

—30 May 1854. Kansas-Nebraska Act, a federal law creating the Kansas Territory and the Nebraska Territory; residents in each region were to decide on the legality of slavery by vote.

—19–20 May 1856. Charles Sumner's "Crime Against Kansas" speech.

—22 May 1856. Preston Brooks beats Sumner in the Senate chamber.

—24 May 1856. The Pottawatomie Massacre: amid violence by supporters on both sides of the slavery debate,

John Brown and company execute five proslavery supporters by sword.

—11 January 1859. Death of Judson Hutchinson.

—1860. John Hutchinson publishes *Hutchinson's Republican Songster.*

—25 November 1884. Asa Hutchinson dies.

—24 November 1892. Death of Abby Hutchinson Patton.

—1 May 1893. President Grover Cleveland officially opens
the World's Columbian Exposition in Chicago.

—25 August 1893. Colored People's Day at the Columbian
Exposition.

—20 February 1895. Death of Frederick Douglass.

—20 October 1908. John Hutchinson dies.

> When you came amongst us strangers
> Having braved the ocean dangers
> Cold perhaps, at first, we met,
> Now we part you with regret.
>
> You have sung in accents clear,
> Strains our souls delight to hear—
> Songs of Freedom, pure and holy
> Pleading for the poor and lowly.
>
> Jesse, Judson, John and Asa,
> Gentle Abby we address you;
> Not as Strangers now we meet you,
> But in Friendship true, we greet you.
>
> —Richard Davis Webb, Farewell to the
> Hutchinson Family Singers, Ireland, 1845

Exposition: American Antislavery Abroad, Racially Mixed Audiences at Home

"We left Boston Saturday afternoon, August 15, leaving friends all
well," wrote Asa. "We sang a song at parting in the time of 'Cranbam-
buli' in which we bid farewell to New England and expressed a hope
that we should have a safe passage in the 'Great Cambria' to the
Mother Country." Eager to test their talents abroad, the Hutchinson
Family Singers quit the personal comfort and professional security of

the United States to tour England and Ireland in 1845. Joining the likes of bugler Frank Johnson and minstrel man Thomas Dartmouth Rice, the Hutchinson troupe was about to enter a select company of American musicians who, in the years before the Civil War, reversed the flow of culture from Europe.[1]

Sailing the Atlantic under steam power alone started in 1838 with the *Sirius* of the St. George Steam Packet Company. A crossing that required six weeks in the 1790s needed only two weeks in the 1840s. The Hutchinsons, with good friend Frederick Douglass, trekked aboard the Cunard steamer *Cambria,* first to Halifax, then east to Liverpool. *Narrative of the Life of Frederick Douglass* had recently revealed Douglass's full identity, and so the famous abolitionist and fugitive slave left his native soil to avoid any likelihood of recapture. That he sent his master a copy of the book only aggravated his jeopardy.

On the ship, Captain Charles Judkins placed Douglass and his white antislavery companion James Buffum in steerage despite their willingness to pay for a more luxurious space. Refusing blacks first-class passage may not have been the official policy of the Cunard line, but it appears to have been standard practice. Douglass and Buffum suffered similar treatment on their return: this time they paid for a cabin, were assured that they would receive one, and then spent the voyage in steerage; amid the ensuing uproar, Samuel Cunard himself guaranteed changes.

Heading to England, the two abolitionists joked of their good fortune to be saving money. Nature, though, took care of all the passengers. Asa noted that the *Cambria* rode the Atlantic like a "wild sea gull," and Buffum, along with his friends in deluxe cabins, John and Judson Hutchinson, wrestled with wicked seasickness.[2]

In calmer seas, the Hutchinsons sang to delight the passengers. Tensions ran high aboard the vessel carrying abolitionists, especially Frederick Douglass, alongside slaveholders and other slavery supporters. The day before the trip ended, Captain Judkins, evidently an atoning ex–slave owner, asked Douglass to address the ship. After dinner and much drinking, passengers were invited to hear the "negro abolition preacher." As Douglass started, a New Orleans man, according to one of travelers, "poked himself into the circle, walked up to the speaker with his hands in his pockets and a 'quid' of tobacco in his mouth." The man listened to the speaker for a bit and then said, "I guess you're a liar." Douglass responded in kind. Tempers flared. "O, I wish I had you in Cuba!" shouted one of Douglass's challengers. "I wish I had him in Savannah!" said another, "We would use him up!"

At some point, the Hutchinsons stepped in with one of their "unrivalled songs." "Like the angel of old," said Douglass, they "closed the lions' mouth, so that, for a time, silence prevailed." The ruckus started again as Douglass lectured. Loud threats volleyed between the two sides, forcing the speaker to stop. Long after Douglass had relinquished the floor, Judkins sent for the irons. Threatening to lock up the passengers proved the only way to control them.

Standing alongside his *Cambria* opponents a few days later, Douglass took some satisfaction when he was admitted to the house of Westminster in Liverpool. By the end of his foreign stay, the black leader would gush about the respect accorded his race in England. Meanwhile, as American papers screamed of the "Riot on Board the Cambria," Asa Hutchinson simply noted that "Frederick Douglass attempted to speak on the quarter deck but was gagged down by a few slave holders and their employees." Over the years, the singer had grown accustomed to volatile display.

In England, Ireland, and Scotland, Douglass utilized the extensive transatlantic antislavery ties to secure venues. That he was met with a warm reception is not surprising. While Ireland and Scotland had very few black residents, a robust abolitionist sentiment permeated the United Kingdom. Following their friend's lead, the Hutchinson Family Singers blazed a reform trail through the country. Some of their ads announced, "MUSIC made subservient to the advancement of PEACE, FREEDOM and VIRTUE." A reviewer at their first English concert established them to be "regular Yankees," "tee-totalers," and "emancipators." The *Birmingham Journal* found that "a high tone of moral sentiment, and a pure spirit of philanthropy, breathes through them all." The group also fostered the same lore which flourished in America: "In the spring they put the seed in the ground," said a Manchester paper, "during the summer go out to sing, and in autumn return to gather in the harvest."

Establishing themselves in the international market did not take much time. Charles Sumner relayed to Henry Longfellow that a friend heard the Hutchinsons "*six* times, & saw Dickens, Foster, Milnes & others, among their audience." British listeners looked for many of the same traits that Americans admired in the group. "Their appearance and manners, like their songs, are characterized by great simplicity." Abby's "intonation is perfect," said one critic, "and her expression so *naïve* and artless as to gain the enthusiastic applause of the audience." And the New Hampshire musicians left no question as to their origin—"No man can listen to the Hutchinson family without feeling that America, has a national music, and none without delightedly acknowledging that 'the family' are happy in their illustrating of the harmony of New England." John, Abby, Judson, and Asa, or at least their stage personae, resonated well with their new viewers. "Right welcome is the Hutchinson Family," said the *London Morning Chronicle*.[3]

A number of negative reports appeared in the British press as well. Some claimed that the American family's repertoire consisted mainly of "English compositions that had their day 20 years back." Others said that the Hutchinson Family Singers "certainly cannot pretend to compete with any of our most finished specimens of professional glee-singing." Foreign reports that made it to American shores, though, celebrated the siblings' accomplishment. There was much to talk about. Meeting English luminaries such as Charles Dickens, the renowned antislavery leader George Thompson, and the popular authors William and Mary Howitt further enhanced the Hutchinsons' already large celebrity.

The Howitts, who would prove lifelong friends, published glowing accounts of Abby and her brothers in *Howitt's Journal of Literature and Popular Progress*. "They have the durability of the granite with the cordial spirit of home," said one piece. Eager fans also followed the Hutchinsons' trip through several public letters from the group. Judson wrote the *Lynn Pioneer* about the stark differences of class he witnessed in Ireland and in England (a theme also found in Asa's private correspondence). On a boat ride from London to Liverpool, so many Irish peasants packed the vessel that the Hutchinsons shared what little space they could find with animals. "Humanity was on a level with beasts," Judson said, "nay not on a level;—for the horses had awnings over them, and Humanity none." Jesse Jr., who was traveling with the Family Singers, described to Horace Greeley at the *New York Tribune* the early stages of a diseased Irish potato crop, which explained the multitudes of poor the group encountered.[4]

Though an ocean away, restless American admirers of the Hutchinsons had a window into what the siblings were doing and thinking. They did not, though, hear of four homesick musicians traveling the globe. Conquering new listeners provided the Hutchinsons a terrific rush, but they had left friends and family behind in exchange for the experience. John and Judson missed their wives and children. Timing for the trip could not have been worse for Asa, whose budding romance took a sabbatical when he boarded the *Cambria*. From London, Asa wrote the antislavery friend who had introduced the young lovers—"O, don't I love the yankees? particularly the girls? God bless them more especially *Lizzy*. I say don't you remember how I told you once in Nantucket . . . how I *loved Lizzy Chace?* I haven't forgotten it—if you have—neither have I forgotten her—neither shall I till I forget that I exist." Born March 14—the same day as Asa but five years later—Elizabeth B. Chace (or Chase) lived in Nantucket, Massachusetts. The daughter of a sea captain, Lizzy made Asa wonder why he had "lived so long a *bacelor*."[5]

Frederick Douglass had also left his wife and children for the trip, yet his reunion with them in 1847 overshadows those of the Hutchinsons, who had returned months earlier in 1846. Douglass had begun his foreign excursion a fugitive from slavery, still legally bound to owner Thomas Auld. In England, Ellen Richardson led a successful campaign to buy his freedom. The purchase upset many American abolitionists, who denounced the effort for dealing with a slave owner. Fortunately some, including the oft-critical William Lloyd Garrison, understood that the exchange was not about "trafficking with slaveholders," but about Douglass's emancipation. When the Hutchinson Family Singers came home, they delighted those on East Boston's wharf with "a pleasing and impressive" rendition of "Home Sweet Home"; Douglass rushed to Lynn from the *Cambria* to embrace his wife and children for the first time ever as an incontestably free man.[6]

The "brave-hearted band" returned from England to rumors of "having amassed comfortable fortunes." Taking time to rest in New Hampshire, the Hutchinson Family Singers resumed performing in the fall. Now with a European success on their résumé, the Hutchinsons played for "extensive" audiences armed with an "abundance of applause."[7]

The clapping stopped when the troupe reached Philadelphia.

Pennsylvania was one of the first states to have enacted emancipation legislation. But the measure freed not a single slave born before the state's emancipation day, 1 March 1780, and relegated children of slaves born after that date to slavery until the age of twenty-eight. No slave, then, had in theory to be freed until 1808, and various subversions of the law perpetuated slavery in Pennsylvania through 1847. In late 1846 and early 1847, anxieties over the growing free black population in Philadelphia flared in the form of resistance to the Hutchinsons. Following several performances which drew racially mixed audiences, the city's mayor informed trustees of Musical Fund Hall that rioting would result from any further desegregated shows. The Hutchinson Family Singers refused to play for white patrons alone. Rather than risk their property, managers for the concert hall closed it to the group.

Racial tensions festered throughout the nineteenth century in Philadelphia, New York, and many other northern cities with significant free black populations. Violence often rained down on African-American communities and on symbols of racial mixing; a New York orphanage for black children was burned during the Civil War, as was an antislavery hall constructed in Philadelphia in the 1830s. Though the Hutchinsons had repeatedly encouraged black listeners at concerts during their career, it was not until the Philadelphia incident that the group drew, and continued to draw, widespread criticism for the practice.

A New York paper dubbed them "Garrison's Nigger Minstrels," and many white Philadelphians stood outraged. "We have a serious charge to make against the managers of the 'Hutchinson family,' for not having announced in their handbills and advertisements, that no distinction of color would be made in admitting persons to their concerts," said a writer to the *Daily Sun*. "It is well known that a distinction is made on all ordinary occasions, and that there are many persons in the community who would on no account, knowingly, place themselves and their families in promiscuous association with the colored race."

Frederick Douglass's new publication, *The North Star,* shot back: the Hutchinsons would "in future contrive to make the poor unhappy mortals who are suffering in body and mind, from the dreadful scourge of colorphobia, understand, that they are not expected to attend the concerts. The Hutchinsons know, as every one else knows, that all diseases are more or less infectious." The *Daily Sun* continued its attack, saying that the African-American community should not be flattered by the "servility of public singers who would condescend to take their money, and sing to them." "If it be servility to take the 'colored person's' money, and give him in exchange that which he pays for," asked the Hutchinsons' black supporters, "what do you call it to take the 'colored person' himself, and give him nothing?"

A Philadelphia cartoonist lampooned the group for supposing blacks equal to whites, suggesting that the singers defended a bunch of unintelligent, disloyal black fans when refusing to support segregated venues (fig. 19). As Abby and one of her brothers perform in the background, a black man and a black women, surrounded by a group of disgusted white onlookers, engage in conversation: "Dat white gal got moss as good eddication as me," says the woman. "I tink I larn dem tunes and join de singers myself." With clear implications about the Hutchinsons' moral character, the two figures decide that the black woman is too "'spectable" to sing in public.

Writing in May 1847 from Plymouth, Massachusetts, where she was enrolled at the Edes Female Seminary, a seventeen-year-old Abby told Mary Howitt about Asa's recent wedding and added, "I suppose our English friends heard through the papers of the excitement we had at Philadelphia. We were very sorry that anything of the kind should happen, and more on account of the coloured people than for ourselves. It is so wrong that they should be excluded on account of their complexion." After the Hutchinson Family Singers debacle, lessees of Musical Fund Hall agreed to two conditions—"That no Anti-Slavery lecture shall be delivered" and "That no colored person may form a portion of any audience."[8]

THE HUTCHINSON FAMILY.

" Wot you tink Missy Phillis; dat consart am berry good music ?" " Berry
well, Sambo.   Dat white gal got moss as good eddication as me.   I tink de
superlatives ob her voice am berry obnoxious."   " Ah, dat am de truff.   Be.
kase dey gib de bobbolition song dat am de reason dat de music sound so
doloriferous dis ebening."   " I tell you wot, Sambo, I tink I larn dem tunes
and join de singers myself.   Den I gib dem de rail colored sound wen I
sing de same."   " Phew! Missy Phillis—you aint in arnest 'bout dat—wot
you want to 'spose yourself for to go 'round wid singers arter dat fashion ?
Young lady, like you, is too 'spectable to 'tand up dar and sing song for
odder people."   "Praps you is right, Sambo.   Praps I better marry dat
white gemman dat advertises for a wife in de Tribune.   Missus tinks dat I
better hab de white gemman."   " Wot dat you say, Missy Phillis !   You
tink you stoop to hab a white man, wen dis darkey hab been payin' 'tention
to you for six monfs.   You is de most onsconciable colored female dat I
ebber seen sense Dorcas Gumbo died."

"The Hutchinson Family" in *Turner's Comic Almanac, 1848* (Philadelphia:
Turner & Fisher, 1847). Courtesy The Library Company of Philadelphia.

Development: Antiwar Culture and Political Antislavery, 1845–1848

The antislavery movement had made great strides since the Hutchinsons had gone to Europe, yet the infighting between political abolitionists and moral abolitionists grew. Trying to keep the sides united
while furthering the antislavery cause, the Hutchinsons got caught in a

tangled web of alliances across varying degrees of reform allegiance; the more people who stood beneath antislavery's umbrella, the more that antislavery, and antislavery alone, became the binding issue. Women's rights, black equality, and a host of other subjects dear to the most ardent social reformers increasingly took a back seat.

Election-day success for abolitionist politicos particularly contributed to the strain. While the Hutchinsons performed in England, New Hampshire voters had selected John P. Hale as the first antislavery activist to the United States Senate. Many abolitionists cheered the event—indeed, cannon blasts shook Concord in celebration—but the victory came with a price, according to antislavery purists.

The senator had been the Democratic representative for New Hampshire until, in January 1845, he broke with his party, condemning the annexation of Texas as a scheme to further slavery. Tossed out by party managers, Hale waged a nasty campaign in 1846, but it would have been useless without securing substantial backing. The Independent Democrats, the political subgroup to which Hale and his antislavery conscience now belonged, did not have the political strength in the state to ensure victory—not even allied with the Liberty Party, whose leaders, after Hale displayed enough antislavery rhetoric, had abandoned their original candidate for the seat.

Hale and friends turned to the Whigs in the winter of 1845–1846 and struck a deal. The Whig Party agreed to support the antislavery senatorial candidate if Hale supporters would help make Anthony Colby, an antislavery Whig, governor of New Hampshire. Both Hale and Colby won, and the coalition proved even stronger than first imagined, splitting other state positions between Independents and Whigs, and sending another Liberty candidate to fill a shortened term in the Senate. The political partnership born out of a shared opposition to slavery used its sudden dominance in the state to deliver resolutions against Texas annexation and the Mexican War, and also promised New Hampshire support for "every just and well-directed effort for the suppression and extermination of that terrible scourge of our race, human slavery."[9]

After the election, Hale's Independent Democrats and the New Hampshire Liberty Party formally united and nominated John Hale as their 1848 presidential candidate. "New Hampshirizing" other states soon developed into a central focus of political abolitionists. Deals and alliances appeared all over the North. At the New York State constitutional convention, the Liberty Party exchanged votes for the Whig Party's lowering of the barriers to black suffrage.

By the late 1840s slavery had become—as it had been in the years before 1820—a catalyst for political bargaining. The Whig Charles Sumner, analyzing antislavery sentiment, said, "In most of the free states it will hold the balance between the two parties, so that neither can succeed without yielding to it in a greater degree." Sumner was only partly right. The two parties he saw squirming in the slavery/antislavery vise would not be the same two to emerge from the workbench. A "Hale storm" had struck the northern political scene.[10]

"I was somewhat amused, a short time ago, at one of the concerts of the Hutchinsons," said Senator Hale to the American and Foreign Anti-Slavery Society, "at following the poor wanderer in one of their songs, in search of 'Down East.'" The wanderer searched everywhere from New York to Maine for "Away Down East," yet he could not find it. Hale envisioned a similar tale if one set out to look for "American Government." "Washington is the very last corner in the Union I would look," he mused. President James K. Polk "will tell you that the first and last article of his political creed is to learn, in the first place, the will of his constituents, and, in the next place, to do it!"

Hale spoke on behalf of a growing number of northerners disgruntled by the Polk presidency. Though the annexation of Texas was all but complete when Polk arrived in office in 1845, it quickly became clear that the president harbored other imperial visions. His administration would settle a dispute over the Oregon Territory through negotiations with the greatest consumer of southern cotton, the British, gaining the territory below the forty-ninth parallel (short of a campaign promise to get "Fifty-four Forty or fight"); but, to the south, Polk clearly desired more than just Texas from Mexico.[11]

In 1845, when Texas became part of the United States, the Mexican government halted diplomatic interaction with its northern neighbor and rejected an offer from Polk to purchase the territory which is today mostly New Mexico and California. Frustrated, the president as commander in chief ordered military units under the command of General Zachary Taylor to the northeastern bank of the Rio Grande, close to the Gulf of Mexico. The Rio Grande, Polk decided unilaterally, was to be the border between Mexico and Texas. In May 1846 Mexican soldiers attacked Taylor's troops, whom they believed had crossed into Mexico. Polk rushed to Congress to obtain a declaration of war. One Iowa citizen rightly assessed the situation: "This is a matter that belongs exclusively to J. K. Polk & Co."

By early 1848 the hostilities had all but ended. American troops stood in Mexico City, and some members of Congress urged Polk to take all of Mexico. In the event, the Treaty of Guadalupe Hidalgo required the United States to pay $15 million in wartime damages, but also provided for the Mexican Cession: Mexico surrendered a little more than half of its territory, a region encompassing parts of present-day Texas, Colorado, Arizona, New Mexico, and Wyoming, and all of California, Utah, and Nevada. Polk's military campaign elevated the United States' status as a key player in the Americas.[12]

For several years the war had stirred controversy. Henry David Thoreau gave an account in "Civil Disobedience" of his refusal to pay a poll tax in protest against the conflict, while James Russell Lowell's satiric *The Biglow Papers* denounced the link between slavery and American expansionism. The Hutchinsons chimed in, too. Using a recent raise given to members of Congress as their fulcrum, they sang "Eight Dollars a Day":

And the next in the order of the day comes the mad cry of war.
While very few of the longest heads can tell what it is for,
But "War Exists" all parties cry and th' enemy we must slay.
So Congress backs the President,—at Eight dollars a day. (fig. 20)

In politics the Democrat David Wilmot wished to end the connection between territorial expansion and the extension of slavery through an 1846 proposal banning human bondage within any territory acquired from Mexico. Though no Congress ever passed the Wilmot Proviso, votes on the measure over the years demonstrate a sectionalism that would eventually cripple American government—northerners in Congress overwhelmingly voted for Wilmot, and southerners voted against it by an even larger margin. The Whig Party sought a way around the regional differences created by slavery and

FOR ONE NIGHT ONLY!

THE

HUTCHINSON

FAMILY!

JUDSON, ABBY, JOHN & ASA,

On their return from New York, respectfully announce to the
citizens of NEW HAVEN that they will give

ONE VOCAL ENTERTAINMENT!

AT EXCHANGE HALL,
Monday Ev'g, May 27.

PROGRAMME.

PART I.

QUARTETTE.

"WE'RE WITH YOU ONCE AGAIN."

Words by Geo. P. Morris.   Music by Hutchinson.

"We're with you once again, kind friends,
No more our footsteps roam;
Where it began our journey ends,
Amid the scenes of home."

QUARTETTE.

Old Clock on the Stairs.

Music by   Hutchinson.
Written by Professor Longfellow, on visiting an ancient and time honored country residence

Somewhat back from the village street,
Stands an old fashioned country seat;
Across its antique Portico,
Tall Poplar Trees their shadows throw,
And from its station in the hall,
An ancient Timepiece says to all,
Forever! Never!
Never! Forever!

SOLO AND CHORUS.

California Song.—GOLD! GOLD! GOLD!!

Words by   Jesse Hutchinson, Jr.
[This Song was written expressly for a Company of Overland Emigrants to California—the Sagamore and Sacramento Company—who left Massachusetts in the Spring of '49.

We're form'd our band, and are all well mann'd,
To journey afar to the promis'd Land,
Where the Golden Ore is rich in store,
On the Banks of the Sacramento Shore.

PART II.

SOLO AND CHORUS.

HORTICULTURAL WIFE.

Written by a confirmed English Gardener, over head and ears in love.

She's my Myrtle, my Geranium,
My Sun-Flower, my Sweet Marjorum.

QUARTETTE.

THE OLD FARM HOUSE.

Melody by I. B. Woodbury.   Arranged by Hutchinson.

After many, many years, how pleasant 'tis to come
To the Old Farm House where we were born,
Our Best, our Childhood's Home.

SOLO.

"IF I WERE A VOICE"

Music by   Hutchinson.

If I were a Voice, a persuasive Voice,
That could travel the wide world through,
I would fly on the beams of the morning light,
And speak to men with a gentle might,
And tell them to be true.
I would fly, I would fly over land and sea,
Wherever a human heart might be,
Telling a tale or singing a song,
In praise of the right, in blame of the wrong.

QUARTETTE.

"GOOD OLD DAYS OF YORE."

A SONG OF HOME.

Words and Music by   Hutchinson.

How my heart is in me burning,
And my inmost soul is yearning,
As my thoughts go backward turning
To the good old days of yore.
When my Father and my Mother,
And each Sister dear and Brother,
Sang and chatted with each other,
Round the good old Cottage Door.
Dear Old Homestead, Cottage Door.

PART III.

Uncle SAM's Farm.

A GENERAL INVITATION TO THE WORLD.

Words by   Jesse Hutchinson, Jr.

Of all the mighty Nations in the east or in the west,
Our glorious Yankee Nation is the greatest and the best;
We have room for all creation and our Banner is unfurled,
With a general invitation to the people of the world.

DESCRIPTIVE SONG.

SHIP ON FIRE!

Melody by   Russell.

The Storm o'er the Ocean,
Flew furious and fast.

CONGRESSIONAL SONG.

"EIGHT DOLLARS A DAY."

Words and Music by   Hutchinson.

At Washington fall once a year do politicians throng,
Contriving there by various arts to make their sessions long;
Aye, many a reason do they give why they're obliged to stay,
But the clearest reason yet adduced, is—"Eight Dollars a Day."

FINALE.

THE OLD GRANITE STATE.

Containing a Family History of the Sons and Daughters of

THE "TRIBE OF JESSE."

TICKETS 50 Cents.   For sale at Skinner & Sperry's Music
Store, Durrie & Peck's Bookstore, at the Tontine, and at the Door.
Concert to commence at 8 o'clock.

From Benham's Cheap Job Engine Press.

[1850]

Poster for the Hutchinson
Family at Exchange Hall,
New Haven, 27 May 1850.
From Misc. Ms. 300 New
Haven Concert Programs
in the Irving S. Gilmore
Music Library of Yale Uni-
versity.

proposed that no territory at all be acquired from the Mexican War. Continuing a traditional Whig opposition to expanding national boundaries, the suggestion sidestepped the faction-causing Wilmot Proviso, giving the party a chance for unity through what was ultimately an antiwar stance.

The Whig Henry Clay, who had lost to Polk in the 1844 election, resurfaced in late 1847 filled with venom for his political opponent and for the war. He promoted the No Territory option while hoping to gain his party's presidential nomination. But the war's end in 1848 undermined Clay's stance. The country got hold of quite a lot of territory with no surefire solution to the debate over slavery that was certain to develop. Yet in a short time the Whig politician had earned much respect from the antiwar contingent in the North.[13]

Though they once had mocked him on their sheet music cover, the Hutchinsons probably started liking Clay more in 1847, particularly after southern Whigs pushed General Taylor for president. Taylor's victory at Buena Vista early in 1847 had turned him into a mythic military man, the kind who often wins elections. Many northerners at first opposed Taylor for his slave ownership and his leadership during what they held to be an unwarranted war. In that context, the Hutchinson Family Singers' acceptance of an 1848 invitation by the Board of Alderman of New York City to a tribute for Henry Clay is understandable.

Jesse Hutchinson, Jr., wrote a song for the occasion, a greeting called "To Harry of the West":

> Come, brothers, rouse, let's hurry out
> To see our honored guest;
> For lo! in every street they shout,
> "Brave Harry of the West!"

After this and several other selections, the New Hampshire vocalists felt they justified their appearance by singing "The Old Granite State" to Clay, slaveholder and gradual emancipationist. With the song's cry of "equal rights for all," the Hutchinson Family Singers thought they advanced abolitionism. One New York paper agreed, noting that the Hutchinsons' music served as an antislavery warning for the guest.

But Henry Clay—of whom it had been said that no man was "more abhorred by the abolitionists"—had earned a distinctive hatred from staunch antislavery activists. That Clay looked less friendly to slavery than Taylor meant very little. "We find it hard to fancy the angel-hearted Abby singing the praise of a notorious trafficker in human flesh," Frederick Douglass roared. "We charitably believe that her heart was not there, and if it was, the angel was not." Douglass concluded with a blow the likes of which he had often defended the singers from: "Alas! a love of popularity has triumphed over their love of principle. Their moorings are loosed, and there is no telling where they will stop."

For every reformer who found the Hutchinson Family Singers' "act so derogatory to their anti-slavery reputation," there was another who saw the performance as "an opportunity" to "influence" Clay "on the side of freedom." But leaders of the movement—Wendell Phillips, William Garrison, and others—thought that the Hutchinsons had gone too far in their bid to expand antislavery's influence, and banned the group from the American Anti-Slavery Society.[14]

The Hutchinson Family Singers were no doubt stunned to be expelled from the very organization which once had helped launch their career. But their reform popularity had long since extended beyond Garrison's friends. After singing antislavery songs in Washington, D.C., in April, the group headed to New York, where they played at a meeting of the American and Foreign Anti-Slavery Society on 9 and 10 May 1848. The Hutchinsons sang along with the Luca boys, four black brothers from New Haven, to an integrated audience. By the next week, leaders of the American Anti-Slavery Society began to rethink their punishment: if the singers would, "through some appropriate medium, frankly and unhesitatingly express their regret," then, Society leaders announced, they might reconsider.

Henry Wright reported on the May standoff: "I am in the Minerva Rooms, on Broadway, in New York city, the commercial emporium of the Western continent. I am sitting by a table, in front of a platform, on which sit Wm. L. Garrison, as President of the American Anti-Slavery Society, Francis Jackson, Wendell Phillips, and others. The hall is full, and we are in a most exciting and pleasant scene. I can term it nothing less than 'The Hutchinsons' Repentance.'"

As was their fashion, the Hutchinson Family Singers startled those in attendance with an impromptu song for emancipation. Garrison then asked, "Do they wish us to take this as evidence of their repentance? Are they sorry for what they have done?" The abolitionist leader went on, "If they are sorry for the deed, we shall hear from them again." No melodies or messages came from the Hutchinson camp that afternoon or evening. The group waited until the next day, 17 May 1848, to sound "their eulogy of Henry Clay." Welcoming the musicians back, Garrison said, "Anti-slavery claims them for her own, and should and will, I trust, have them to be *all* her own."[15]

Working for political abolitionist organizations in the heat of the summer of 1848 was certainly not what Garrison had in mind. But the Hutchinson Family Singers and many other antislavery supporters saw an opportunity for a grand political alliance. The lost impact of the antiwar position had combined with a rise in sectional concerns over slavery to create a volatile political landscape in which Hale, the very man who had become synonymous with forming successful political combinations, would find his presidential campaign undone by the chance for an even greater assemblage. In August, Whigs searching for an option to the party's presidential candidate, the slave owner Zachary Taylor; Independent Democrats with no other available forum for their antislavery ideas; and Liberty Party members looking for the big victory at the polls which had so far eluded them, traveled to Buffalo, New York, to form a political union capable of seriously influencing, if not winning, the upcoming presidential election.

Between ten and twenty thousand delegates packed the convention. By the second day, they decided on a platform of opposition to the expansion of slavery, the separation of the federal government from slavery, and support for cheaper postage and government, as well as tax reform, internal improvements, and free homesteads. The meeting then moved to pick a presidential candidate. John P. Hale, the Liberty Party's nominee, was rather quickly dismissed. His party's leaders had come to Buffalo ready to barter Hale's position for leverage, and they would trade it for a "thorough Liberty platform." Former President Martin Van Buren emerged as the best-liked option for the new party. Benjamin F. Butler, who as a Union general was later to cause a stir by

protecting runaway slaves from their southern owners during the Civil
War, soothed Van Buren doubters by claiming that the ex-president
would ban slavery in the District of Columbia if elected.

During the convention Butler often called for the Hutchinsons,
but only Jesse Jr. had made it to Buffalo. Time and again, Jesse gathered
volunteers to sing. The crowd "rapturously received" the songs with
"repeated cheers and laughter."

> Let the people shout together,
> In the old free states;
> We're the friends of freedom,
> And our motto is free soil,

wrote Jesse for a song he called "The Old Free States":

> O! the south begins to tremble,
> In the old slave states,
> For their days are numbered,
> And 'tis written on the wall.

"Free Soil" became the party's mantra and name, while "FREE SOIL,
FREE LABOR, FREE SPEECH AND FREE MEN" emblazoned party emblems.
More than ten years earlier Lydia Maria Child had suggested that free
workers were necessarily more productive than enslaved workers; "a
very brief glance will show that slavery is inconsistent with economy,
whether domestic or political," she said in *An Appeal in Favor of
That Class of Americans Called Africans.* Those in Buffalo emphatically
agreed. The Free Soil Party was the first significant antislavery political
party to steer clear of civil rights ideas for African Americans in their
platform. Black leaders Frederick Douglass and Henry Bibb did address the convention, and most blacks supported the new party, but
Free Soilers ran the gamut from former Liberty Party men who understood the near impossibility of a winning national party founded on
equal rights to candidly racist ex-Democrats who embraced Free Soil
as a means to keep blacks out of new American territories. "The oppressed and downtrodden of the world look to this country for homes;

and if we allow slavery to be introduced into the territories of the South and West, these people can never find a home there," cautioned Benjamin Butler, who remained silent on black Americans while showing deep concern for white immigrants. "Free labor cannot exist where slavery holds sway."[16]

The Hutchinson Family Singers had intended to travel to Buffalo for the meeting, but "circumstances," Jesse Jr. said, "forbid it." We do not know what happened, though back in June 1848, when Frederick Douglass's *North Star* visited the Hutchinsons in Milford, "We found Asa hoeing, Jordan [Judson] building a stone fence, and John ploughing." Perhaps the singers didn't want to break summer vacation before their arduous fall touring schedule kicked in. Whatever the reason, they did not visit the Free Soil meeting in August. Meanwhile, the *North Star* reversed its criticism of the Hutchinson Family Singers over the Clay incident—"Here were a company of the most popular vocalists in this country. . . . Instead of being out constantly seeking sordid gold, which they have only to seek, in order to find, [they are] deliberately working away on their farms."[17]

The agricultural vocalists did join the political fray in September 1848 when they appeared at a New Hampshire Free Soil convention in Concord, "the largest and most enthusiastic Convention that has assembled here for years," according to the *Democrat and Freeman*. John's journal for the fall records playing "a Free Soil song that brought down the house" in Worcester, Massachusetts, and in other New England locations. The 291,804 Free Soil votes (14 percent of the total) in the national election marked a decided increase of almost five times the Liberty Party's 1844 results. Yet Van Buren did not win a single state. Only in Vermont, Worcester County, upstate New York, northeastern Illinois, and southeastern Wisconsin did the Free Soil candidate earn a plurality, and in rare cases a majority, of the popular ballot.

The Free Soil Party had hurt northern Democrats the most. Whigs, too repulsed to vote for a man who once had stood as a symbol of Jacksonian democracy, did not turn to the new organization en masse. In New York, where Van Buren ran in second place, the Free Soil Party tipped the state's large electoral balance—and thirty-two of the thirty-four New York congressional posts—to the Whigs. Free Soilers also sent twelve members to Congress. But the effect of the third party is not told by the numbers. The threat of losing voters to an antislavery party forced northern Whigs and northern Democrats to more fully showcase a commitment against slavery's extension.

For all the talk about the land obtained from Mexico, nothing much had been done with it by the time Taylor ascended to the presidency in 1849. Endless fights abounded over whether each territory would enter the Union as a free or slave state, or whether the residents of the territory should be allowed to decide the question. The Hutchinson Family Singers were always on the side of keeping slavery out. But their own internal divisions were becoming harder to handle. Abby told Mary Howitt, "We sang like angels sometimes on the stage, and then rushed off and say to each other—why didn't you sing better, and some other sharp speeches which singers and sinners only know how to make." In 1849 the Hutchinsons found themselves on a list cataloging "the field of Human Greatness," along with Shakespeare, Mozart, and Benjamin Franklin. How much longer the group could hold such stature would soon be in doubt.[18]

Recapitulation, Opening: Abby's Retirement, 1849

"Thanks for a slice of the wedding cake," said William Lloyd Garrison, "and our best wishes for the happiness of the parties." On 28 February 1849 Abby Hutchinson married Ludlow Patton in New York City. "ABBY HUTCHINSON NO MORE" ran the headline in a New York paper, as if the nineteen-year-old had died. "This nest of brothers, with a sister in it," noted the *National Era,* "has been robbed." The dramatics were appropriate. Not only was the "American Jenny Lind" no longer single, but her union with Ludlow ushered in a new phase for the singing troupe (fig. 21).[19]

Ludlow wrote Frederick Douglass, "I want Abby as my private companion, and not as an amusement for the crowds." He expected his wife to "retire to the shades" and "happiness . . . of private life." Patton's ideas were not the rantings of an overprotective spouse; they represented a normal expectation for wedded women in the 1840s. Jenny Lind, upon becoming Jenny Goldschmidt during her American tour, faced a similar fate. A little more than a decade after Abby's marriage, the media mocked Mary Todd Lincoln for refusing to retire to "private

Portrait of Abby Hutchinson by Frank Carpenter. Courtesy The Lynn Museum and Historical Society, Lynn, Massachusetts.

womanhood" following her husband's assassination. Abby's calling, as one journalist summed it, now rested in the anticipation that her "musical powers, sweet face, and modest deportment, will descend to another generation." Abby was now "wholly absorbed in another, and we shall here from her no more."

In 1841 a resilient seventy-four-year-old John Quincy Adams said that "while a remnant of physical power is left me to write and speak, the world will retire from me before I shall retire from the world." Abby never had such an option. The marriages of John, Judson, and Asa increased tensions in the musical group, but had never threatened its existence during the 1840s. Though members of the Hutchinson Family Singers proved strong advocates for women's rights in the upcoming years, they lived this reality: married men were free to pursue whatever calling they wished; married women were free to raise a family and, if brothers and husbands allowed, were fortunate to appear on stage.[20]

Soon after the wedding, Abby Hutchinson Patton fell severely ill. For a while, the family feared that they might lose her. Readers of the *Saturday Evening Post, Scientific American,* and other publications tracked the young woman's illness. Apparently doctors advised Abby to fast, which she did for an extended period. Further details were not disclosed, but she had convalesced enough by the fall of 1849 to move from Milford for treatment at a water-cure establishment. The relocation must have worked because in 1850 the young singer took the stage again with her brothers. Abby's retirement was real, yet never absolute. By 1851 lingering questions of her still working forced a public renouncement of professional ties to her brothers in the publication the *Message Bird.* "Brothers speak in whispers light," Abby would soon sing on stage in "The Brides Departure"; "'Tis my last, my last good night." In upcoming years, though, she used a variety of charitable causes—from antislavery events to benefits for the Five Points Mission in New York—as excuses to rejoin the singing troupe.

Abby's departure undermined the Family Singers' already deteriorating dynamic. As Frederick Douglass had predicted, the brothers presented "a lonely aspect" without their sister. "After church 'Judson & John & Asa' had a 'scuffle' away in the bushes," noted Asa in the 1850s—the three, especially John and Asa, increasingly and easily lost patience with one another without their sister nearby. Meanwhile, newspaper reports over the next decade recorded Judson's loosening grip—"*Judson Hutchinson, one of the Hutchinson Family Singers, is insane,*" reported the *Saturday Evening Post.*[21]

Their personal troubles aside, there is no denying the entrenchment of the Hutchinson Family Singers and their do-good musical philosophy in popular consciousness throughout the 1850s. Minstrels had loved poking fun at the Hutchinsons as far back as the early

1840s—the Ethiopian Serenaders' "The Old Virginny State" from 1844 turned the message of the "Old Granite State" on its head. Notably, even during the Hutchinson Family Singers' decline, minstrels still found them a worthy target. At 633 Broadway in New York during the 1855 concert season, "the principal members of the original and well known Christy's Minstrels" gave a series of what they claimed to be "Chaste and Fashionable" concerts in which their headline act was a burlesque called "The Hutchinson Family."

While the content of the Christy's act is unknown, the group was an easy quarry, for New York audiences remained well versed in the Hutchinsons' mannerisms and presentations. The minstrels undoubtedly scorned the Hutchinson Family Singers' beliefs, highlighting their controversies over playing for desegregated audiences; in keeping with the tradition of burlesque parody, the Christy's show surely removed the Hutchinson Family Singers' from their lofty post as reform musicians, rendering them in something less than a beatific mode.[22]

The Hutchinson Family Singers had collected enough renown by 1846 to endure without a family-styled stage presentation. Yet something went wrong. Clearly, Abby's retirement alone was not the reason for the group's demise. The Hutchinsons' continued efforts for an integrated America, combined with the group's metamorphosis into a band of bickering brothers, eventually would complete the push of the Hutchinson Family Singers to the fringe of the cultural landscape. Papers had lavished praise on the group in 1845 even while they sang "the most ultra sentiments in the city of New York." "Citizens of Baltimore!" read an 1852 announcement, "are you willing to be insulted by a band of abolitionists, singing strains of fanaticism?" Where once the Virginia politician Henry Wise claimed to enjoy a 1844 Hutchinsons performance, during the political campaign of 1855, a Virginia senator called the "songs of the Hutchinson family" a declaration "against that greatest of all liberties, the liberty of conscience."[23]

A growing sectionalism in the United States was only part of the problem. The limits on reform speech had shifted. By the 1850s the enlarged antislavery body in the North had not formed according to the Hutchinsons' ideals. Unlike the most mainstream Free Soilers (and their progeny in the Republican Party founded in 1854), members of the Hutchinson Family Singers held fast to notions of racial tolerance, if not racial equality, for the American nation. ("How nobly they cling to the principles of liberty and humanity," praised Frederick Douglass in 1855.) White supremacy, though, proved more potent for politicians and popular entertainers. Music and musicians offering a blend of sympathy, piety, and strict racial hierarchy—think of Stephen Collins Foster—gained the most attention.

At one point, politicians could turn to the intermediary stances of extending the line set by the Missouri Compromise or to popular sovereignty—letting the people in a territory vote on the issue of slavery—to satisfy both the proslavery and antislavery public. But by 1854 these two options had dissolved. The Missouri Compromise was killed by the Kansas-Nebraska Act (1854), which gave residents the right to decide the fate of slavery in those two territories, and in turn the fairness of popular sovereignty was undone by the Democrat Stephen Douglas, who had suggested it as a means of bringing slavery to areas once considered free. Violent struggles to plant as many supporters in the new territories as necessary to shift the vote further sullied a ballot-based solution. After the 1855 congressional election, the remaining party that could claim to hold North and South together under its auspices, the Democratic Party, would lose viability in the North, the victim of antislavery sentiment and the emergence of the Know-Nothing Party, a nativist organization whose members swore not to vote for a Catholic or any foreign-born candidate.

The Hutchinson Family Singers knew firsthand of the American enmity between Protestants and Catholics. New Hampshire's constitution prohibited Catholics from some state offices, and already back in 1844, before the great migrations of Irish Catholics to the United States, several concerts of the Hutchinsons had failed to attract large audiences when they played in Baltimore's Calvert Hall. "The Protestants don't like to go into Calvert Hall because it is owned by Catholics," said Asa.

A tremendous influx of 2,939,000 immigrants into the United States between 1845 and 1854—a figure representing 14.5 percent of the 1845 population—exacerbated these tensions. Nearly 41 percent of those immigrants, about 1,200,000, came from Ireland. Many of the newcomers were quickly swept into the Democratic Party's efficient urban political machines. Whigs and antislavery reformers thus shared a degree of loathing for the foreign-born who would spurn their political beliefs. The rise of the Know-Nothings worked hand-in-hand with a lot of what antislavery politicians had to offer—rural northerners who backed these platforms revered free labor, Protestantism, temperance, and nativism, turning the Catholic, hard-drinking Irish into the enemy.[24]

An antislavery and Know-Nothing alliance could not succeed, though, for the very reason that Benjamin Butler once explained to Free Soilers: to ease the strain of new immigrants on American urban centers, free states were needed to attract foreign-born workers to western expanses. Immigrants played an important role in free-labor antislavery thought, making the nativist party, already repugnant to some for its bigoted stance, even less attractive. So after extensive Know-Nothing victories in 1854 nearly squashed the Whig Party, Whig politicians like Charles Seward and Abraham Lincoln abandoned their sinking ship for the newly formed Republican Party. "As a nation, we began by declaring that 'all men are created equal,'" said Lincoln. "Now we practically read it as 'all men are created equal, except negroes.' When the Know-Nothings get control, it will read 'all men are created equal, except negroes, foreigners, and Catholics.'"[25]

In 1856 John Brown and his sons killed five Kansas settlers who allegedly supported slavery. A few days earlier, hundreds of proslavery men from Missouri had sacked an antislavery newspaper and other "free" buildings in Lawrence, Kansas. Armed conflict between proslavery and antislavery forces tore through the territory of Kansas, an experiment in popular sovereignty gone wrong. "You are now called to redress a great transgression," proclaimed Republican Charles Sumner at the start of a speech to Congress entitled "The Crime Against Kansas."

Sumner reported only the violent acts of proslavery forces in his speech, while singling out South Carolina's Senator Andrew Pickens Butler as a leader of the so-called Slave Power. Two days later, Preston Brooks, Butler's cousin, beat Sumner nearly to death on the Senate floor. The attack outraged northerners to such an extent that the wave of nativist sentiment which the Know-Nothing Party was riding in 1856, and which many thought would help them capture the presidency, crashed, and was soon swept out by an antislavery fervor. Fol-

lowing the election, the Republicans and Democrats stood as two pil-
lars of American politics ready to trade blows across slavery's sectional-
ized divide.[26]

Recapitulation, Closing: The End of the Hutchinson Family Singers

A quick visit with the Hutchinson family in the 1850s shows why the
singing troupe's legacy should stem from their 1840s music and activism. On the surface, it appears that the group thrived in the years
just before the Civil War. And a look at their campaign songs over the
years—"Get Off the Track!" (1844; Liberty Party), "The Old Free
States" (1848; Free Soil Party), and "Lincoln and Liberty" (1860; Republican Party)—certainly helps to explain the mindset of antislavery politics. The brash cries of the two earlier songs promise a steam-
rolling for those opposed to antislavery. The 1860 piece seeks salvation
through a leader:

> Hurrah for the choice of the nation!
> Our chieftain so brave and so true;
> We'll go for the great reformation,
> For Lincoln and Liberty too!

A more personal change, though, lurks beneath any study of the
group's songs. To state it plainly, it was not the group which thrived
as the Civil War approached. Collaborative endeavors among the siblings diminished as the 1850s progressed—indeed, John Hutchinson
published on his own *Hutchinson's Republican Songster,* which included
"Lincoln and Liberty." While they were to remain reformers in thought
and in action, members of the Hutchinson Family Singers had begun
to squander a most powerful asset, their voice as a group, choosing instead to act as individuals. The result equaled an end to the exceptional
success of their brand of musical advocacy.[27]

Eighteen fifty-three: With the national political dialogue around
slavery's expansion distilling to its two most extreme positions, free soil
or enslaved soil, the Hutchinson Family Singers (without Abby) could

not capitalize on or really influence the situation, though they had helped establish a vibrant cultural space for such a discussion. The musicians now worked, even in the minds of many northerners, as radicals advocating amalgamation and civil rights for blacks. In their stead, Harriet Beecher Stowe and *Uncle Tom's Cabin* fulfilled the mission. The soap-opera-like serialization of the novel titillated readers with its Christian portrayal of the wrongs of slavery. *Uncle Tom's Cabin* meant many different things to readers, but, as William Lloyd Garrison pointed out in his review, Stowe certainly embraced the idea of "African colonization." In closing, Stowe directs readers to educate and Christianize freed slaves in the North, and then "let them go to Africa."[28]

Asa Hutchinson saw the transformation of antislavery in the wake of Stowe's work. He surmised that the famous antislavery statement, "Am I not a man and brother?" had changed—"Am I not a man and *Uncle?*" he scribbled in his journal. For those who chose to ignore Stowe's final instructions, the novel "was a voice of God in behalf of the oppressed." So taken by the Christian ideals exemplified in the work, Asa wrote Stowe for permission to stage the novel (likely without the colonizationist ending). She refused. Asa turned to music, writing the melody for "Little Topsy's Song" in 1853. Eliza Cook's lyrics celebrated Little Eva's ability to see the good in Topsy while deriding her "Ole Missus" and the merciless institution of slavery:

> This is Topsy's human song
> Topsy's cute and clever,
> Hurrah then for the white child's work
> Humanity forever!

Frederick Douglass wrote, "This song deserves a wide circulation; and it will have it."[29]

In 1853, to defend herself against charges that she had presented a fictionalized slavery in her novel, Stowe published *A Key to Uncle Tom's Cabin,* revealing the real events which provided the basis of her tale. ("The facts are *stranger* and *stronger* than the fiction," wrote one Bostonian on the book.) For the Hutchinson Family Singers, it was a difficult year, with familial tensions running high. "Judsons relations" despised Elizabeth Chace Hutchinson, Asa's wife, and the bass singer could not fathom why. "'There's rott in Denmark'—I think I shall sell my farm from Milford," said an angry Asa. "Separation is needfull and we must obey." Deciding to move away from his parents and siblings, though, would not stop the jealousies—those "great engines of Satan" —rampant within the singing troupe.

One night Judson would criticize John if he sang poorly, and the next John would complain about Asa's singing. For a group that had been together for so long, such petty disputes seemed out of place. But the truth was that the three young Hutchinson boys had grown to become three very different men—comments such as "No Union among us brothers, each one for himself" abound in Asa's journal. Life on the road, even in the 1850s, led to salacious encounters to which Asa saw his brothers fall victim. When Asa overheard Judson and John speaking with their friend Jesse Briggs about "*Mormons* and women's rights," he could not help but crack that the three men "have got three wrong wives." "They long for others to satisfy their lives," Asa noted. "Thank God I'm happy with *One wife*. And to her Constant & true through life."

John and Judson no doubt stood irritated by Asa's moralizing, for he too had experienced doubts, "struggles & love temptation." But the biggest reason for the infighting came from the smaller spotlight now shining on the singers. At the peak of their fame in the 1840s, there had been plenty of acclaim to spread around. Now, playing nightly for $50 to $100 of profit, the trio faced consistent disappointment compared with an earlier era. Asa even looked forward to the group's demise: "I think we shall have as much peace separated—I shall live with my wife bless God."[30]

By 1853 Jesse Hutchinson, Jr., had already removed himself from his musical brothers. Disagreements with them had led Jesse to manage the Barker Family in 1849 and also, in 1851, his brothers' hated rivals, the Alleghanians—"those Alleghanians, little heads, hardly know enough to pick up Chicken S-t-!," Asa once blasted. Jesse took both these groups to California. Emotionally exhausted from the deaths of his father and his wife, Susan Hartshorn Hutchinson, in 1851, Jesse not only headed the Alleghanians but also became, like many who sought

fortune out West, quite a speculator, his name linked to such endeavors as "Dr. Robinson's remedy for the fever and ague," as well as the
production and sale of "unbolterd (or Graham) flour."

Traveling through Panama on his way home in 1853, Jesse caught
"Panama fever" (yellow fever). "Reverse of fortune," he said, under-
stating his situation in a letter to Asa. Not only was Jesse penniless, but
his health forced him to stop at the Cumminsville Water Cure in Ohio.
Newspapers reported that Jesse visited the institution to see Judson,
whose "state of raving insanity" following a Hutchinson Family Singers concert in Cleveland had landed him there. But these reports were
false. Jesse was ill, and Asa received a telegraph on 8 April from his Uncle Leavitt that Judson was on his way to Cumminsville.

Five days later, John and Asa waited impatiently at the post office
for more news. Some came in the form of a letter from their brother
Andrew, to whom Judson had telegraphed, "Jesse is worse. Joshua and
Asa come immediately." Joshua, though, was out of reach in Pennsylvania, so Asa tried to persuade John to come with him. John wanted to
bring his wife. Asa chose not to waste any time and hurried to New
York.

"Jesse is sinking fast," read the next telegraph, so Asa and his wife
left for Ohio on 19 April at 5 P.M. During one quick stop on 20 April,
Asa sent a message asking Leavitt for Jesse's current status, requesting a
return response at the station in Cleveland. Asa and Lizzie changed
trains at Cleveland without word. "No telegraph from Jesse yet. I dont
know that he is alive. I fear he is dead!" Asa even asked the conductor
whether any bodies had been loaded on the train. Finally Leavitt's telegraph arrived: "Jesse is better."

In Cumminsville, Asa met up with Judson and saw Jesse for the
first time—"O poor Jesse looked like a corpse." The two mended their
differences. Asa guessed that his brother would not live through the
night, but he did. Still, Jesse, confident the end was near, began con-
fessing to Asa that he was "wrong to love Martha when Susan was still
alive" and regretted letting Susan die without his sympathy.

John and Joshua soon arrived in Ohio. On 24 April the brothers
gathered around Jesse to read aloud passages from the *Key to Uncle
Tom's Cabin*—the "high Moral of Mrs Stowes book is second only to
the book of God," Asa said. "Key to Uncle Tom full of instruction.

Homely women write the best books." Screaming, screeching, Jesse soon fell into a delirium. His end looked near. Judson, horrified by the events, wished for his brother's death.

On 30 April the brothers learned more troubling news—their brother Zephaniah had died one week earlier in Illinois. All agreed not to tell Jesse. In May doctors started treating Jesse with a diet of candy, gingerbread, and "Arrabia" juice. On 9 May, Asa read more of the *Key* to Jesse—they concluded that "slavery is the foundation of every evil."

John, Asa, and Judson performed on 13 May. A few days before the show, the three had a fierce fight. Asa asked whether his wife Lizzie could sing with the group, pointing out to his brothers that each of them had brought his children on stage at one time or another. "Judson and John were so bitter," cried Asa. "One little song in an obscure country village—we gave a concert to 200 people—Lizzie did not sing."

On 15 May, Asa stood fanning Jesse for more than two hours. "Calmly quietly. without a struggle." Jesse Hutchinson, Jr., died at six in the morning. Frederick Douglass served notice in his paper: "Jesse Hutchinson died yesterday at a Water Cure establishment near Cincinnati."[31]

Douglass should have added another few lines: "The torch has been passed. When Jesse was ill the Hutchinson Family Singers chose not to sing, but to read to their sick relation."

Several years later, President Lincoln "twice closed his eyes and partially went to sleep" during a concert of John Hutchinson. Members of the Hutchinson Family Singers—who, collectively, had proved "that music has power over the human soul, to inspire it with noble thoughts and fill it with holy aspirations"—induced slumber playing apart.[32]

On 20 October 1908 the *New York Times* reported that "while attempting to light a gas stove Mr. Hutchinson fell after he had opened the valve." The statement is clear, but the circumstances of John's death were not. We don't know whether the singer's heart stopped during the act of turning on a stove or whether he started the gas to stop his heart. Abby had died in 1892, Frederick Douglass in 1896. John had outlasted all of his many siblings, his reform friends, his wife, and even his sons,

Henry John (who died at the age of thirty-nine in 1884) and Judson Whittier (who died at thirty-six in 1898). Loneliness and isolation took from John far more than his eighty-seven years ever did.

The story of the Hutchinson Family Singers should be an uplifting one. Each member of the troupe strove to summon interest in a range of social reforms from the 1840s until their deaths. There is no denying that while the musicians were flawed like all individuals, they were also unshakable reformers and performers. Not even loss of life could separate Asa from his instrument—"At the foot of the casket stood the old violincello that had for so many thousand times responded to the delicate touch of the fingers now stiff in death," read the *Glencoe Register* in 1884.[33]

Yet each Hutchinson seemingly paid a price for their early and fantastic rise to fame. Asa died a poor relative to the three other Hutchinson Family Singers; John died forlorn, Judson distressed; and Abby died after more than forty years under Ludlow's wealth and authority.

One of the three brothers' last attempts to promote social progress together opened the way to a permanent spilt of what remained of the singing troupe in 1855. At the time, the trio had been thinking seriously of going to Kansas to found a town to help antislavery forces there make the state slave free. Talked out of that dangerous endeavor by a New Hampshire friend, the three journeyed instead to McLeod County, Minnesota, where the they became majority shareholders in the town of Hutchinson. With five acres planned for "Humanity's Church" and ideas that the town would be a place where "woman shall enjoy equal rights with man," John, Judson, and Asa kept up their reform idealism.[34]

Yet Asa was the only brother to actually move to Hutchinson, an act which nearly fractured the sibling singing trio forever. Each brother and his respective family now independently carried the group's legacy. On occasion, the three appeared in concert together, but more often separate singing troupes distinguished by the word *tribe*—Hutchinson Family Singers, Tribe of John, for example—stalked the nation (fig. 22). Though he wrote one last hit song—"Tenting Tonight" with Walter Kittredge during the Civil War—Asa would squander the bulk of his fortune speculating in Colorado silver mines. Living in Hutchin-

Ticket for the Original Hutchinson Family, Tribes of John and Jesse. Courtesy The Lynn Museum and Historical Society, Lynn, Massachusetts.

son, away from the centers of American music and culture, only furthered his decline.

Divisions in family and in antislavery reform proved too much for Judson Hutchinson. After singing at a benefit for the Boston church of the black Baptist minister Leonard Grimes, the mercurial musician publicly attacked Frederick Douglass. During the Grimes event, Douglass had lectured that the Constitution, as he read it, was an antislavery document—a barb aimed at William Lloyd Garrison and the American Anti-Slavery Society, who argued the opposite.

Ever since his trip to Europe, Douglass had gradually distanced himself from Garrison and his organizations. The Hutchinsons, too, had often drifted from Garrison's line, particularly in their deep involvement with political antislavery. Yet Judson Hutchinson felt used by Douglass at the 1855 Boston event. Douglass had made the same allegations in public before, but Judson would have none of it. "It was not manly or just," Judson wrote in a letter that he personally delivered to Garrison at the *Liberator.* "I despise the slave who calls the *Constitution anti-slavery,* which admits *his* countrymen to be represented in Congress as cattle"—strong words against a man who was no longer a slave and with whom Judson had shared rooms, and even beds, over the years.[35]

John and Asa remained silent about the charge. A somewhat gracious Douglass, amused by the letter, called Judson an "impulsive and warm-hearted man, saying often, and doing often, that of which his

better judgment disapproves." Then Douglass chided Judson once
more for having sung to Henry Clay in 1848.[36]

Four years later, in the winter of 1858–1859, John Hutchinson
worried over his brother's mental state. Thinking a busy mind health-
ier than an idle one, John put Judson to work on some of the renova-
tions taking place in a cottage at High Rock in Lynn. (Most of the time
Judson minded a fire drying some newly plastered walls.)

On Tuesday afternoon, 11 January, as the Hutchinsons sat down
for tea, Judson went missing. John found his brother in an unfinished
basement of the small house next door. "I could see his form, apparently standing as though he was in one of his moody fits of abstrac-
tion," he wrote years later. "As I got within a few feet of him I saw a line
about his neck."

"Alas!" mourned the *Liberator* when announcing the "Melancholy Suicide," "for this sad termination of his earthly existence." Privately, Garrison gave John reason for hope: "Of course, he knew not
what he did. But he no longer 'sees through a glass darkly'—every fet-
ter is broken—his spirit is free—and *all is well!*" The *New York Times*
avoided revealing the cause of Judson's end, choosing instead to announce the "Death of Another Member of the Hutchinson Family."[37]

By the start of the Civil War, Abby wasn't really allowed to appear
on stage (though her actions reveal a yearning to do so), Judson was
dead, and Asa and John were seeking separate recognition for their
music and reform ideals in the Tribes of Asa and John. In the years
ahead, the three remaining Hutchinson Family Singers gave their best
for the Republican Party, temperance, women's rights, Union soldiers,
freedmen, industrial labor, and the Baptist Church. And all three suffered longing for a fame the likes of which they had known in earlier
times.[38]

What happened to the Hutchinsons after the war is no mystery.
Though interfamilial squabbles had torn apart the original Hutchinson Family Singers, the death knell sounded for the ideals that the
group, as a collective, had once held, and, as individuals, continued to
hold in the postbellum age when a different worldview came to the
fore. Exasperated by the experience of civil war, the nation slowly grav-
itated to the feeling that ideas should not develop into faith—a wari-

ness of transcendent beliefs opened the way for a more critical method of seeing the world. Talk of the millennium had suddenly become quaint.[39]

Coda to Part First: John and Fred, the 1893 Danvers Meeting, the 1893 World Expo, and the Trajectory of Black and White Antebellum Reform

Curiously missing from the ranks gathered in the Danvers Town Hall for the 1893 antislavery commemoration had been Frederick Douglass. Though invited, the heralded reformer did not attend. He explained in a letter to those convened in Danvers that "to see Parker Pillsbury, the man who was perhaps the source of more terror to the proslavery church and clergy of his day than any other, and to see John Hutchinson, the only remaining one of the Hutchinson Family which gave its youth, beauty, and transcendent musical genius to the cause of the slave, would compensate me for any trouble a long journey would require at my hands." Yet Douglass refused such reimbursement. The most famous antislavery activist still alive spent the year before the Danvers convention recharging his reform zeal, and by the time of the Anti-Slavery Commemorative meeting, he was in no mood to celebrate.

At the root of Douglass's renewed social awareness was a friendship with Ida B. Wells. Wells's journalism exposed the economic and racial impulses behind southern lynchings that had commonly been attributed to blacks' licentious nature. After reading her work, Douglass was appalled with himself, bemoaning that he "had begun to believe it true that there was an increased lasciviousness on the part of Negroes." After the Civil War the black leader's frustration with the results of his earlier apocalyptic reform visions forced him to choose between idealism and practicality. Douglass, like many other abolitionists, had chosen a more conservative path as the North and South reconciled. He wrote about innate differences between blacks and whites, a position he once had refuted, and even made peace with his former master. By the 1890s, though, Douglass started to see new openings for activism, grumbling that recent years had been filled with "reaction and darkness" and that "the air has been filled with reconciliations between those who fought for freedom and those who fought for slavery."

And so Douglass searched for answers. Sometimes he turned to his aging abolitionist colleagues. Early in 1892 he singled out John G. Whittier, Robert Purvis, and Parker Pillsbury as the only remaining worthies from the old antislavery days. But if his absence from the Danvers commemoration was any sign, Douglass understood that his old friends, by and large, were not the reformers they once had been. Their critique of American life at the close of the century never, despite their good intentions, sounded as urgent or as important as it had in the 1840s and 1850s. Douglass, like his comrades in Danvers, was concerned with remembering the days of emancipation—in fact, one of his black critics, the Rev. Alexander Crummell, came to see the famous spokesman's obsession with slavery's past as a hindrance to the contemporary struggle of African Americans. But when Douglass came across the writings of Wells, he found a new place and a new inspiration for his voice.[40]

In April 1893 Douglass was not in Danvers but at his post as the commissioner of the Republic of Hayti pavilion at the World's Columbian Exposition in Chicago, a position he had acquired as the former U.S. ambassador to the Caribbean nation. The four hundredth anniversary of Columbus's discovery of the New World inspired the massive affair, a gala showcasing the future of human progress. During this international venue blacks were presented as an amusing sideshow. Nothing better demonstrated this than Colored People's Day at the fair in August. The event, which was supposed to showcase black artists and black achievement, quickly turned into a mockery; Douglass arrived early only to discover that the fairground vendors had been stocked with watermelons. Not amused, he stormed off.[41]

Douglass, unlike Ida Wells and other black leaders, believed that Colored People's Day offered an opportunity to highlight black accomplishment. So despite his early disappointment, the famous orator returned at 2:30 to take his place in the afternoon festivities. Following the introductions, Douglass began reading a piece entitled "The Race Problem in America." White hecklers interspersed throughout the crowd interrupted. Douglass tried to continue but could not. The combination of critics and the summer heat appeared to be too much for the aged speaker. Seemingly defeated, he threw down his speech and then his glasses. Douglass, however, did not retreat. He found again the thunderous voice of his youth and started, "Men talk of the Negro problem. . . . There is no Negro problem. The problem is whether the American people have loyalty enough, honor enough, patriotism enough, to live up to their own Constitution." One hour later, he finished.[42]

Douglass shunned the Danvers event because he preferred to be on the front lines of the African-American struggle for recognition at a global showcase. In 1893 he felt little exuberance over the ending of slavery. Reawakened to the struggles of his race, Douglass recommitted himself to the fight. Celebrating the end of slavery would have been not only trite but useless for the enraged reformer. What he found in Chicago upset him. In the end many fairgoers rejoiced in comic representations that white Americans held of blacks and trusted the "scientific" ideology on exhibit that placed blacks near the bottom of the evolutionary scale. Simply put, "the White City took no account of the inhumanity endured by black Americans." Douglass had lived through slavery, and what he saw in 1893 looked strikingly similar. Blacks were living in virtual slavery, chained by poverty, violence, disenfranchisement, and racism. The predominately white conventioneers who gathered on a spring day in Massachusetts—a group once at the forefront of the battle against slavery—were largely powerless to combat these new problems. In Danvers sat a most painful proof of how far apart race relations in the country had drifted. In Chicago it was on display.[43]

After the Danvers meeting, John Wallace Hutchinson found his way to Chicago in the summer of 1893. There he spent roughly six months wandering the fairgrounds, singing at a variety of events, and mingling with luminaries. He remembered visiting Frederick Douglass as one of his first orders of business upon arriving (fig. 23 and fig. 24). John's memoirs focus more upon his own accomplishments in Chicago, like singing "The Sword of Bunker Hill" on Massachusetts Day, than upon his friend's troubles within the "white walls" of the Exposition. John attended the 24 June inauguration of the Hayti Building. Chicago papers reported that "the exercises were very appro-

Frederick Douglass. Courtesy The Lynn Museum and Historical Society, Lynn,
Massachusetts.

priately opened with a song, 'The Millennium,' by dear John Hutchinson, who has so often sung in the cause of the freedom of the black
people as he now sung in their triumph."

One presumes that the "triumph" of black Americans is the ending of legalized slavery in the country. But many other problems had
since surfaced. Indeed, the account obscured a striking fact: black musicians were relegated to spaces outside the fairgrounds. During the
festivities on Hayti Day, John and every other speaker and singer was
accompanied by the all-white Iowa State Band. In order for visitors to
hear black musicians, they had to search for performances off of the
fairgrounds midway or wander into one of many establishments cater-
ing to exhausted fairgoers outside of the Exposition. Here, away from

An older John Hutchinson. Courtesy The Lynn Museum and Historical Society, Lynn, Massachusetts.

the fair, people could hear a black composer, pianist, and cornetist from Sedalia, Missouri, named Scott Joplin render his interpretations of the latest musical craze, called ragtime.[44]

The infamous Colored People's Day at the fair fell on 25 August 1893. John Hutchinson sang one of "his inimitable songs" during the day's festivities, at which he was only one of several featured white musicians. His thoughts on a day set aside for African Americans remain unknown because, other than a newspaper clip mentioning his own involvement in the revelry, John recorded nearly nothing about the event. While Ida B. Wells declared that Douglass's impromptu speech "had done more to bring our cause to the attention of the American people than anything else which had happened during the fair," John, perhaps accustomed to Douglass's passion, never mentioned Douglass's name in the context of this occasion.[45]

At the Columbian Exposition, John stumbled upon an aging Indian chief who spoke about lost tribal lands for which his tribe had never been compensated. The emotional singer immediately broke out in a sorrowful tune that the Hutchinson Family Singers had often performed, about an Indian escaping fate by paddling his canoe out to sea. "The foaming billow shall be my grave," he sang, "for I'll not die the white man's slave."

Linking Native Americans to white enslavement, John's performance did not go over well. His voice failed to summon a righteous indignation of the kind that he desired. The Indian chief responded to John's emphatic "whoops that accompany the song" by opening "his eyes very wide." The musician's attempt to demonstrate caring and sympathy had failed. The chief, dumbstruck by the strange man screaming bastardized Indian war cries, was not impressed. John sang about the hopelessness of some idealized Indian; the chief, demonstrating a very modern sensibility, had come to Chicago trying to find a legal or political means to plead his case. In this the Indian leader was hardly a pioneer. The Oglala chief Red Cloud had stopped fighting railroads in 1872 and traveled to Washington to carry on through diplomacy. These leaders understood that their struggles centered around rights and land, not, as John's song suggested, around a choice between nature or slavery.[46]

That John dealt with issues using images of the greatest evil he had ever known, slavery, was not surprising. Unfortunately, many reformers of John's age agreed with his assessment of Native Americans. For most of the other social dilemmas facing Americans at the close of the century, though, John Hutchinson could offer a voice of hope. The travesty facing the old singer in the 1890s was that fewer Americans were listening to him, especially on issues of race. The Hutchinson Family Singers' importance always had rested on their ability to communicate reform in a way that reached a broad spectrum of northern whites. At their best, the Hutchinson Family Singers and other artists representing the culture of antebellum reform united an antislavery movement factionalized by different reform strategies and opinions. Often in exchange for promises of a Christian world cleansed of sin (and savagery), the Hutchinson Family Singers convinced many whites to embrace antislavery. With the millennium nowhere in sight by the late 1890s and with the North and South desperate to heal the scars of war, much of that white audience for racial reform had disappeared.

John lost African-American listeners in the 1890s as well. Before the war, the Hutchinson Family Singers had earned a significant free black following. Asa was enthralled when, at a concert in Boston, there were "many *Coloured* persons present, sitting in as good seats as the *Whites!!*" But following the end of Reconstruction, the African-American community was often more interested in (and, more often, forced into) building an identity for themselves, leaving white sympathizers, like John, on the sidelines. Black men and women increasingly took charge of their own communities and their own destinies.[47]

Even though he had fewer listeners, John did not always shelter himself at celebrations like the one in Danvers. John was willing to stand up in song and in deed for various causes, and while his diagnosis of contemporary issues was a bit dated, the fact that mainstream white America was not interested in what he had to say was more important. People were far more fascinated with what John once had been—"This will be your only chance of a lifetime. He will receive a grand ovation," said ads for his shows in the 1890s—than with what he currently promoted. By performing at a variety of Douglass's events in Chicago, the old bard demonstrated his support for what Douglass was trying to do. John Hutchinson's singing of "The Millennium," though, highlights how he clung to a religious vision of social change often rejected by late-nineteenth-century reformers. (Asa had clung to the vision as well. Abby, though far removed from the public spotlight after her marriage, sought a different vision of social betterment: "My religion is to educate people how to work—then give them work and pay them for it," she said to John in 1891.) Standing on the platform near Douglass on Colored Americans' Day, John must have felt pride in his friend and sadness over the condition of his country.

Black Americans were very much a part of the Chicago fair experience as visitors, speakers, workers, and performers, but the African-American vanguard looked to further this inclusion. The Civil War had greatly reshaped power relations in America, advantaging the weak to the detriment of their antagonists, but it hardly represented a complete turnaround. In the space that did open up, Frederick Douglass and many younger African-American leaders in politics, culture, and religion expressed discontent. They led the wake-up call to white America that blacks were now poised for a fuller participation in American society. This notion, voiced prominently in the collaborative publication entitled *The Reason Why the Colored American Is Not in the World's Columbian Exposition,* advocated a new period of civil rights activism.[48]

John Hutchinson's friendship with Frederick Douglass continued strong until the black leader's death in 1895. Almost immediately after the fair closed at the end of October 1893, John introduced Douglass and also sang at a lecture held in Boston's People's Church. A little later the former slave wrote the introduction to John's two-volume memoir, an opportunity that thrilled both men. And when Douglass died, John asked to sing at his funeral. The real difference between the two was that John found some solace in being a relic from days past, while Douglass battled against being an "antique abolitionist."[49]

Samuel May wrote in 1874 that "it will be very difficult for most readers at this day to comprehend the extent and force of the hostility to the Abolitionists in 1835." It was a sentiment widely echoed by former antislavery advocates at such celebrations as the one in Danvers. This would not have been the case had they stood by Douglass's side in Chicago. There they would have felt transported back in time. John and his Danvers colleagues were living in a world that increasingly sanctioned everything that they had once battled against. Disenfranchisement, lynching, sharecropping, and other means were now employed to reinforce the nation's racial stratification. There was little need for actual slavery when this new system of oppression kept power safely in white hands.

By the close of the century, Americans could have used a reform group appealing to an interracial audience as even some black Americans were beginning to suffer from a "fading racial memory." The commemoration of emancipation in Washington, D.C., which had taken place every year since Congress first freed slaves in the District on 17 April 1862, was now a celebration shunned by the African-American elite and virtually ignored by the younger generations, for whom the event lacked meaning. Douglass had closed one of his first public speeches by exclaiming that prejudice "hangs around my neck like a heavy weight." More than fifty years later his words continued to ring true. Douglass could not tolerate it; John celebrated one victory, and did his best to fight for another.

"I hope the American people will never underrate the influence of the songs of the Hutchinson family," said Wendell P. Garrison in 1891. "I wish we had another such, attuned to the times and needs of the present hour."[50]

Many years later, a writer noticed a bust of John Hutchinson at the sculptor Adelaide Johnson's gallery at 5 East Thirty-sixth Street in New York City. The statue John—whose real life counterpart had died three months earlier—resembled an "Old Testament Prophet." John and his siblings had, Mary Howitt once said, "calculated to produce a moral era," one addressing needs and concerns of a growing commercial republic. The Hutchinson Family Singers' sound—founded upon revival melodies and the religious singings of the 1820s and 1830s—was not, though, a music equipped to speak to many different generations. Through their continued good deeds, their preacherlike perseverance, and, no doubt, their wealth, members of the Hutchinson Family Singers had lingered on in the public eye long after the sweet family harmony collapsed. Without the opportunity to record their music in their own voice, the Hutchinson Family Singers as John, Asa, Abby, and Judson eventually deliquesced into mere notes on sheet music pages.

Had you walked out of Johnson's studio in 1908, a satisfying song might have caught your ear—"There's a good time coming boys, wait a little longer." You stop, pause, glance back in the studio at John's cast face. Walking away, you could swear that you heard the Hutchinson Family Singers' "There's a Good Time Coming":

> We may not live to see the day,
> But earth shall glisten in the ray,
> Of the good time coming.[51]

Appendix
Lyrics to Select Hutchinson Family Singers Songs

Get Off the Track!

Ho! the Car Emancipation
Rides majestic thro' our nation
Bearing on its train the story,
LIBERTY! a Nation's Glory.
Roll it along, Roll it along,
Roll it along, Thro' the Nation
Freedom's Car Emancipation.

First of all the trains and greater,
Speeds the dauntless *Liberator*
Onward cheered amid hosannas,
And the waving of Free Banners.
Roll it along, Roll it along,
Roll it along, Spread your Banners
While the people shout hosannas.

Men of various predilections,
Frightened, run in all directions,
Merchants, Editors, Physicians,
Lawyers, Priests, and Politicians.
Get Out of the Way! Get Out of the Way!
Get Out of the Way! every station,
Clear the track of 'mancipation.

Let the Ministers and Churches
Leave behind sectarian lurches;
Jump on board the Car of Freedom
Ere it be too late to need them.
Sound the Alarm! Sound the Alarm!
Sound the Alarm! Pulpit's thunder!
Ere too late, you see your blunder.

Politicians gazed, astounded.
When, at first, our Bell resounded;
Freight trains are coming, tell these Foxes,
With our *Votes* and *Ballot Boxes.*
Jump for your Lives! Jump for your Lives!
Jump for your Lives! Politicians,
From your dangerous false positions.

Rail Roads to Emancipation
Cannot rest on *Clay* foundation
And the tracks of *"The Magician"*
Are but *Rail Roads* to perdition.
Pull up the rails! Pull up the rails!
Pull up the rails! Emancipation
Cannot rest on such foundation.

All true friends of Emancipation,
Haste to Freedom's Rail Road Station;
Quick into the Cars get seated,
All is ready and completed.
Put on the Steam! Put on the Steam!
Put on the Steam! All are crying,
And the Liberty Flags are flying.

Now, again the bell is tolling,
Soon you'll see the car wheels rolling;
Hinder not their destination,
Chartered for Emancipation.
Wood up the fire! Wood up the fire!
Wood up the fire! keep it dashing
While the train goes onward dashing.

Hear the mighty car wheels humming!
Now, look out! *The Engine's coming!*
Church and Statesmen! hear the thunder!
Clear the track! or you'll fall under.

Get off the track! Get off the track!
Get off the track! all are singing
While the *Liberty Bell* is ringing.

On triumphant, see them bearing,
Through sectarian rubbish tearing;
Th' Bell and Whistle and the Steaming,
Startles thousands from their dreaming.
Look out for the cars! Look out for the cars!
Look out for the cars! while the Bell rings,
Ere the sound your funeral knell rings.

See the people run to meet us,
At the Depots thousands greet us;
All take seats with exultation,
In the Car Emancipation.
Huzza! Huzza! Huzza! Huzza!
Huzza! Huzza! Emancipation
Soon will bless our happy nation.
Huzza! Huzza!! Huzza!!!

By Jesse Hutchinson, Jr. (Boston: Jesse Hutchinson, Jr., 1844)

The Millennium
"What do I see! Ah! Look, behold!
The Glorious day by Prophets told,
Has dawn'd and now is near,
Me-thinks I hear from yonder plain,
With shouts of gladness loud proclaim,
The Millennium is here!

See freedom's star that shines so bright,
It sheds its ray of truth and light,
O'er mountain, rock, and sea,
And like the mighty march of mind,
Had sought and bless'd all human kind,
And set the bondman free.

No dungeons, chains, or gibbets here,
No groans of prisoners in despair,
Are heard to mar the scene;
But Peace as once on Bethlehem's plain
By Angels sung, has come again,
And earth is all serene.

The voice of war is heard no more,
The cannon with its deadly roar,
Is hushed in silence now;
All implements of death you see,
Are changed from war to husbandry,
The pruning hook and plough.

Salvation to our God proclaim,
This is the glorious, peaceful reign,
The nations now shall know;
The kingdoms of this world are given
To Christ, the Lord of earth and heaven,
Predicted long ago.

By Caleb and Joshua Hutchinson (Boston: Wm. H. Oakes, 1847)

The Old Granite State

We have come from the mountains,
We have come from the mountains,
We have come from the mountains of the Old Granite State.
We're a band of brothers,
We're a band of brothers,
We're a band of brothers and we live among the hills.

With a band of music,
With a band of music,
With a band of music, We are passing 'round the World.
We have left our aged parents,
We have left our aged parents,
We have left our aged parents in the Old Granite State.

We obtained their blessing,
We obtained their blessing,
We obtained their blessing, And we bless them in return.
Good old fashion'd singers,
Good old fashion'd singers,
Good old fashion'd singers. They can make the air resound.

We have eight other Brothers,
And of Sisters, just another,
Besides our Father, and our Mother, in the Old Granite State.
With our present number,
There are fifteen in the tribe;
Thirteen sons and daughters, And their history we bring.

Yes while the air is ringing,
With their wild mountain singing,
We the news to you are bringing, from the Old Granite State.
'Tis the Tribe of Jesse,
'Tis the Tribe of Jesse,
'Tis the Tribe of Jesse, And their several names we sing.

David, Noah, Andrew, Zephy, (aniah)
Caleb, Joshua, Jess, and Beny, (jamin)
Judson, Rhoda, John and Asa, and Abbe are our names:
We're the Sons of Mary,
Of the Tribe of Jesse,
And we now address ye, With our native mountain song.

We are all real Yankees,
We are all real Yankees,
We are all real Yankees, from the Old Granite State.
And by prudent guessing,
And by prudent guessing,
And by prudent guessing, We shall whittle through the world.

Liberty is our motto,
Liberty is our motto,

Equal liberty is our motto in the Old Granite State.
We despise oppression,
We despise oppression,
We despise oppression and we cannot be enslaved.

Yes we're friends of emancipation,
And we'll sing the proclamation,
'Til it echoes through our nation from the Old Granite State
That the Tribe of Jesse,
That the Tribe of Jesse
That the Tribe of Jesse are the friends of equal rights.

We are all Washingtonians,
Yes we're all Washingtonians,
Heav'n bless the Washingtonians of the Old Granite State.
We are all teetotalers,
We are all teetotalers,
We are all teetotalers and have signed the temperance pledge.

Now three cheers altogether,
Should Columbia's people ever,
Yankee hearts none can sever in the Old Sister States.
Like our sires before us,
We will swell the chorus,
'Til the Heavens o'er us shall rebound the loud hussa.
Hurrah! hurrah! hurrah!
By the Hutchinson Family (Boston: Oliver Ditson, 1843)

Slavery Is a Hard Foe to Battle
I looked to the South and I looked to the West,
And I saw slavery old Slavery a coming,
With four Northern dough faces hitched up in front,
Driving freedom to the other side of Jordan.
    Then take off coats and roll up sleeves,
    Slavery is a hard foe to battle I believe.

Slavery and freedom they both had a fight,
And the whole North came up behind 'em;
Hit slavery a few knocks with a free ballot box,
Sent it staggering to the other side of Jordan.
> Then rouse up the North, the sword unsheath,
> Slavery is a hard foe to battle I believe.

If I was the Legislature of these United States,
I'd settle the great question accordin';
I'd let every slave go free over land, and on the sea,
And let them have a little hope this side of Jordan.
> Then rouse up the free, the sword unsheath,
> Freedom is the best road to travel I believe.

The South have their school where the masters learn to rule,
And they lord it o'er the free states accordin';
But sure they'd better quit e'er they raise the yankee grit,
And we tumble 'em over t'other side of Jordan.
> Then wake up the North, sword unsheath,
> Slavery is a hard foe to battle I believe.

But the day is drawing nigh that Slavery must die,
And every one must do his part accordin';
Then let us all unite to give every man his right, (and woman too!)
And we'll get our pay the other side of Jordan.
> Then wake up the North, sword unsheath,
> Freedom is the best road to travel I believe.

By Judson Hutchinson (New York: Horace Waters, 1855)

Notes

Prelude

1. John Wallace Hutchinson, *Story of the Hutchinsons (Tribe of Jesse)*, ed. Charles E. Mann (Boston: Lee and Shepard, 1896), 1:267.

2. Ibid., 1:267–268.

3. Ken Emerson, *Doo-Dah! Stephen Foster and the Rise of American Popular Culture* (New York: Da Capo, 1998), 93. For the most complete list of songs performed by the Hutchinson Family Singers, see Dale Cockrell, ed., *Excelsior: Journals of the Hutchinson Family Singers, 1842–1846* (Stuyvesant, N.Y.: Pendragon, 1989), 393–406.

4. David Blight, Introduction, *Narrative of the Life of Frederick Douglass* (New York: Bedford St. Martin's, 2003), 18. John Ashworth, *Slavery, Capitalism, and Politics in Antebellum America,* vol. 1, *Commerce and Compromise, 1820–1850* (New York: Cambridge University Press, 1995). David M. Potter, *Impending Crisis, 1848–1861,* completed and ed. Don E. Ferenbacher (New York: Harper Torchbooks, 1976). Whitman cited in David Reynolds, *Beneath the American Renaissance: The Subversive Imagination in the Age of Emerson and Melville* (Cambridge: Harvard University Press, 1988), 104; see also 92 for the importance of reform in antebellum culture. For reform as defining the essential meaning of the years before the Civil War, see Ron Eyerman and Andrew Jamison, *Music and Social Movements: Mobilizing Traditions in the Twentieth Century* (Cambridge: Cambridge University Press, 1998), 1–6. Elizabeth B. Clark, "'The Sacred Rights of the Weak': Pain, Sympathy, and the Culture of Individual Rights in Antebellum America," *Journal of American History* 82 (Sept. 1995):463–493. For the link between religion, reform, and culture, see Robert Laurence Moore, "Religion, Secularization, and the Shaping of the Culture Industry in Antebellum America," *American Quarterly* 41, no. 2 (June 1989):216–242, and Robert Laurence Moore, *Selling God: American Religion in the Marketplace of Culture* (New York: Oxford University Press, 1994).

5. For the Hutchinsons' experiences and meetings abroad, see Cockrell, *Excelsior,* 315–316. Peter F. Walker, *Moral Choices: Memory, Desire, and Imagination in Nineteenth-Century American Abolition* (Baton Rouge: Louisiana State University Press, 1978), 85. Hannah Webb in Cockrell, *Excelsior,* 326. *Guardian,* ibid., 329.

6. Clark, "'Sacred Rights,'" 470–473. On the importance of religion to the creative process in the nineteenth century, see Debora Silverman, *Van Gogh and Gauguin: The Search for Sacred Art* (New York: Farrar, Straus and Giroux, 2000). Donald Scott expertly described early-nineteenth-century cultural growth: "Itinerancy had certainly been a part of the cultural and social landscape of seventeenth- and eighteenth-century New England. But the difference is one of range and scale: by the 1830s and 1840s a staggering number and variety of entertainers and performers, purveyors of this or that kind of lore or doctrine, agents or missionaries of one society or another, and peddlers of some cultural good or another were coursing their way from town to town across New England and New York"; Scott, "Itinerant Lecturers and Lecturing in New England, 1800–1850,"

in *Itinerancy in New England and New York,* ed. Peter Benes (Boston: Boston University Press, 1986), 65. Moore, *Selling God,* especially chapter 2. R. Whitney Cross is often credited with the "discovery" of the importance of Christian revivals in the antebellum era in his seminal study, *Burned-Over District: The Social and Intellectual History of Enthusiastic Religion in Western New York, 1800–1850* (Ithaca: Cornell University Press, 1950). For the influence of religious thought on the antislavery movement, see Ronald G. Walters, *Antislavery Appeal: American Abolitionism After 1830* (New York: Norton, 1978). Jon Butler, *Awash in a Sea of Faith: Christianizing the American People* (Cambridge: Harvard University Press, 1990), especially chapters 6 and 9.

7. Though an excellent study, Eric Lott's famous book *Love and Theft: Blackface Minstrelsy and the American Workingclass* (New York: Oxford University Press, 1995) treats minstrelsy as a rather static event, as if minstrel shows in 1835 and 1855 were the same. John G. Blair, "Nineteenth-Century Exports of American Entertainment Forms," in *"Here, There, and Everywhere": The Foreign Politics of American Popular Culture,* ed. Reinhold Wagnleitner and Elaine Tyler May (Hanover, N.H.: University Press of New England, 2000), 17–33. For the change of minstrelsy over time, see Dale Cockrell, *Demons of Disorder: Early Blackface Minstrels and Their World* (New York: Cambridge University Press, 1997). See also Philip F. Gura, "America's Minstrel Daze," review of *Demons of Disorder* by Dale Cockrell; *Raising Cain: Blackface Performance from Jim Crow to Hip Hop* by W. T. Lhamon, Jr.; *Behind the Burnt Cork Mask: Early Blackface Minstrelsy and Antebellum American Culture* by William J. Mahar, *New England Quarterly* 72, no. 4 (Dec. 1999):602–616. Greg Tate, ed., *Everything But the Burden: What White People Are Taking from Black Culture* (New York: Broadway, 2003). One forty-niner clearly distinguished between early and late minstrel music. Of the most popular music in the West in 1849, he wrote: "It is not real 'darkey' music exactly, I admit; but certainly plantation songs, as written, for instance, by Stephen Foster, are the most popular songs among us"; cited in Emerson, *Doo-Dah,* 10. Images that adorned minstrel sheet music covers also gradually moved toward depictions more appropriate for parlor performance and display; see Stephanie Dunson, "The Minstrel in the Parlor: Nineteenth-Century Sheet Music and the Domestication of Blackface Minstrelsy," *ATQ: Nineteenth Century Literature and Culture* 16, no. 4 (Dec. 2002):241–256. For decline of minstrelsy and Foster's turn away from minstrelsy, see also "Who Writes Our Songs," *Dwight's Journal of Music,* 14 May 1859, 52. Quotation from "The Christy Minstrels," *Times* (London), 27 Dec. 1870, 4.

8. Jesse Hutchinson and B. Covert, "Welcome to Jenny Lind" (Boston: Oliver Ditson, 1850). Hutchinson, *Story of the Hutchinsons,* 1:268. See Bluford Adams's account of the meeting, *E Pluribus Barnum: The Great Showman and the Making of U.S. Popular Culture* (Minneapolis: University of Minnesota Press, 1997), 63.

9. Frederick Douglass to John W. Hutchinson, 18 Nov. 1894, Biddleford, in *Memorabilia of the Hutchinson Family* (Gift of Mrs. Viola Hutchinson Campbell to the Lynn Historical Society, 1920), 31. When the British abolitionist Algernon Cooper mocked Lind's reverence for the American flag—she had said that "the oppressed of all nations worship thee"—he was one of many reformers who chided her for remaining silent about American slaves. Cooper, Letter to the Editor, *Times* (London), 8 Oct. 1850, 7. Richard D. Brown, *Knowledge Is Power: The Diffusion of Information in Early America, 1700–1865* (New York: Oxford University Press, 1989), 35. Moore, *Selling God,* 3–39.

10. Nicknames used in "Exeter-Hall," *Times* (London), 23 Oct. 1861, 10. Lind cited in

Adams, *E Pluribus Barnum*, 63. For the sale of Lind see, for example, "The Fifteenth National Anti-Slavery Bazaar, Faneuil Hall, Boston," *Liberator*, 22 Dec. 1848, 203. Joseph Roach is quite critical of the Barnum-Lind marketing of reform and piety; see "Barnumizing Diaspora: The 'Irish Skylark' Does New Orleans," *Theatre Journal* 50, no. 1 (1998):39–51. For a more positive and feminist take on Lind's tour, see Sherry Lee Linkon, "Reading Lind Mania: Print Culture and the Construction of Nineteenth Century Audiences," *Book History* 1, no. 1 (1998):94–106. For more on the marketing of Lind, see W. Porter Ware and Thaddeus C. Lockard, *P. T. Barnum Presents Jenny Lind: The American Tour of the Swedish Nightingale* (Baton Rouge: Louisiana State University Press, 1980), 3, 7, 9, 12, 19–20, 24–28, 37, 41.

11. Simon Schama, "Sail Away," *New Yorker*, 31 May 2004:39–43. Cockrell, *Excelsior*, 321–323. *Western Christian Advocate* in "Profitable Singing," *Anti-Slavery Bugle* (Salem), Hutchinson Family Singers Collection, box 1, item 4, Wadleigh Memorial Public Library, Milford, N.H. (hereafter WMPL 1, 4).

12. "Meeting of the Massachusetts Anti-Slavery Society at the Free Church in Haverhill," *Liberator*, 7 April 1843, 56. "Boston—Sunday, March 31, 1844," in Cockrell, *Excelsior*, 244–245. *Christian Citizen*, WMPL 1, 4. Jesse Hutchinson, Jr., also responded to the *Western Christian Advocate* claim, calling it completely false. See his article from the *Lynn Pioneer*, WMPL 1, 3.

13. Asa Hutchinson, "London—Monday, February 9, 1846," in Cockrell, *Excelsior*, 343. Stuart Blumin, *The Emergence of the Middle Class: Social Experience in the American City, 1760–1900* (New York: Cambridge University Press, 1989), 109–110. Asa Hutchinson, "Tuesday, January 23, 1844," in Cockrell, *Excelsior*, 201. John Hutchinson, "8 Aug 1851," ibid., 383.

14. Mason critic cited in Carol A. Pemberton, *Lowell Mason: A Bio-Bibliography* (New York: Greenwood, 1988), 21. Charles Grier Sellers, *Market Revolution: Jacksonian America, 1815–1846* (New York: Oxford University Press, 1991). Moore, *Selling God*. Gilbert Hobbs Barnes, *Antislavery Impulse, 1830–1844* (New York: D. Appleton-Century, 1933), 56. More recently, David Blight called Garrison a "professional radical," a term that nicely summarizes his reform calling and his profession. "Modern Voices: David Blight on William Lloyd Garrison," 10 July 2004 <http://www.pbs.org/wgbh/aia/part4/4i2980.html>. James T. Kloppenberg, *Virtues of Liberalism* (New York: Oxford University Press, 1998), 47. William Lloyd Garrison to Joshua Hutchinson, 3 April 1874, in *A Brief Narrative of the Hutchinson Family: Sixteen Sons and Daughters of the "Tribe of Jesse"* (Boston: Lee and Shepard, 1874), 6.

15. Mrs. William B. Rotch (Patty McLane Botch) to Mrs. McKay, 10 June 1951, Milford, N.H., in *Milford Cabinet and Wilton Journal*, 28 June 1951, folder 920.H9766ba, New Hampshire State Library, Concord, New Hampshire. Landmark designation issued by the National Music Council and Exxon, "Hutchinson Homestead Is Designated as a Landmark of American Music," *Cabinet and Wilton Journal*, 19 Aug. 1976. Cara Reese, "The Tribe of Jesse," *Commercial Gazette* (Pittsburgh), 15 Aug. 1891, WMPL 3, 96. Joshua Hutchinson, *Brief Narrative*.

16. Alan Lewis, "Hutchinson Family," 13 Oct. 2005 <http://www.geocities.com/unclesamsfarm/hutchinsons.htm>. For the reception of antislavery throughout the nation see James Brewar Stewart, *Holy Warriors: The Abolitionists and American Slavery* (New York: Hill and Wang, 1976), especially chapter 3, "Mobs and Martyrs: The Dynamics of Moral Suasion." Brown, *Knowledge*, 35. Letter to the Editor, *National Era*, 21

Nov. 1850, 187. Mary Howitt, "What Are the Hutchinsons Doing?" *Howitt's Journal,*
WMPL 1, 8; "Miss Abby Hutchinson," *Phrenological Almanac* (Jan. 1848), WMPL 1, 8;
American Phrenological Journal (June 1847), WMPL 1, 7; "Married," WMPL 1, 9; "The
Hutchinsons," WMPL 1, 9; "The Hutchinson Family," WMPL 1, 9; "The Hutchin-
sons," WMPL 1, 9; "The Popular Singers," *Scientific American* 47, no. 1 (13 Aug. 1846):2;
"Madame Rumor," WMPL 1, 12; "Oh, Sweet," WMPL, 1, 14; "Abby Hutchinson,"
WMPL 1, 24; "Garrison's Nigger Minstrels," *New York Sunday,* WMPL 1, 32; "We Re-
gret," WMPL 1, 36; "Judson Hutchinson," WMPL 1, 35; "The Hutchinson Family,"
WMPL 1, 37; "It Is Jesse Hutchinson," WMPL 1, 38.

17. Charles Sumner and President Tyler were just two of many political figures who
supported the Hutchinson Family Singers. For Lowell factory girls as fans of the singers,
see *Lowell Offering* 4 (Aug. 1844):237–240, in Nicholas E. Tawa, *High-Minded and Low-
Down: Music in the Lives of Americans, 1800–1861* (Boston: Northeastern University
Press, 2000), 204–205. For Whitman on the Hutchinsons, see David S. Reynolds, "'I
Hear America Singing': Walt Whitman and the Music of His Time," 11 April 2002
(1999) <http://www.americancomposers.org/whitman2.htm>. Perhaps the best analy-
sis of class division via a cultural event for the antebellum era is Peter Buckley, "To the
Opera House: Culture and Society in New York City, 1820–1860," Ph.D. diss., State
University of New York at Stony Brook, 1984. Richard Middleton, *Studying Popular
Music* (Philadelphia: Open University Press, 1990), 3–11. Stuart Hall, "Notes on De-
constructing 'the Popular,'" in *People's History and Socialist Theory,* ed. Ralph Samuel
(New York: Routledge, 1981). Raymond Williams, "Base and Superstructure in Marxist
Cultural Theory," in *Rethinking Popular Culture,* ed. Michael Schudson and Chandra
Mukerji (Berkeley: University of California Press, 1991). Lawrence Levine, *Highbrow/
Lowbrow: The Emergence of Cultural Hierarchy in America* (Cambridge: Harvard Uni-
versity Press, 1988).

18. David K. Dunaway, "Folk Protest and Political Music in the United States," *Journal of American Folklore* 105, no. 417 (Summer 1992):374; David K. Dunaway, "Folk-Top-
ical Recordings and American Left-wing Politics," *Journal of American Folklore* 110, no.
438 (Fall 1997):418. Betty Wang, "Folksongs as Regulators of Politics," in *The Study of
Folklore,* ed. Alan Dundes (Englewood Cliffs, N.J.: Prentice Hall, 1965), 308–313. For the
Hutchinsons as the link to current social change and musical performance, see Richard
Harrington, "Facing the Music: Singing to Change the World," *Washington Post,* 15 Sept.
2000.

19. "Women and Temperance," *New York Times,* 2 Sept. 1853, 1. Robinson song included in George W. Clark, *Liberty Minstrel* (New York: Saxton and Miles, 1844), 173.
George W. Clark, *Harp of Freedom* (New York: Miller, Orton and Mulligan, 1856).

20. *Exhibition of Vocal and Instrumental Music in the Center Church . . . on June 4th,
1844, with the Juvenile Class of More Than Two Hundred and Fifty Pupils* ([New Haven?]:
Hitchcock and Stafford, 1844). "Destitute Children of Seamen," *New York Times,* 4 Jan.
1852, 3. "Afternoon Session," *District School Journal of the State of New York* 11, no. 5 (Aug.
1850):73. "Queries and Answers," *New York Times,* 24 Apr. 1909, BR266. "Queries and
Answers," *New York Times,* 3 Dec. 1944, BR19. Eyerman and Jamison, *Music and Social
Movements,* 1–6. The most popular song of the Hutchinsons in the twentieth century
was "Tenting Tonight," written by a friend of the singers named Walter Kittredge. The
Civil War ballad was a success for Asa Hutchinson and his family, but it was not written
until after the original Hutchinson Family Singers had disbanded. The song can be

found in guitar manuals and in general collections of American music. For examples, see Irwin Silber and Jerry Silverman, *Songs from Singout! Traditional and Contemporary Folk Songs* (New York: Oak Publications[, 197?]), and Margaret Braford Boni, ed., *Fireside Book of Favorite American Songs* (New York: Simon and Schuster, 1952).

21. "Discussion in Spiritualism," *New York Times,* 6 Mar. 1855, 8. For the dream, see coverage in the *Liberator,* 4 Mar. 1854, and Cockrell, *Excelsior,* 206–207. H. C. Wright, "Old England and New England Laborers on Land Contrasted," *Liberator,* 26 May 1848, 81. Frank B. Carpenter, "Abraham Lincoln: Personal Recollections and Incidents of a Six Months' Sojourn in the White House During the Lincoln Administration," *Peterson Magazine* 6, no. 3 (Mar. 1896):234. For the increase in and diversity of antebellum cultural offerings, see Donald Scott, "The Popular Lecture and the Creation of a Public in Mid-Nineteenth Century America," *Journal of American History* 66 (Mar. 1980):791–809.

22. Charles Hamm linked the Hutchinsons to the tradition of singing in protest, but incorrectly calls them unique in their time. They were unique for their commercial success and their devotion to reform. Many others sang for reform without any popularity, and others, like Henry Russell, were popular but disingenuous as reformers. Hamm, *Yesterdays: Popular Song in America* (New York: Norton, 1979). By tracing the trajectory of the tradition of reform music and its tie to the Hutchinson Family Singers, we can see the abolitionist endeavor in a more positive light; to understand how the abolitionists failed, see Merton Dillon, "The Failure of the Abolitionists," *Journal of Southern History* 25, no. 2 (May 1959):159–177, and, on the ambiguity of abolitionism's success, see Stewart, *Holy Warriors,* chapter 8. "The Hutchinson Family Singers," *New York Times,* 31 Jan. 1965, X13. "Television This Week," *New York Times,* 22 Aug. 1965, X15. Richard Harrington, "Facing the Music: Singing to Change the World," *Washington Post,* 15 Sept. 2000, 40. Robert Shelton, "'Freedom Songs' Sweep North," *New York Times,* 6 Jul. 1963, 7.

23. Mary Blake, "What Today Means to You," *Washington Post,* 4 Jan. 1932, 8.

24. Serge Denisoff distinguishes between two types of protest songs: "magnetic" tunes and songs that attract new adherents to the movement; "rhetorical" songs proclaim dissent without offering a solution. The music of the Hutchinson Family Singers fits in both categories, but certainly operated on a more complicated level. Denisoff, *Sing a Song of Social Significance* (Bowling Green, Ohio: Bowling Green University Press, 1972). Ron Eyerman and Andrew Jamison explain why Denisoff's distinction fails to capture the relationship between music and reform in *Music and Social Movements,* 1–6, 43. As pious domesticity developed into a seemingly universal condition in the North, the power of sentimental culture peaked. Clark, "'Sacred Rights." Jane Tompkins, *Sensational Designs: The Cultural Work of American Fiction, 1790–1860* (New York: Oxford University Press, 1985).

25. Abraham Lincoln, "Facts for the People" (n.p., 1858). Dinesh D'Souza, "Lincoln: Tyrant, Hypocrite, or Consummate Statesman?" *American History,* April 2005.

26. John Stauffer, *Black Hearts of Men: Radical Abolitionists and the Transformation of Race* (Cambridge: Harvard University Press, 2001). Douglass in John Stauffer, "Frederick Douglass and the Aesthetics of Freedom," manuscript for *Raritan Review,* 23 May 2004. "Garrison's Nigger Minstrels," *New York Sunday,* WMPL 1, 32. *Evening Transcript* in Cockrell, *Excelsior,* 151.

27. Eyerman and Jamison, *Music and Social Movements,* 12. Eric Foner, *Tom Paine and Revolutionary America* (New York: Oxford University Press, 1976). Joan D. Hedrick,

Harriet Beecher Stowe (New York: Oxford University Press, 1995). Emerson in John Byron Wilson, "Activities of the New England Transcendentalists in the Dissemination of Culture," Ph.D. diss., University of North Carolina, Chapel Hill, 1941, 6.

Part First

1. James Brewar Stewart, *Holy Warriors: The Abolitionists and American Slavery* (New York: Hill and Wang, 1976). Ira Berlin, Barbara Fields, et al., *Slaves No More: Three Essays on the Civil War and Emancipation* (Cambridge: Cambridge University Press, 1992). Steven Hahn, *A Nation Under Our Feet: Black Political Struggles in the Rural South from Slavery to the Great Migration* (Cambridge: Harvard University Press, 2003). James McPherson, *Drawn with the Sword: Reflections of the Civil War* (New York: Oxford University Press, 1997). Rogers M. Smith, *Civic Ideals* (New Haven: Yale University Press, 1997).

2. Hahn, *Nation Under Our Feet.* "Howard University Classes," *Washington Post,* 29 May 1901, 9. Philip V. Bohlman, "Ontologies of Music," in *Rethinking Music,* ed. Nicholas Cook and Mark Everist (New York: Oxford University Press, 1999), 20.

3. For the precedence of healing over civil rights, see David Blight, *Race and Reunion: The Civil War in American Memory* (Cambridge: Harvard University Press, 2001). James Freeman Clarke cited in Ronald G. Walters, *Antislavery Appeal: American Abolitionism After 1830* (New York: Norton, 1978), 140. See also ibid., 142–144.

4. Many have discussed the role of abolitionists after the Civil War. It was once thought that because Reconstruction failed, abolitionists must have stopped pressing for social change. James McPherson's *Abolitionist Legacy: From Reconstruction to the NAACP* (Princeton: Princeton University Press, 1976) shows that the activists did not retreat, claiming that their legacy is found in many institutions and programs they initiated in the postbellum era. "John W. Hutchinson," *New York World,* 6 Jan. 1900, in Hutchinson Family Singers Collection, box 3, item 128, Wadleigh Memorial Public Library, Milford, N.H. (hereafter WMPL 3, 128).

5. Asa Hutchinson, "Sunday June 4th 1843," *Excelsior: Journals of the Hutchinson Family Singers, 1842–1846,* ed. Dale Cockrell (Stuyvesant, N.Y.: Pendragon, 1989), 153.

6. This chapter on the Hutchinsons deals with the success and failure of the abolitionists in terms of cultural abolitionism. As antislavery musicians, the Hutchinson Family Singers were "movement intellectuals," who translated the political and social activities of the abolitionists into music meant for widespread consumption—for a better definition of the movement intellectuals see Lawrence Goodwyn, *Populist Moment: A Short History of the Agrarian Revolt in America* (New York: Oxford University Press, 1978), and Ron Eyerman, *Cultural Trauma: Slavery and the Formation of African American Identity* (Cambridge: Cambridge University Press, 2001). There is an increasing recognition of the power of culture, especially in terms of redefining traditions, and its significance to society as a whole. Many earlier works on the antislavery movement hold that only those who worked within the strictest definition of political activity were significant. I argue that the members of the Hutchinson Family Singers did not give up their goals for a more progressive America but that, in effect, times had changed and the Hutchinsons were unable to change with them, thus losing a certain vitality which was the cornerstone of their popularity. For discussions on the legacy of abolitionism see

Merton Dillon, "The Failure of the Abolitionists," *Journal of Southern History* 25, no. 2 (May 1959):159–177; George Frederickson, *Inner Civil War: Northern Intellectuals and the Crisis of the Union* (1965; Urbana: University of Illinois Press, 1992); Stanley M. Elkins, *Slavery: A Problem in American Institutional and Intellectual Life* (Chicago: University of Chicago Press, 1959); John L. Thomas, *Liberator: William Lloyd Garrison, A Biography* (Boston: Little, Brown, 1963); These works hold that an anti-institutional bias led abolitionists to failure. As can be seen from the Hutchinson Family Singers' music, the abolitionists were not against institutions, per se, just institutions and traditions that did not serve their ideals. Thus the Hutchinson Family Singers, who disliked blackface minstrelsy, transformed the popular musical form into something that aligned with their antislavery ideology. Likewise the Hutchinsons withdrew from organized religion—an action called Come-Outerism—believing that the church supported slavery. For a more positive view of the abolitionists' work and the centrality of their actions in the nineteenth century, see Henry Mayer, *All on Fire: William Lloyd Garrison and the Abolition of Slavery* (New York: St. Martin's, 1998). Stewart's *Holy Warriors* attempts an evenhanded account of the antislavery crusade but favors a traditional political view of social movements and offers a rather ambiguous legacy for abolitionist activists. For recent works on the power of culture, see Jane Tompkins, *Sensational Designs: The Cultural Work of American Fiction, 1790–1860* (New York: Oxford University Press, 1985); Chandra Mukerji and Michael Schudson, eds., *Rethinking Popular Culture: Contemporary Perspectives in Cultural Studies* (Berkeley: University of California Press, 1991); Joan D. Hedrick, *Harriet Beecher Stowe: A Life* (New York: Oxford University Press, 1995); Jean Fagan Yellin and John C. Van Horne, eds. *Abolitionist Sisterhood: Women's Political Culture in Antebellum America* (Ithaca: Cornell University Press, 1994).

7. In the vast records of the meeting, the weather on the day of the meeting was not mentioned. This leads one to believe that the temperature and conditions were rather normal for that time of year. My figure was surmised by taking the average temperature of April in the region from 1895 until 1910 (with 1895 the earliest for which there are data available), National Climactic Data Center, 9 Dec. 2002 <http://lwf.ncdc.noaa.gov/oa/ncdc.html>. *Old Anti-Slavery Days: Proceedings of the Commemorative Meeting, Held by the Danvers Historical Society, at the Town Hall, Danvers, April 26, 1893, With Introduction, Letters, and Sketches* (Danvers: Danvers Mirror Print, 1893), 1–2.

8. Photo and list of participants are in *Old Anti-Slavery Days*, xxviii–xxix. See the forty-four-star flag, U.S. Flag Page, 1 Mar. 2002 <www.usflag.org/the.44.star.flag.html>.

9. Much in the same way some current scholars herald the civil rights era as the "Second Reconstruction," the Rev. Austin Willey declared the Civil War the "Second Revolution"; *History of the Antislavery Cause in State and Nation* (Portland, Maine: Brown Thurston and Hoyt, Fogg and Donham, 1886), 30.

10. Mayer, *All on Fire*, 51–55. David W. Bartlett, *Modern Agitators; or, Pen Portraits of Living American Reformers* (New York: Miller, Orton and Mulligan, 1855), 111–112. Dillon, "The Failure of American Abolitionists," in *Abolitionism and American Reform*, ed. John R. McKivigan (New York: Garland, 1999), 255. Wendell Phillips Garrison and Francis Jackson Garrison, *William Lloyd Garrison, 1805–1879: The Story of His Life Told by His Children*, 4 vols. (Boston: Houghton, Mifflin, 1885). To understand Garrison's eventual acceptance of violence to end slavery during the Civil War we must turn to Lewis Perry: "To end war and slavery—to end anarchy in the bad sense of lawlessness—the guiding strategy was to abolish human government and to institute the government of God";

Radical Abolitionism: Anarchy and the Government of God in Antislavery Thought (Ithaca: Cornell University Press, 1973), 270.

11. Donald Yacovone, *Samuel Joseph May and the Dilemmas of the Liberal Persuasion* (Philadelphia: Temple University Press, 1991), 3, 31, 40–41, 61. Samuel Joseph May, *Memoir of Samuel Joseph May* (Boston: Roberts Brothers, 1874), 50–51, 260. Mayer, *All on Fire*, 103–104, 199, 186, 387, 571, 412, 620. Walters, *Antislavery Appeal*, 25. Lydia Maria Child, *An Appeal in Favor of That Class of Americans Called Africans* (New York: John S. Taylor, 1836), iii. Albert J. Von Franck, *Trials of Anthony Burns: Freedom and Slavery in Emerson's Boston* (Cambridge: Harvard University Press, 1998), 20.

12. C. A. Bartol, *Senatorial Character: A Sermon in West Church, Boston, Sunday, 15th of March, After the Decease of Charles Sumner* (Boston: A. Williams, 1874), 6.

13. *A Memorial of Charles Sumner from the City of Boston* (Boston: Rockwell and Churchill, 1874), 87–100. See also David Herbert Donald's excellent study of Sumner, *Charles Sumner and the Rights of Man* (New York: Knopf, 1970). Donald Scott, "The Popular Lecture and the Creation of a Public in Mid-Nineteenth Century America," *Journal of American History* 66 (March 1980): 796. William G. Rowland, *Literature and the Marketplace* (Lincoln: University of Nebraska Press, 1997), 1–16. For a more thorough explanation of Humboldt and the unity of all things, see Aaron Sachs, "The Humboldt Current: Avant-Garde Exploration and Environmental Thought in Nineteenth-Century America," Ph.D. thesis, Yale University, 2004. Charles Sumner to Wendell Phillips, 4 Feb. 1845, in Irving H. Bartlett, *Wendell and Ann Phillips: The Community of Reform, 1840–1880* (New York: Norton, 1979), 150. Bartol, *Senatorial Character*, 40. Hooley's Minstrels in Robert Toll, *Blacking Up: The Minstrel Show in Nineteenth-Century America* (New York: Oxford University Press, 1974), 116.

14. David M. Potter, *Impending Crisis, 1848–1861,* completed and ed. Don E. Ferenbacher (New York: Harper Torchbooks, 1976), 139, 209, 210–211, 220–221. *Memorial of Sumner.*

15. John B. Pickard, Introduction to *Letters of John Greenleaf Whittier* (Cambridge: Harvard University Press, 1975), 1:xix, xviii, xiv. Bartlett, *Modern Agitators,* 243. See also Thomas Wentworth Higginson to Mother, 10 July 1859, *Letters and Journals of Thomas Wentworth Higginson, 1846–1906,* ed. Mary Thatcher Higginson (Boston: Houghton Mifflin, 1921), 107. John Greenleaf Whittier to Thomas J. Mumford, 3 Nov. 1871, *Letters,* 3:151. W. Sloane Kennedy, *John Greenleaf Whittier: His Life, Genius, and Writings* (Boston: S. E. Cassino, 1882), 9. John B. Pickard, "Whittier's Abolitionist Poetry," *Memorabilia of John Greenleaf Whittier* (Hartford: Emerson Society, 1968), 109. Van Wyck Brooks, *Flowering of New England, 1815–1865* (New York: Dutton, 1937), 400, 398, 401. Poem included on the broadside *Am I Not a Man and a Brother?* (n.p., 1837). John Greenleaf Whittier, "Stanzas," *Early Poems of John Greenleaf Whittier Comprising Mogg Megone, The Bridal of Pennacock, Legendary Poems, Voices of Freedom, and Songs of Labor* (New York: Houghton, Mifflin, 1885), 137. See explanatory notes in Pickard, *Letters,* 2:637. For more examples of Whittier's reporting through poetry see Whittier, "Lines on the Adoption of Pinckney's Resolutions," "The World's Convention of the Friends of Emancipation, Held in London in 1840," "Lines, Written for the Meeting of the Antislavery Society, at Chatham Street Chapel, N.Y., 1834," *Early Poems,* 226–228, 170–178, 162–163. Whittier also wrote public letters about current events; see Whittier to *Essex Transcript,* 6 Oct. 1843; Whittier to *Essex Transcript,* 20 May 1844, *Letters,* 1:607, 638.

16. Kennedy, *Whittier,* 99–100. Brooks, *Flowering of New England,* 398–399. Pickard, Introduction to *Letters,* 1:xv. Whittier is included among those American writers listed in the Poet's Corner dedicated in St. John the Divine Church in New York during the 1980s. Frederick Douglass, *Anti-Slavery Movement: A Lecture by Frederick Douglass Before the Rochester Ladies' Anti-Slavery Society* (Rochester: Press of Lee, Mann and Co., 1855), 40.

17. Pickard, Introduction to *Letters,* 1:xxi, xxxv. Whittier to Samuel May, 27 Mar. 1840, *Letters,* 1:402. Thomas Wentworth Higginson also relayed Whittier's negative remarks about Garrison in 1849; *Letters and Journals,* 8. Whittier tried to reach out to Garrison to form a united antislavery coalition after an 1854 incident involving Anthony Burns, a fugitive slave captured in Boston and ordered by a judge to be returned to Virginia, but Garrison would not join forces with the political or the violent. See Von Franck, *Trials of Anthony Burns,* 228. Also mentioned in Catherine Clinton, *Harriet Tubman: The Road to Freedom* (New York: Little, Brown, 2004), 111.

18. In Massachusetts white men between thirty and forty years old in 1850 could expect to live for another twenty-eight to thirty-four years, while white women in the same range could expect another thirty to thirty-five years, Information Please, "Life Expectancy by Age, 1850–1999," 26 Feb. 2002 <http://www.infoplease.com/ipa/A0005140.html>. Mayer, *All on Fire,* 620. H.B.B, "Memorial Meeting for Maria Weston Chapman," in Lewis Ford, *Variety Book Containing Life Sketches and Reminiscences* (Boston: Geo. E. Crosby, 1892), 53. Stacey M. Robertson, *Parker Pillsbury: Radical Abolitionist, Male Feminist* (Ithaca: Cornell University Press, 2000), 184–185. William S. McFeely, *Frederick Douglass* (New York: Norton, 1991), 359–360.

19. Mayer, *All on Fire,* 628, 620. Whittier also wrote a poem upon the death of Charles Sumner; see *A Memorial,* 98.

20. John Wallace Hutchinson, *Story of the Hutchinsons (Tribe of Jesse),* ed. Charles E. Mann (Boston: Lee and Shepard, 1896), 1:382–384. Quotation in Whittier to John Wallace Hutchinson, 6 Mar. 1862, *Letters,* 3:29. This letter is also included in Hutchinson, *Story of the Hutchinsons,* 1:397. Whittier to John W. Hutchinson, 2 Dec. 1874, in *Story of the Hutchinsons,* 2:336. Whittier to Abigail Hutchinson Patton, 1889, *Letters,* 2:744. Abby Hutchinson Patton to John G. Whittier, 14 Dec. 1889, Pickard-Whittier Papers, b MS Am 1844, Harvard University Library. Copy of John G. Whittier to Abby Hutchinson Patton, 23 Dec. 1889, Pickard-Whittier Papers.

21. John Hutchinson, *Story of the Hutchinsons,* 2:191. Roland H. Woodwell, *John Greenleaf Whittier: A Biography* (Haverhill: DBL Commercial, 1985), 529. "The Poet Whittier Buried: Thousands Looked Upon the Face of the Patriotic Bard," *New York Times,* 11 Sept. 1892, 8. Asa Hutchinson, "Close His Eyes His Work Is Done" (Boston: Oliver Ditson, 1863).

22. Susan B. Anthony to John W. Hutchinson, 9 Dec. 1892, *Memorabilia of the Hutchinson Family,* Gift of Mrs. Viola Hutchinson Campbell to the Lynn Historical Society, 1920. Abby Hutchinson Patton to John Hutchinson, 6 June 1891, *Story of the Hutchinsons,* 2:381. Abby Hutchinson Patton, *A Handful of Pebbles* (privately printed, 1891). "Obituary," *New York Mail and Express,* 26 Nov. 1892; "Mrs. Abby Hutchinson Patton," *New York Herald,* 26 Nov. 1892; "One of the Hutchinsons. Death of a Woman Who Had Charmed Thousands with Her Songs," *New York Times,* 26 Nov. 1892; "Abby Hutchinson Patton Dead," *New York World,* 26 Nov. 1892; "Funeral of the Late Abby

Hutchinson Patton," *New Hampshire Republican,* 29 Nov. 1892, WMPL 3, 105. "Sung the People's Songs. Death at Her Home of Mrs. Abby Hutchinson Patton," 26 Nov. 1892, *Memorabilia of the Hutchinson Family,* 96.

23. John Hutchinson, *Story of the Hutchinsons,* 2:152–233. "High Rock Card of Inquiries" (Lynn: n.p., 1888), WMPL 3, 98. *The Seventieth Birthday Anniversary of John W. Hutchinson, (Tribe of John and Jesse,) At Tower Cottage, High Rock, Lynn, Mass. January Fifth, 1891* (Lynn: Nichols, 1891). "Sings to Save," WMPL 3, 130. "Aged Singer in Cigarette War," *Boston Journal,* 16 Dec. 1901, WMPL 3, 129. "He'll Sing Against Use of Cigarettes: Millionaire John W. Hutchinson, 81 Years Old, to Start on Tour," *American* (Chicago), 25 Dec. 1901, WMPL 3, 129. "John W. Hutchinson," *New York World,* 16 Jan. 1900, WMPL 3, 128.

24. Mrs. Mary A. Livermore to John W. Hutchinson, 20 Aug. 1903, *Memorabilia of the Hutchinson Family,* 33. "Peace Song At Bridal: Mrs. Everest, of this City, and J. W. Hutchinson Wed," *Washington Post,* 25 Aug. 1906, 3. "John W. Hutchinson's Relatives Wish Him Declared Insane, Last of Famous Family, Nearly 80, He Is Said to Have Asked 20-Year-Old Girl to Marry Him—Is Known Nationally as a Singer—Has Much Property," *Boston Morning Post,* 16 July 1900, WMPL 3, 128. Letter from Susan B. Anthony, *Life and Work of Susan B. Anthony: Including the Triumphs of Her Last Years, Account of Her Death and Funeral and Comments of the Press,* vol 3., ed. Ida Husted Harper (Indianapolis: Hollenbeck, 1908), 407.

25. "John W Hutchinson of Lynn has appeared in court in Salem to prove his sanity. He called at the Pointer office last week. Uncle John is evidently o.k.," WMPL, 1, 117. Carol Brink, *Harps in the Wind: The Story of the Singing Hutchinsons* (New York: Macmillan, 1947), 287. "John Hutchinson's Oxen Cremated," WMPL 1, 117. In the end, John gave his ample holdings of land in Minnesota to his family and turned over his estate on High Rock to the city of Lynn to be made into a park; see "Good News from High Rock," WMPL 3, 99. John Hutchinson, *Story of the Hutchinsons,* 2:184. "The Last Minstrel," n.p., n.d., WMPL 3, 129. *Old Anti-Slavery Days,* 4. "Still Famous in Slavery Days," *Washington Post,* 27 April 1893, 1.

26. Mrs. Mary A. Livermore to John W. Hutchinson, 20 Aug. 1903, *Memorabilia of the Hutchinson Family,* 33. Brink, *Harps in the Wind,* 287. "Obituary," *New York Mail and Express,* 26 Nov. 1892; "Mrs. Abby Hutchinson Patton," *New York Herald,* 26 Nov. 1892; "One of the Hutchinsons. Death of a Woman Who Had Charmed Thousands with Her Songs," *New York Times,* 26 Nov. 1892; "Abby Hutchinson Patton Dead," *New York World,* 26 Nov. 1892; "Funeral of the Late Abby Hutchinson Patton," *New Hampshire Republican,* 29 Nov. 1892, WMPL 3, 105. "Sung the People's Songs. Death at Her Home of Mrs. Abby Hutchinson Patton," 26 Nov. 1892, *Memorabilia of the Hutchinson Family,* 96. John Hutchinson, *Story of the Hutchinsons,* 2:200. John W. Hutchinson, "Address and Song by John W. Hutchinson," reported by Edward Noble and others, *Old Anti-Slavery Days,* 4.

27. Perley Derby, *Hutchinson Family* (Salem: Essex Institute, 1870), 29. John Hutchinson, *Story of the Hutchinsons,* 1:3, 5. Von Franck, *Trials of Anthony Burns,* xi, 59–60. Annette Gordon-Reed, *Thomas Jefferson and Sally Hemings: An American Controversy* (Charlottesville: University Press of Virginia, 1998). Joseph J. Ellis, *American Sphinx: The Character of Thomas Jefferson* (New York: Vintage, 1998). Stewart, *Holy Warriors,* 27–33. Stephanie Smallwood, "Commodified Freedom: Interrogating the Limits of Anti-Slavery Ideology in the Early Republic," *Journal of the Early Republic* 24, no. 2 (Summer 2004): 298. If, as Walter Johnson suggests, we gain more by defining slavery and freedom

as "concretely intertwined and ideologically symbiotic," then Jefferson's ideas are less contradictory and more complementary. See Johnson, "The Pedestal and the Veil: Rethinking the Capitalism/Slavery Question," *Journal of the Early Republic* 24, no. 2 (Summer 2004): 306. David Brion Davis, "The Emergence of Immediatism in British and American Thought," *Mississippi Valley Historical Review* 49, no. 2 (Sept. 1962), 209–230. Adam Rothman, "The Expansion of Slavery in the Deep South, 1790–1820," Ph.D. thesis, Columbia University, 2000. Rogers M. Smith, *Civic Ideals* (New Haven: Yale University Press, 1997). Eric Foner, *The Story of American Freedom* (New York: Norton, 1998).

28. "New Hampshire Indians Have Gone But Their Names at Least Remain," *Historical New Hampshire* 7, no. 2 (October 1952). Hoxie Neal Fairchild, *Noble Savage: A Study in Romantic Naturalism* (New York: Columbia University Press, 1928), 1–2. A Horace Bushnell speech in 1851 accomplished many of the same convenient omissions that John Hutchinson did in 1893; see Laurel Thatcher Ulrich, *Age of Homespun* (New York: Knopf, 2001), 24. See also a poem celebrating "The redman soon knock'd under" and New Hampshire's founding, George Kent, "The Old Granite State," *Festival of the Friends of New Hampshire . . . Celebrated in Boston, November 7, 1849* (Boston: James French, 1849), 87.

29. Frederick Jackson Turner, *Frontier in American History* (New York: Holt, 1920). Philip J. Deloria, *Playing Indian* (New Haven: Yale University Press, 1998), 3. Rebecca Solnit, *River of Shadows: Eadweard Muybridge and the Technological Wild West* (New York: Viking, 2003), 73. James T. Kloppenberg, *Virtues of Liberalism* (New York: Oxford University Press, 1998), 11–12. Eric Foner, *Reconstruction: America's Unfinished Revolution, 1863–1877* (New York: HarperCollins, 1989). Blight, *Race and Reunion*. John Stauffer, "Frederick Douglass and the Aesthetics of Freedom," manuscript for *Raritan Review*, 23 May 2004.

30. John Hutchinson, *Old Anti-Slavery Days*, 4. The term for such a shared memory is "cultural trauma"; see Eyerman, *Cultural Trauma*, 2–5. Stauffer, "Frederick Douglass." Elizabeth B. Clark, "'The Sacred Rights of the Weak': Pain, Sympathy, and the Culture of Individual Rights in Antebellum America," *Journal of American History* 82 (Sept. 1995):463–493.

31. Dale Cockrell, Review of Carol Brink, *Harps in the Wind: The Singing Hutchinsons of New Hampshire* (1947; New York: Da Capo, 1980), in *American Music* 1, no. 2 (Summer 1983): 86. George W. Latimer to John W. Hutchinson, 22 Nov. 1843, *Story of the Hutchinsons*, 2:350. Ibid., 2:309. Joshua Hutchinson, *A Brief Narrative of the Hutchinson Family: Sixteen Sons and Daughters of the "Tribe of Jesse"* (Boston: Lee and Shepard, 1874), 68. John G. Whittier to John W. Hutchinson, 2 Dec. 1874, *Story of the Hutchinsons*, 2:336. Gerrit Smith to John W. Hutchinson, 30 June 1874, ibid., 2:338. *Seventieth Birthday Anniversary*, 9. John Hutchinson, *Story of the Hutchinsons*, 2:170. Brink, *Harps in the Wind*. Philip D. Jordan, *Singin' Yankees* (Minneapolis: University of Minnesota Press, 1946).

32. Asa J. Davis, "The George Latimer Case: A Benchmark Case in the Struggle for Freedom," Thomas A. Edison Papers, 7 Nov. 2004 <http://edison.rutgers.edu/latimer/glatcase.htm>. John Hutchinson, *Story of the Hutchinsons*, 1:70–71. Cockrell, *Excelsior*, 91–94, 388. Joshua Hutchinson to John Hutchinson, 6 Aug. 1874, *Story of the Hutchinsons*, 2:354–355. Frederick Douglass, Introduction to Hutchinson, *Story of the Hutchinsons*, 1:xviii. Douglass, *Life and Times of Frederick Douglass* (Hartford: Park, 1883), 601. Asa Hutchinson, "Saturday, April 27, 1844," in Cockrell, *Excelsior*, 267.

33. Aaron Porter, "Address," *Old Anti-Slavery Days*, 45.

34. John Hutchinson, *Old Anti-Slavery Days,* 4. Parker Pillsbury, *Acts of the Anti-Slavery Apostles* (Boston: Cupples, Upham, 1884), 80.

35. George B. Bartlett, "Relics of the Mighty Past," *Old Anti-Slavery Days,* 25. *Old Anti-Slavery Days,* 26–27.

36. George T. Downing, *Old Anti-Slavery Days,* 33. Garrison and Garrison, *William Lloyd Garrison,* 1:290.

37. Frederick Douglass, Introduction to Hutchinson, *Story of the Hutchinsons,* 1:xvii–xviii. Elizabeth Cady Stanton, *Eighty Years and More, 1815–1897: Reminiscences of Elizabeth Cady Stanton* (New York: European Publishing, 1898), 131. Rebecca Solnit, *Savage Dreams: A Journey into the Landscape Wars of the American West* (New York: Vintage, 1994), 69.

38. John W. Hutchinson, *Old Anti-Slavery Days,* 33.

39. George W. Putnam, *Old Anti-Slavery Days,* 50–51.

40. Lucy Stone, "Address," *Old Anti-Slavery Days,* 39. See also *Old Anti-Slavery Days,* 32–42. Peter Randolph, "Address," *Old Anti-Slavery Days,* 55–56. Hutchinson, *Story of the Hutchinsons,* 2:204–205.

41. *Old Anti-Slavery Days,* 59–60, 121. A. P. Putnam, "Introductory Chapter: Danvers and the Abolitionists," in *Old Anti-Slavery Days,* viii, 100.

42. Fernald in William Odel, "Slavery in Colonial Portsmouth," *Historical New Hampshire* 21, no. 3 (Autumn 1966): 11, 3. Geospatial and Statistical Data Center, University of Virginia, 8 Nov. 2004 <http://fisher.lib.virginia.edu>. Lorenzo J. Greene, "Slave-Holding New England and Its Awakening," *Journal of Negro History* 13, no. 4 (Oct. 1928): 492–533. Leon Litwack, *North of Slavery: The Negro in the Free States, 1790–1860* (Chicago: University of Chicago Press, 1961), 3. James Oliver Horton and Lois E. Horton, *In Hope of Liberty: Culture, Community, and Protest Among Northern Free Blacks, 1700–1860* (New York: Oxford University Press, 1997), 72. Ira Berlin, *Many Thousands Gone: The First Two Centuries of Slavery in North America* (Cambridge: Harvard University Press, 1998), 47, 58, 229. William D. Pierson, *Black Yankees: The Development of Afro-American Sub-Culture in Eighteenth-Century New England* (Amherst: University of Massachusetts Press, 1988). "Anti-Slavery Convention at Milford," *Herald of Freedom* (Concord), 20 Nov. 1840, 154. A. J. Coolidge and J. B. Mansfield, *A History and Description of New England, General and Local* (Boston: A. J. Coolidge, 1859), 1:396. The first antislavery meeting in Milford was probably held in October 1835 in the schoolhouse of district number ten; Edith Hunter, *A Brief History of the Public Schools of Milford, New Hampshire, 1738–1972* (Wethersfield Center, Vt.: Hunter, 1973), 29. Garrison, *Liberator,* 13 Mar. 1840, cited in Walters, *Antislavery Appeal,* 14. Stewart, *Holy Warriors,* chapter 3.

43. David Goodwin, *Historical Sketch of the Town of Milford, New Hampshire, 1846,* ed. Milford Historical Society (Milford: Cabinet, 1987), 8, 11–13. In the national election of 1848 Milford cast 46 Whig votes, 75 Democratic, and 176 Free Soil; in the 1852 governor's race, 179 for Free Soil, 81 for Whig, and 98 for the Democrats. Goodwin recorded elections in 1854 and 1856 as those between "anti-slavery" and "pro slave." Voters overwhelmingly preferred the antislavery candidate—in the 1856 election nearly three out of four Milford votes were for John C. Fremont. Cockrell, *Excelsior,* 93–94. For a broader view of the factionalization and politicization of the antislavery movement, see Stewart, *Holy Warriors* (1976), 94–123.

44. John W. Quist, "'The Great Majority of Our Subscribers are Farmers': The

Michigan Abolitionist Constituency of the 1840s," in McKivigan, *Abolitionism and American Reform*, 221. Walters, *Antislavery Appeal*, 3–18.

45. Sarah H. Southwick, *Reminiscences of Early Anti-Slavery Days* (Boston: privately printed, 1893), 11. Walters, *Antislavery Appeal*, 27. Mayer, *All on Fire*, 200–205.

46. George Storrs, *Mob, Under the Pretence of Law, or the Arrest and Trial of Rev. George Storrs at Northfield, N.H.* (Concord: Elbridge G. Chase, 1835), 3, 6–7. John L. Myers, "The Major Effort of Antislavery Agents in New Hampshire, 1835–1837," *Historical New Hampshire* 26, no. 3 (Fall 1971): 3–27. For oxen version, Mayer, *All on Fire*, 197. For horses, Stewart, *Holy Warriors* (1976), 63. Ford, *Variety Book*, 22. Foster in Sallie Holley, *A Life for Liberty: Anti-Slavery and Other Letters of Sallie Holley*, ed. John White Chadwick (New York: Putnam, 1899), 6. Whittier in Stewart *Holy Warriors* (1976), 73. Pillsbury, *Acts*, 266, 318.

47. Pillsbury, *Acts*, 102. Burns recalled that "Milford was once the hotbed of abolitionism. . . . It contained a splendid set of men and women who early espoused the cause of the slave," in Winifred A. Wright, *Granite Town: Milford, New Hampshire, 1901/1978* (Canaan, N.H.: Phoenix, 1979), 13. Milford was also a station on the Underground Railroad and housed Harriet E. Wilson. Wilson, author of *Our Nig* (1859), was not only the first black woman but the first black person to publish a novel in the United States. She resided a short distance from the home of the Hutchinson Family Singers. See Barbara A. White, "'Our Nig' and the She-Devil: New Information about Harriet Wilson and the 'Bellmont' Family," *American Literature* 56, no. 1 (Mar. 1993): 19–52.

48. Pillsbury, *Acts*, 102. "Anti-Slavery Convention at Milford," *Herald of Freedom*, 20 Nov. 1840, 154.

49. "Anti-Slavery Convention at Milford," *Herald of Freedom*, 20 Nov. 1840, 154.

50. Hutchinson, *Story of the Hutchinsons*, 1:8–9. "Declaration of Faith," *Church Covenant, and Catalogue of Members of the Baptist Church in Milford, N.H., August, 1859* (Milford: Boutwell's Book and Job Office, 1859), 17–19. Hutchinson, *Story of the Hutchinsons*, 1:21, 2:239–240. Perry, *Radical Abolitionism*, xi–xiii. Cockrell, *Excelsior*, xxiv. "The performances," *Farmer's Cabinet* (Amherst), 13 Nov. 1840, n.p. Brink, *Harps in the Wind*, 8–9. Hutchinson, *Story of the Hutchinsons*, 1:35–36.

51. This is not to say that there wasn't significant interest in music within the antislavery movement prior to 1843. "In reading and singing hymns of triumph and martyrdom," said Maria Weston Chapman in 1836, "our minds receive a general idea of something high and heroic." But even the use of antislavery hymns increases after the Hutchinsons' reform-singing success. Maria Weston Chapman, ed., *Songs of the Free, and Hymns of Christian Freedom* (Boston: Isaac Knapp, 1836), 90, cited in Vicki Eaklor, *American Antislavery Songs: A Collection and Analysis* (New York: Greenwood, 1988), xxi. For other collections of pre–Hutchinson Family Singer abolitionist hymns, see *Hymn for the Quarterly Meeting of the Mass. Anti-Slavery Society. Monday, March 28, 1836* (Boston: n.p., 1836); Edwin Hatfield, ed., *Freedom's Lyre; or, Psalms, Hymns, and Sacred Songs, for the Slave and His Friends* (New York: S. W. Benedict, 1840); *Hymns and Songs for the Friends of Freedom* (Middletown: C. H. Pelton, 1842); John A. Collins, ed., *Anti-Slavery Picknick: A Collection of Speeches, Poems, Dialogues, and Songs; Intended for Use in Schools and Anti-Slavery Meetings* (Boston: H. W. Williams, 1842).

52. Robertson, *Parker Pillsbury*, 64. Jacob B. Moore, "History of Newspapers Published in New Hampshire," *American Quarterly Register* 13 (Nov. 1840):174.

53. "N.H. Vocalists," *Nashua Gazette,* 9 Oct. 1845. Lawrence, "Obbligato: 1839," 55. Cockrell, *Excelsior,* xxi–xxiv, xxvii. Tompkins, *Sensational Designs,* 8.

54. N. P. Rogers, "The New Hampshire 'Rainers,'" *Herald of Freedom,* 10 June 1842, 63.

55. Rogers, "The Hutchinsons Again," *Herald of Freedom,* 15 Jul. 1842, 83.

56. Rogers, "The Hutchinson Singers" [from the *Herald of Freedom,* 11 Aug. 1842], *Liberator,* 30 Dec. 1842, 208. John Greenleaf Whittier, Introduction to *Letters of Lydia Maria Child* (Boston: Houghton, Mifflin, 1883), ix. Kennedy, *John Greenleaf Whittier,* 99–100. Brooks, *Flowering of New England,* 399. Carolyn L. Karcher, "Rape, Murder, and Revenge in 'Slavery's Pleasant Homes': Lydia Maria Child's Antislavery Fiction and the Limits of the Genre," in *Culture of Sentiment: Race, Gender, and Sentimentality in Nineteenth-Century America,* ed. Shirley Samuels (New York: Oxford University Press, 1992), 60. Whittier's biographer takes a stronger stance on his isolation due to his abolitionism; see Elizabeth Gray Vining, *Mr. Whittier: A Biography* (New York: Viking, 1974). Lori Ginzburg, *Women in Antebellum Reform* (Wheeling, Ill.: Harlan Davidson, 2000), 65. Economic History Services, 3 Oct. 2002 <http://eh.net/hmit/ppowerusd>. Rogers, "The Hutchinson Singers," 208. Judson Hutchinson, "14 Diferent Springs Here," in Cockrell, *Excelsior,* 40. John Hutchinson, "August 5th/42," ibid., 43. Judson Hutchinson, "Franklin [NH] July 14, 1842," ibid., 7.

57. Rogers, "The Hutchinson Singers," 208. Davis, "Emergence of Immediatism," 212–228. Frederick Douglass, in the 1840s and 1850s, saw a clear relationship between cultural works and reform. To Douglass, writes Stauffer, "Art was the engine of social change." Stauffer, "Frederick Douglass."

58. *Journal of the American Temperance Union* 1 (January 1837):1. Charles T. Young, *Temperance Song Book of the Mass. Temperance Union* (Boston: Kidder and Wright, 1842), 3. *Lover's Forget-Me-Not, and Songs of Beauty: A Choice Collection of Sentimental, Comic, and Temperance Songs, with All the Late Negro Melodies* (Philadelphia: John B. Perry, 1847), 149–210. *Temperance Hymns* (Nashua: n.p.[, 184?]). William Ellery Channing, "Popular Amusements," *Western Messenger* 4 (Jan. 1838):344. See also Lawrence, "Obbligato: 1843," 231.

59. Lucretia Mott, "Letter Dated 4th mo., 4th, 1843," *James and Lucretia Mott: Life and Letters,* ed. Anna Davis Hallowell (Boston: Houghton, Mifflin, 1884), 241–242.

60. Jean Fagin Yellin, *Women and Sisters: The Antislavery Feminists in American Culture* (New Haven: Yale University Press, 1989). Walters, *Antislavery Appeal,* 25. James Gibbons, "11 mo., 28, 1840," in Abby Hopper Gibbons, *Life of Abby Hopper Gibbons: Told Chiefly Through Her Correspondence,* ed. Sarah Hopper Emerson (New York: Putnam, 1896) 1:97. Hallowell, *James and Lucretia Mott,* 241. Mott, ibid., 324.

61. Frederick Douglass, *Narrative of Frederick Douglass,* ed. David Blight (New York: St. Martin's, 2003). Revelations cited in Perry, *Radical Abolitionism,* 93. Perry, *Radical Abolitionism,* 92–103.

62. Solnit, *Savage Dreams,* 43, 69. Andrew Hutchinson in Asa Hutchinson, 4 Mar. 1853, Diary, Manuscript Division, American Antiquarian Society, Worcester, Mass. Denison Gould, *"Rains Finely Today": The Diary and Account Book of Denison Gould During the Years 1817 to 1865,* Harrison C. Baldwin, ed. (Milford, N.H.: Cabinet, 1974), 104. Ballou in Perry, *Radical Abolitionism,* 132.

63. Perry, *Radical Abolitionism,* 108–109. "Thomas Parnell Beach," *Herald of Freedom,* 16 Dec. 1842, 170. "Rally! Rally!! Rally!!!," *Herald of Freedom,* 23 Dec. 1842, 174. "Rally! Rally!! Rally!!!," *Herald of Freedom,* 30 Dec. 1842, 179.

64. John R. French, "Beach Is Out!" *Herald of Freedom,* 30 Dec. 1842, 178. "Anti-Slavery Convention, Milford," *Herald of Freedom,* 13 Jan. 1843, 185. Nathaniel P. Rogers, "Milford Convention," *Herald of Freedom,* 13 Jan. 1843, 186.

65. Rogers, "Milford Convention," 186. "Anti-Slavery Convention, Milford," 185. Perry, *Radical Abolitionism,* 109.

66. "Anti-Slavery Convention, Milford," 185. Rogers, "Milford Convention," 186.

67. Rogers, "Milford Convention," 186. "Anti-Slavery Hymns and Songs," *Herald of Freedom,* 17 Feb. 1843, 208.

68. Rogers, "Anti-Slavery Melody," *Liberator,* 20 Jan. 1843, 10. "Eleventh Annual Meeting of the Massachusetts Anti-Slavery Society," *Liberator,* 3 Feb. 1843, 19.

69. Nathaniel P. Rogers, "Anniversary of the Massachusetts A.S. Society in Faneuil Hall" [from the *Herald of Freedom*], *Liberator,* 24 Feb. 1843, 32. Stanton, *Eighty Years and More,* 130–131.

70. Rogers, "Anniversary."

71. William Garrison, "Concerts in Boston by the Hutchinson Family," *Liberator,* 24 Feb. 1843, 81. "Vocal Concert," *Liberator,* 24 Feb. 1843, 81.

72. "Anniversary in New-York," *Liberator,* 28 Apr. 1843.

73. J. A. Collins to I. C. Ray et al., 28 Apr. 1842, "Slavery in the United States Collection," box 1, folder 5, Manuscript Division, American Antiquarian Society. McFeeley, *Frederick Douglass,* 91–103.

74. For public meetings over books and "the diversity of forms and styles" see Walters, *Antislavery Appeal,* 21–22.

75. Advertisement in scrapbook at Minnesota Historical Society; its deceptive nature in Cockrell, *Excelsior,* 85. *American Music Journal* in Vera Brodsky Lawrence, "Rondo," *Strong on Music: The New York Music Scene in the Days of George Templeton Strong,* vol. 1, *1836–1849* (Chicago: University of Chicago, 1988), xxvii. These sentiments were widely echoed. The *Knickerbocker* (New York), for example, proclaimed that "there is a wide and general taste for the fine arts in this country, and New-York boasts as many enlightened connoisseurs as could be found in any city of the same extent in Europe"; 2, no. 3 (Mar. 1833):194. Henry C. Watson, *Musical History, Biography and Criticism* (New York: Henry G. Daggers, 1845), ix–x.

76. Asa B. Hutchinson, "New York May 10th, Wednesday Evening," in Cockrell, *Excelsior,* 112.

77. Asa B. Hutchinson, "Tuesday May 9th," ibid., 115.

78. Emerson in Thomas Wentworth Higginson, *Cheerful Yesterdays* (Boston: Houghton, Mifflin, 1898), 327. Also in Pillsbury, *Acts,* 326. *Weekly Herald,* 13 May 1842, cited in Cockrell, *Excelsior,* 116. Garrison to *Liberator,* 9 May 1843, in *Letters of William Lloyd Garrison,* ed. Walter M. Merrill (Cambridge: Belknap, Harvard University Press, 1973) 3:156–158. See also Cockrell, *Excelsior,* 117.

79. Nathaniel P. Rogers, "Anti-Slavery Melody," *Liberator,* 20 Jan. 1843, 10. "Eleventh Annual Meeting of the Massachusetts Anti-Slavery Society," *Liberator,* 3 Feb. 1843, 19. William Lloyd Garrison, "Concerts in Boston by the Hutchinson Family," *Liberator,* 24 Feb. 1843, 81. Rogers, "Anniversary." Rogers, "Milford Convention," 186.

80. *Liberator,* 26 May 1843, 81. See also Cockrell, *Excelsior,* 117. Asa Hutchinson, "Wednesday May 10th" and "Thursday New York May 11th," ibid., 117.

81. Asa Hutchinson, "Sunday Morning May 14th" and "New York Thursday Eve," ibid., 122, 140.

82. Cockrell, *Excelsior,* 160–161.

83. "The Hutchinsons," *Herald of Freedom,* 23 June 1843, 71. "A Public Meeting," *Liberator,* 31 Mar. 1843, 51. "Notice," *Liberator,* 21 Apr. 1843, 63. "Notice," *Liberator,* 24 Mar. 1843, 47. "Andover," *Liberator,* 31 Mar. 1843, 50. "The Old Granite State," *Liberator,* 26 May 1843, 88. "Meeting of the Massachusetts Anti-Slavery Society at the Free Church in Haverhill," *Liberator,* 7 Apr. 1843, 56. H. W. Foster, "Lowell Picnic," *Liberator,* 11 Aug. 1843, 127.

84. "Meeting of the Massachusetts Anti-Slavery Society at the Free Church in Haverhill," 56. Stauffer, "Douglass," 22–23.

85. *Twelfth Annual Report, Presented to the Massachusetts Anti-Slavery Society, By its Board of Managers, January 24, 1844* (Boston: Oliver Johnson, 1844), 70, 78–79. Benjamin Quarles, "Sources of Abolitionist Income," in McKivigan, *Abolitionism and American Reform,* 210.

86. Frederick Douglass, Introduction to Hutchinson, *Story of the Hutchinsons,* 1:xvii. Frederick Douglass to John Hutchinson, 18 Nov. 1894, *Memorabilia of the Hutchinson Family,* 31. Burns in Von Franck, *Trials of Anthony Burns,* 258. "The Hutchinson Family," *Pennsylvania Freeman,* 18 Jan. 1844. Solnit, *River of Shadows,* 114. John A. Collins, William Lloyd Garrison, Wendell Phillips, Francis Jackson, and Henry W. Williams, Letter to H. B. Couring, 1843, Slavery in the United States Collection. "New-England Anti-Slavery Convention," *Liberator* [from the *Practical Christian*], 30 June 1843, 102.

Part Second

1. Andrew Jackson, *President Jackson's Farewell Address to the People of the United States* (New York: J. W. Bell, n.d.). Marc M. Arkin, "The Federalist Trope: Power and Passion in Abolitionist Rhetoric," *Journal of American History* 88, no. 1 (June 2001):78.

2. Adam Rothman, "The Expansion of Slavery in the Deep South, 1790–1820," Ph.D. thesis, Columbia University, 2000, 4, 7, 16, 30, 60.

3. John Wallace Hutchinson, *Story of the Hutchinsons (Tribe of Jesse),* ed. Charles E. Mann (Boston: Lee and Shepard, 1896), 1:1–11.

4. A. J. Coolidge and J. B. Mansfield, *A History and Description of New England, General and Local* (Boston: A. J. Coolidge, 1859), 1:580. Andrew E. Rothovius, "How Hillsborough County Towns Were Named," *Olden Time: New Hampshire Historical Letter* 1, no. 9 (Sept. 1949):2. League of Women Voters of the Milford Area, N.H., *Know Your Town* (Milford: League of Women Voters of the Milford Area, 1974), 9. Winifred A. Wright, *Granite Town: Milford, New Hampshire, 1901/1978* (Canaan, N.H.: Phoenix, 1979), 7. George Allen Ramsdell, *History of Milford* (Concord, N.H.: Rumford, 1901), 6. John Hayward, *Gazetteer of New Hampshire* (Boston: John P. Jewett), 100.

5. Christopher Clark, *Roots of Rural Capitalism: Western Massachusetts, 1780–1860* (Ithaca: Cornell University Press, 1990), 63. Christopher M. Jedrey, *World of John Cleaveland: Family and Community in Eighteenth-Century New England* (New York: Norton, 1979), 164. Norman Allen Baxter, *History of Freewill Baptists: A Study in New England Separatism* (Rochester: American Baptist Historical Society, 1957), 18.

6. Steven Hahn and Jonathan Prude, eds., Introduction to *Countryside in the Age of Capitalist Transformation: Essays in the Social History of Rural America* (Chapel Hill: University of North Carolina Press, 1985), 3. Hutchinson, *Story of the Hutchinsons,* 1:6.

7. Cassius Marcellus Clay, "Divorce.—Beauty in Women.—Physical Laws.—Slavery," *Writings of Cassius Marcellus Clay: Including Speeches and Addresses,* ed. Horace Greeley (New York: Harper, 1848), 238. Clark, *Roots of Rural Capitalism,* 26. Steven Mintz and Susan Kellogg, *Domestic Revolutions: A Social History of American Family Life* (New York: Free Press, 1988). Steven Mintz, *Huck's Raft: A History of American Childhood* (Cambridge: Harvard University Press, 2004), 77.

8. See print of Polly in Hutchinson, *Story of the Hutchinsons,* 2:277. Olive Maria Warner, *Memories, 1792–1872: A Sketch of the Life of Lauretta Jewett Hutchinson* (Gilhead, Conn.: privately printed, 1899), 14–15.

9. R. D. Muzzey to Rev. Dr. Davis, 1862, in Hutchinson, *Story of the Hutchinsons,* 1:6–7. *Excelsior: Journals of the Hutchinson Family Singers, 1842–1846,* ed. Dale Cockrell (Stuyvesant, N.Y.: Pendragon, 1989), 87–88. Hutchinson, *Story of the Hutchinsons,* 1:470–471. Polly Hutchinson in Asa Hutchinson, "29 Mar. 1844," in Cockrell, *Excelsior,* 241.

10. Thomas Dublin, "Women and Outwork in a Nineteenth-Century New England Town: Fitzwilliam, New Hampshire, 1830–1850," in Hahn and Prude, *Countryside,* 51. Joshua Hutchinson remembered this divide clearly: his father at the plough and his mother at the "old spinning-wheel and loom," *A Brief Narrative of the Hutchinson Family: Sixteen Sons and Daughters of the Tribe of Jesse* (Boston: Lee and Shepard, 1874), 12. Carroll Smith-Rosenberg, "The Female World of Love and Ritual," in *Disorderly Conduct: Visions of Gender in Victorian America* (New York: Oxford University Press, 1985), 60.

11. Hutchinson, *Story of the Hutchinsons,* 1:20. Clark, *Roots of Rural Capitalism,* 24–27. E. Anthony Rotundo, *American Manhood: Transformations in Masculinity from the Revolution to the Modern Era* (New York: Basic, 1993). Hutchinson, *Story of the Hutchinsons,* 2:241–242; 1:14. "Milford Convention," *Herald of Freedom,* 13 Jan. 1843, 163. Asa Hutchinson, "Milford June 5th 1843," in Cockrell, *Excelsior,* 145. Mintz and Kellogg, *Domestic Revolutions,* 19, 45. A patriarchal dominance was a common occurrence. For Lauretta Hutchinson's father (unrelated to the Hutchinson Family Singers) and his "well-regulated household" see Warner, *Memories,* 2. Jesse Hutchinson's paternal dominance exhibited a certain "gloomy Calvinist determinism" that later religious traditions would seek to overturn; Paul E. Johnson and Sean Wilentz, *Kingdom of Matthias: A Story of Sex and Salvation in Nineteenth-Century America* (New York: Oxford University Press, 1994), 7.

12. Workers of the Federal Writers' Project of the Works Progress Administration for the State of New Hampshire, *New Hampshire: A Guide to the Granite State* (Boston: Houghton Mifflin, 1938), 44. Fruit was the major crop of the region, but hop cultivation was especially popular along the banks of the Souhegan River; see Coolidge and Mansfield, *History and Description of New England,* 1:580. "The Hutchinson Family," *Arthur's Lady's Magazine of Elegant Literature and Fine Arts,* Aug. 1844, 75. Hutchinson, *Story of the Hutchinsons,* 1:12. Clark, *Roots of Rural Capitalism,* 25. "Milford Convention," *Herald of Freedom* (Concord), 13 Jan, 1843, 163. Asa Hutchinson, "4 May 1843," "14 May 1844," in Cockrell, *Excelsior,* 107, 277. Hutchinson, *Story of the Hutchinsons,* 1:67, 143, 470, 6. Hutchinson, *Brief Narrative,* 11. Mintz, *Huck's Raft,* 77.

13. Catherine E. Kelly, *In the New England Fashion: Reshaping Women's Lives in the Nineteenth Century* (Ithaca: Cornell University Press, 1999), 5. Mintz and Kellogg, *Domestic Revolutions,* 19, 45. Mintz, *Huck's Raft.* Rotundo, *American Manhood,* 4. Ronald G. Walters, *Antislavery Appeal: American Abolitionism After 1830* (New York: Norton, 1978), 93.

14. Hutchinson, *Story of the Hutchinsons,* 1:4, 283. Perley Derby, *Hutchinson Family* (Salem: Essex Institute Press, 1870), 49.

15. Truman Abell, *New-England Farmer's Diary and Almanac, 1822* (Windsor, Vt.: Ebenezer Hutchinson, 1822). Wolfgang Schivelbusch, *Railway Journey: The Industrialization of Time and Space in the Nineteenth Century* (Berkeley: University of California Press, 1986), 1. Hutchinson, *Story of the Hutchinsons,* 1:18. For an example of the frequency of wood cutting and splitting see Moses Porter, "Diary for the Year 1824, Kept by Moses Porter," *Historical Collections of the Danvers Historical Society* 1 (1913):31–51. Derby, *Hutchinson Family,* 49. Hutchinson, *Brief Narrative,* 12. Hutchinson, *Story of the Hutchinsons,* 2:235–236. Asa Burnham Hutchinson, *Book of Brothers or the History of the Hutchinson Family* (New York: Hutchinson Family, 1852), 9–10.

16. Judson Hutchinson, "30 July 1842," in Cockrell, *Excelsior,* 36. Joshua Hutchinson, *Brief Narrative,* 11. Asa Hutchinson, "4 May 1843," in Cockrell, *Excelsior,* 107.

17. Farmland in Rebecca Solnit, *Savage Dreams: A Journey into the Landscape Wars of the American West* (New York: Vintage, 1994), 272. Leo Marx, *The Machine in the Garden: Technology and the Pastoral Ideal in America* (1964; New York: Oxford University Press, 1999). "A Farmer's Life and a Farmer's Duties," *Farmer's Monthly Visitor,* 15 Jan. 1839, 10. Coolidge and Mansfield, *History and Description of New England,* 1:397. *Constitution, Bye-Laws and Act of Incorporation of the Hillsborough Society for the Promotion of Agriculture and Domestic Manufactures* (Amherst: Elijah Mansur, 1821), 8. Asa Hutchinson, "January 5, 1853," *Diary, 1853,* Manuscript Department, American Antiquarian Society. Viola Hutchinson Campbell, *Memories of a Busy Life* (Plymouth: Rogers Print, 1926), 26.

18. *Celebration of Hundredth Anniversary of the Incorporation of Milford, New Hampshire, June 26, 1894* (Milford: Cabinet Print, 1894), 52. Abell, *New-England Farmer's Diary and Almanac, 1822.* Clark, *Roots of Rural Capitalism,* 25. Carol Brink, *Harps in the Wind: The Story of the Singing Hutchinsons* (New York: Macmillan, 1947), 3–7. Hutchinson, *Story of the Hutchinsons,* 1:3–7. Wright, *Granite Town,* 11. Porter, "Diary for the Year 1824," 31–34, 36, 39, 42, 45, 46. Hutchinson, *Story of the Hutchinsons,* 1:5.

19. Hutchinson, *Story of the Hutchinsons,* 1:8–10. Derby, *Hutchinson Family,* 49. Coolidge and Mansfield, *History and Description of New England,* 1:397, 580. *Early Milford Homes* (n.p., 1976?). For examples of international goods available in the New Hampshire countryside, see the *Farmers' Museum, or Literary Gazette* (Walpole), 16 June 1800. As T. H. Breen has recently suggested, historians have done a poor job recognizing the vast availability of British commercial goods in America, including rural areas, long before the so-called Market Revolution, and what this might mean for the sudden swell in consumerism in the nineteenth century. See Breen, *Marketplace of Revolution: How Consumer Politics Shaped American Independence* (New York: Oxford University Press, 2004), and John L. Brooke's review of the work, "Consumer Virtues in America?" *Reviews in American History* 32, no. 3 (Sept. 2004):329–340. Martin Bruegel, "'Time That Can Be Relied Upon': The Evolution of Time Consciousness in the Mid-Hudson Valley, 1790–1860," *Journal of Social History* 28 (Spring 1995): 548–549. Charles T. Jackson, *First Annual Report on the Geology of the State of New Hampshire* (Concord: Cyrus Barton, 1841), 557.

20. Hutchinson, *Story of the Hutchinsons,* 2:236. Mintz, *Huck's Raft,* 59.

21. Smith-Rosenberg, "Female World," 70–71. Carroll Smith-Rosenberg, "Hearing Women's Words," in *Disorderly Conduct,* 28. Lydia Maria Child to Abby Hopper Gibbons, 6 Nov. 1842, *Life of Abby Hopper Gibbons: Told Chiefly Through Her Correspondence,* ed. Sarah Hopper Emerson (New York: Putnam, 1896), 125. Fanny J. Crosby [Mrs. Alexander Van Alstyne], *Memoirs of Eighty Years: The Story of Her Life, Told by Herself: An-*

cestry, Childhood, Womanhood, Friendships, Incidents, and History of Her Songs and Hymns (Boston: James H. Earle & Company, 1906), 72.

22. William Lloyd Garrison to Ann Phillips, 20 April 1848, in Irving Bartlett, *Wendell and Ann Phillips: The Community of Reform, 1840–1880* (New York: Norton, 1979), 225. James Gibbons in *Life of Abby Hopper Gibbons,* 127. Jesse certainly did not attend college, which was where many nineteenth-century men forged their homosocial bonds; see E. Anthony Rotundo, "Romantic Friendship: Male Intimacy and Middle-Class Youth in the Northern United States, 1800–1900," *Journal of Social History* 23, no. 1 (1989): 1–25. Rotundo, *American Manhood.*

23. John Lewis in Nicholas Marshall, "'In the Midst of Life We Are in Death': Affliction and Religion in Antebellum New York," in *Mortal Remains: Death in Early America,* ed. Nancy Isenberg and Andrew Burstein (Philadelphia: University of Pennsylvania Press, 2003), 176. Hutchinson, *Story of the Hutchinsons,* 2:236. Hutchinson, *Brief Narrative,* 13, 53, 15. Marshall, "'In the Midst of Life,'" 186, 179. Asa Hutchinson, "Over the River" (Boston: Henry Tolman, 1860).

24. Hutchinson, *Story of the Hutchinsons,* 2:235–285; quotations from 2:236, 238.

25. Ibid., 1:328; 2:237–243. David Jaffee, "Peddlers of Progress and the Transformation of the Rural North, 1760–1860," *Journal of American History* 78 (1991):511–535; David Jaffee, "The Village Enlightenment in New England, 1760–1820," *William and Mary Quarterly* 47 (1990): 327–346. Bruegel, "'Time,'" 547–564. John Ashworth, *Slavery, Capitalism, and Politics in Antebellum America,* vol. 1, *Commerce and Compromise, 1820–1850* (New York: Cambridge University Press, 1995). John Ashworth, "The Relationship Between Capitalism and Humanitarianism," in *Antislavery Debate: Capitalism and Abolitionism as a Problem in Historical Interpretation,* ed. Thomas Bender (Berkeley: University of California Press, 1992), 180–199. Jeanne Boydston, *Home and Work: Housework, Wages, and the Ideology of Labor in the Early Republic* (New York: Oxford University Press, 1994). Charles Sellers, *Market Revolution: Jacksonian America, 1815–1846* (New York: Oxford University Press, 1994).

26. Hutchinson, *Story of the Hutchinsons,* 1:328, 2:237–243. Lowell Mason to Father, Mother, Sister, & Brothers, 8 June 1814, Savannah, Georgia, in Lowell Mason Papers, MSS 33, box 4, folder 7, Music Library, Yale University. George W. Anderson to Lowell Mason, 12 June 1827, Savannah, Lowell Mason Papers, box 4, folder 29. Jarrett Burch, *Adiel Sherwood: Baptist Antebellum Pioneer in Georgia* (Macon: Mercer University Press, 2003), 18, 48. Robert W. John, "Origins of the First Music Educators Convention," *Journal of Research in Music Education* 13, no. 4 (1965):207–219. Henry L. Mason, *Lowell Mason: His Life and Work, 1792–1872* (n.p., n.d.), 19–96, 197–235, in Lowell Mason Papers, box 12, Yale University. Nathan O. Hatch, *The Democratization of American Christianity* (New Haven: Yale University Press, 1989), 147–157. Richard Crawford, *The American Musical Landscape: The Business of Musicianship from Billings to Gershwin* (Berkeley: University of California Press, 1993), 51. Economic History Services, 11 Apr. 2006 <http://eh.net/hmit/compare>. Carol A. Pemberton, *Lowell Mason: A Bio-Bibliography* (New York: Greenwood, 1988), 7–20, student quotation, 4, Mason quotation, 18. Michael Broyles, *"Music of the Highest Class": Elitism and Populism in Antebellum Boston* (New Haven: Yale University Press, 1992), 66–67, 88. Mason felt so strongly about the simplicity of sacred music that he favored chant, unaccompanied singing, in church.

27. Hutchinson, *Story of the Hutchinsons,* 1:328, 2:237–243. Mason, *Lowell Mason,* 197. Chuck Klosterman, "The Pretenders," *New York Times,* 17 Mar. 2002. Joshua's and

the church's role in the training of the Hutchinson Family Singers has been sadly ignored. From the start the Hutchinsons displayed a depth of musical knowledge—especially in composition and instrumental technique—which hinted at some kind of formal training. They could not have acquired such tremendous skills, as one writer suggested, through their enthusiastic rehearsals behind a large rock in their family's fields alone. See Brink, *Harps in the Wind*, 7.

28. Hutchinson, *Brief Narrative*, 12–30. Hutchinson, *Story of the Hutchinsons*, 1:12. Richard D. Brown, "The Emergence of Urban Society in Rural Massachusetts, 1760–1820," *Journal of American History* 61 (June 1974):32, 48. "Stoves. Jesse Hutchinson, Jr. Stove Dealer, Lynn Mass.," *Lynn Directory and Register for the Year 1841* (Lynn: Benjamin F. Roberts, 1841), 12. "Free Soil Songs, Composed and Sung at the Buffalo Convention, August 9th and 10th 1848, by Messrs. Hutchinson, Jewell, Bates and Foster, of Massachusetts," *Buffalo Republic . . . Extra. Official Proceedings of the National Free Soil Convention, Assembled at Buffalo, N.Y., August 9th and 10th, 1848* (E. A. Maynard, 1848), 23.

29. Judson Hutchinson, "The Standing Collar" (Boston: Geo. P. Reed, 1851). Hutchinson, *Story of the Hutchinsons*, 2:260–261. Hutchinson, *Brief Narrative*, 41. Newspaper article in Hutchinson, *Story of the Hutchinsons*, 2:258.

30. Hutchinson, *Brief Narrative*, 47–50. Hutchinson, *Story of the Hutchinsons*, 1:261–263. Asa Hutchinson, "Asa B. Hutchinson, Last Will, Given Dec. 16, 1869," and "Assignment of Policy, Milwaukee Aug. 30, 1878," Asa B. Hutchinson and Family Papers, 1842–1937, Minnesota Historical Society, MSS microfilm roll 1. *Power and Blessing of a True Womanhood Illustrated in the Life, Labors, and Death of Mrs. Elizabeth C. Hutchinson of the Hutchinson Family, (Tribe of Asa)* (Minneapolis: Johnson and Smith, 1875).

31. Hutchinson, *Brief Narrative*, 53–55. Hutchinson, *Story of the Hutchinsons*, 2:269–274.

32. Songbooks (listing only the lyrics to songs, usually citing a well-known melody to which the words could be sung) were more common in the eighteenth century than were tune books. Crawford, *American Musical Landscape; American Sacred Music Imprints, 1698–1810: A Bibliography* (Worcester: American Antiquarian Society, 1990). Cyrus B. Phillips, *The Musical Self Instructor, Containing Five Hundred Questions and Answers Relative to the Science of Music, with Appropriate Examples, Tables &c. Comprising About Twenty Chapters; and Designed Chiefly for Students* (Burlington, N.J.: J. L. Powell, 1828). Crawford, *American Musical Landscape*, 49.

33. Gilbert Chase, *America's Music from Pilgrims to the Present*, rev. 3rd ed. (Urbana: University of Illinois Press, 1987), 33. Hutchinson, *Story of the Hutchinsons*, 1:11. Wright, *Granite Town*, 12. E. D. Sanborn, *Churches of New-Hampshire: An Historical Discourse, Delivered Before the General Association of New-Hampshire, at Littleton, Sept. 11, 1876* (Britstol, N.H.: R. W. Musgrove, 1876), 21. Arthur Wallace Peach, "The Reverend Joel Winch—Pioneer Minister," *Proceedings of the Vermont Historical Society* 9, no. 4 (December 1941):249. Adin Ballou, *Autobiography of Adin Ballou, 1803–1890*, ed. William S. Heywood (Lowell: Vox Populi, 1890), 42.

34. Nationalism quotation in Anne M. Boylan, *Sunday School: The Formation of an American Institution, 1790–1880* (New Haven: Yale University Press, 1988), 3. Hatch, *Democratization of American Christianity*, 147–148.

35. William B. Towne, *An Historical Address Delivered in the Town Hall at Amherst, January 19, 1874, on the Occasion of the Hundredth Anniversary of the Dedication of the Congregational Meeting-House* (Concord, 1874), 17, 28. *Manual of the First Congrega-*

tional Church Founded Nov. 19, 1738 (Milford, N.H., 1916). George A. Ramsdell, *Oration Delivered at the Dedication of the Town House, at Milford, N.H., April 29, 1870* (n.p., 1870), 5. *New England Narrative: A Record of One Hundred and Seventy-Five Years of History Compiled for the Anniversary Celebration in 1963 of the First Congregational Church of Milford, New Hampshire* (n.p., 1963), 20. *Declaration of Faith, Church Covenant, and Catalogue of Members of the Baptist Church in Milford, N.H., August, 1859* (Milford: Boutwell's Book and Job Office, 1859), 12, 15. Derby, *Hutchinson Family,* 48. *Murder of Caroline H. Cutter by the Baptist Ministers and Baptist Churches* (n.p., n.d.), 13. Hutchinson, *Story of the Hutchinsons,* 1:3.

36. Baxter, *History of Freewill Baptists,* 2, 18, 20, 36, 37, 116–117. *Burmah's Great Missionary. Records of the Life, Character, and Achievements of Adoniram Judson* (New York: Edward H. Fletcher, 1854), 445. Jon Butler, "Enthusiasm Decried: The Great Awakening as Interpretive Fiction," *Journal of American History* 69, no. 2 (Sept. 1982):305–325.

37. *Burmah's Great Missionary,* 365, 445. Joan Jacobs Brumberg, *Mission for Life* (New York: Free Press, 1980), xiii, 1–5. Baxter, *History of Freewill Baptists,* 66.

38. Internalization of sin in Susan Juster, *Disorderly Women: Sexual Politics and Evangelicalism in Revolutionary New England* (Ithaca: Cornell University Press, 1994), 154. Elizabeth Clark, "'The Sacred Rights of the Weak': Pain, Sympathy, and the Culture of Individual Rights in Antebellum America," *Journal of American History* 82, no. 2 (Sept. 1995):463–473.

39. *Declaration of Faith,* 11. Baxter, *History of Freewill Baptists,* 74. Johnson and Wilentz, *Kingdom of Matthias,* 7–10. *Fifth Annual Report of the New-Hampshire Baptist Sabbath School Union Presented at the Annual Meeting Held at Rumney, June 25, 1833* (Concord: Chase and Dunlap, 1833), 14–24. Jon Butler, *Awash in a Sea of Faith: Christianizing the American People* (Cambridge: Harvard University Press, 1990), 145. Hatch, *Democratization of American Christianity,* 95, 157. Janet Moore Lindemen, "A World of Baptists: Gender, Race, and Religious Community in Pennsylvania and Virginia, 1689–1825," Ph.D. thesis, University of Minnesota, 1994, 170–172. George A. Levesque, "Inherent Reformers—Inherited Orthodoxy: Black Baptists in Boston, 1800–1873," *Journal of Negro History* 60, no. 4 (Oct. 1975):494. "First Annual Meeting of the New-Hampshire Baptist Anti-Slavery Society. Held at Troy, Oct. 24, 1838," *Proceedings of the New-Hampshire Baptist State Convention . . . at Troy, Oct. 23 & 24, 1838* (Concord: Baptist Register Office, 1838), 35. *History of the First Congregational Church, Milford, New Hampshire* (Milford: First Congregational Church, 1938), 12.

40. Johnson and Wilentz, *Kingdom of Matthias,* see the Baptist patriarchy as a reaction to the female empowerment of Protestant evangelicalism, yet before the era of great revivals, the Baptist Church had retreated from gender equality in church governance. Indeed, by the 1830s the Baptists of Milford promote the middle-class, Finneyite revolution which Johnson claims they battled. For Baptists and the language of gender, Juster, *Disorderly Women,* 3, 6, 12, 42, 124–126, 140.

41. Lindemen, "A World of Baptists," 81–88. Boylan, *Sunday School,* 142–143. *Declaration of Faith,* 11.

42. Hutchinson, *Story of the Hutchinsons,* 1:14–15, 21. *Declaration of Faith,* 13. Edith Hunter, *A Brief History of the Public Schools of Milford, New Hampshire, 1738–1972* (Wethersfield Center, Vt.: Hunter, 1973), 24. The Hutchinson Family Singers' uncle Andrew Hutchinson supervised the Milford Sabbath Schools for many years; see *Fifth Annual Report of the New-Hampshire Baptist Sabbath School Union Presented at the Annual*

Meeting Held at Rumney, June 25, 1833 (Concord: Chase and Dunlap, 1833), 38. Boylan, *Sunday School,* 22–25, 142–143. Robert Lawrence Moore, *Selling God: American Religion in the Marketplace of Culture* (New York: Oxford University Press, 1994), 62–65.

Intermission (Bridge to Part Third)

1. *Proceedings of the Baptist Convention of the State of New-Hampshire at Their Ninth Annual Meeting at Jaffrey, June 26, 27 & 28, 1834* (Concord: Eastman, Wenster, 1834), 27. *Proceedings of the Baptist Convention of the State of New-Hampshire, at Their Seventh Annual Meeting in Portsmouth, June 27 & 28, 1832* (Concord: Chase and Dunlap, 1832), 38. *Proceedings of the New-Hampshire Baptist State Convention, New-Hampshire Branch of the N.H. Education Society, N. Hampshire Baptist Sabbath School Union, and the New-Hampshire Branch of the Baptist General Tract Society, at their Annual Meetings; and also the Organization of the New-Hampshire Foreign Bible Society, at Milford, October 18, 19, and 20, 1836* (Concord: Stevens and Young, 1836), 20, 26–28, 12–13.

2. *Proceedings . . . at Jaffrey,* 27. *Proceedings . . . in Portsmouth,* 38. *Proceedings . . . at Milford, October 18, 19, and 20, 1836,* 20, 26–28, 12–13. E. D. Sanborn, *Churches of New-Hampshire: An Historical Discourse, Delivered Before the General Association of New-Hampshire, at Littleton, Sept. 11, 1876* (Bristol, N.H.: R. W. Musgrove, 1876), 21–22. Robert Laurence Moore, *Selling God: American Religion in the Marketplace of Culture* (New York: Oxford University Press, 1994), 67–73.

3. *Proceedings of the Fourth Annual Meeting of the Baptist Convention of the State of New-Hampshire . . . June 24th & 25th, 1829* (Concord: Office of the Bartholomew Press, Printed by George Hough, 1829), 17, 5–6. Nathan O. Hatch, *The Democratization of American Christianity* (New Haven: Yale University Press, 1989), 3, 5. *Proceedings of the Fourth Annual Meeting,* 34. *Proceedings of the Baptist Convention of the State of New-Hampshire at their Eighth Annual Meeting in Rumney, June 26 & 27, 1833* (Concord: Chase and Dunlap, 1833), 25. Samuel Everett, "The Baptist Church," *New-England Baptist Register* 23, no. 1 (June 8, 1831). "Declaration of Faith," *Church Covenant, and Catalogue of Members of the Baptist Church in Milford, N.H., August, 1859* (Milford: Boutwell's Book and Job Office, 1859), 17–19. John Wallace Hutchinson, *Story of the Hutchinsons (Tribe of Jesse),* ed. Charles E. Mann (Boston: Lee and Shepard, 1896), 1:21, 2:239–240. *Proceedings of the Baptist Convention of the State of New-Hampshire at their Ninth Annual Meeting at Jaffrey, June 26, 27 & 28, 1834* (Concord: Eastman, Wenster, 1834), 27. Samuel Osgood, "Letter from New-Hampshire, Oct. 1836," *Western Messenger* 4 (Dec. 1837):238–239. Ebenezer E. Cummings, *Annals of the Baptist Churches in New Hampshire,* in *An Anthology of Early Baptists,* ed. Terry Wolever (Springfield, Mo.: Particular Baptist, 2001).

4. Harrison Gray Otis in Hatch, *Democratization of American Christianity,* 3. Sanborn, *Churches of New-Hampshire,* 17, 21. Arthur Wallace Peach, ed., "The Reverend Joel Winch," *Proceedings of the Vermont Historical Society* 9, no. 4 (Dec. 1941):235–240. Lucy N. Colman, *Reminiscences* (Buffalo: H. L. Green, 1891), 1–13. Polly Hutchinson in Hutchinson, *Story of the Hutchinsons,* 1:22. Moore, *Selling God,* 67–73.

5. Louis P. Masur, *1831: Year of Eclipse* (New York: Hill and Wang, 2001), 64, 68. F. A. Cox and J. Hoby, *Baptists in America: A Narrative of the Deputation from the Baptist Union in England, to the United States and Canada* (London: T. Ward, 1836), 223.

6. William G. McLoughlin, *Revivals, Awakenings, and Reform: An Essay on Religion*

and Social Change in America, 1607–1977 (Chicago: University of Chicago Press, 1978), 112. Moore, *Selling God,* 44–45, 77. Robert Laurence Moore, "Religion, Secularization, and the Shaping of the Culture Industry in Antebellum America," *American Quarterly* 41, no. 2 (June 1989):217, 228–230. David Grimstead, *American Mobbing, 1828–1861* (New York: Oxford University Press, 1998). Peter George Buckley, "To the Opera House: Culture and Society in New York City, 1820–1860," Ph.D. diss., State University of New York at Stony Brook, 1984.

7. Daniel W. Paterson, "Word, Song, and Motion: Instruments of Celebration Among Protestant Radicals in Early Nineteenth-Century America," in *Celebration: Studies in Festivity and Ritual,* ed. Victor Turner (Washington, D.C.: Smithsonian Institution Press, 1982). Cartwright cited in McLoughlin, *Revivals, Awakenings, and Reform,* 136. In recording numbers, religious leaders and others used their increasing numeracy to see the world differently than they had before; Patricia Cline Cohen, *A Calculating People: The Spread of Numeracy in Early America* (New York: Routledge, 1999).

8. Moore, *Selling God,* 43–45, 52–56. Minister cited ibid., 45. Elizabeth B. Clark, "'The Sacred Rights of the Weak': Pain, Sympathy, and the Culture of Individual Rights in Antebellum America," *Journal of American History* 82 (Sept. 1995):478. T. Gregory Garvey, *Creating the Culture of Reform in Antebellum America* (Athens: University of Georgia Press, 2006), 32. Scott Gac, "The Eternal Symphony Afloat: The Transcendentalists' Quest for a National Culture," *ATQ: Nineteenth Century Literature and Culture* 16, no. 3 (Sept. 2002):156–157. David Brion Davis, "The Emergence of Immediatism in British and American Thought," *Mississippi Valley Historical Review* 49, no. 2 (Sept. 1962):209–230. Colin Campbell, *Romantic Ethic and the Spirit of Modern Consumerism* (Oxford: Basil Blackwell, 1987). Leon Chai, *Romantic Foundations of the American Renaissance* (Ithaca: Cornell University Press, 1987). Michael T. Gilmore, *American Romanticism and the Marketplace* (Chicago: University of Chicago Press, 1985). Charles Capper, *Margaret Fuller: An American Romantic Life* (New York: Oxford University Press, 1992). John Colby, *Life, Experience and Travels of John Colby, Preacher of the Gospel* (Rochester, N.Y.: E. Peck, 1827), 70.

9. Robert Abzug, *Cosmos Crumbling: American Reform and the Religious Imagination* (New York: Oxford University Press, 1994), 35–37. Alfred F. Young, *The Shoemaker and the Tea Party: Memory and the American Revolution* (Boston: Beacon, 1999). Alan Taylor, "From Fathers to Friends of the People: Political Personas in the Early Republic," in *New Perspectives on the Early American Republic: Essays from the Journal of the Early Republic, 1981–1991,* ed. Ralph D. Gray and Michael A. Morrison (Urbana: University of Illinois Press, 1994), 139–163. McLoughlin, *Revivals, Awakenings, and Reform,* 99–100. Hatch, *Democratization of American Christianity.*

10. Hutchinson, *Story of the Hutchinsons,* 1: 239–240. Peach, "The Reverend Joel Winch," 240.

11. Hatch, *Democratization of American Christianity.* Abzug, *Cosmos Crumbling,* 79–80. John Stauffer, *Black Hearts of Men: Radical Abolitionists and the Transformation of Race* (Cambridge: Harvard University Press, 2002), 14–20. Moore, *Selling God,* 3–11, 17–39, 72–73. Donald G. Mathews, "The Second Great Awakening as an Organizing Process, 1780–1830," *American Quarterly* 21 (1969):22–43. David Reynolds, *Beneath the American Renaissance: The Subversive Imagination in the Age of Emerson and Melville* (Cambridge: Harvard University Press, 1988). John W. Frick, *Theatre, Culture, and Temperance Reform in Nineteenth-Century America* (New York: Cambridge University Press,

2003). Moore, "Religion," 217–219, 228–230; Twain quotation on 216. James W. Carey, *Communication as Culture: Essays on Media and Society* (1989; New York: Routledge, 1992). McLoughlin, *Revivals, Awakenings, and Reform,* 99–100; national religion quotation on 106.

12. James T. Kloppenberg, *Virtues of Liberalism* (New York: Oxford University Press, 1998), 35–41. Swisshelm in Peter F. Walker, *Moral Choices: Memory, Desire, and Imagination in Nineteenth-Century American Abolition* (Baton Rouge: Louisiana State University Press, 1978), 102–103, 138.

13. Sean Wilentz, *Chants Democratic: New York City and the Rise of the American Working Class* (New York: Oxford University Press, 1984). McLoughlin, *Revivals, Awakenings, and Reform,* 99–100; Jackson quotation on 139; Finney quotation on 126. Andrew Jackson may be incorrectly identified as the author of the quotation; see Gerald L. Priest, "Revival and Revivalism: A Historical and Doctrinal Evaluation," *Detroit Baptist Seminary Journal* 1 (Fall 1996):242, n. 71. Moore, *Selling God,* 87.

14. Glenn C. Altschuler and Stuart M. Blumin, *Rude Republic: Americans and Their Politics in the Nineteenth Century* (Princeton: Princeton University Press, 2000), 46; Democrat cited on 36.

15. *Harrison Eagle,* 25 June 1840. Altschuler and Blumin, *Rude Republic,* 21–37.

16. George W. Julian, *Political Recollections, 1840–1872* (Chicago: Jansen, McClurg, 1884), 17–18.

17. Ibid., 17–18. David N. Johnson, *Sketches of Lynn or Changes of Fifty Years* (Lynn: Thos. P. Nichols, 1880), 174. For the 1844 election, the Whigs offered up *Whig Songs for 1844* (Fragment at the Library Company of Philadelphia) and *National Clay Minstrel and True Whig's Pocket Companion for the Presidential Canvass of 1844* (Philadelphia: George Hood, 1843).

18. Hutchinson, *Story of the Hutchinsons,* 1:25–27. *Harrison Eagle,* 25 June 1840. Altschuler and Blumin, *Rude Republic,* 62. John's observations further a premise stated by Altschuler and Blumin that "the 1840 election . . . attracted vast numbers of Americans who had been, and perhaps continued to be, only superficially interested in politics," 36.

19. Altschuler and Blumin, *Rude Republic,* 36–37.

20. Thomas Dublin, *Transforming Women's Work: New England Lives in the Industrial Revolution* (Ithaca: Cornell University Press, 1994), xv–14, 33, 231. Christopher Clark, ed., *The Diary of an Apprentice Cabinetmaker: Edward Jenner Carpenter's "Journal," 1844–45* (Worcester: American Antiquarian Society, 1989), 304. Richard D. Brown, "The Emergence of Urban Society in Rural Massachusetts, 1760–1820," *Journal of American History* 61 (June 1974):30. Steven Mintz, *Huck's Raft: A History of American Childhood* (Cambridge: Harvard University Press, 2004), 75.

21. Francis Silsbee, "Francis Silsbee's Odyssey, 1831," ed. Alan R. Booth, *Essex Institute Historical Collections* 100 (1964):68. Milford Civic Club, *Milford: The Granite Town of New Hampshire* (Milford: Cabinet, 1940), 5. Workers of the Federal Writers' Project of the Works Progress Administration for the State of New Hampshire, *New Hampshire: A Guide to the Granite State* (Boston: Houghton Mifflin, 1938), 195–198. G. W. H., "Letter from Buffalo," 24 Oct. 1837, *Western Messenger* 4 (Dec. 1837):245.

22. Jonathan Prude, "Town-Factory Conflicts in Antebellum Rural Massachusetts," in *Countryside in the Age of Capitalist Transformation: Essays in the Social History of Rural America,* ed. Steven Hahn and Jonathan Prude (Chapel Hill: University of North Carolina Press, 1985), 80–83. Ronald G. Walters, "The Mass Media and Popular Culture," in

Encyclopedia of the United States in the Twentieth Century, ed. Stanley Kutler (New York: Scribner's, 1996), 4:1461. Henry Russell, *Cheer, Boys, Cheer!* (London: John Macqueen, 1895), 5. Excursionist in David Jaffee, "The Village Enlightenment in New England, 1760–1820," *William and Mary Quarterly* 47, no. 3 (July 1990):339–340. Michael T. Gilmore, *American Romanticism and the Marketplace* (Chicago: University of Chicago Press, 1985), 1–17.

23. Dona Brown, *Inventing New England: Regional Tourism in the Nineteenth Century* (Washington, D.C.: Smithsonian Institution Press, 1995), 1–13, 23–25. Arthur Schlesinger, Jr., *Age of Jackson* (Boston: Little, Brown, 1945), 5.

24. Brown, *Inventing New England,* 4. Raymond J. O'Brien, *American Sublime: Landscape and Scenery of the Lower Hudson Valley* (New York: Columbia University Press, 1981), 6–11, 280. The tie between the antebellum love of landscape and industrialization is one example of using an idealized past (in this case pastoral scenes of nature) as a "sanctuary from the awful present" (11). Also see David Lowenthal, "The American Scene," *Geographical Review* 58, no. 1 (Jan. 1968):61–88. One hundred years later, romanticism beat back industrial advance (instead of working with it) as beauty was deemed a vital public resource in the National Environmental Policy Act of 1969; O'Brien, *American Sublime,* 30.

25. Brown, *Inventing New England,* 41–43. Silsbee, "Francis Silsbee's Odyssey," 63–65.

26. Silsbee, "Francis Silsbee's Odyssey," 62–67. G. W. H., "Letter from Buffalo," 244. Martineau in Frederick Tuckerman, "Gleanings from the Visitors' Album of Ethan Allen Crawford," *Appalacia* 14, no. 4 (June 1919):381.

27. Silsbee, "Francis Silsbee's Odyssey," 63. Mary A. Hale, "A Trip to the White Mountains in 1840," *Essex Institute Historical Collection* 83 (1947):28. Asa Hutchinson, "September 29th, 1844," in *Excelsior: Journals of the Hutchinson Family Singers, 1842–1846,* ed. Dale Cockrell (Stuyvesant, N.Y.: Pendragon, 1989), 293.

28. Lowenthal, "American Scene," 61. Tuckerman, "Gleanings," 374–383. Brown, *Inventing New England,* 34, 45–48.

29. Brown, *Inventing New England,* 52–74. John F. Sears, *Sacred Places: American Tourist Attractions in the Nineteenth Century* (Amherst: University of Massachusetts Press, 1998), 73–74. James Duane Squires, *The Granite State of the United States: A History of New Hampshire from 1623 to the Present* (New York: American Historical, 1956), 270–271. Wolfgang Schivelbusch, *Railway Journey: The Industrialization of Time and Space in the Nineteenth Century* (Berkeley: University of California Press, 1986), 9.

30. William Willis Hayward, *History of Hancock, New Hampshire, 1764–1889* (Lowell: Vox Populi, 1889), 229–230. Clark, *Diary,* 304. Moore, *Selling God,* 72–73. Winifred A. Wright, *Granite Town: Milford, New Hampshire, 1901/1978* (Canaan, N.H.: Phoenix, 1979), 12. Robert A. Gross, "Transcendentalism and Urbanism: Concord, Boston, and the Wider World," *Journal of American Studies* 18, no. 3 (1984):362–363, 368–381, quotation from 369. Charles Sellers, *Market Revolution: Jacksonian America, 1815–1846* (New York: Oxford University Press, 1991).

31. Mintz, *Huck's Raft,* 86. *Catalogue of the Officers and Members of Milford Female Seminary, for the Fall Term of 1835, and the Spring, Summer & Fall Terms of 1836* (Amherst: R. Boylston, 1836), 7–11. Charles Burroughs, *An Address on Female Education, Delivered in Portsmouth, New-Hampshire, October 26, 1827* (Portsmouth: Childs and March, 1827), 6. Samuel Cornish in Shirley Yee, *Black Women Abolitionists: A Study in Activism, 1820–1860* (Knoxville: University of Tennessee Press, 1992), 49. David Goodwin, *Historical*

Sketch of the Town of Milford New Hampshire, 1846, ed. Milford Historical Society (Milford: Cabinet, 1987), 7. Frank Carpenter's 1892 article from the *Home Journal* in Hutchinson, *Story of the Hutchinsons,* 2:269–275. Hayward, *History of Hancock,* 229–230.

Part Third

1. *The Original Hutchinson Family: "Tribes of John & Jesse" and Miss Jenniebelle Neal* (n.p.: C.P. Shaw and H.J. Hutchinson, 1881). "Music and Musicians," *Church's Musical Visitor,* Nov. 1881, 40. Farmer's Cabinet in *Excelsior: Journals of the Hutchinson Family Singers, 1842–1846,* ed. Dale Cockrell (Stuyvesant, N.Y.: Pendragon, 1989), xxiv. John Wallace Hutchinson, *Story of the Hutchinsons (Tribe of Jesse),* ed. Charles E. Mann (Boston: Lee and Shepard, 1896), 1:35–36.

2. Lord Chesterfield in Karen Alquist, *Democracy at the Opera* (Urbana: University of Illinois Press, 1997), 10–11.

3. A "List of Letters" held in Lynn shows mail available for "Hutchinson J Jr," *Lynn Record,* 14 Jan. 1835. "New Stoves, at Hutchinson's," *Lynn Freeman and Essex County Whig,* 17 Oct. 1840. See similar ad in *Lynn Freeman,* 24 Oct. 1840. See advertisements for Jesse, Zephaniah, and Perley and Stoneham in *Lynn Directory and Register for the Year 1841* (Lynn: Benjamin F. Roberts, 1841), 12, 47–48, back cover. Perley Derby reports that Jesse removed to Lynn in 1836; see *Hutchinson Family* (Salem: Essex Institute, 1870), 77.

4. "Family Concert," *Lynn Freeman and Essex County Whig,* 13 Feb. 1841. Ad reprinted in Cockrell, *Excelsior,* xxvi.

5. Lawrence Buell, *New England Literary Culture from Revolution Through Renaissance* (New York: Cambridge University Press, 1986). Gilbert Chase, *America's Music from Pilgrims to the Present,* rev. 3rd ed. (Urbana: University of Illinois Press, 1987), 131–133. Hutchinson, *Story of the Hutchinsons,* 1:37–38.

6. Hutchinson, *Story of the Hutchinsons,* 1:39–40.

7. Cockrell, *Excelsior,* xxiv–xxvii. Aeolian harp, Berlioz, and Emerson in Thomas L. Hankins and Robert J. Silverman, *Instruments and the Imagination* (Princeton: Princeton University Press, 1995), 87, 99, 108. Hutchinson, *Story of the Hutchinsons,* 1:44–45. Hoxie Neale Fairchild, *The Noble Savage: A Study in Romantic Naturalism* (New York: Columbia University Press, 1928), 1. Asa Burnham Hutchinson, *Book of Brothers or the History of the Hutchinson Family* (New York: Hutchinson Family, 1852), 19.

8. Hutchinson, *Story of the Hutchinsons,* 1:44–45.

9. Hutchinson, *Book of Brothers,* 11. Elias Nason and George J. Varney, *A Gazetteer of the State of Massachusetts* (Boston: B. B. Russell, 1890), 430–432. Stuart Blumin, *The Emergence of the Middle Class: Social Experience in the American City, 1760–1900* (New York: Cambridge University Press, 1989), 299–300. William S. McFeely, *Frederick Douglass* (New York: Norton, 1991), 92. "A Concert of Ancient Music," *Lynn Record,* 15 Mar. 1837. "Mozart Society," *Lynn Record,* 10 May 1837. "Joice Heth," *Lynn Record,* 1 Feb. 1837. "Old Hampshire Slavery Society," *Lynn Record,* 1 Feb. 1837. "Anti-Slavery Lecture," *Lynn Record,* 15 Mar. 1837. "At a Meeting of the Lynn Anti-Slavery Society," *Lynn Record,* 20 Sept. 1837. David N. Johnson, *Sketches of Lynn or Changes of Fifty Years* (Lynn: Thos. P. Nichols, 1880), 1–11.

10. "Stoves, Jesse Hutchinson, jr.," *Lynn Freeman and Essex County Whig*, 16 Oct. 1841. Hutchinson, *Story of the Hutchinsons*, 1:39–40. "Singing School," *Lynn Freeman and Essex County Whig*, 19 Jan. 1842.

11. Greil Marcus, "Stories of a Bad Song," *Threepenny Review* 104 (Winter 2006):7. Cockrell, *Excelsior*, xxi–xxiv. Ignatz Moscheles, *Recent Music and Musicians: As Described in the Diaries and Correspondence of Ignatz Moscheles*, trans. A. D. Coleridge (1873; New York: Da Capo, 1970), 93–95, 128–129. Hans Nathan, "The Tyrolese Family Rainer, and the Vogue of Singing Mountain-Troupes in Europe and America," *Musical Quarterly* 32, no. 1 (Jan. 1946):63–79; quotation from 66. G. J. Webb and Lowell Mason, *Odeon: A Collection of Secular Melodies, Arranged and Harmonized for Four Voices. Designed for Adult Singing Schools, and for Social Music Parties* (Boston: J. H. Wilkins and R. B. Carter, 1837). Lowell Mason cited in the Rainers' advertisement, *Soiree Musicale, the Celebrated Rainer Family, or Tyrolese Minstrels* (Boston: Clapp, 1840).

12. Margaret Fuller, "Lives of the Great Composers," *Dial*, 10 Sept. 1841, 148–203. Scott Gac, "The Eternal Symphony Afloat: The Transcendentalists' Quest for a National Culture," *ATQ: Nineteenth Century Literature and Culture* 16, no. 3 (Sept. 2002):151. Robinson in Nicholas Tawa, *High-Minded and Low-Down: Music in the Lives of Americans, 1800–1860* (Boston: Northeastern University Press, 2000), 18. Denise Von Glahn, *Sounds of Place: Music and the American Cultural Landscape* (Boston: Northeastern University Press, 2003), 17–35. William Brooks, "The Flowering of Vocal Music in America," "Anthony Philip Heinrich," liner notes, *The Flowering of Vocal Music in America*, New World Records 80467. Peter F. Walker, *Moral Choices: Memory, Desire, and Imagination in Nineteenth-Century American Abolition* (Baton Rouge: Louisiana State University Press, 1978), 19. Irving H. Bartlett, *Wendell and Ann Phillips: The Community of Reform, 1840–1880* (New York: Norton, 1979), 3. Cockrell, *Excelsior*, xxi–xxii. Baltimore paper in Nathan, "Tyrolese Family Rainer," 72. Ibid., 70–72. Margaret Fuller, "Entertainments of the Past Winter," *Dial*, July 1842, 50, 71.

13. Hutchinson, *Story of the Hutchinsons*, 1:46, 2:296. "Concert," *Lynn Freeman and Essex County Whig*, 4 Dec. 1841. Contrary to my findings, Dale Cockrell suggests that it was Rainers' influence that precipitated the Hutchinsons' first performances in concert in 1840; *Excelsior*, xxiv. Nathan, "Tyrolese Family Rainer," 71–75.

14. "Vocal and Instrumental Concert," *Lynn Freeman and Essex County Whig*, 19 Jan. 1842.

15. Hutchinson, *Story of the Hutchinsons*, 1:46, 2:296. Singing style and yodeling in Nathan, "Tyrolese Family Rainer," 70, 77. "Family Concert by the Aeolian Vocalists!" *Lynn Freeman and Essex County Whig*, 26 Feb. 1842.

16. Conversion factors vary widely, but expenses of $190 in 1842 are probably equivalent to somewhere between $4,000 and $40,000 in 2005 dollars. Economic History Services, "What Is Its Relative Value in US Dollars?" 17 Apr. 2006 <http://eh.net/hmit/compare>. Asa Hutchinson, "Weare July 11th 1842," "Bethlehem, N.Y. August 7th/1842," "Rutland July 24th 1842," "1842 Rutland Vt July 24th," "Milford Nov 26th 1842," in Cockrell, *Excelsior*, 3–4, 47, 23, 83.

17. See various journal entries from Asa and Judson Hutchinson in Cockrell, *Excelsior*, 7–8, 16, 21–23, 28, 30, 32, 37–38, 45–46, 50, 60.

18. Judson Hutchinson, "Franklin [NH] July 14, 1842 18 miles from Concord," in Cockrell, *Excelsior*, 7–8.

19. Nathaniel Peabody Rogers, "The Hutchinsons Again," *Herald of Freedom,* 15 July 1842, 83. Asa Hutchinson, "Hanover July 21th," in Cockrell, *Excelsior,* 17–18. "That Concert," *Nashua Gazette and Hillsborough County Advertiser,* 8 Nov. 1842.

20. Asa Hutchinson, "July 15th 1842," in Cockrell, *Excelsior,* 8. Asa Hutchinson, "August 14th 1842," ibid., 61. "Social Aspects of the Forties," *Lippincott's Magazine of Popular Literature and Science* 25 (Jun. 1880):755. Mintz, *Huck's Raft,* 72–75. Robert H. Abzug, *Cosmos Crumbling: American Reform and the Religious Imagination* (New York: Oxford University Press, 1994), chapters 4 and 7. Hutchinson, *Story of the Hutchinsons,* 1:41–42. *Proceedings of the Fourth Annual Meeting of the Baptist Convention of the State of New-Hampshire . . . June 24th & 25th, 1829* (Concord: Bartholomew Press and George Hough, 1829), 6. Jack S. Blocker, *American Temperance Movements: Cycles of Reform* (Boston: Twayne, 1989), 3–12. Elizabeth B. Clark, "'The Sacred Rights of the Weak': Pain, Sympathy, and the Culture of Individual Rights in Antebellum America,'" *Journal of American History* 82, no. 2 (Sept. 1995):486. "Great Temperance Meeting—the Ball Rolling On," *Lynn Freeman and Essex County Whig,* 10 June 1841. "Concert by the Aeolians," *Lynn Freeman and Essex County Whig,* 22 April 1843. "Celebrations on the Fourth," *Farmers' Cabinet* (Amherst), 8 July 1842. "Mass Temperance Convention," *Nashua Gazette and Hillsborough County Advertiser,* 10 Aug. 1843. Cockrell, *Excelsior,* 388.

21. N. P. Rogers, "The New-Hampshire 'Rainers,'" *Herald of Freedom,* 10 June 1842, 63. Leon Chai, *Romantic Foundations of the American Renaissance* (Ithaca: Cornell University Press, 1987), xi, 6. Asa Hutchinson, "Hanover July 15th 1842," in Cockrell, *Excelsior,* 8. H. H., "Letter to the Editor," *Essex County Washingtonian,* 29 Sept. 1842. Ralph Waldo Emerson, "Art," *Essays: First and Second Series* (1883; New York: Vintage, 1990), 201. See also Vera Brodsky Lawrence, *Strong on Music: The New York Music Scene in the Days of George Templeton Strong, 1836–1849* (New York: Oxford University Press, 1988), 1:lvi.

22. Asa Hutchinson, "Saratoga Springs Tuesday P.M. Aug 2d," "Sept 1st 1842," in Cockrell, *Excelsior,* 37–38, 80. Ibid., 38–40. Richard Crawford, *American Musical Life: A History* (New York: Norton, 2001), 423–425. James Trotter, *Music and Some Highly Musical People* (Boston: Lee and Shepard, 1878), 306–308.

23. *Evening Journal,* 10 Aug. 1842, in Cockrell, *Excelsior,* 58. *Microscope* (Albany), 20 Aug. 1842, ibid., 67.

24. Asa B. Hutchinson, "Albany August 14th/42," "Schenectady NY Aug 16th/42," ibid., 62–63. John Hutchinson, "John H.," ibid., 78.

25. U.S. Census Bureau, "Table 7. Population of the 100 Largest Urban Places: 1840," 15 Jun. 1998, 62 <www.census.gov/population/documentation/twps0027/tab07.txt>. New York State Museum, "Albany Population," 6 Nov. 2002 <http://www.nysm. nysed.gov/albany/population.html>. CensusRecords.Net, "New York City Census Records," 6 Nov. 2002 <http://www.censusrecords.net/cities/new_york_city_census. htm>. Sidney Redner, "Population of Boston, 1790–1990," 6 Nov. 2002 <http:// physics.bu.edu/~redner/projects/population/cities/boston.html>. U.S. Census Bureau, "Table 1. Rank by Population of the 100 Largest Urban Places, Listed Alphabetically by State: 1790–1990," 15 Jun. 1998, 6 Nov. 2002 <http://www.census.gov/population/ documentation/twps0027/tab01.txt>. Asa Hutchinson, "Albany August 22d 1842," in Cockrell, *Excelsior,* 68. Dale Cockrell estimated that the paying audience for the August 22 show was between 104 and 152 persons, not including an undisclosed quantity of free tickets that the Hutchinson Family Singers always handed out; ibid., 69. Asa Hutchin-

son, "Aug 23d Tuesday," ibid., 69–70. One earlier private concert was in Bethlehem, New York, near the beginning of August; see Asa Hutchinson, "Bethlehem August 7th/ 42," ibid., 48. Hutchinson, *Story of the Hutchinsons,* 1:60. *Evening Journal* in Cockrell, *Excelsior,* 70. Asa Hutchinson, "23d August 1842," "Thursday Aug 25th," "Saturday August 27th 1842," ibid., 71–74. Derby, *Hutchinson Family,* 102. Hutchinson, *Book of Brothers,* 29.

26. Asa Hutchinson, "Sabath day Aug 28th/42," "Monday Aug 29th/42," "Tuesday Morning Aug 30th," "Tuesday Aug 30th/42," in Cockrell, *Excelsior,* 75–77. Judson Hutchinson, "Monday Aug 29 42," ibid., 76. Economic History Services, 7 Nov. 2002 <http://eh.net/hmit/ppowerusd>. Cockrell, *Excelsior,* 69. Rogers, "The Hutchinsons Again," 83. Bathsheba H. Morse Crane, *Life, Letters, and Wayside Gleanings, for the Folks at Home* (Boston: J. H. Earle, 1880), 480.

27. Asa Hutchinson, "Albany August 28th," "Monday Aug 29th/42," in Cockrell, *Excelsior,* 74, 76. Donald Scott, "Itinerant Lecturers and Lecturing in New England, 1800–1850," in *Itinerancy in New England and New York,* ed. Peter Benes (Boston: Boston University Press, 1986), 65. Asa Hutchinson, "Sabath day Aug 28th/42;" "Sept 1st 1842," in Cockrell, *Excelsior,* 75, 80.

28. Judson Hutchinson, "Sunday Night, Aug 14 10 1/2 o'Clock," in Cockrell, *Excelsior,* 61–63. John Hutchinson, "July 26 42," ibid., 29.

29. Ibid., 81–87. Asa Hutchinson, "Milford Nov 26th 1842," ibid., 82–89. Judson Hutchinson, "Whitehall July 25/42," ibid., 26. Hutchinson, *Story of the Hutchinsons,* 1:69. "Benefit Concert by the Aeolian Vocalists," *Farmers' Cabinet,* 28 Oct. 1842. For a similar ad for the benefit concert on 29 October 1842, see Cockrell, *Excelsior,* 87.

30. Rogers, "The Hutchinson Singers," *Liberator,* 30 Dec. 1842, 208. "Case of Thomas P. Beach," *Liberator,* 18 Nov. 1842, 183. It appears that Jesse Hutchinson may have been composing songs at other antislavery meetings in the Boston area as well, as an unnamed source of music appears in "Anti-Slavery Soiree," *Liberator,* 30 Dec. 1842, 206. John A. Collins, ed., *Anti-Slavery Picknick: A Collection of Speeches, Poems, Dialogues, and Songs; Intended for Use in Schools and Anti-Slavery Meetings* (Boston: H. W. Williams, 1842). *Hymns and Songs for the Friends of Freedom* (Middleton: C. H. Pelton, 1842). Maria Weston Chapman, ed., *Songs of the Free, and Hymns of Christian Freedom* (Boston: Isaac Knapp, 1842). See also Vicki L. Eaklor, *American Antislavery Songs: A Collection and Analysis* (New York: Greenwood, 1988).

31. Asa Hutchinson, "New York Monday May 22," "New York Tuesday Morning May 23d 1843," "New York May 24th Wednesday P.M.," in Cockrell, *Excelsior,* 137–138. Cockrell lists thirteen songs for 1843, ibid., 161–163. There were also: "The Cot Were [sic] We Were Born" (New York: Firth and Hall, 1843); "We Are Happy and Free" (New York: Firth and Hall, 1843). Library of Congress, "Music for a Nation" <http://memory.loc.gov/ammem/mussmhtml/mussmhome.html>. The list of popular music by decade on the site was culled from Julius Mattfeld's *Variety Music Cavalcade, 1620–1969,* 3rd ed. (Englewood Cliffs, N.J.: Prentice-Hall, 1971).

32. Asa Hutchinson, "Milford Nov 26th 1842," in Cockrell, *Excelsior,* 83. "C. H. Ditson Dead; Music Publisher," *New York Times,* 16 May 1929, 29. "C. H. Ditson Left $6,935,938 Estate," *New York Times,* 15 Oct. 1931, 33. The material on early publishing was shaped by a generous phone conversation in November 2001 with Richard J. Wolfe in Philadelphia. See also Wolfe, *Early American Music Engraving and Printing: A History of Music Publishing in America from 1787 to 1825 with Commentary on Earlier and Later Prac-*

tices (Urbana: University of Illinois Press, 1980). For the variety of publishers see the collection of Hutchinson Family Singers music at the New Hampshire Historical Society, Concord. "As Sung By the Hutchinsons," see "Oh! Home of My Boyhood, My Own Country Home" (Boston: Oliver Ditson, 1847). T. Bircher, "Band of Young Apostles, A Poetic Address to the Celebrated Hutchinson Family" (Boston: Stephen W. Marsh, 1846). Lori Merish, *Sentimental Materialism: Gender, Commodity Culture, and Nineteenth-Century American Literature* (Durham: Duke University Press, 2000), 16.

33. Oliver Ditson to Mr. Asa B. Hutchinson, 9 Apr. 1864, Asa B. Hutchinson and Family Papers, 1842–1937, Minnesota Historical Society, Manuscript Division, microfilm roll 1. Asa B. Hutchinson, "Receipt, Oliver Ditson & Co.," 1877, Asa B. Hutchinson and Family Papers, microfilm roll 1. Oliver Ditson, "Notice of Receipt," Asa B. Hutchinson and Family Papers, microfilm roll 1. Hutchinson, *Story of the Hutchinsons,* 1:418. For the variety of sheet music covers see the collection of Hutchinson Family Singers' music at the New Hampshire Historical Society, Concord, New Hampshire. "Editors' Book Table," *Godey's Lady's Book* 34 (May 1847):270.

34. J. Judson Hutchinson, "Cape Ann" (New York: Firth and Hall, 1843). See copy of the song at the Library of Congress for handwritten note on its receipt. Sandy Paton, "New England Traditions in Folk Music," *Brave Boys* (New Word Records 80239), liner notes, 21–23. Cockrell, *Excelsior,* xxviii. Asa Hutchinson, "Tuesday Aug 30th/42," ibid., 77.

35. Jesse Hutchinson, "King Alcohol" (Boston: Oliver Ditson, 1843). Asa Hutchinson, "Boston May 8th 1843," "Thursday New York May 11th," in Cockrell, *Excelsior,* 108–111, 117–119. Ibid., 108–119.

36. *The Granite Songster, Containing the Poetry as Sung by the Hutchinson Family, at their Concerts* (Boston: Asa Hutchinson, 1847). Asa Hutchinson, "Milford, Tuesday, June 6th 1843," "Friday Washington, February 2, 1844," "London, February 5, 1846," in Cockrell, *Excelsior,* 154, 216, 339–340. Chase, *America's Music,* 197. R. T. Trall, "Topics of the Month," *Water-Cure Journal* 23, no. 5 (May 1857):109. "Old Hundred" in Brian Roberts, "'Slavery Would Have Died of That Music': The Hutchinson Family Singers and the Rise of Popular-Culture Abolitionism in Early Antebellum-Era America, 1842–1850," *Proceedings of the American Antiquarian Society* 114, no. 2 (2004):334. Hutchinson, *Story of the Hutchinsons,* 1:87. Moore in Cockrell, *Excelsior,* 340.

37. Tawa, *High-Minded and Low-Down.* Asa Hutchinson, "New York May 12th," "New York May 14th 1843," in Cockrell, *Excelsior,* 120, 126. Ibid., 120–121, 285. *Tribune,* 26 May 1843, in Cockrell, *Excelsior,* 141.

38. Judson Hutchinson and Henry Wadsworth Longfellow, "Excelsior" (New York: Firth and Hall, 1843). David Brion Davis, "The Emergence of Immediatism in British and American Antislavery Thought," *Mississippi Valley Historical Review* 49, no. 2 (Sept. 1962):229. Brooks, "Flowering of Vocal Music." Diane Ackerman, "Language at Play," in *In Fact: The Best of Creative Nonfiction,* ed. Lee Gutkind (New York: Norton, 2005), 179. Longfellow quotation in Cockrell, *Excelsior,* 373. Fairchild, *Noble Savage.* Jason Toynbee, "Music, Culture, and Creativity," in *Cultural Study of Music: A Critical Introduction,* ed. Martin Clayton, Trevor Herbert, and Richard Middleton (New York: Routledge, 2003), 103–110. Howard S. Becker, *Art Worlds* (Berkeley: University of California Press, 1982). Jon Guttman, "Napoleon's Coronation Cost Him a Chance at Musical Immortality," *Military History* 21, no. 5 (Dec. 2004):6. Philip V. Bohlman, "Ontologies of Music," in *Rethinking Music,* ed. Nicholas Cook and Mark Everist (New York: Oxford University

Press, 1999), 30. Cockrell, *Excelsior,* 378. Charles Sumner to Henry Wadsworth Longfellow, 12 August 1846, in *Selected Letters of Charles Sumner,* ed. Beverly Wilson Palmer. (Boston: Northeastern University Press, 1990), 1:174. Newspaper reviews of the song in Cockrell, *Excelsior,* 324, 373, 378. See also Chase, *America's Music,* 197.

39. Judson Hutchinson and George P. Morris, "My Mother's Bible" (New York: Firth and Hall, 1843). George P. Morris, "My Mother's Bible," in *Poems* (New York: Charles Scribner, 1853), 85–86. Lewis Perry, *Radical Abolitionism: Anarchy and the Government of God in Antislavery Thought* (Ithaca: Cornell University Press, 1973), 92–94. Asa Hutchinson, "Milford, May 19th, Sunday, 1844," in Cockrell, *Excelsior,* 278–279.

40. "Editor's Book Table," *Godey's Magazine and Lady's Book* (Mar. 1844), 150. Asa Hutchinson, "Wednesday, February 21, 1844," in Cockrell, *Excelsior,* 230–231. Hogarth, *Daily News* (London), 26 Feb. 1846, ibid., 371.

41. "The Old Granite State" as national anthem, Cockrell, *Excelsior,* 161.

Part Fourth

1. Asa Hutchinson, "Philadelphia, Jan. 3, 1844," "Philadelphia, Jan. 4, 1844," "Philadelphia, Jan. 10th, 1844," "Philadelphia, Jan. 13th, 1844," in *Excelsior: The Journals of the Hutchinson Family Singers, 1842–1846,* ed. Dale Cockrell (Stuyvesant, N.Y.: Pendragon, 1989), 169–171, 181–182, 187–188. *Public Ledger,* ibid., 170. *Christian Observer,* ibid., 171–172. *Saturday Courier,* ibid., 182. John Wallace Hutchinson, *Story of the Hutchinsons (Tribe of Jesse),* ed. Charles E. Mann (Boston: Lee and Shepard, 1896), 1:110–111. Nathaniel P. Willis to Asa Hutchinson, 12 Aug. 1844, 6991-F, Barrett-Willis, Manuscript Department, University of Virginia Library.

2. Asa Hutchinson, "Philadelphia, Jan. 11, 1844," in Cockrell, *Excelsior,* 183–184. Miss F.A.C., "The Granite State Minstrels," *Sun,* ibid., 184–185.

3. George Pope Morris, "The Land of Washington," *Poems,* Project Gutenberg ETexts, 27 Dec. 2002 <ftp://ibiblio.org/pub/docs/books/gutenberg/etext01/mrrsp10.txt>. Asa Hutchinson, "Baltimore, Jan. 22nd, 1844," in Cockrell, *Excelsior,* 200.

4. Asa Hutchinson, "Baltimore, Jan. 22nd, 1844." Patricia Cline Cohen, *A Calculating People: The Spread of Numeracy in Early America* (1982; New York: Routledge, 1999), 4–5. U.S. Census Bureau, "Table 7. Population of the 100 Largest Urban Places: 1840," 6 Nov. 2002 <www.census.gov/population/documentation/twps0027/tab07.txt>. Lydia Maria Child, *The American Anti-Slavery Almanac, for 1843* (New York: American Anti-Slavery Society, 1842).

5. Asa Hutchinson, "Philadelphia, Jan. 3, 1844," "Philadelphia, Jan. 4th, 1844," "Philadelphia, Jan. 8, 1844," in Cockrell, *Excelsior,* 169–171, 176–177. Asa Hutchinson, "Hanover July 15," "Hanover July 15th 1842," Hanover, Monday July 18th," "New York May 10th," "Thursday New York May 11th," "New York May 14th 1843," "New York Sunday Eve May 21," "New York Tuesday Morning," "Philadelphia, Jan. 12th, 1844," "Tuesday, January 23, 1844," "Friday morning, Baltimore, January 26th, 1844," "Boston—Wednesday Morning, April 3, 1844," "Hartford, April 17, 1844," "H (Abby stops me) Hallowell, M.E. (Down East) Sunday, September 29th, 1844," "Lowell, Mass. March 5th, 1845," ibid., 11–14, 112, 117, 128, 135–137, 186, 201–203, 208–209, 245, 257, 293, 307. Abby Kelley to Messrs. and Miss Hutchinson, Dover, 21 Aug. 1844, Manuscripts, Schlesinger Library, Radcliffe Institute, Harvard University.

6. Though Dale Cockrell suggests that "Mary Lincoln" was Mary Ware Lincoln, the publication of Mary Hersey Lincoln's writings proves otherwise; see Theodora Cabot, "Young Reformers Climb Mount Washington," *New England Quarterly* 6, no. 1 (Mar. 1933):158–172. Cockrell, *Excelsior,* 293.

7. Quotations from White Mountain journey from Mary Lincoln in Cabot, "Young Reformers." N. P. Rogers, "Milford Convention," *Herald of Freedom,* 13 Jan. 1843, 186.

8. Asa Hutchinson, "January 26th, 1844," in Cockrell, *Excelsior,* 209.

9. Henry W. Rugg, *Presidents of the United States* (New York: Hurst, 1890), 72–87. Richard H. Sewell, *Ballots for Freedom: Antislavery Politics in the United States* (New York: Norton, 1976), 62–63. David M. Potter, *Impending Crisis, 1848–1861,* completed and ed. Don E. Ferenbacher (New York: Harper Torchbooks, 1976). Michael F. Holt, *Fate of Their Country: Politicians, Slavery Extension, and the Coming of the Civil War* (New York: Hill and Wang, 2004), 8–41. John Ashworth, *Slavery, Capitalism, and Politics in the Antebellum Republic* (New York: Cambridge University Press, 1995), 418–422.

10. Asa Hutchinson, "January 31st, 1844," "February 1, 1844," "February 2, 1844," "February 4, 1844," "February 6, 1844," "February 10, 1844," "February 12, 1844," in Cockrell, *Excelsior,* 212–215, 217–219, 222–223, 226–229. Nick Hornby, *Songbook* (New York: Riverhead, 2003). *Whig Standard,* 6 Feb. 1844, cited in Cockrell, *Excelsior,* 223. Unidentified newspaper clipping from Washington, D.C., Wadleigh Memorial Public Library, Hutchinson Family Singers Collection box 1, item 12 [hereafter WMPL 1, 12]. Columnist: R. H. Howard, "The Hutchinson Family as Reformers," *Our Day* 7 (1897):279. Hutchinson, *Story of the Hutchinsons,* 1:101. Cheryl Harris, "Whiteness as Property," *Harvard Law Review* 106 (June 1993):1709–1791. Mary Niall Mitchell, "Rose-bloom and Pure White, Or So It Seemed," *American Quarterly* 54, no. 3 (Sept. 2002): 369–410.

11. Cockrell, *Excelsior,* 397. Clay in Sewell, *Ballots for Freedom,* 48. Jesse Hutchinson, Jr., "Get Off the Track!" (Boston: Jesse Hutchinson, Jr., 1844). David Brion Davis, *Antebellum American Culture: An Interpretive Anthology* (Lexington, Mass.: D. C. Heath, 1979), 353–366. Wolfgang Schivelbusch, *Railway Journey: The Industrialization of Time and Space in the Nineteenth Century* (Berkeley: University of California Press, 1986), 2–16. Henry Russell, *Cheer! Boys, Cheer!* (London: John McQueen, 1895), 69. P., "The Hutchinsons," *Herald of Freedom,* 18 Apr. 1845, 14. "The Salem Convention," *Liberator,* 11 April 1844, 63. *Atlas, Morning Chronicle,* and *National Anti-Slavery Standard* cited in Cockrell, *Excelsior,* 258–259, 302, 309. "Get Out of the Way!" *Whig Songs for 1844* (fragment at the Library Company of Philadelphia).

12. Nathaniel P. Rogers, "New England Convention," *Liberator,* 21 June 1844. *Eleventh Annual Report, Presented to the Massachusetts Anti-Slavery Society, By Its Board of Managers, January 23, 1843* (Boston: Oliver Johnson, 1843), 85. Sewell, *Ballots for Freedom,* 110–111. David Goodwin, *Historical Sketch of the Town of Milford, New Hampshire, 1846,* ed. Milford Historical Society (Milford: Cabinet, 1987), 8, 11–13. Cockrell, *Excelsior,* 93–94. Jarius Lincoln, *Anti-Slavery Melodies: For the Friends of Freedom* (Hingham, Mass.: Elijah B. Gill, 1843), 3. "Anti-Slavery Melodies," *Liberator,* 29 Dec. 1843, 206.

13. H. C. Wright, "Old England and New England Laborers on Land Contrasted," *Liberator,* 26 May 1848, 81. Lewis Perry, *Radical Abolitionism* (Ithaca: Cornell University Press, 1973), 97. John Hutchinson reported Russell's lost dollar figure at $13,000 in his memoirs; either way it was a healthy amount, the equivalent of at least a quarter of a million 2005 dollars; Hutchinson, *Story of the Hutchinsons,* 1:98. Economic History Services,

"What Is Its Relative Value in US Dollars?" 13 Oct. 2005 <http://eh.net/hmit/compare/>. Asa Hutchinson, "Sandy Hill Friday July 29th 1842," "Philadelphia, Jan. 4th, 1844," "Philadelphia January 5th, 1844," "Tuesday, January 23, 1844," "Friday A.M., Milford, March 29, 1844," "Milford, May 8, 1845," in Cockrell, *Excelsior,* 33, 171–172, 201, 240–241. Ibid., 161, 172–173. Ashworth, *Slavery, Capitalism, and Politics,* 350–355. Holt, *Fate of Their Country,* 40–41. Stuart Blumin, *The Emergence of the Middle Class: Social Experience in the American City, 1760–1900* (New York: Cambridge University Press, 1989), 109–110. John, Asa, Judson, and their brother David secured more land in Milford in 1849, which they then sold to the Milford school system in 1853. John and Jesse purchased the land immediately surrounding High Rock, a preeminent spot in Lynn, Massachusetts. Winifred A. Wright, *Granite Town: Milford, New Hampshire, 1901/1978* (Canaan, N.H.: Phoenix, 1979), 487, 501. Hutchinson, *Story of the Hutchinsons,* 1:136. "General Notes," *New York Times,* 9 Mar. 1902, 6.

14. Christopher Clark, *Communitarian Moment: The Radical Challenge of the Northampton Association* (Ithaca: Cornell University Press, 1995), xi–14, 220–223. Davis, *Antebellum American Culture,* 348–351. Asa Hutchinson, "Jan. 9th, 1844," in Cockrell, *Excelsior,* 179–180. Thanks to James Green of the Library Company of Philadelphia for pointing out the correlation between currency and a ticket of the Hutchinson Family Singers. "Reminiscences of Brook Farm," *Old and New* 3, no. 4 (Apr. 1871):425. Ripley to Emerson, 9 Nov. 1840, in Sterling F. Delano, *Brook Farm: The Dark Side of Utopia* (Cambridge: Harvard University Press, 2004), 61. Ibid., xiv, 60–63.

15. Cockrell, *Excelsior,* 102, 272. Hutchinson, *Story of the Hutchinsons,* 1:135–137. Asa Hutchinson, "Jan. 29th, 1853," *1853 Diary,* American Antiquarian Manuscript Department. Perley Derby, *Hutchinson Family* (Salem: Essex Institute Press, 1870), 49–50. "Property Convention," *Liberator,* 10 Mar. 1843. Clark, *Communitarian Moment,* xi, 1, 88, 111. Asa Hutchinson, "Saturday, April 27, 1844," in Cockrell, *Excelsior,* 264–268. "Deaths in the Hutchinsons Circle," *Liberator,* 3 Jan. 1845, 3.

16. "Weekly List of Remittances," *Herald of Freedom,* 16 June 1843, 67. Asa Hutchinson, "Wednesday, April 10, 1844," in Cockrell, *Excelsior,* 251–252. Cockrell, "Appendix B: Concert Itineraries," "Appendix C: Repertory of the Hutchinson Family," in *Excelsior,* 390–392, 394–406. "No Union with Slaveholders!" *Liberator,* 14 June 1844, 95. Jesse Hutchinson, Jr., "The Old Free States," *Buffalo Republic . . . Extra. Official Proceedings of the National Free Soil Convention, Assembled at Buffalo, N.Y., August 9th and 10th, 1848.* (n.p., 1848?). "Essex County Anti-Slavery Meeting," *Liberator,* 31 Mar. 1843, 50. Wright, *Granite Town,* 487.

17. Peter Benes, ed., *Itinerancy in New England and New York* (Boston: Boston University Press, 1986). Philip F. Gura and James F. Bollman, *America's Instrument: The Banjo in the Nineteenth Century* (Chapel Hill: University of North Carolina Press, 1999). Rebecca Solnit, *River of Shadows: Eadweard Muybridge and the Technological Wild West* (New York: Viking, 2003), 19. Lydia Maria Child, "Letter From New-York XXVII, September 8, 1842," *Letters From New-York: A Portrait of New York on the Cusp of its Transformation into a Modern City,* ed. Bruce Mills (Athens: University of Georgia Press, 1998), 120.

18. Samuel A. Eliot, *Address Before the Boston Academy of Music, on the Opening of the Odeon, Aug. 5, 1835* (Boston: Perkins, Marvin, 1835), 13. Robert Laurence Moore, *Selling God: American Religion in the Marketplace of Culture* (New York: Oxford University Press, 1994). Richard Bushman, *Refinement of America: Persons, Houses, Cities* (New York:

Vintage, 1993), 313–331. Karen Halttunen, *Confidence Men and Painted Women: A Study of Middle-Class Culture in America* (New Haven: Yale University Press, 1982), 98–99. Catherine Kelly, "'Well Bred Country People': Sociability, Social Networks, and the Creation of a Provincial Middle Class, 1820–1860," *Journal of the Early Republic* 19 (Fall 1999):465. Adin Ballou, *Autobiography of Adin Ballou, 1803–1890,* ed. William S. Heywood (Lowell: Vox Populi, 1890), 42. B., "The Claims of Vocal Music," *New Hampshire Magazine: Devoted to Literature, Education, Moral, and Religious Reading,* ed. E. D. Boylston (Manchester: n.p., 1843–1844), 1:33–34, 37. Margaret Fuller cited in Ora Frishberg Saloman, "American Writers on Beethoven, 1838–1849: Dwight Fuller, Cranch, Story," *American Music* 8 (1990):18. Scott Gac, "The Eternal Symphony Afloat: The Transcendentalists' Quest for a National Culture," *ATQ: Nineteenth Century American Literature and Culture* 16, no. 3 (Sept. 2002):156–157. Gilbert Chase, *America's Music From Pilgrims to the Present,* rev. 3rd ed. (Urbana: University of Illinois Press, 1987), 133. "Music," *New Hampshire Magazine* 1 (1843–1844):272.

19. John Pitkin Norton, "19 Mar. 1844," Diary, group 367, series II, box 4, folder 20, John Pitkin Norton Papers, Manuscript and Archives, Yale University, 222–223. Phelps cited in Kelly, "'Well Bred,'" 455–456. Margaret Fuller, *Summer on the Lakes, in 1843* (Urbana: University of Illinois Press, 1991), 40. Charles Capper, *Margaret Fuller: An American Romantic Life* (New York: Oxford University Press, 1992), 35, 53, 56, 228. Bushman, *Refinement of America. Catalogue of the Officers and Members of Milford Female Seminary, for the Fall Term of 1835, and the Spring, Summer, and Fall Terms of 1836* (Amherst: R. Boylston, 1836), 11. William Ellery Channing, "Popular Amusements," *Western Messenger* 4 (Jan. 1838):344. Ada R. Parker [Adaline Rice Parker] to Mrs. Emily Greene, 5 Mar. 1841, in *Letters of Ada R. Parker* (Boston: Crosby and Nichols, 1863), 18–19.

20. Christopher Clark, *Diary of an Apprentice Cabinetmaker: Edward Jenner Carpenter's "Journal," 1844–45* (Worcester: American Antiquarian Society, 1989), 312, 324, 335, 346, 349, 350, 357, 360, 375, 384, 394. It is clear from the Hutchinson Family Singers' concern over their ticket prices that fifty cents was a lot to spend on entertainment. Yet many laborers in cities and towns spent twenty-five cents or more on tickets for events. Certainly not everyone spends within his means, but historians often suggest that workers who went to concerts were doing so. A better understanding is needed of tickets prices in relation to yearly income. For a discussion of pricing and the Post Office, see Michel S. Foley, "A Mission Unfulfilled: The Post Office and the Distribution of Information in Rural New England, 1821–1835," *Journal of the Early Republic* 17, no. 4 (Winter 1997): 623–624. The *Lowell Offering* in Nicholas E. Tawa, *High-Minded and Low-Down: Music in the Lives of Americans, 1800–1861* (Boston: Northeastern University Press, 2000), 204–205.

21. Anna Quincy Thaxter, "Tuesday Jan. 27, 1846," "7 January 1845," Papers, 1816–1918, Manuscript Collection, American Antiquarian Society, Worcester, Mass., octavo #1. Carpenter, "Tuesday May 21th," *Diary,* 335, 346. Keans and Mrs. Peters quotation from Thaxter, "October 26, 1846," Papers, octavo #4.

22. Thaxter, "Jan. 3, 1846," Papers, octavo #2; "Oct. 5, 1846," "Oct. 2, 1846," Papers, octavo #3, 87, 85; "October 24, 1846," "Nov. 3, 1846," Papers, octavo #4.

23. Thaxter, "Tuesday, Dec. 8, 1846," Papers, octavo #4. Firth, Hall, and Pond, *Catalogue of Music, Published by Firth, Hall & Pond, Publishers and Importers of Music* (New York: J. A. Fraetas, 1846).

24. John Pitkin Norton, "26 Feb. 1843," "23 Feb. 1844," "26 Feb 1844," "27 Feb 1844," "18 Mar. 1844," "19 Mar. 1844," "29 Mar. 1844," Diaries, folder 20, 56, 199–223; "29 May 1844," Diaries, folder 21, 39.

25. Aaron Rice Dutton, "Letter to Mary Dutton," 1835? Dutton Family Papers, Special Collections, Divinity Library, Yale University, RG 63, box 1. Mary Dutton, "Letter to brothers," 31 Aug. 1835, Dutton Family Papers, RG 63, box 2, folder 24. Dorcas Dutton, "Letter to Mary Dutton," 7 Sept. 1835, Dutton Family Papers, RG 63, box 1.

26. "Reminiscences of Brook Farm," 425. *Evening Transcript* in Cockrell, *Excelsior,* 151.

27. Eric Foner, *Free Soil, Free Men, Free Labor* (1970; New York: Oxford University Press, 1995). Asa Hutchinson, "April 27, 1844," in Cockrell, *Excelsior,* 267. John W. Hutchinson to Wendell Phillips, 22 Mar. 1867, MS Am 1953, Wendell Phillips Papers, Harvard University.

28. George Henry Lewes, *The Principles of Success in Literature,* cited in Ben Yagoda, *Sound on the Page: Great Writers Talk About Style and Voice in Writing* (New York: Harper-Resource, 2004), 9. Crayon, "The Hutchinson Family (From the *New-Englander*)," *North Star,* 5 Dec. 1850. The romanticized tale of the Hutchinson Family Singers as farmers (which, of course, was partially true) is analogous to the urban legends which have propelled many modern-day hip-hop performers to great fame; Ethan Brown, *Queens Reigns Supreme: Fat Cat, 50 Cent and the Rise of the Hip-Hop Hustler* (New York: Anchor, 2005), xxii.

29. Isabelle Lehuu, "Sentimental Figures: Reading *Godey's Lady's Book* in Antebellum America," in *Culture of Sentiment: Race, Gender, and Sentimentality in Nineteenth-Century America,* ed. Shirley Samuels (New York: Oxford University Press, 1992), 73, 82. Joan L. Severa, *Dressed for the Photographer: Ordinary Americans and Fashion, 1840–1900* (Kent, Ohio: Kent State University Press, 1995), 2. "The Patton Family," *Founders and Builders of the Oranges,* in Hutchinson Family Singer collection at the Wadleigh Memorial Public Library, Milford, New Hampshire. "The Hutchinson Family," *Arthur's Lady's Magazine of Elegant Literature and Fine Arts,* Aug. 1844, 76.

30. Elizabeth B. Clark, "'The Sacred Rights of the Weak': Pain, Sympathy, and the Culture of Individual Rights in Antebellum America," *Journal of American History* 82 (Sept. 1995):486–487. Halttunen, *Confidence Men and Painted Women,* 56–91. Aristotle, *On Rhetoric,* in Yagoda, *Sound on the Page,* 5. Robert G. Allen, *Horrible Prettiness: Burlesque and American Culture* (Chapel Hill: University of North Carolina, 1991), 84–87. "The Hutchinsons. From the Philadelphia Citizen," *Nashua Gazette,* 8 May 1845.

31. Asa Burnham Hutchinson, *Book of Brothers or the History of the Hutchinson Family* (New York: Hutchinson Family, 1852), 25–26. Asa Hutchinson, "Hanover July 15th 1842," in Cockrell, *Excelsior,* 13. Frederick Douglass, "Hutchinson Family," *North Star,* 3 Oct. 1850. "Thanksgiving in Prison," *New York Tribune,* WMPL 1, 5. Cassius Clay to Miss Abby Hutchinson, 14 Sept. 1848, Archives, Hutchins Library, Berea College. "The Hutchinson Family Singers," *New York Tribune,* 15 May 1843, 4. Henry Whittemore, "The Patton Family," from *Founders and Builders of the Oranges,* in Hutchinson Family Singers collection, Wadleigh Memorial Public Library, Milford, N.H. Ludlow Patton first heard the Hutchinsons on May 13, 1843; WMPL 1, 25. Patton cited in Cockrell, *Excelsior,* 119.

32. Cockrell, *Excelsior,* 286. *Lowell Offering* 4 (August 1844):237–240, in Tawa, *High-*

Minded and Low-Down, 204–205. "Editor's Book Table," *Godey's Lady's Book* 28 (Mar. 1844):150. "Abby Hutchinson Patton," uncited article, WMPL 3, 106. *John Bull,* 14 Feb. 1846, in Cockrell, *Excelsior,* 366.

33. Catherine Esther Beecher, *A Treatise on Domestic Economy: For the Use of Young Ladies at Home, and at School* (Boston: Marsh, Capen, Lyon, and Webb, 1841). Andrew Jackson Downing, *Cottage Residences; Or, A Series of Designs for Rural Cottages and Cottage Villas, and Their Gardens and Grounds* (New York: Wiley and Putnam, 1842). Adam W. Sweeting, *Reading Houses and Building Books: Andrew Jackson Downing and the Architecture of Popular Antebellum Literature* (Hanover: University Press of New England, 1996), 44, 49–50. Lori Merish, *Sentimental Materialism: Gender, Commodity Culture, and Nineteenth-Century American Literature* (Durham: Duke University Press, 2000), 141. "Farm House Architecture," *Farmer's Monthly Visitor,* 30 Sept. 1840, 129–130. Thomas Wentworth Higginson, *Cheerful Yesterdays* (Boston: Houghton Mifflin, 1898), 118.

34. Blumin, *Emergence of the Middle Class,* 1. Jane Tompkins, *Sensational Designs: The Cultural Work of American Fiction, 1790–1860* (New York: Oxford University Press, 1985). Clark, "'Sacred Rights of the Weak.'" Saidiya V. Hartmann correctly warns that sympathy was hardly a cure-all for the nation's racial dilemma: *Scenes of Subjection: Terror, Slavery, and Self-Making in Nineteenth-Century America* (New York: Oxford University Press, 1997). Michael Schudson, *Good Citizen: A History of American Civic Life* (New York: Martin Kessler, 1998), 206. Stephanie Dunson, "The Minstrel in the Parlor: Nineteenth-Century Sheet Music and the Domestication of Blackface Minstrelsy," *ATQ: Nineteenth Century Literature and Culture* 16, no. 4 (December 2002):246, 251. Stephanie Dunson, "The Minstrel in the Parlor: Nineteenth-Century Sheet Music and the Domestication of Blackface Minstrelsy," Ph.D. diss., University of Massachusetts, 2004. Philip F. Gura, "America's Minstrel Daze," review of *Demons of Disorder,* by Dale Cockrell; *Raising Cain: Blackface Performance from Jim Crow to Hip Hop,* by W. T. Lhamon, Jr.; *Behind the Burnt Cork Mask: Early Blackface Minstrelsy and Antebellum American Culture,* by William J. Mahar, *New England Quarterly* 72, no. 4 (Dec. 1999):602–616. Ken Emerson, *Doo-Dah! Stephen Foster and the Rise of American Popular Culture* (New York: Da Capo, 1998), 93. Eric Lott, *Love and Theft: Blackface Minstrelsy and the American Working Class* (New York: Oxford University Press, 1995). Cockrell, *Excelsior,* 259. Hutchinson, *Story of the Hutchinsons,* 1:114.

35. Frederick Douglass, "The Hutchinson Family. Hunkerism," *North Star,* 27 Oct. 1848. Lott, *Love and Theft,* 15. Douglass, *The Anti-Slavery Movement: A Lecture by Frederick Douglass Before the Rochester Ladies' Anti-Slavery Society* (Rochester: Lee, Mann, 1855), 40. William W. Austin, *Susanna, Jeanie, and the Old Folks at Home: The Songs of Stephen C. Foster from His Time to Ours* (New York: Macmillan, 1975), xxiv, 10. John Jeremiah Sullivan, "Horseman, Pass By," *Harper's Magazine,* Oct. 2002, 43–59.

Finale

1. Asa Hutchinson, "August 16, 1845," *Excelsior: Journals of the Hutchinson Family Singers, 1842–1846,* ed. Dale Cockrell (Stuyvesant, N.Y.: Pendragon, 1989), 315. Richard Crawford, *American Musical Life* (New York: Norton, 2001), 423–425. Robert C. Toll, *Blacking Up: The Minstrel Show in Nineteenth-Century America* (New York: Oxford University Press, 1974), 28, 30, 196. Lucretia Mott also found portraits painted by American

artists when visiting Manchester, England, in 1840; see Mott, *Slavery and "The Woman Question": Lucretia Mott's Diary, 1840,* ed. Frederick B. Tolles (Haverford, Penn.: Friends' Historical Association, 1952), 16.

2. Simon Schama, "Sail Away," *New Yorker,* 24 May 2004, 39. Frederick Douglass, *Narrative of the Life of Frederick Douglass, An American Slave* (Boston: Anti-Slavery Office, 1845). John Blassingame, Introduction to *Narrative of the Life of Frederick Douglass, An American Slave* (New Haven: Yale University Press, 2001), xxiii. William S. McFeely, *Frederick Douglass* (New York: Norton, 1991), 116–118, 120, 137. Cockrell, *Excelsior,* 312. Asa Hutchinson, "Sunday evening, August 24th, 1845," "Monday evening, 11½ o'clock," in Cockrell, *Excelsior,* 319.

3. McFeely, *Frederick Douglass,* 120–127, 131. Schama, "Sail Away," 39. Asa Hutchinson, "Monday evening," "Royal Mail Ship Cambria," in Cockrell, *Excelsior,* 320–321. Douglass to William Lloyd Garrison, 1 Sept. 1845, ibid., 322–323. George Warburton, *Hochelaga; or, England in the New World* (New York: Wiley and Putnam, 1846), 2:194. Warburton also cited in Cockrell, *Excelsior,* 321–322. *Mercury* (Liverpool), 12 Sept. 1845, ibid., 324. "Black Faces and White Money [from the London Atlas]," *Liberator,* 14 May 1847, 77. "Anti-Slavery Minstrels [from the Manchester Report]," *Lynn Pioneer,* in Hutchinson Family Singer Collection, Wadleigh Memorial Public Library, box 1, item 1 [hereafter WMPL 1, 1]. "Music" in Cockrell, *Excelsior,* 360. "Concert of the Hutchinson Family [from the Birmingham Journal]," *Liberator,* 15 May 1856, 77. John Blassingame, *Frederick Douglass Papers* (New Haven: Yale University Press, 1979) 1:62–65, 82–83. *Freedman's Journal* (Dublin) in *Washington Mirror,* WMPL, 1, 1. Charles Sumner to Henry W. Longfellow, 12 Aug. 1846, in *Selected Letters of Charles Sumner,* ed. Beverly Wilson Palmer (Boston: Northeastern University Press, 1990), 1:174. "The Hutchinson Family," *London Morning Chronicle,* 11 Feb. 1846, WMPL 1, 1.

4. *Times* (London), 12 Feb. 1846, in Cockrell, *Excelsior,* 352. *Atlas* (London), 14 Feb. 1846, ibid., 368. Abby Hutchinson Patton to my dear brothers John and Asa and to their families, Rome, 11 Dec. 1874, in Asa B. Hutchinson and Family Papers, 1842–1937, Minnesota Historical Society, Manuscript Division. Mary Howitt, "The Hutchinson Family," *Salem Register,* WMPL 1, 3. Judson Hutchinson to *Lynn Pioneer,* 16 Oct. 1845, WMPL 1, 5. Asa B. Hutchinson to Isaiah Ray, London, 23 Feb. 1846, Slavery in the United States Collection, box 1, folder 5, Manuscript Division, American Antiquarian Society. Jesse Jr. in Cockrell, *Excelsior,* 326.

5. Asa B. Hutchinson to Isaiah Ray, Cockrell, *Excelsior,* 326. Lizzie Chace to Mr. Isaiah C. Ray, New Bedford, 31 May 1846, Slavery in the United States Collection, box 1, folder 5, Manuscript Division, American Antiquarian Society. Asa Huchinson, "London, Saturday morning, March 7, 1846," in Cockrell, *Excelsior,* 357.

6. McFeely, *Frederick Douglass,* 143–145. "A Pleasing Incident," *Springfield Republican,* WMPL 1, 2.

7. Elizabeth P. Roberts, "Farewell Song Inscribed to the Hutchinson Family," *Eclectic Magazine of Foreign Literature* 9, no. 2 (Oct. 1846):289. "The popular singers," *Scientific American* 1, no. 47 (13 Aug. 1846):2. "The return," *Scientific American* 2, no. 9 (21 Nov. 1846):70.

8. James Oliver Horton and Louis E. Horton, *In Hope of Liberty: Culture Community and Protest Among Northern Free Blacks, 1700–1860* (New York: Oxford University Press, 1996). Ira Berlin, *Many Thousands Gone: The First Two Centuries of Slavery in North America* (Cambridge: Harvard University Press, 1998). "Garrison's Nigger Minstrels

[from the *Daily Sun*]," *New York Sunday Era,* WMPL 1, 32. J. D., "The Hutchinsons," *North Star,* 21 April 1848. "The Hutchinson Family," *Turner's Comic Almanac for 1848* (Philadelphia: Turner and Fisher, 1847). Abby Hutchinson to Mary Howitt, Plymouth, 5 May 1847, in "What Are the Hutchinsons Doing?" in *Howitt's Journal,* n.d., WMPL 1, 8. See also Abby Hutchinson to Mary Howitt, Plymouth, 5 May 1847, in "The Hutchinsons," *Lynn Pioneer and the Herald of Freedom,* 2 Sept. 1847. Frank Carpenter in John Wallace Hutchinson, *Story of the Hutchinsons (Tribe of Jesse),* ed. Charles E. Mann (Boston: Lee and Shepard, 1896), 2:270. "Exclusion of Colored People from Miss Stone's Lecture on Woman's Rights," *North Star,* 10 Feb. 1854.

9. Richard H. Sewell, "John P. Hale and the Liberty Party," *New England Quarterly* 37, no. 2 (June 1964):200–223. Richard H. Sewell, *Ballots for Freedom: Antislavery Politics in the United States, 1837–1860* (New York: Norton, 1976), 128–129.

10. Sewell, *Ballots for Freedom,* 129–131.

11. Hale in "American and Foreign Anti-Slavery Society," *National Era,* 18 May 1848, 80. John Ashworth, *Slavery, Capitalism, and Politics in the Antebellum Republic* (New York: Cambridge University Press, 1995), 431–433. Michael Holt, *The Fate of Their Country* (New York: Hill and Wang, 2004), 25.

12. Holt, *Fate of Their Country,* 14–18. William Salter, Letter to Eliab Parker, 23 Jan. 1847, in *The Letters of Eliab Parker Mackintire of Boston, Written Between 1835 and 1863, to Reverend William Salter of Burlington, Iowa,* ed. Phillip Dillon Jordan (New York: New York Public Library, 1936), 25–26. Shelley Streeby, *American Sensations: Class, Empire, and the Production of Popular Culture* (Berkeley: University of California Press, 2002), 6–9.

13. Henry David Thoreau, *Civil Disobedience* (Boston: Godine, 1969). James Russell Lowell, *Biglow Papers* (Cambridge, Mass.: G. Nichols, 1848). Jesse Hutchinson, Jr., and Judson Hutchinson, "Eight Dollars a Day" (Boston: Oliver Ditson, 1848). Holt, *Fate of Their Country,* 38–41.

14. Holt, *Fate of Their Country,* 40–41. "From the New York Eagle. The Hutchinsons, H. Clay, and the Abolitionists," *Liberator,* 31 Mar. 1848, 50. "Visitor of the Hutchinsons to Mr. Clay," *North Star,* 17 Mar. 1848. "Tied to an Anchor," *Liberator,* 11 Nov. 1842, 179. "Alluding to the prostitution of their fine vocal powers to the service of Henry Clay, by the Hutchinsons, Douglass in his North Star," *Liberator,* 31 Mar. 1848, 50. Jesse Hutchinson, Jr., to William Lloyd Garrison, 5 April 1848, *Liberator,* 28 Apr. 1848, 66. L. P. to Frederick Douglass, "The Hutchinsons," *North Star,* 31 Mar. 1848.

15. Lewis Tappan to John Scoble, 15 May 1848, in "Correspondence of Lewis Tappan and Others with the British and Foreign Anti-Slavery Society," *Journal of Negro History* 12, no. 3 (July 1927):418. Jesse Hutchinson, Jr., to William Lloyd Garrison, 66. "The Hutchinsons in Washington," *Lynn Pioneer and Herald of Freedom,* 3 May 1848. Henry C. Wright to Richard and Anne Allen, "The Hutchinsons' Repentance," *Liberator,* 19 May 1848, 79. "From the Chronotype. The Hutchinsons," *Liberator,* 26 May 1848, 81. "From the Lynn Pioneer. The Hutchinsons Repentance," *Liberator,* 2 June 1848, 85.

16. David M. Potter, *Impending Crisis, 1848–1861,* ed. Don E. Ferenbacher (New York: Harper Torchbooks, 1976), 59–61, 76–81. "Free Soil Convention," *National Era,* 17 Aug. 1848, 130. Sewell, *Ballots for Freedom,* 155–161. "Old Free States" in *Buffalo Republic. Extra. Official Proceedings of the National Free Soil Convention, Assembled at Buffalo, N.Y., August 9th and 10th, 1848* (n.p., n.d.). Lydia Maria Child, *An Appeal in Favor of That Class of Americans Called Africans* (New York: John S. Taylor, 1836), 76. Eric Foner, "Politics and

Prejudice: The Free Soil Party and the Negro," *Journal of Negro History* 50, no. 4 (Oct. 1965):239–256. "Benjamin F. Butler's Speech," *National Era,* 31 Aug. 1848, 137.

17. Jesse Hutchinson, Jr., "The Hutchinsons," *North Star,* 16 June 1848. "Eastern Tour," *North Star,* 9 June 1848.

18. "New Hampshire Free Soil Convention," *North Star,* 29 Sept. 1848. Hutchinson, *Story of the Hutchinsons,* 1:244. Sewell, *Ballots for Freedom,* 167–169. Holt, *Fate of Their Country,* 46–48. Abby Hutchinson Patton to my dear brothers John and Asa and to their families, 11 Dec. 1874, in Asa B. Hutchinson and Family, Papers, 1842–1937, Manuscript Division, Minnesota Historical Society, Minneapolis. L. A. Hine, "Relations of Marriage to Greatness," *National Era* 3, no. 46 (15 Nov. 1849):181.

19. "Abby Hutchinson No More [from *New York Commercial*]," *Liberator,* 16 Mar. 1849, 43. "Letters from the Capital," *National Era,* 18 Mar. 1852, 46. Garrison, notation to "Abby Hutchinson No More." Crayon, "The Hutchinson Family [from *New-Englander,*" *North Star,* 5 Dec. 1850.

20. Frederick Douglass, "This charming little songstress," *North Star,* 5 Oct. 1849. Hutchinson, *Story of the Hutchinsons,* 2:166. Lora Romero, *Home Fronts: Domesticity and Its Critics in the Antebellum United States* (Durham: Duke University Press, 1997), 29. "Oh, Sweet Little Abby Hutchinson," clipping in WMPL 1, 14. James Parton, Horace Greeley, and others, *Eminent Women of the Age* (Hartford: S. M. Betts, 1868), 388. John Quincy Adams, *Memoirs of John Quincy Adams, Comprising Portions of His Diary from 1795–1848,* ed. Charles Francis Adams (Philadelphia: Lippincott, 1874), 10:450. A quick note on the Hutchinson Family Singers and women's rights (and women's suffrage): though the group played at many events for women's causes, the status they held during these conventions had largely been earned through antislavery. Indeed, the index of John's *Story of the Hutchinsons* makes no mention of women's issues (but women's rights and women's suffrage are mentioned in the book), and when Abby Hutchinson died, Elizabeth Cady Stanton noted the group's influence "in the war for freedom" (clearly meaning antislavery) but not in women's suffrage; Stanton in *Story of the Hutchinsons,* 2:281.

21. "Gleanings," *Literary Union: A Journal of Progress, In Literature and Education, Religion,* 18 Aug. 1849, 317. "Clippings," *Saturday Evening Post,* 18 Aug. 1849, 2. "A Case of Long Fasting," *Scientific American* 5.9 (17 Nov. 1849), 69. "The Hutchinson Family's Concert," *New York Times,* 11 Nov. 1853, 4. Douglass, "This charming." Abby Hutchinson in the *Message Bird,* 1 April 1851, 10, in Vera Brodsky Lawrence, *Strong on Music: The New York Musical Scene in the Days of George Templeton Strong* (Chicago: University of Chicago, 1995), 2:202. Bernard Covert and Capt. Patten, "Brothers Speak in Whispers Light or the Brides Departure" (Boston: A. & J. P. Ordway, 1850). "General Summary," *National Era,* 25 Mar. 1858, 47. Asa Hutchinson, "Jan 2," Diary, 1853, American Antiquarian Society, Manuscript Department. *Utica Daily Gazette,* 31 Jan. 1851. "Judson Hutchinson," *Saturday Evening Post,* 2 Nov. 1850, 2.

22. Ethiopian Serenaders in Sarah Meer, "Competing Representations: Douglass, the Ethiopian Serenaders, and Ethnic Exhibition in London," in *Liberating Sojourn: Frederick Douglass and Transatlantic Reform,* ed. Alan J. Rice and Martin Crawford (Athens: University of Georgia Press, 1999), 152. Ad for Christy's Minstrels cited in Lawrence, *Strong on Music,* 2:643. Robert C. Allen, *Horrible Prettiness: Burlesque and American Culture* (Chapel Hill: University of North Carolina Press, 1991), 101–117.

23. "The Hutchinsons Threatened With a Mob!" *Liberator,* 26 Mar. 1852, 1. P., "The Hutchinsons," *Herald of Freedom,* 18 Apr. 1845, 14. James P. Hambleton, *A History of the Political Campaign in Virginia in 1855* (Richmond: Randolph, 1856), 92.

24. Potter, *Impending Crisis,* 160–177, 244–251. Douglass, "A Letter From the Editor," *Frederick Douglass's Paper,* 2 Feb. 1855. William E. Gienapp, *Origins of the Republican Party, 1852–1856* (New York: Oxford University Press, 1987), 22, 120–121. Asa Hutchinson, "January 23, 1844," in Cockrell, *Excelsior,* 201, 208.

25. Foner, "Politics and Prejudice," 236–237. Holt, *Fate of Their Country,* 114–115. Lincoln in T. Gregory Garvey, *Creating the Culture of Reform in Antebellum America* (Athens: University of Georgia Press, 2006), 25.

26. Holt, *Fate of Their Country,* 115–120. Foner, "Politics and Prejudice," 249. Potter, *Impending Crisis,* 199.

27. John Hutchinson, ed., *Hutchinson's Republican Songster, for the Campaign of 1860* (New York: O. Hutchinson, 1860). John Hutchinson, ed., *Connecticut Wide-Awake Songster* (New Haven: n.p., 1860).

28. James Brewer Stewart, *Holy Warriors: The Abolitionists and American Slavery* (1976; New York: Hill and Wang, 1996), 164–165. William Lloyd Garrison, "Uncle Tom's Cabin," *Liberator,* 26 Mar. 1852, 50. Harriet Beecher Stowe, *Uncle Tom's Cabin* (Boston: John P. Jewett, 1852), 319.

29. Asa Hutchinson, "January 12," Diary, 1853, American Antiquarian Society, Manuscript Department. Austin Willey, *History of the Antislavery Cause in State and Nation* (Portland, Maine: Brown, Thurston and Hoyt, Fogg and Dunham, 1886), 389. Ralph Eugene Lund, *Century Magazine* 115 (January 1928):336. Asa Hutchinson and Eliza Cook, "Little Topsy's Song" (Boston: Oliver Ditson, 1853). Another Stowe song performed by the Hutchinsons: Martha Hill, "The Ghost of Uncle Tom" (New York: Horace Waters, 185?). Frederick Douglass, "Little Topsey's Song," *Frederick Douglass's Paper.* 30 Sept. 1853.

30. Eliab Parker, Letter to William Salter, 10 May 1853, *Letters of Eliab Parker Mackintire,* 85. Asa Hutchinson, "Lewiston Maine Jan 1," "Jan. 5 Portland," "March 11 1853," "March 13," Diary, 1853.

31. M. S. Prime, "Around the Horn in '49," *Overland Monthly and Out West Magazine* 8, no. 43 (July 1886):93. Asa Hutchinson, "March 9," "April 8 1853," "April 13," "April 15," "April 18," "April 20," "April 22," "April 23," "April 24," "April 26," "April 27," "May 2," "May 3," "May 9," "May 10," "May 12," "May 13," "May 15," Diary, 1853. "Jesse Hutchinson," clipping in WMPL 1, 38. Perley Derby, *Hutchinson Family* (Salem: Essex Institute Press, 1870), 49, 77–78. "Jesse Hutchinson," *Frederick Douglass's Paper,* 1 April 1853. "Jesse Hutchinson Turned Flour Dealer," *Frederick Douglass's Paper,* 25 Feb. 1853. "Gleanings of News," *Frederick Douglass's Paper,* 13 May 1853. "Jesse Hutchinson," *Frederick Douglass's Paper,* 20 May 1853. "Death of Jesse Hutchinson," *Liberator,* 20 May 1853, 88. "The Cincinnati Forgeries—Death of Jesse Hutchinson, & c," *New York Times,* 18 May 1853, 1. "Jesse Hutchinson—The Hutchinson Family," *Illustrated News,* 4 June 1853, 356.

32. On Lincoln, Mary Aston Rice Livermore, *My Story of the War: A Woman's Narrative* (Hartford: A. D. Worthington, 1896), 638. On Hutchinsons, Revilo, "The Progressive Friends," *National Era,* 24 May 1855, 97.

33. Derby, *Hutchinson Family.* W. W. Satterlee, *In Memoriam: The Power and Blessing of True Womanhood Illustrated in the Life, Labors, and Death of Elizabeth C. Hutchinson of the Hutchinson Family (Tribe of Asa)* (Minneapolis: Johnson and Smith, 1875). "Obituary

Notes," *New York Times,* 7 Jan. 1884, 4. "Death of Mrs. Asa B. Hutchinson," *Minneapolis Tribune,* 22 Dec. 1874. W. W. Satterlee, "Obituary of Mrs. Elizabeth B. Hutchinson," *Citizen* (Minneapolis), 14 Jan. 1874. "Funeral of Asa B. Hutchinson," *Glencoe Register,* 4 Dec. 1884, in WMPL 2, 88. "Death of Asa Hutchinson," *New York Times,* 1 Dec. 1884, 2.

34. "Founding of the Town by the Hutchinson Singers," *Collections of the Minnesota Historical Society* (St. Paul: Minnesota Historical Society, 1872–1920), 10, no. 1:70–77.

35. "Insanity of One of the Hutchinson Family [from *Roch. Dem.* Monday]," *Liberator,* 25 Oct. 1850, 171. "Judson Hutchinson Insane [from *Syr. Standard*]," *Frederick Douglass Paper,* 31 Oct. 1850. Judson J. Hutchinson, "A Prompt Disclaimer," *Liberator* 26 Jan. 1855, 14.

36. Hutchinson, "Prompt Disclaimer," 14. Frederick Douglass, "A Prompt Disclaimer," *Frederick Douglass's Paper,* 23 Feb. 1855.

37. Hutchinson, *Story of the Hutchinsons,* 1:362. Derby, *Hutchinson Family,* 78. "Melancholy Suicide," *Liberator,* 14 Jan. 1859, 6. Garrison to John Hutchinson, Boston, 15 Mar. 1859, in *Letters of William Lloyd Garrison,* ed. Louis Ruchames (Cambridge: Belknap, Harvard University Press, 1975), 4:266–267; also in Hutchinson, *Story of the Hutchinsons,* 2:345–46. "Death of Another Member of the Hutchinson Family," *New York Times,* 13 Jan. 1859, 4.

38. Hutchinson, *Hutchinson's Republican Songster.* George Birdseye, "America's Song Composers," *Potter's American Monthly,* 12 Feb. 1879, 145. John W. Hutchinson, *A History of the Adventures of John W. Hutchinson and His Family in the Camps of the Army of the Potomac* (Boston: S. Chism, 1864), 10–20. Simon Cameron, Secretary of War, to John W. Hutchinson, 14 Jan. 1862, in *Memorabilia of the Hutchinson Family,* Gift of Mrs. Viola Hutchinson Campbell to the Lynn Historical Society, 1920, 5. Lydia Maria Child to Friend Hutchinson, Wayland, 19 Jan. 1862, ibid., 11. Joseph Jackson to John Hutchinson, Alexandria, 18 Jan. 1862, ibid., 7. Horace Greeley, *American Conflict: A History of the Rebellion in the United States of America, 1860–'65, Its Causes, Incidents, and Results* (Hartford: O. D. Case, 1866), 1:629. Benson J. Lossing, *Our Country* (New York: Johnson, Wilson, 1875–1878), 6:1577–1578. O. O. Howard to Rev. A. Toomer [?], 21 Mar. 1870, *Memorabilia,* 23. Review of *History of the War in America* by Horace Greeley, *Christian Recorder,* 24 Sept. 1864. "News Items," *Saturday Evening Post,* 15 Feb. 1862, 3. "The Levee at the White House," *Memphis Daily Appeal,* 6 Feb. 1862, 3. "The Hutchinson Family," *Christian Recorder,* 7 Mar. 1863. "Singing of the Hutchinson Family," *Christian Recorder,* 30 Mar. 1861. "Academy of Music," *Vanity Fair* 5 (28 June 1862):302. "General Notes," *New York Times,* 6 Mar. 1873, 5. Ad for Hutchinson Family benefit concert for the Penn Relief Association, *Saturday Evening Post,* 31 Jan. 1863, 2. "Grand Temperance Demonstration," *New York Times,* 7 May 1872, 7. "In J. W. Hutchinson's Honor," *New York Times,* 3 Jan. 1896, 6. "'Bon Voyage' to Miss Willard," *New York Times,* 20 Apr. 1896, 5. "Seventy-Third Anniversary of the American Baptist Missionary Union," *Baptist* 67, no. 7 (July 1887):1. "Capitol Chat," *Washington Post,* 21 Mar. 1898, 6.

39. Louis Menand, *The Metaphysical Club: A Story of Ideas in America* (New York: Farrar, Straus, and Giroux, 2001), ix–xii.

40. Frederick Douglass to the Danvers Historical Society, 29 Mar. 1893, *Old Anti-Slavery Days: Proceedings of the Commemorative Meeting, Held by the Danvers Historical Society, at the Town Hall, Danvers, April 26, 1893, with Introduction, Letters and Sketches* (Danvers: Danvers Mirror Print, 1893), 62. Douglass to Ida B. Wells, 25 Oct. 1892, cited in McFeely, *Frederick Douglass,* 362. Douglass to Marshall Pierce, 18 Feb. 1892, ibid., 360.

Ibid., 359–371. John Stauffer, "Frederick Douglass and the Aesthetics of Freedom," *Raritan Review,* forthcoming. Christopher Robert Reed, *"All the World Is Here!" The Black Presence at White City* (Bloomington: Indiana University Press, 2000), 7.

41. Reed, *"All the World Is Here!"* xv–xxii, 22. While Reed argues that the fair laid the groundwork for an American society more accepting of its black citizens by hiring some black workers, his examples clearly show how segregated and demeaning the fair experience was. McFeely, *Frederick Douglass,* 359–371.

42. McFeely, *Frederick Douglass,* 367. Douglass cited ibid., 371. Robert Rydell, Introduction to *The Reason Why the Colored American Is Not in the World's Columbian Exposition,* by Ida Wells and others (1893; Chicago: University of Illinois Press, 1999), xxx–xxxi.

43. Quotation from McFeely, *Frederick Douglass,* 372.

44. Hutchinson, *Story of the Hutchinsons,* 2:205–217. Chicago paper cited ibid., 2:208. Reed, *"All the World Is Here!"* 70.

45. *Chicago News* cited in Hutchinson, *Story of the Hutchinsons,* 2:211, 208. Reed, *"All the World Is Here!"* 70. Ida B. Wells cited in McFeely, *Frederick Douglass,* 371. "New-Hampshire's Sons Celebrate at the World's Fair," WMPL 3, 97.

46. Hutchinson Family Singers, *The Hutchinson Family's Book of Words* (New York: Baker, Godwin, 1852), 32. The song John offered is similar in theme to Henry Russell, "The Indian Hunter" (New York: Firth, Hall and Pond, n.d.). See also Vance Randolph, ed., *Ozark Folksongs* (Columbia: State Historical Society of Missouri, 1950), 297. Hutchinson, *Story of the Hutchinsons,* 2:216–217. Eliza Cook, ed., *Poetical Works of Mary Howitt* (Boston: Phillips, Sampson, 1857), 360. Hutchinson, *Story of the Hutchinsons,* 1:340–353. John W. Hutchinson, *Book of Brothers; (Second Series) Being a History of the Adventures of John W. Hutchinson and His Family in the Camps of the Army of the Potomac* (Boston: S. Chism, 1864), 22. Derby, *Hutchinson Family,* 104. Rebecca Solnit, *Savage Dreams: A Journey into the Landscape Wars of the American West* (New York: Vintage, 1994), 276. Rebecca Solnit, *River of Shadows: Eadweard Muybridge and the Technological Wild West* (New York: Viking, 2003), 73. David Roediger, "The Pursuit of Whiteness: Property, Terror, and National Expansion, 1790–1860," in *Colored White: Transcending the Racial Past* (Berkeley: University of California, 2002), 131.

47. David Brion Davis, "The Emergence of Immediatism in British and American Thought," *Mississippi Valley Historical Review* 49, no. 2 (Sep. 1962):209–230. Asa Hutchinson, "June 2d 1843," in Cockrell, *Excelsior,* 150–151. Ron Eyerman, *Cultural Trauma: Slavery and the Formation of African American Identity* (Cambridge: Cambridge University Press, 2001). Steven Hahn, *A Nation Under Our Feet: Black Political Struggles in the Rural South from Slavery to the Great Migration* (Cambridge: Harvard University Press, 2003). Eric Foner, *Reconstruction: America's Unfinished Revolution, 1863–1877* (New York: Harper and Row, Publishers, 1988).

48. John's ad, *Town Hall, Milford, Thursday, Nov. 2* ([Milford?]: N.p., 1893?). Abby Hutchinson Patton to John W. Hutchinson, 16 April 1891, New York, in Hutchinson, *Story of the Hutchinsons,* 2:380. Elizabeth B. Clark, "'The Sacred Rights of the Weak': Pain, Sympathy, and the Culture of Individual Rights in Antebellum America," *Journal of American History* 82 (Sept. 1995):475, 492. McFeely, *Frederick Douglass,* 369. Reed, *"All the World Is Here!"* 190, 139. Ida B. Wells and others, *Reason Why the Colored American Is Not in the World's Columbian Exposition.*

49. John W. Hutchinson to Helen Pitts Douglass, 22 Feb. 1895, in McFeely, *Frederick*

Douglass, 382. "Tributes of Two Races: White and Colored Attend Funeral of Frederick Douglass," *New York Times,* 26 Feb. 1895, 2.

50. Samuel Joseph May, *Memoir of Samuel Joseph May* (Boston: Roberts Brothers, 1874), 156. Reed, *"All the World Is Here!"* 34–35. Douglass in McFeely, *Frederick Douglass,* 94. Cheryl I. Harris, "Whiteness as Property," *Harvard Law Review* 1993 (June):1707–1791. David W. Blight, *Race and Reunion: The Civil War in American Memory* (Cambridge: Harvard University Press, 2001), 5, 13–14, 31, 57, 387. Wendell P. Garrison to John Wallace Hutchinson, Orange, N.J., 1 Jan. 1891, in *Seventieth Birthday Anniversary of John W. Hutchinson, (Tribe of John and Jesse,) at Tower Cottage, High Rock, Lynn, Mass. January Fifth, 1891* (Lynn: Nichols, 1891), 25.

51. "In New Jersey," *New York Times,* 26 Jan. 1908. "John W. Hutchinson Dead," *New York Times,* 30 Oct. 1908, 9. "Obituary Notes," *New York Times,* 14 Apr. 1884, 5. "Mrs. Adelaide Johnson Is the Sculptor of Suffrage," *Washington Post,* 4 Apr. 1909, M9. Mary Howitt, "Memoir of Elihu Burritt," in Elihu Burritt, *Thoughts and Things at Home and Abroad* (Boston: Phillips, Sampson, 1864), vi. Hutchinson Family, "There's a Good Time Coming" (Boston: Oliver Ditson, 1846).

Index